A Bloomsbury Group Reader

A Bloomsbury Group Reader

Edited by

S. P. Rosenbaum

BLACKWELL
Oxford UK & Cambridge USA

Copyright © Basil Blackwell Ltd 1993
Copyright © Specific contributions as given in the Acknowledgements 1993
Copyright © Notes and arrangement, S. P. Rosenbaum 1993

First published 1993

Blackwell Publishers
108 Cowley Road
Oxford OX4 1JF
UK

238 Main Street
Cambridge, Massachusetts 02142
USA

British Library Cataloguing in Publication Data
A CIP catalogue record for this book is available from
the British Library.

Library of Congress Cataloging-in-Publication Data
A Bloomsbury group reader / edited by S. P. Rosenbaum.
    p.   cm.
  Includes bibliographical references and index.
  ISBN 0-631-17318-8 (alk. paper). – ISBN 0-631-19059-7 (pbk.:
alk. paper)
    1. English literature—20th century.   2. Bloomsbury group.
I. Rosenbaum, S. P. (Stanford Patrick), 1929–   .
PR1149.B65   1993
828'. 9120808—dc20
                                                                    92-44808
                                                                    CIP

Typeset in on 11 pt Sabon by Best-set Typesetters
Printed in Great Britain by T.J. Press Ltd Padstow, Cornwall
This book is printed on acid-free paper

Contents

Contents

Introduction

The purpose of *A Bloomsbury Group Reader* is to present a representative selection of shorter writings by Virginia Woolf, E. M. Forster, Lytton Strachey, Roger Fry, Desmond MacCarthy, Clive Bell, Leonard Woolf, John Maynard Keynes, and Vanessa Bell. Everything that the Group wrote they tried to write well, and there is an abundant variety of illuminating and delightful reading to be found in shorter prose works of Bloomsbury's novelists, biographers, critics, and even political economists.

The writings of the Bloomsbury Group continue to interest readers more than a century after the births of their authors. While the beauty of their visual art is being increasingly recognized, and the Group's lifestyles still attract biographers, it is in Bloomsbury's books that their greatest achievements are to be found. Yet the very reputation of the Bloomsbury's Group's full-length works has overshadowed their other writings and deterred readers from enjoying the wide diversity of their briefer works. The unavailability of many of these writings has been a further difficulty.

Because literary form was important to Bloomsbury, all the works chosen here are complete in themselves, though some are also parts of larger works. The only abridgments are those done by the authors themselves. The works selected were also all written for some kind of reading (or listening) public, and therefore selections from Bloomsbury diaries or correspondence have not been included. Ellipses and footnotes in the selections are those of the authors; in some pieces, however, square-bracketed identifications have occasionally been interpolated. Several of the titles have been changed, and these have been noted in the brief commentary that is provided for each selection. Titles, quotation marks, capitalization, abbreviations, and spelling have been made broadly consistent throughout the selections. Misprints and other obvious mistakes have also been silently corrected.

The arrangement of Bloomsbury's shorter works is by their forms to indicate their diversity and suggest various interconnections among them. The genres of literary works are not rigid, of course, and many of the pieces selected could be put under other headings in this reader. There are essays that might be forewords, and talks that could be essays, biographies that are memoirs, and memoirs that are stories. Bloomsbury writers particularly enjoyed the modernist mixing of forms, combining fact with fiction, polemics with aesthetics, humour with history.

The general order in which Bloomsbury's kinds of writing have been presented is from the objective to the subjective, as it were – from genres in which the writer's presence is least felt in the work to those in which it may be dominant. The sequence from stories, biographies, and essays, through reviews, polemics, and talks, to travel writings and memoirs is framed by the forewords and afterwords written for some of Bloomsbury's books. Several familiar texts, such as E. M. Forster's 'What I Believe' or Virginia Woolf's 'Mr Bennett and Mrs Brown', have been included here, but others are rarely read: Virginia Woolf's biography of her great-aunt has not yet been collected, and Desmond MacCarthy's introduction to the first Post-Impressionist Exhibition catalogue, as well as Leonard Woolf's very early review of Freud, have not, as far as I know, ever been reprinted.

All discussions of Bloomsbury have, sooner or later, to explain what is meant by the Bloomsbury Group. For the purposes of this collection, the Group is assumed to be an informal but lifelong association of English friends and relations, some of whom met at the turn of the century as undergraduates at Cambridge and then extended college relationships among their families in London. At the centre of the Group were Leslie Stephen's daughters Vanessa, who married Clive Bell, and Virginia, who married Leonard Woolf. Lytton Strachey and his cousin Duncan Grant were the principal Bloomsbury members from the Strachey family. And, through Cambridge, Roger Fry, E. M. Forster, Saxon Sydney-Turner, John Maynard Keynes, Desmond MacCarthy and his wife Mary became associated with the Group. In the 1920s the members of Bloomsbury confirmed their association by founding the Memoir Club to celebrate their friendships and laugh over their individual or shared experiences. Younger members of Bloomsbury were associated with the Group later, the most prominent writer among them being David Garnett. The selections for this reader have been drawn only from the original members, however, and not even all of them are represented, so extensive are the shorter writings of Bloomsbury.

A *Bloomsbury Group Reader* is something of a sequel to *The Bloomsbury Group: A Collection of Memoirs, Commentary, and Criticism* that I edited in 1975. The focus in this selection is on the writings of the Group rather than their lives, for it is Bloomsbury's writings that ultimately justify the interest in their lives. The first collection was undertaken, as I noted at the time, in preparation for the writing of a literary history of the Bloomsbury Group. This reader is partly a result of that continuing history, the first volume of which was published as *Victorian Bloomsbury* in 1987, and the second as *Edwardian Bloomsbury* in 1993. The third volume will be called *Georgian Bloomsbury*.

Acknowledgements

The editor and publishers wish to thank King's College Cambridge and the Society of Authors as literary representatives of the E. M. Forster estate for E. M. Forster: 'The Emperor Babur', 'Cnidus', 'Me, Them and You', *Abinger Harvest*, © 1936; 'What I Believe', 'The Complete Poems of C. P. Cavafy', 'In My Library', *Two Cheers for Democracy*, ed. Oliver Stallybrass, © 1951, 1972; 'My Recollections', *Marianne Thornton*, © 1956; 'A View without a Room', *A Room with a View*, ed. Oliver Stallybrass, © 1977. The Society of Authors as agents for the Strachey Trust for: Lytton Strachey: 'Art and Indecency', *The Really Interesting Question*, ed. Paul Levy, © 1972; 'Lancaster Gate', *Lytton Strachey by Himself*, ed. Michael Holroyd, © 1971. David Higham Associates and Hugh Cecil and the Estate of Desmond MacCarthy for: Desmond MacCarthy: 'Two Historic Houses', 'Disraeli,' 'To Desmond MacCarthy Aet 22', *Portraits*, © 1931. Hugh Cecil and the Estate of Desmond MacCarthy for: Desmond MacCarthy: 'The Post-Impressionists', *Manet and the Post-Impressionists*, 1910; 'The New St Bernard', *Independent Review*, 1903; 'The Job of a Dramatic Critic', *The Listener*, 1939. Mrs Angelica Garnett for: Vanessa Bell: 'Notes on Virginia's Childhood', © 1974. The Hogarth Press and the Executors of the Leonard Woolf Estate for: Leonard Woolf: 'Pearls and Swine', *Stories of the East*, © 1921; 'Herbert Spencer', 'The Gentleness of Nature', *Essays*, © 1927; *Fear and Politics*, © 1925. The Estate of Leonard Woolf for: Leonard Woolf: 'Freud's *Psychopathology of Everyday Life*'; 'Coming to London'. Sidgwick and Jackson for: E. M. Forster, 'Introduction', 'The Point of It', *Collected Short Stories of E. M. Forster*, © 1948. Alfred A. Knopf for: E. M. Forster: 'Introduction', 'The Point of It', *The Collected Tales of E. M. Forster*, © 1947. Royal Economic Society and Macmillan, London and Basingstoke, for: John Maynard Keynes: 'Newton the Man',

'Mr Lloyd George', 'On Reading Books', 'Julian Bell', 'Economic Possibilities for Our Grandchildren', *Collected Writings of John Maynard Keynes*, ed. Donald Moggridge et al., 1972, 1982. Cambridge University Press, New York, for: John Maynard Keynes: 'Newton the Man', 'Mr Lloyd George', 'On Reading Books', 'Julian Bell', 'Economic Possibilities for our Grandchildren', *Collected Writings of John Maynard Keynes*, ed. Donald Moggridge et al., © 1972, 1982. Chatto and Windus and the executors of the Clive Bell Estate for: Clive Bell: 'Wilcoxism', 'The Artistic Problem', *Since Cézanne*, © 1922; 'Ibsen', *Pot-Boilers*, © 1918; 'Maynard Keynes', *Old Friends*, © 1956. The Hogarth Press and the Executors of the Virginia Woolf Estate for: Virginia Woolf: 'Mrs Dalloway in Bond Street', *The Complete Shorter Fiction*, ed. Susan Dick, 1985, 1989; 'Old Bloomsbury', *Moments of Being*, ed. Jeanne Schulkind, © 1976, 1985. Harcourt, Brace, Jovanovich and the Executors of the Virginia Woolf Estate for: Virginia Woolf: *The Common Reader*, First and Second Series, © 1925, 1932; 'Mrs Dalloway in Bond Street', *The Complete Shorter Fiction*, ed. Susan Dick, 1985, 1989; 'An Essay in Criticism', *Granite and Rainbow*, © 1958; 'Old Bloomsbury', *Moments of Being*, ed. Jeanne Schulkind, © 1976, 1985; 'Professions for Women', *The Death of the Moth*, © 1942.

Finally, the editor is grateful to Naomi Black and Andrew McNeillie for suggested inclusions and exclusions, and to Ann Bone for careful editing. The painting on the cover was kindly suggested by Richard Shone.

Toronto   S. P. R.

Part I

Forewords

Four forewords begin *A Bloomsbury Group Reader*. Virginia Woolf's is a critical credo, Lytton Strachey's is a manifesto, Roger Fry's is a disclaimer, and E. M. Forster's a backward glance over his short stories.

1

Virginia Woolf: The Common Reader

A Bloomsbury Group Reader begins and ends with The Common Reader *of Virginia Woolf. She introduced her first collection of literary essays in 1925 with a brief sketch of the common reader borrowed from Samuel Johnson's conception of a reader who was neither critic nor scholar. To this Woolf added the notion that such a reader might also be creative. Bloomsbury found eighteenth-century rationality and common sense a relief after Romanticism and Victorianism, and Virginia Woolf shared a number of Johnson's critical convictions; nevertheless there is still something ironical in the invoking of Johnson to support her very different critical and biographical writings.*

There is a sentence in Dr Johnson's 'Life of Gray' which might well be written up in all those rooms, too humble to be called libraries, yet full of books, where the pursuit of reading is carried on by private people. '... I rejoice to concur with the common reader; for by the common sense of readers, uncorrupted by literary prejudices, after all the refinements of subtilty and the dogmatism of learning, must be finally decided all claim to poetical honours.' It defines their qualities; it dignifies their aims; it bestows upon a pursuit which devours a great deal of time, and is yet apt to leave behind it nothing very substantial, the sanction of the great man's approval.

The common reader, as Dr Johnson implies, differs from the critic and the scholar. He is worse educated, and nature has not gifted him so generously. He reads for his own pleasure rather than to impart knowledge or correct the opinions of others. Above all, he is guided by an instinct to create for himself, out of whatever odds and ends he can come by, some kind of whole – a portrait of a man, a sketch of an age, a theory of the art of writing. He never ceases, as he reads, to run up some rickety and ramshackle fabric which shall give him the temporary satisfaction of looking sufficiently like the real object to allow of affection, laughter, and argument. Hasty, inaccurate, and superficial, snatching now this poem, now that scrap of old furniture, without caring where he finds it or of what nature it may be so long as it serves his purpose and rounds his structure, his deficiencies as a critic are too obvious to be pointed out; but if he has, as Dr Johnson maintained, some say in the final distribution of poetical honours, then, perhaps, it may be worth while to write down a few of the ideas and opinions which, insignificant in themselves, yet contribute to so mighty a result.

2

Lytton Strachey:
Preface to *Eminent Victorians*

Virginia Woolf dedicated The Common Reader *to Lytton Strachey, whose* Eminent Victorians *had appeared towards the end of 1918. Strachey's preface to the ironical biographies of Cardinal Manning, Florence Nightingale, Dr Arnold, and General Gordon is a Bloomsbury manifesto that shows the influence of the First World War. Abandoning the method of scrupulous narration, Strachey proclaims the modern biographer's need for art and for freedom of spirit. Fragmentary rather than systematic truth was all that Strachey could manage, but within this restricted scope is a profound Bloomsbury belief in the value of human beings for their own sakes. The note of exposé on which the preface ends is sounded in one of the pseudo-quotations that Strachey was fond of making up.*

The history of the Victorian Age will never be written: we know too much about it. For ignorance is the first requisite of the historian – ignorance, which simplifies and clarifies, which selects and omits, with a placid perfection unattainable by the highest art. Concerning the Age which has just passed, our fathers and our grandfathers have poured forth and accumulated so vast a quantity of information that the industry of a Ranke would be submerged by it, and the perspicacity of a Gibbon would quail before it. It is not by the direct method of a scrupulous narration that the explorer of the past can hope to depict that singular epoch. If he is wise, he will adopt a subtler strategy. He will attack his subject in unexpected places; he will fall upon the flank, or the rear; he will shoot a sudden, revealing searchlight into obscure recesses, hitherto undivined. He will row out over that great ocean of material, and lower down into it, here and there, a little bucket, which will bring up to the light of day some characteristic specimen, from those far depths, to be examined with a careful curiosity. Guided by these considerations, I have written the ensuing studies. I have attempted, through the medium of biography, to present some Victorian visions to the modern eye. They are, in one sense, haphazard visions – that is to say, my choice of subjects has been determined by no desire to construct a system or to prove a theory, but by simple motives of convenience and of art. It has been my purpose to illustrate rather than to explain. It would have been futile to hope to tell even a *précis* of the truth about the Victorian age, for the shortest *précis* must fill innumerable volumes. But, in the lives of an ecclesiastic, an educational authority, a woman of action, and a man of adventure, I have sought to examine and elucidate certain fragments of the truth which took my fancy and lay to my hand.

I hope, however, that the following pages may prove to be of interest from the strictly biographical no less than from the historical point of view. Human beings are too important to be treated as mere symptoms of the past. They have a value which is independent of any temporal processes – which is eternal, and must be felt for its own sake. The art of biography seems to have fallen on evil times in England. We have had, it is true, a few masterpieces, but we have never had, like the French, a great biographical tradition; we have had no Fontenelles and Condorcets, with their incomparable *éloges*, compressing into a few shining pages the manifold existences of men. With us, the most delicate and humane of all the branches of the art of writing has been relegated to the journeymen of letters; we do not reflect that it is perhaps as difficult to write a good life as to live one. Those two fat volumes, with which it is our custom to commemorate the dead – who does not know them, with their ill-digested masses of material, their slipshod style, their tone of tedious panegyric, their lamentable lack of selection, of detachment, of design? They are as familiar as the *cortège* of the undertaker, and wear the same air of slow, funereal barbarism. One is tempted to suppose, of some of them, that they were composed by that functionary, as the final item of his job. The studies in this book are indebted, in more ways than one, to such works – works which certainly deserve the name of Standard Biographies. For they have provided me not only with much indispensable information, but with something even more precious – an example. How many lessons are to be learnt from them! But it is hardly necessary to particularize. To preserve, for instance, a becoming brevity – a brevity which excludes everything that is redundant and nothing that is significant – that, surely, is the first duty of the biographer. The second, no less surely, is to maintain his own freedom of spirit. It is not his business to be complimentary; it is his business to lay bare the facts of the case, as he understands them. That is what I have aimed at in this book – to lay bare the facts of some cases, as I understand them, dispassionately, impartially, and without ulterior intentions. To quote the words of a Master – 'Je n'impose rien; je ne propose rien: j'expose.'

3

Roger Fry:
Introduction to *A Sampler of Castile*

---

*Art, fragmentariness, and freedom of spirit are also claimed by Roger Fry
in his introduction to* A Sampler of Castile, *published by Leonard and
Virginia Woolf's Hogarth Press in 1923 with sixteen plates of drawings
by Fry to accompany his Castilian descriptions. Visual and verbal representation are closely allied in Bloomsbury's work, and especially Fry's.
Fry's introduction might have been placed among the travel writings of
this collection (where another selection from his sampler is given), but as
an introduction disingenuously disavowing any concern for the reader, it
also has a place among Bloomsbury's forewords.*

This book makes no pretensions except one, namely – that it was not
written for you, my reader, but solely for myself. It was written so that
I might let some of all those variegated, vivid, and odd impressions run
themselves clear on to paper before they became part of the vague mist
of blurred images which move like ghosts in the dim world of the past.
It has been botched together from scraps written at odd moments in halls
of hotels when dinner lingered, in waiting-rooms, in trains, and even
trams; whenever or wherever, in short, the chance of crystallizing some
of these haunting images in words presented itself to a capricious and
unmethodical mind.

How then, you will ask, did it ever come into your hands? That is the
result of the Devil's usual little manoeuvre which I trust you know as well
as I. One is standing near the edge of an attractive ravine, when he comes
up and politely says, 'If you are thinking of trying to get down there, I

should strongly dissuade you; it really is rather dangerous, and you never know what may happen. But just a little way down there, you see that convenient ledge: from there you can get the whole prospect, and the way is quite easy. There is nothing irrevocable in going down that far: you can always turn back.' Every time this happens one forgets how slippery those ledges are, what an easy slide it is from writing to publishing. So now, I find myself approaching that nasty bump at the bottom, and there is no way out of it. After all, the slide down is pleasant enough while it lasts; in fact, I should feel rather disappointed if the Hogarth Press broke down and I found myself safely back on the brink. I expect the Devil knew that all along.

It was not written for you, then, good reader; but now that I find the printer is going to get these sheets, after all I begin to think of you – you must either have been to Spain or not been to Spain. In a book that has to do with travel one may presume that those who have been to the country in question are easily interested; for either they will enjoy explaining to every one how wrong-headed, misled, and ill-equipped the author is, how false his generalizations and how feeble his impressions, or they will begin writing, 'How true!' – 'How just!' – 'Quite so' in the margin, and in either case they are well occupied. But you, reader, who have not been to Spain, how can I suppose that I can hand over to you, through language, the faintest image of a single moment's physical sensation? And, now I come to think of it, I expect the best chance is, if one does not happen to have genius, not to think of you at all but only of my own sensations – which is precisely what I have done.

To be *innocente* is, I am told, the worst thing that can happen to one in Spain. *Innocente* is one of those apparently harmless little words, like *stupido* in Italian, which one had better not use. To be *innocente*, not to be up to snuff, to be a mug, and generally out of it, is a fate too terrible to be accepted by a Spaniard. He must always be in the know and have the tip, not indeed given to him, but got by his native intuition. I find it simpler to avoid complications by accepting the ultimate disgrace from the beginning. I write, therefore, as an *innocente*; however absurd my generalizations may be, I cannot fall lower. I have complete liberty to think as I like. In short, I can enjoy the position of being envied by no one.

4

E. M. Forster:
Introduction to *Collected Short Stories*

Forster once thought his short stories to be his best work. In the intro-duction he wrote to his collected stories of 1947, he humorously deprecates them as fantasies that the god Hermes might conduct 'to a not too terrible hereafter'. Forster had defined fantasy in Aspects of the Novel *as a bar of light across fiction that asks readers to accept the impossible, but not all of his collected stories are actually fantasies, even by this definition. As an irreverent account of creativity's vagaries, how-ever, Forster's introduction is a characteristic Bloomsbury text.*

These fantasies were written at various dates previous to the first world-war, and represent all that I have accomplished in a particular line. Much has happened since; transport has been disorganized, frontiers rectified on the map and in the spirit, there has been a second world-war, there are preparations for a third, and Fantasy to-day tends to retreat or to dig herself in or to become apocalyptic out of deference to the atom-bomb. She can be caught in the open here by those who care to catch her. She flits over the scenes of Italian and English holidays, or wings her way with even less justification towards the countries of the future. She or he. For Fantasy, though often female, sometimes resembles a man, and even functions for Hermes who used to do the smaller behests of the gods – messenger, machine-breaker, and conductor of souls to a not-too-terrible hereafter.

The opening item, 'The Story of a Panic', is the first story I ever wrote and the attendant circumstances remain with me vividly. After I came

down from Cambridge – the Cambridge to which I have just returned –
I travelled abroad for a year, and I think it was in the May of 1902 that
I took a walk near Ravello. I sat down in a valley, a few miles above the
town, and suddenly the first chapter of the story rushed into my mind as
if it had waited for me there. I received it as an entity and wrote it out as
soon as I returned to the hotel. But it seemed unfinished and a few days
later I added some more until it was three times as long; as now printed.
Of these two processes, the first – that of sitting down on the theme as if
it were an anthill – has been rare. I did it again next year in Greece, where
the whole of 'The Road from Colonus' hung ready for me in a hollow
tree not far from Olympia. And I did it, or rather tried it on, a third time,
in Cornwall, at the Gurnard's Head. Here, just in the same way, a story
met me, and, since the 'Panic' and 'Colonus' had both been published
and admired, I embraced it as a masterpiece. It was about a man who was
saved from drowning by some fishermen, and knew not how to reward
them. What is your life worth? £5? £5,000? He ended by giving nothing,
he lived among them, hated and despised. As the theme swarmed over
me, I put my hand into my purse, drew out a golden sovereign – they
existed then – and inserted it into a collecting box of the Royal Lifeboat
Institution which had been erected upon the Gurnard's Head for such
situations as this. I could well afford it. I was bound to make the money
over and again. Calm sea, flat submerged rock whereon my hero was to
cling and stagger, village whence his rescuers should sally – I carried
off the lot, and only had to improvise his wife, a very understanding
woman. 'The Rock' was the title of this ill-fated effort. It was a complete
flop. Not an editor would look at it. My inspiration had been genuine
but worthless, like so much inspiration, and I have never sat down on a
theme since.

One of my novels, *The Longest Journey*, does indeed depend from an
encounter with the genius loci, but indirectly, complicatedly, not here to
be considered. Directly, the genius loci has only inspired me thrice, and
on the third occasion it deprived me of a sovereign. As a rule, I am set
going by my own arguments or memories, or by the motion of my pen,
and the various methods do not necessarily produce a discordant result.
If the reader will compare the first chapter of 'The Story of a Panic',
caught straight off the spot it describes, with the two subsequent chapters, in which I set myself to wonder what would happen afterwards, I do
not think he will notice that a fresh hemisphere has swung into action.
All a writer's faculties, including the valuable faculty of faking, do con-
spire together thus for the creative act, and often do contrive an even
surface, one putting in a word here, another there.

The other stories call for little comment from their author. 'The

Machine Stops' is a reaction to one of the earlier heavens of H. G. Wells. 'The Eternal Moment', though almost an honest-to-God yarn, is a meditation on Cortina d'Ampezzo. As for 'The Point of It', it was ill-liked when it came out by my Bloomsbury friends. 'What *is* the point of it?' they queried thinly, nor did I know how to reply.

Original publication was in two volumes. The first was named after 'The Celestial Omnibus', and was dedicated 'To the Memory of the Independent Review.' This was a monthly, controlled by an editorial board of friends who had encouraged me to start writing; another friend, Roger Fry, designed the book-cover and end-paper. The second volume came out many years later. It was called *The Eternal Moment*, and I dedicated it 'To T. E. in the absence of anything else.' T. E. was Lawrence of Arabia.

Now that the stories are gathered together into a single cover, and are sailing further into a world they never foresaw, should they be dedicated anew? Perhaps, and perhaps to a god. Hermes Psychopompus suggests himself, who came to my mind at the beginning of this introduction. He can anyhow stand in the prow and watch the disintegrating sea.

Part II

Stories

Bloomsbury's fiction for most readers means their novels, yet E. M. Forster, Leonard Woolf, and Virginia Woolf all published collections of short stories as well. The three included here are interesting in themselves and also good introductions to the kinds of novels each wrote.

5

E. M. Forster: The Point of It

E. M. Forster's are the best known of Bloomsbury's short stories. 'The Point of It' was written in 1911, after Howards End *and before* Maurice. *Forster included it in a 1928 collection called* The Eternal Moment *after one of the stories. 'The Point of It' is another story of an eternal moment. In a later Memoir Club paper on the poet A. E. Housman, Forster said the Bloomsbury friends who disliked the story (see p. 12) were the Stracheys. Fantasies on meaning of life were certainly not likely to appeal to Lytton, yet a poem of his entitled 'When We Are Dead a Thousand Years' impressed Forster and may lie behind the story. Although Forster could not tell the Stracheys what the point of the story was, he wrote later in his memoir that its theme was about affection shattering the gates of hell – a theme he had told Housman he found memorably expressed in his poem 'Hell Gate'. Housman was not impressed either. In its combination of imaginative fantasy and realistic satire, 'The Point of It' is a very Forsterian story.*

I

'I don't see the point of it,' said Micky, through much imbecile laughter.

Harold went on rowing. They had spent too long on the sand-dunes, and now the tide was running out of the estuary strongly. The sun was setting, the fields on the opposite bank shone bright, and the farm-house where they were stopping glowed from its upper windows as though filled to the brim with fire.

'We're going to be carried out to sea,' Micky continued. 'You'll never win unless you bust yourself a bit, and you a poor invalid, too. I back the sea.'

They were reaching the central channel, the backbone, as it were, of the retreating waters. Once past it, the force of the tide would slacken, and they would have easy going until they beached under the farm. It was a glorious evening. It had been a most glorious day. They had rowed out to the dunes at the slack, bathed, raced, eaten, slept, bathed and raced and eaten again. Micky was in roaring spirits. God had never thwarted him hitherto, and he could not suppose that they would really be made late for supper by an ebbing tide. When they came to the channel, and the boat, which had been slowly edging upstream, hung motionless among the moving waters, he lost all semblance of sanity, and shouted:

> 'It may be that the gulfs will wash us down,
> It may be we shall touch the Happy Isles,
> And see the great Achilles, whom we knew.'

Harold, who did not care for poetry, only shouted. His spirits also were roaring, and he neither looked nor felt a poor invalid. Science had talked to him seriously of late, shaking her head at his sunburnt body. What should Science know? She had sent him down to the sea to recruit, and Micky to see that he did not tire himself. Micky had been a nuisance at first, but common sense had prevailed, as it always does among the young. A fortnight ago, he would not let the patient handle an oar. Now he bid him bust himself, and Harold took him at his word and did so. He made himself all will and muscle. He began not to know where he was. The thrill of the stretcher against his feet, and of the tide up his arms, merged with his friend's voice towards one nameless sensation; he was approaching the mystic state that is the athlete's true though unacknowledged goal: he was beginning to be.

Micky chanted, 'One, two – one, two,' and tried to help by twitching the rudder. But Micky had imagination. He looked at the flaming windows and fancied that the farm was a star and the boat its attendant satellite. Then the tide was the rushing ether stream of the universe, the interstellar surge that beats for ever. How jolly! He did not formulate his joys, after the weary fashion of older people. He was far too happy to be thankful. 'Remember now thy Creator in the days of thy youth,' are the words of one who has left his youth behind, and all that Micky sang was 'One, two.'

Harold laughed without hearing. Sweat poured off his forehead. He put on a spurt, as did the tide.

'Wish the doctor could see you,' cried Micky.

No answer. Setting his teeth, he went berserk. His ancestors called to him that it was better to die than to be beaten by the sea. He rowed with gasps and angry little cries, while the voice of the helmsman lashed him to fury.

'That's right – one, two – plug it in harder. . . . Oh, I say, this is a bit stiff, though. Let's give it up, old man, perhaps.'

The gulls were about them now. Some wheeled overhead, others bobbed past on the furrowed waters. The song of a lark came faintly from the land, and Micky saw the doctor's trap driving along the road that led to the farm. He felt ashamed.

'Look here, Harold, you oughtn't to – I oughtn't to have let you. I – I don't see the point of it.'

'Don't you?' said Harold with curious distinctness. 'Well, you will some day,' and so saying dropped both oars. The boat spun round at this, the farm, the trap, the song of the lark vanished, and he fell heavily against the rowlock. Micky caught at him. He had strained his heart. Half in the boat and half out of it, he died, a rotten business.

II

A rotten business. It happened when Michael was twenty-two, and he expected never to be happy again. The sound of his own voice shouting as he was carried out, the doctor's voice saying, 'I consider you responsible,' the coming of Harold's parents, the voice of the curate summarizing Harold's relations with the unseen – all these things affected him so deeply that he supposed they would affect him for ever. They did not, because he lived to be over seventy, and with the best will in the world, it is impossible to remember clearly for so long. The mind, however sensitive and affectionate, is coated with new experiences daily; it cannot clear itself of the steady accretion, and is forced either to forget the past or to distort it. So it was with Michael. In time only the more dramatic incidents survived. He remembered Harold's final gesture (one hand grasping his own, the other plunged deep into the sea), because there was a certain aesthetic quality about it, not because it was the last of his friend. He remembered the final words for the same reason. 'Don't you see the point of it? Well, you will some day.' The phrase struck his fancy, and passed into his own stock; after thirty or forty years he forgot its origin. He is not to blame; the business of life snowed him under.

There is also this to say: he and Harold had nothing in common except youth. No spiritual bond could survive. They had never discussed theology or social reform, or any of the problems that were thronging Michael's brain, and consequently, though they had been intimate enough, there was nothing to remember. Harold melted the more one thought of him. Robbed of his body, he was so shadowy. Nor could one imagine him as a departed spirit, for the world beyond death is surely august. Neither in heaven nor hell is there place for athletics and aimless good temper, and if these were taken from Harold, what was left? Even if the unseen life should prove an archetype of this, even if it should contain a sun and stars of its own, the sunburn of earth must fade off our faces as we look at it, the muscles of earth must wither before we can go rowing on its infinite sea. Michael sadly resigned his friend to God's mercy. He himself could do nothing, for men can only immortalize those who leave behind them some strong impression of poetry or wisdom.

For himself he expected another fate. With all humility, he knew that he was not as Harold. It was no merit of his own, but he had been born of a more intellectual stock, and had inherited powers that rendered him worthier of life, and of whatever may come after it. He cared for the universe, for the tiny tangle in it that we call civilization, for his fellow-men who had made the tangle and who transcended it. Love, the love of humanity, warmed him; and even when he was thinking of other matters, was looking at Orion perhaps in the cold winter evenings, a pang of joy, too sweet for description, would thrill him, and he would feel sure that our highest impulses have some eternal value, and will be completed hereafter. So full a nature could not brood over death.

To summarize his career.

Soon after the tragedy, when he in his turn was recruiting, he met the woman who was to become his helpmate through life. He had met her once before, and had not liked her; she had seemed uncharitable and hard. Now he saw that her hardness sprang from a morality that he himself lacked. If he believed in love, Janet believed in truth. She tested all men and all things. She had no patience with the sentimentalist who shelters from the world's rough and tumble. Engaged at that time to another man, she spoke more freely to Michael than she would otherwise have done, and told him that it is not enough to feel good and to feel that others are good; one's business is to make others better, and she urged him to adopt a profession. The beauty of honest work dawned upon the youth as she spoke. Mentally and physically, he came to full manhood, and, after due preparation, he entered the Home Civil Service – the British Museum.

Here began a career that was rather notable, and wholly beneficial to humanity. With his ideals of conduct and culture, Michael was not content with the official routine. He desired to help others, and, since he was gifted with tact, they consented to the operation. Before long he became a conciliatory force in his department. He could mollify his superiors, encourage his inferiors, soothe foreign scholars, and show that there is something to be said for all sides. Janet, who watched his rise, taxed him again with instability. But now she was wrong. The young man was not a mere opportunist. He always had a sincere opinion of his own, or he could not have retained the respect of his colleagues. It was really the inherent sweetness of his nature at work, turned by a woman's influence towards fruitful ends.

At the end of a ten years' acquaintance the two married. In the interval Janet had suffered much pain, for the man to whom she had been engaged had proved unworthy of her. Her character was set when she came to Michael, and, as he knew, strongly contrasted with his own; and perhaps they had already interchanged all the good they could. But the marriage proved durable and sufficiently happy. He, in particular, made endless allowances, for toleration and sympathy were becoming the cardinal points of his nature. If his wife was unfair to the official mind, or if his brother-in-law, an atheist, denounced religion, he would say to himself, 'They cannot help it; they are made thus, and have the qualities of their defects. Let me rather think of my own, and strive for a wider outlook ceaselessly.' He grew sweeter every day.

It was partly this desire for a wider outlook that turned him to literature. As he was crossing the forties it occurred to him to write a few essays, somewhat retrospective in tone, and thoughtful rather than profound in content. They had some success. Their good taste, their lucid style, the tempered Christianity of their ethics, whetted the half-educated public, and made it think and feel. They were not, and were not intended to be, great literature, but they opened the doors to it, and were indubitably a power for good. The first volume was followed by 'The Confessions of a Middle-aged Man'. In it Michael paid melodious tribute to youth, but showed that ripeness is all. Experience, he taught, is the only humanizer; sympathy, balance and many-sidedness cannot come to a man until he is elderly. It is always pleasant to be told that the best is yet to be, and the sale of the book was large. Perhaps he would have become a popular author, but his wife's influence restrained him from writing anything that he did not sincerely feel. She had borne him three children by now – Henry, Catherine, and Adam. On the whole they were a happy family. Henry never gave any trouble. Catherine took after her mother. Adam, who was wild and uncouth, caused his father some anxiety. He could not understand him, in spite of careful observation, and they never became real friends. Still, it was but a little cloud in a large horizon. At home, as in his work, Michael was more successful than most men.

Thus he slipped into the fifties. On the death of his father he inherited a house in the Surrey hills, and Janet, whose real interests were horticultural, settled down there. After all, she had not proved an intellectual woman. Her fierce manner had misled him and perhaps herself into believing it. She was efficient enough in London society, but it bored her, for she lacked her husband's pliancy, and aged more rapidly than he did. Nor did the country suit her. She grew querulous, disputing with other ladies about the names of flowers. And, of course, the years were not without their effect on him, too. By now he was somewhat of a valetudinarian. He had given up all outdoor sports, and, though his health remained good, grew bald, and rather stout and timid. He was against late hours, violent exercise, night walks, swimming when hot, muddling about in open boats, and he often had to check himself from fidgeting the children. Henry, a charming sympathetic lad, would squeeze his hand and say, 'All right, father.' But Catherine and Adam sometimes frowned. He thought of the children more and more. Now that his wife was declining, they were the future, and he was determined to keep in touch with them, remembering how his own father had failed with him. He believed in gentleness, and often stood between them and their mother. When the boys grew up he let them choose their own friends. When Catherine, at the age of nineteen, asked if she might go away and earn some money as a lady gardener, he let her go. In this case he had his reward, for Catherine, having killed the flowers, returned. She was a restless, scowling young woman, a trial to her mother, who could not imagine what girls were coming to. Then she married and improved greatly; indeed, she proved his chief support in the coming years.

For, soon after her marriage, a great trouble fell on him. Janet became bedridden, and, after a protracted illness, passed into the unknown. Sir Michael – for he had been knighted – declared that he should not survive her. They were so accustomed to each other, so mutually necessary, that he fully expected to pass away after her. In this he was mistaken. She died when he was sixty, and he lived to be over seventy. His character had passed beyond the clutch of circumstance and he still retained his old interests and his unconquerable benignity.

A second trouble followed hard on the first. It transpired that Adam was devoted to his mother, and had only tolerated home life for her sake. After a brutal scene he left. He wrote from the Argentine that he was sorry, but wanted to start for himself. 'I don't see the point of it,' quavered Sir Michael. 'Have I ever stopped him or any of you from starting?' Henry and Catherine agreed with him. Yet he felt that they understood their brother better than he did. 'I have given him freedom all his life,' he continued. 'I have given him freedom, what more does he want?' Henry, after hesitation, said, 'There are some people who feel that freedom cannot be given. At least I have heard so. Perhaps Adam is like that. Unless he took freedom he might not feel free.' Sir Michael disagreed. 'I have now studied adolescence for many years,' he replied, 'and your conclusions, my dear boy, are ridiculous.'

The two rallied to their father gallantly; and, after all, he spent a dignified old age. Having retired from the British Museum, he produced a little aftermath of literature. The great public had forgotten him, but the courtliness of his 'Musings of a Pensioner' procured him some circulation among elderly and educated audiences. And he found a new spiritual consolation. *Anima naturaliter Anglicana*, he had never been hostile to the Established Church; and, when he criticized her worldliness and occasional inhumanity, had spoken as one who was outside her rather than against her. After his wife's death and the flight of his son he lost any lingering taste for speculation. The experience of years disposed him to accept the experience of centuries, and to merge his feeble personal note in the great voice of tradition. Yes; a serene and dignified old age. Few grudged it to him. Of course, he had enemies, who professed to see through him, and said that Adam had seen through him too; but no impartial observer agreed. No ulterior motive had ever biassed Sir Michael. The purity of his record was not due to luck, but to purity within, and his conciliatory manner sprang from a conciliated soul. He could look back on failures and mistakes, and he had not carried out the ideals of his youth. Who has? But he had succeeded better than most men in modifying those ideals to fit the world of facts, and if love had been modified into sympathy and sympathy into compromise, let one of his contemporaries cast the first stone.

One fact remained – the fact of death. Hitherto, Sir Michael had never died, and at times he was bestially afraid. But more often death appeared as a prolongation of his present career. He saw himself quietly and tactfully organizing some corner in infinity with his wife's assistance; Janet would be greatly improved. He saw himself passing from a sphere in which he had been efficient into a sphere which combined the familiar with the eternal, and in which he would be equally efficient – passing into it with dignity and without pain. This life is a preparation for the next. Those who live longest are consequently the best prepared. Experience is the great teacher; blessed are the experienced, for they need not further modify their ideals.

The manner of his death was as follows. He, too, met with an accident. He was walking from his town house to Catherine's by a short cut through a slum; some women were quarrelling about a fish, and as he passed they appealed to him. Always courteous, the old man stopped, said that he had not sufficient data to judge on, and advised them to lay the fish aside for twenty-four hours. This chanced to annoy them, and they grew more angry with him than with one another. They accused him of 'doing them', of 'getting round them', and one, who was the worse for drink, said, 'See if he gets round that,' and slapped him with the fish in the face. He fell. When he came to himself he was lying in bed with one of his headaches.

He could hear Catherine's voice. She annoyed him. If he did not open his eyes, it was only because he did not choose.

'He has been like this for nearly two years,' said Henry's voice.

It was, at the most, ten minutes since he had fallen in the slum. But he did not choose to argue.

'Yes, he's pretty well played out,' said a third voice – actually the voice of Adam; how and when had Adam returned? 'But, then, he's been that for the last thirty years.'

'Gently, old boy,' said Henry.

'Well, he has,' said Adam. 'I don't believe in cant. He never did anything since Mother died, and damned little before. They've forgotten his books because they aren't first-hand; they're rearranging the cases he arranged in the British Museum. That's the lot. What else has he done except tell people to dress warmly, but not too warm?'

'Adam, you really mustn't –'

'It's because nobody speaks up that men of the old man's type get famous. It's a sign of your sloppy civilization. You're all afraid – afraid of originality, afraid of work, afraid of hurting one another's feelings. You let anyone come to the top who doesn't frighten you, and as soon as he dies you forget him and knight some other figurehead instead.'

An unknown voice said, 'Shocking, Mr Adam, shocking. Such a dear old man, and quite celebrated, too.'

'You'll soon get used to me, nurse.'

The nurse laughed.

'Adam, it is a relief to have you,' said Catherine after a pause. 'I want you and your boy to help me with mine.' Her voice sounded dimmer; she had turned from her father without a word of farewell. 'One must profit by the mistakes of others . . . after all, more heroism. . . . I am determined to keep in touch with my boy –'

'Larrup him,' said Adam. 'That's the secret.' He followed his sister out of the room.

Then Henry's delightful laugh sounded for the last time. 'You make us all feel twenty years younger,' he said; 'more like when –'

The door shut.

Sir Michael grew cold with rage. This was life, this was what the younger generation had been thinking. Adam he ignored, but at the recollection of Henry and Catherine he determined to die. If he chose, he could have risen from bed and driven the whole pack into the street. But he did not choose. He chose rather to leave this shoddy and ungrateful world. The immense and superhuman cynicism that is latent in all of us came at last to the top and transformed him. He saw the absurdity of love, and the vision so tickled him that he began to laugh. The nurse, who had called him a dear old man, bent over him, and at the same moment two boys came into the sick-room.

'How's grandpapa?' asked one of them – Catherine's boy.

'Not so well,' the nurse answered.

There was a silence. Then the other boy said, 'Come along, let's cut.'

'But they told us not to.'

'Why should we do what old people tell us? Dad's pretty well played out, and so's your mother.'

'Shocking; be off with you both,' said the nurse; and, with a little croon of admiration, Catherine's boy followed his cousin out of the room. Their grandfather's mirth increased. He rolled about in the bed; and, just as he was grasping the full irony of the situation, he died, and pursued it into the unknown.

III

Micky was still in bed. He was aware of so much through long melancholy dreams. But when he opened his mouth to laugh, it filled with dust. Choosing to open his eyes, he found that he had swollen enormously, and lay sunk in the sand of an illimitable plain. As he expected, he had no occasion greatly to modify his ideals; infinity had merely taken the place of his bedroom and of London. Nothing moved on its surface except a few sand-pillars, which would sometimes merge into each other as though confabulating, and then fall with a slight hiss. Save for these, there was no motion, no noise, nor could he feel any wind.

How long had he lain here? Perhaps for years, long before death perhaps, while his body seemed to be walking among men. Life is so short and trivial, that who knows whether we arrive for it entirely, whether more than a fraction of the soul is aroused to put on flesh? The bud and the blossom perish in a moment, the husk endures, and may not the soul be a husk? It seemed to Micky that he had lain in the dust for ever, suffering and sneering, and that the essence of all things, the primal power that lies behind the stars, is senility. Age, toothless, dropsical age; ungenerous to age and to youth; born before all ages, and outlasting them; the universe as old age.

The place degraded while it tortured. It was vast, yet ignoble. It sloped downward into darkness and upward into cloud, but into what darkness, what clouds! No tragic splendour glorified them. When he looked at them he understood why he was so unhappy, for they were looking at him, sneering at him while he sneered. Their dirtiness was more ancient than the hues of day and night, their irony more profound; he was part of their jest, even as youth was part of his, and slowly he realized that he was, and had for some years been, in Hell.

All around him lay other figures, huge and fungous. It was as if the plain had festered. Some of them could sit up, others scarcely protruded from the sand, and he knew that they had made the same mistake in life as himself, though he did not know yet what the mistake had been; probably some little slip, easily avoided had one but been told.

Speech was permissible. Presently a voice said, 'Is not ours a heavenly sky? Is it not beautiful?'

'Most beautiful,' answered Micky, and found each word a stab of pain. Then he knew that one of the sins here punished was appreciation; he was suffering for all the praise that he had given to the bad and mediocre upon earth; when he had praised out of idleness, or to please people, or to encourage people; for all the praise that had not been winged with passion. He repeated 'Most beautiful,' and the sky quivered, for he was entering into fuller torments now. One ray of happiness survived: his wife could not be in this place. She had not sinned with the people of the plain, and could not suffer their distortion. Her view of life had proved right after all; and, in his utter misery, this comforted him. Janet should again be his religion, and as eternity dragged forward and returned upon itself and dragged forward she would show him that old age, if rightly managed, can be beautiful; that experience, if rightly received, can lead the soul of man to bliss. Then he turned to his neighbour, who was continuing his hymn of praise.

'I could lie here for ever,' he was saying. 'When I think of my restlessness during life – that is to say, during what men miscall life, for it is death really – this is life – when I think of my restlessness on earth, I am overcome by so much goodness and mercy, I could lie here for ever.'

'And will you?' asked Micky.

'Ah, that is the crowning blessing – I shall, and so will you.'

Here a pillar of sand passed between them. It was long before they could speak or see. Then Micky took up the song, chafed by the particles that were working into his soul.

'I, too, regret my wasted hours,' he said, 'especially the hours of my youth. I regret all the time I spent in the sun. In later years I did repent, and that is why I am admitted here where there is no sun; yes, and no wind and none of the stars that drove me almost mad at night once. It would be appalling, would it not, to see Orion again, the central star of whose sword is not a star but a nebula, the golden seed of worlds to be. How I dreaded the autumn on earth when Orion rises, for he recalled adventure and my youth. It was appalling. How thankful I am to see him no more.'

'Ah, but it was worse,' cried the other, 'to look high leftward from Orion and see the Twins. Castor and Pollux were brothers, one human, the other divine; and Castor died. But Pollux went down to Hell that he might be with him.'

'Yes; that is so. Pollux went into Hell.'

'Then the gods had pity on both, and raised them aloft to be stars whom sailors worship, and all who love and are young. Zeus was their father, Helen their sister, who brought the Greeks against Troy. I dreaded them more than Orion.'

They were silent, watching their own sky. It approved. They had been cultivated men on earth, and these are capable of the nicer torments hereafter. Their memories will strike exquisite images to enhance their pain. 'I will speak no more,' said Micky to himself. 'I will be silent through eternity.' But the darkness prised open his lips, and immediately he was speaking.

'Tell me more about this abode of bliss,' he asked. 'Are there grades in it? Are there ranks in our heaven?'

'There are two heavens,' the other replied, 'the heaven of the hard and of the soft. We here lie in the heaven of the soft. It is a sufficient arrangement, for all men grow either hard or soft as they grow old.'

As he spoke the clouds lifted, and, looking up the slope of the plain, Micky saw that in the distance it was bounded by mountains of stone, and he knew, without being told, that among those mountains Janet lay, rigid, and that he should never see her. She had not been saved. The darkness would mock her, too, for ever. With him lay the sentimentalists, the conciliators, the peacemakers, the humanists, and all who have trusted the warmer vision; with his wife were the reformers and ascetics and all sword-like souls. By different paths they had come to Hell, and Micky now saw what the bustle of life conceals: that the years are bound either to liquefy a man or to stiffen him, and that Love and Truth, who seem to contend for our souls like angels, hold each the seeds of our decay.

'It is, indeed, a sufficient arrangement,' he said; 'both sufficient and simple. But answer one question more that my bliss may be perfected; in which of these two heavens are the young?'

His neighbour answered, 'In neither; there are no young.'

He spoke no more, and settled himself more deeply in the dust. Micky did the same. He had vague memories of men and women who had died before reaching maturity, of boys and unwedded maidens and youths lowered into the grave before their parents' eyes. Whither had they gone, that undeveloped minority? What was the point of their brief existence? Had they vanished utterly, or were they given another chance of accreting experiences until they became like Janet or himself? One thing was certain: there were no young, either in the mountains or the plain, and perhaps the very memory of such creatures was an illusion fostered by cloud.

The time was now ripe for a review of his life on earth. He traced his decomposition – his work had been soft, his books soft, he had softened his relations with other men. He had seen good in everything, and this is itself a sign of decay. Whatever occurred he had been appreciative, tolerant, pliant. Consequently he had been a success; Adam was right; it was the moment in civilization for his type. He had mistaken self-criticism for self-discipline, he had muffled in himself and others the keen, heroic edge. Yet the luxury of repentance was denied him. The fault was his, but the fate humanity's, for everyone grows hard or soft as he grows old.

'This is my life,' thought Micky; 'my books forgotten, my work superseded. This is the whole of my life.' And his agony increased, because all the same there had been in that life an elusive joy which, if only he could have distilled it, would have sweetened infinity. It was part of the jest that he should try, and should eternally oscillate between disgust and desire. For there is nothing ultimate in Hell; men will not lay aside all hope on entering it, or they would attain to the splendour of despair. To have made a poem about Hell is to mistake its very essence; it is the imagination of men, who will have beauty, that fashion it as ice or flame. Old, but capable of growing older, Micky lay in the sandy country, remembering that once he had remembered a country – a country that had not been sand. . . .

He was aroused by the mutterings of the spirits round him. An uneasiness such as he had not noted in them before had arisen. 'A pillar of sand,' said one. Another said, 'It is not; it comes from the river.'

He asked, 'What river?'

'The spirits of the damned dwell over it; we never speak of that river.'

'Is it a broad river?'

'Swift, and very broad.'

'Do the damned ever cross it?'

'They are permitted, we know not why, to cross it now and again.'

And in these answers he caught a new tone, as if his companions were frightened, and were finding means to express their fear. When he said, 'With permission, they can do us no harm,' he was answered, 'They harm us with light and a song.' And again, 'They harm us because they remember and try to remind.'

'Of what would they remind us?'

'Of the hour when we were as they.'

As he questioned a whisper arose from the low-lying verges. The spirits were crying to each other faintly. He heard, 'It is coming; drive it back over the river, shatter it, compel it to be old.' And then the darkness was cloven, and a star of pain broke in his soul. He understood now; a torment greater than any was at hand.

'I was before choice,' came the song. 'I was before hardness and softness were divided. I was in the days when truth was love. And I am.'

All the plain was convulsed. But the invader could not be shattered. When it pressed the air parted and the sand-pillars fell, and its path was filled with senile weeping.

'I have been all men, but all men have forgotten me. I transfigured the world for them until they preferred the world. They came to me as children, afraid; I taught them, and they despised me. Childhood is a dream about me, experience a slow forgetting: I govern the magic years between them, and am.'

'Why trouble us?' moaned the shades. 'We could bear our torment, just bear it, until there was light and a song. Go back again over the river. This is Heaven, we were saying, that darkness is God; we could praise them till you came. The book of our deeds is closed; why open it? We were damned from our birth; leave it there. O, supreme jester, leave us. We have sinned, we know it, and this place is death and Hell.'

'Death comes,' the voice pealed, 'and death is not a dream or a forgetting. Death is real. But I, too, am real, and whom I will I save. I see the scheme of things, and in it no place for me, the brain and the body against me. Therefore I rend the scheme in two, and make a place, and under countless names have harrowed Hell. Come.' Then, in tones of inexpressible sweetness, 'Come to me all who remember. Come out of your eternity into mine. It is easy, for I am still at your eyes, waiting to look out of them; still in your hearts, waiting to beat. The years that I dwelt with you seemed short, but they were magical, and they outrun time.'

The shades were silent. They could not remember.

'Who desires to remember? Desire is enough. There is no abiding home for strength and beauty among men. The flower fades, the seas dry up in the sun, the sun and all the stars fade as a flower. But the desire for such things, that is eternal, that can abide, and he who desires me is I.'

Then Micky died a second death. This time he dissolved through terrible pain, scorched by the glare, pierced by the voice. But as he died he said, 'I do desire,' and immediately the invader vanished, and he was standing alone on the sandy plain. It had been merely a dream. But he was standing. How was that? Why had he not thought to stand before? He had been unhappy in Hell, and all that he had to do was to go elsewhere. He passed downwards, pained no longer by the mockery of its cloud. The pillars brushed against him and fell, the nether darkness went over his head. On he went till he came to the banks of the infernal stream, and there he stumbled – stumbled over a piece of wood, no vague substance, but a piece of wood that had once belonged to a tree. At his impact it moved, and water gurgled against it. He had embarked. Some one was rowing. He could see the blades of oars moving towards him through the foam, but the rower was invisible in cloud. As they neared mid-channel the boat went more slowly, for the tide was ebbing, and Micky knew that once carried out he would be lost eternally; there was no second hope of salvation. He could not speak, but his heart beat time to the oars – one, two. Hell made her last effort, and all that is evil in creation, all the distortions of love and truth by which we are vexed, came surging down the estuary, and the boat hung motionless. Micky heard the pant of breath through the roaring, the crack of muscles; then he heard a voice say, 'The point of it . . .' and a weight fell off his body and he crossed mid-stream.

It was a glorious evening. The boat had sped without prelude into sunshine. The sky was cloudless, the earth gold, and gulls were riding up and down on the furrowed waters. On the bank they had left were some sand-dunes rising to majestic hills; on the bank in front was a farm, full to the brim with fire.

6

Leonard Woolf: Pearls and Swine

Leonard Woolf wrote 'Pearls and Swine' out of his experience as an imperial civil servant in Ceylon. Later in Growing: An Autobiography of the Years 1904–1911 *he borrowed the story's description of the dead Arab diver in recounting the administration of the pearl fishery. When Woolf asked Forster's advice about his story, he was encouraging and praised the descriptions of the two deaths. He also complained a little that the story reminded him of the scold in Kipling and left him peevish, as Conrad did. Woolf's dramatic monologue form and some of the story's content – the allegorical Mr White's death, for instance – are obviously influenced by Conrad's 'Heart of Darkness'. While the three stories that Woolf collected in* Stories of the East *(1921) are haunted by Kipling and Conrad, the attitudes expressed in all of them became part of what Woolf called in* Growing *his 'education as an anti-imperialist'.*

I had finished my hundred up – or rather he had – with the Colonel and we strolled into the smoking room for a smoke and a drink round the fire before turning in. There were three other men already round the fire and they widened their circle to take us in. I didn't know them, hadn't spoken to them or indeed to anyone except the Colonel in the large gaudy uncomfortably comfortable hotel. I was run down, out of sorts generally, and – like a fool, I thought now – had taken a week off to eat, or rather to read the menus of interminable table d'hôte dinners, to play golf and to walk on the 'front' at Torquay.

I had only arrived the day before, but the Colonel (retired) a jolly tubby little man – with white moustaches like two S's lying side by side on the top of his stupid red lips and his kind choleric eyes bulging out on a life which he was quite content never for a moment to understand – made it a point, my dear Sir, to know every new arrival within one hour after he arrived.

We got our drinks and as, rather forgetting that I was in England, I murmured the Eastern formula, I noticed vaguely one of the other three glance at me over his shoulder for a moment. The Colonel stuck out his fat little legs in front of him, turning up his neatly shoed toes before the blaze. Two of the others were talking, talking as men so often do in the comfortable chairs of smoking rooms between ten and eleven at night, earnestly, seriously, of what they call affairs, or politics, or questions. I listened to their fat, full-fed, assured voices in that heavy room which smelt of solidity, safety, horsehair furniture, tobacco smoke, and the faint civilized aroma of whisky and soda. It came as a shock to me in that atmosphere that they were discussing India and the East: it does you know every now and again. Sentimental? Well, I expect one is sentimental about it, having lived there. It doesn't seem to go with solidity and horsehair furniture: the fifteen years come back to one in one moment all in a heap. How one hated it and how one loved it!

I suppose they had started on the Durbar and the King's visit. They had got on to Indian unrest, to our position in India, its duties, responsibilities, to the problem of East and West. They hadn't been there of course, they hadn't even seen the brothel and café chantant at Port Said suddenly open out into that pink and blue desert that leads you through Africa and Asia into the heart of the East. But they knew all about it, they had solved, with their fat voices and in their fat heads, riddles, older than the Sphinx, of peoples remote and ancient and mysterious whom they had never seen and could never understand. One was, I imagine, a stock-jobber, plump and comfortable with a greasy forehead and a high colour in his cheeks, smooth shiny brown hair and a carefully grown small moustache: a good dealer in the market; sharp and confident, with a loud voice and shifty eyes. The other was a clergyman: need I say more? Except that he was more of a clergyman even than most clergymen, I mean that he wore tight things – leggings don't they call them? or breeches? – round his calves. I never know what it means: whether they are bishops or rural deans or archdeacons or archimandrites. In any case I mistrust them even more than the black trousers: they seem to close the last door for anything human to get in through the black clothes. The dog collar closes up the armour above, and below, as long as they *were* trousers, at any rate some whiff of humanity might have eddied up the legs of them and touched bare flesh. But the gaiters button them up finally, irremediably, for ever.

I expect he was an archdeacon: he was saying:

'You can't impose Western civilization upon an Eastern people – I believe I'm right in saying that there are over two hundred millions in our Indian Empire – without a little disturbance. I'm a Liberal you know, I've been a Liberal my whole life – family tradition – though I grieve to say I could *not* follow Mr Gladstone on the Home Rule question. It seems to me a good sign, this movement, an awakening among the people. But don't misunderstand me, my dear Sir, I am not making any excuses for the methods of the extremists. Apart from my calling – I have a natural horror of violence. Nothing can condone violence, the taking of human life, it's savagery, terrible, terrible.'

'They don't put it down with a strong enough hand,' the stock-jobber was saying almost fiercely. 'There's too much Liberalism in the East, too much namby-pambyism. It's all right here, of course, but it's not suited to the East. They want a strong hand. After all they owe us something: we aren't going to take all the kicks and leave them all the halfpence. Rule 'em, I say, rule 'em, if you're going to rule 'em. Look after 'em, of course: give 'em schools, if they want education – schools, hospitals, roads, and railways. Stamp out the plague, fever, famine. But let 'em know you are top dog. That's the way to run an eastern country: I'm a white man, you're black; I'll treat you well, give you courts and justice; but I'm the superior race, I'm master here.'

The man who had looked round at me when I said 'Here's luck!' was fidgeting about in his chair uneasily. I examined him more carefully. There was no mistaking the cause of his irritation. It was written on his face, the small close-cut white moustache, the smooth firm cheeks with the deep red-and-brown glow on them, the innumerable wrinkles round the eyes, and above all the eyes themselves, that had grown slow and steady and unastonished, watching that inexplicable, meaningless march of life under blazing suns. He had seen it, he knew. 'Ah,' I thought, 'he is beginning to feel his liver. If he would only begin to speak, we might have some fun.'

'H'm, h'm,' said the Archdeacon. 'Of course there's something in what you say. Slow and sure. Things may be going too fast, and, as I say, I'm entirely for putting down violence and illegality with a strong hand. And after all, my dear Sir, when you say we're the superior race you imply a duty. Even in secular matters we must spread the light. I believe – devoutly – I am not ashamed to say so – that we are. We're reaching the people there, it's the cause of the unrest, we set them an example. They desire to follow. Surely, surely we should help to guide their feet. I don't speak without a certain knowledge. I take a great interest, I may even say that I play my small part, in the work of one of our great missionary societies. I see our young men, many of them risen from the people, educated often, and highly educated (I venture to think), in Board Schools. I see them go out full of high ideals to live among those poor people. And I see them when they come back and tell me their tales honestly, unostentatiously. It is always the same, a message of hope and comfort. We are getting at the people, by example, by our lives, by our conduct. They respect us.'

I heard a sort of groan, and then, quite loud, these strange words: 'Kasimutal Rameswaramvaraiyil terintavan.'

'I beg your pardon,' said the Archdeacon, turning to the interrupter.

'I beg yours. Tamil, Tamil proverb. Came into my mind. Spoke without thinking. Beg yours.'

'Not at all. Very interesting. You've lived in India? Would you mind my asking you for a translation?'

'It means "he knows everything between Benares and Rameswaram." Last time I heard it, an old Tamil, seventy or eighty years old, perhaps – he looked a hundred – used it of one of your young men. The young man, by the bye, had been a year and a half in India. D'you understand?'

'Well, I'm not sure I do: I've heard, of course, of Benares, but Rameswaram, I don't seem to remember the name.'

I laughed; I could not help it; the little Anglo-Indian looked so fierce. 'Ah!' he said, 'you don't recollect the name. Well, it's pretty famous out there. Great temple – Hindu – right at the southern tip of India. Benares, you know, is up north. The old Tamil meant that your friend knew everything in India after a year and a half: *he* didn't, you know, after seventy, after seven thousand years. Perhaps you also don't recollect that the Tamils are Dravidians? They've been there since the beginning of time, before we came, or the Dutch or Portuguese or the Muhammadans, or our cousins, the other Aryans. Uncivilized, black? Perhaps, but, if they're black, after all it's *their* suns, through thousands of years, that have blackened them. They ought to know, if anyone does: but they don't, they don't pretend to. But you two gentlemen, you seem to know everything between Kasimutal – that's Benares – and Rameswaram, without having seen the sun at all.'

'My dear sir,' began the Archdeacon pompously, but the jobber interrupted him. He had had a number of whiskies and sodas, and was quite heated. 'It's very easy to sneer: it doesn't mean because you've lived a few years in a place . . .'

'I? Thirty. But they – seven thousand at least.'

'I say, it doesn't mean because you've lived thirty years in a place that you know all about it. Ramisram, or whatever the damned place is called, I've never heard of it and don't want to. You do, that's part of your job, I expect. But I read the papers, I've read books too, mind you, about India. I know what's going on. One knows enough – enough – data: East and West and the difference: I can form an opinion – I've a right to it even if I've never heard of Ramis what d'you call it. You've lived there and you can't see the wood for the trees. We see it because we're out of it – see it at a distance.'

'Perhaps,' said the Archdeacon 'there's a little misunderstanding. The discussion – if I may say so – is getting a little heated – unnecessarily, I think. We hold our views. This gentleman has lived in the country. He holds others. I'm sure it would be most interesting to hear them. But I confess I didn't quite gather them from what he said.'

The little man was silent: he sat back, his eyes fixed on the ceiling. Then he smiled:

'I won't give you views,' he said. 'But if you like I'll give you what you call details, things seen, facts. Then you can give me *your* views on 'em.'

They murmured approval.

'Let's see, it's fifteen, seventeen years ago. I had a district then about as big as England. There may have been twenty Europeans in it, counting the missionaries, and twenty million Tamils and Telegus. I expect nineteen millions of the Tamils and Telegus never saw a white man from one year's end to the other, or if they did, they caught a glimpse of me under a sun helmet riding through their village on a fleabitten grey Indian mare. Well, Providence had so designed it that there was a stretch of coast in that district which was a barren wilderness of sand and scrubby thorn jungle – and nothing else – for three hundred miles; no towns, no villages, no water, just sand and trees for three hundred miles. O, and sun, I forgot that, blazing sun. And in the water off the shore at one place there were oysters, millions of them lying and breeding at the bottom, four or five fathoms down. And in the oysters, or some of them, were pearls.

'Well, we rule India and the sea, so the sea belongs to us, and the oysters are in the sea and the pearls are in the oysters. Therefore of course the pearls belong to us. But they lie in five fathoms. How to get 'em up, that's the question. You'd think being progressive we'd dredge for them or send down divers in diving dresses. But we don't, not in India. They've been fishing up the oysters and the pearls there ever since the beginning of time, naked brown men diving feet first out of long wooden boats into the blue sea and sweeping the oysters off the bottom of the sea into baskets slung to their sides. They were doing it centuries and centuries before we came, when – as someone said – our ancestors were herding swine on the plains of Norway. The Arabs of the Persian Gulf came down in dhows and fished up pearls which found their way to Solomon and the Queen of Sheba. They still come, and the Tamils and Moormen of the district come, and they fish 'em up in the same way, diving out of long wooden boats shaped and rigged as in Solomon's time, as they were centuries before him and the Queen of Sheba. No difference, you see, except that we – Government I mean – take two-thirds of all the oysters fished up: the other third we give to the diver, Arab or Tamil or Moorman, for his trouble in fishing 'em up.

'We used to have a Pearl Fishery about once in three years. It lasted six weeks or two months just between the two monsoons, the only time the sea is calm there. And I had, of course, to go and superintend it, to take Government's share of oysters, to sell them, to keep order, to keep out K. D.'s – that means Known Depredators – and smallpox and cholera. We had what we called a camp, in the wilderness, remember, on the hot sand down there by the sea: it sprang up in a night, a town, a big town of thirty or forty thousand people, a little India, Asia almost, even a bit of Africa. They came from all districts: Tamils, Telegus, fat Chetties, Parsees, Bombay merchants, Sinhalese from Ceylon, the Arabs and their negroes, Somalis probably, who used to be their slaves. It was an immense gamble; everyone bought oysters for the chance of the prizes in them: it would have taken fifty white men to superintend that camp properly: they gave me one, a little boy of twenty-four fresh-cheeked from England, just joined the service. He had views, he had been educated in a Board School, won prizes, scholarships, passed the Civil Service "Exam". Yes, he had views; he used to explain them to me when he first arrived. He got some new ones I think before he got out of that camp. You'd say he only saw details, things happen, facts, data. Well, he did that too. He saw men die – he hadn't seen that in his Board School – die of plague or cholera, like flies, all over the place, under the trees, in the boats, outside the little door of his own little hut. And he saw flies, too, millions, billions of them all day long buzzing, crawling over everything, his hands, his little fresh face, his food. And he smelt the smell of millions of decaying oysters all day long and all night long for six weeks. He was sick four or five times a day for six weeks; the smell did that. Insanitary? Yes, very. Why is it allowed? The pearls, you see, the pearls; you must get them out of the oysters as you must get the oysters out of the sea. And the pearls are very often small and embedded in the oyster's body. So you put all the oysters, millions of them, in dug-out canoes in the sun to rot. They rot very well in that sun, and the flies come and lay eggs in them, and maggots come out of the eggs and more flies come out of the maggots; and between them all, the maggots and the sun, the oysters' bodies disappear, leaving the pearls and a little sand at the bottom of the canoe. Unscientific? Yes, perhaps; but after all it's our camp, our fishery – just as it was in Solomon's time? At any rate, you see, it's the East. But whatever it is, and whatever the reason, the result involves flies, millions of them and a smell, a stench – Lord! I can smell it now.

'There was one other white man there. He was a planter, so he said, and he had come to "deal in" pearls. He dropped in on us out of a native boat at sunset on the second day. He had a red face and a red nose, he was unhealthily fat for the East: the whites of his eyes were rather blue and rather red; they were also watery. I noticed that his hand shook, and that he first refused and then took a whisky and soda – a bad sign in the East. He wore very dirty white clothes and a vest instead of a shirt; he apparently had no baggage of any sort. But he was a white man, and so he ate with us that night and a good many nights afterwards.

'In the second week he had his first attack of D. T. We pulled him through, Robson and I, in the intervals of watching over the oysters. When he hadn't got D. T., he talked: he was a great talker, he also had views. I used to sit in the evenings – they were rare – when the fleet of boats had got in early and the oysters had been divided, in front of my hut and listen to him and Robson settling India and Asia, Africa too probably. We sat there in our long chairs on the sand looking out over the purple sea, towards a sunset like blood shot with gold. Nothing moved or stirred except the flies which were going to sleep in a mustard tree close by; they hung in buzzing clusters, billions of them on the smooth leaves and little twigs; literally it was black with them. It looked as if the whole tree had suddenly broken out all over into some disease of living black currants. Even the sea seemed to move with an effort in the hot, still air; only now and again a little wave would lift itself up very slowly, very wearily, poise itself for a moment, and then fall with a weary little thud on the sand.

'I used to watch them, I say, in the hot still air and the smell of dead oysters – it pushed up against your face like something solid – talking, talking in their long chairs, while the sweat stood out in little drops on their foreheads and trickled from time to time down their noses. There wasn't, I suppose, anything wrong with Robson, he was all right at bottom, but he annoyed me, irritated me in that smell. He was too cocksure altogether, of himself, of his School Board education, of life, of his "views". He was going to run India on new lines, laid down in some damned Manual of Political Science out of which they learn life in Board Schools and extension lectures. He would run his own life, I daresay, on the same lines, laid down in some other text book or primer. He hadn't seen anything, but he knew exactly what it was all like. There was nothing curious, astonishing, unexpected, in life, he was ready for any emergency. And we were all wrong, all on the wrong tack in dealing with natives! He annoyed me a little, you know, when the thermometer stood at 99, at 6 P.M., but what annoyed me still more was that they – the natives! – were all wrong too. They too had to be taught how to live – and die, too, I gathered.

'But his views were interesting, very interesting – especially in the long chairs there under the immense Indian sky, with the camp at our hands – just as it had been in the time of Moses and Abraham – and behind us the jungle for miles, and behind that India, three hundred millions of them listening to the piping voice of a Board School boy. They are the inferior race, these three hundred millions – mark race, though there are more races in India than people in Peckham – and we, of course, are superior. They've stopped somehow on the bottom rung of the ladder of which we've very nearly, if not quite, reached the top. They've stopped there hundreds, thousands of years; but it won't take any time to lead 'em up by the hand to our rung. It's to be done like this: by showing them that they're our brothers, inferior brothers; by reason, arguing them out of their superstitions, false beliefs; by education, by science, by example, yes, even he did not forget example, and White, sitting by his side with his red nose and watery eyes, nodded approval. And all this must be done scientifically, logically, systematically: if it were, a Commissioner could revolutionize a province in five years, turn it into a Japanese India, with all the ryots as well as all the vakils and students running up the ladder of European civilization to become, I suppose, glorified Board School angels at the top. "But you've none of you got any clear plans out here," he piped, "you never work on any system; you've got no point of view. The result is" – here, I think, he was inspired, by the dead oysters, perhaps – "instead of getting hold of the East, it's the East which gets hold of you."

'And White agreed with him, solemnly, at any rate when he was sane and sober. And I couldn't complain of his inexperience. He was rather reticent at first, but afterwards we heard much – too much of his experiences – one does, when a man gets D. T. He said he was a gentleman, and I believe it was true; he had been to a public school, Cheltenham or Repton. He hadn't, I gathered, succeeded as a gentleman at home, so they sent him to travel in the East. He liked it, it suited him. So he became a planter in Assam. That was fifteen years ago, but he didn't like Assam: the luck was against him – it always was – and he began to roll; and when a man starts rolling in India, well – He had been a clerk in merchants' offices; he had served in a draper's shop in Calcutta; but the luck was always against him. Then he tramped up and down

India, through Ceylon, Burma; he had got at one time or another to the
Malay States, and, when he was very bad one day, he talked of cultivat-
ing camphor in Java. He had been a sailor on a coasting tramp; he had
sold horses (which didn't belong to him) in the Deccan somewhere; he
had tramped day after day begging his way for months in native bazaars;
he had lived for six months with, and on, a Tamil woman in some little
village down in the south. Now he was "dealing in" pearls. "India's got
hold of me," he'd say, "India's got hold of me and the East."

'He had views too, very much like Robson's, with additions. "The
strong hand" came in, and "rule". We ought to govern India more; we
didn't now. Why, he had been in hundreds of places where he was the
first Englishman that the people had ever seen. (Lord! think of that!) He
talked a great deal about the hidden wealth of India and exploitation. He
knew places where there was gold – workable too – only one wanted a
little capital – coal probably and iron – and then there was this new stuff,
radium. But we weren't go-ahead, progressive, the Government always
put difficulties in his way. They made "the native" their stalking-horse
against European enterprise. He would work for the good of the native,
he'd treat him firmly but kindly – especially, I thought, the native women,
for his teeth were sharp and pointed and there were spaces between each,
and there was something about his chin and jaw – *you* know the type, I
expect.

'As the fishing went on we had less time to talk. We had to work. The
divers go out in the fleet of three hundred or four hundred boats every
night and dive until midday. Then they sail back from the pearl banks
and bring all their oysters into an immense Government enclosure where
the Government share is taken. If the wind is favourable, all the boats get
back by 6 P.M. and the work is over at 7. But if the wind starts blowing
off shore, the fleet gets scattered and boats drop in one by one all night
long. Robson and I had to be in the enclosure as long as there was a boat
out, ready to see that, as soon as it did get in, the oysters were brought
to the enclosure and Government got its share.

'Well, the wind never did blow favourably that year. I sat in that
enclosure sometimes for forty-eight hours on end. Robson found man-
aging it rather difficult, so he didn't like to be left there alone. If you get
two thousand Arabs, Tamils, Negroes, and Moormen, each with a bag or
two of oysters, into an enclosure a hundred and fifty yards by a hundred
and fifty yards, and you only have thirty timid native "subordinates" and
twelve native policemen to control them – well, somehow or other he
found a difficulty in applying his system of reasoning to them. The first
time he tried it, we very nearly had a riot; it arose from a dispute between
some Arabs and Tamils over the ownership of three oysters which fell out

of a bag. The Arabs didn't understand Tamil and the Tamils didn't understand Arabic, and, when I got down there, fetched by a frightened constable, there were sixty or seventy men fighting with great poles – they had pulled up the fence of the enclosure for weapons – and on the outskirts was Robson running round like a distracted hen with a white face and tears in his blue eyes. When we got the combatants separated, they had only killed one Tamil and broken nine or ten heads. Robson was very upset by that dead Tamil, he broke down utterly for a minute or two, I'm afraid.

'Then White got his second attack. He was very bad: he wanted to kill himself, but what was worse than that, before killing himself, he wanted to kill other people. I hadn't been to bed for two nights and I knew I should have to sit up another night in that enclosure as the wind was all wrong again. I had given White a bed in my hut: it wasn't good to let him wander in the bazaar. Robson came down with a white face to tell me he had "gone mad up there again". I had to knock him down with the butt end of a rifle; he was a big man and I hadn't slept for forty-eight hours, and then there were the flies and the smell of those dead oysters.

'It sounds unreal, perhaps a nightmare, all this told here to you behind blinds and windows in this –' he sniffed – 'in this smell of – of – horsehair furniture and paint and varnish. The curious thing is it didn't seem a nightmare out there. It was too real. Things happened, anything might happen, without shocking or astonishing. One just did one's work, hour after hour, keeping things going in that sun which stung one's bare hands, took the skin off even my face, among the flies and the smell. It wasn't a nightmare, it was just a few thousand Arabs and Indians fishing up oysters from the bottom of the sea. It wasn't even new, one felt; it was old, old as the Bible, old as Adam, so the Arabs said. One hadn't much time to think, but one felt it and watched it, watched the things happen quietly, unastonished, as men do in the East. One does one's work, – forty-eight hours at a stretch doesn't leave one much time or inclination for thinking, – waiting for things to happen. If you can prevent people from killing one another or robbing one another, or burning down the camp, or getting cholera or plague or small-pox, and if one can manage to get one night's sleep in three, one is fairly satisfied; one doesn't much worry about having to knock a mad gentleman from Repton on the head with the butt end of a rifle between-whiles.

'I expect that's just what Robson would call "not getting hold of India but letting India get hold of you". Well, I said I wouldn't give you views and I won't: I'm giving you facts: what I want, you know, too is to give you the feeling of facts out there. After all that is data for your views, isn't it? Things here *feel* so different; you seem so far from life, with windows and blinds and curtains always in between, and then nothing ever happens, you never wait for things to happen, never watch things happening here. You are always doing things somehow – Lord knows what they are – according I suppose to systems, views, opinions. But out there you live so near to life, every morning you smell damp earth if you splash too much in your tin bath. And things happen slowly, inexorably by fate, and you – you don't do things, you watch with the three hundred millions. You feel it there in everything, even in the sunrise and sunset, every day, the immensity, inexorableness, mystery of things happening. You feel the whole earth waking up or going to sleep in a great arch of sky; you feel small, not very powerful. But who ever felt the sun set or rise in London or Torquay either? It doesn't: you just turn on or turn off the electric light.

'White was very bad that night. When he recovered from being knocked down by the rifle, I had to tie him down to the bed. And then Robson broke down – nerves, you know. I had to go back to the enclosure and I wanted him to stay and look after White in the hut – it wasn't safe to leave him alone even tied down with cord to the camp bed. But this was apparently another emergency to which the manual system did not apply. He couldn't face it alone in the hut with that man tied to the bed. White was certainly not a pretty sight writhing about there, and his face – have you ever seen a man in the last stages of D. T.? I beg your pardon, I suppose you haven't. It isn't nice, and White was also seeing things, not nice either: not snakes you know as people do in novels when they get D. T., but things which had happened to him, and things which he had done – they weren't nice either – and curious ordinary things distorted in a most unpleasant way. He was very much troubled by snipe: hundreds of them kept on rising out of the bed from beside him with that shrill "cheep! cheep!" of theirs: he felt their soft little feathered bodies against his bare skin as they fluttered up from under him somewhere and flew out of the window. It threw him into paroxysms of fear, agonies: it made one, I admit, feel chilly round the heart to hear him pray one to stop it.

'And Robson was also not a nice sight. I hate seeing a sane man break down with fear, mere abject fear. He just sat down at last on a cane-bottomed chair and cried like a baby. Well, that did him some good, but he wasn't fit to be left alone with White. I had to take White down to the enclosure, and I tied him to a post with coir rope near the table at which I sat there. There was nothing else to do. And Robson came too and sat there at my side through the night watching White, terrified but fascinated.

'Can you picture that enclosure to yourself down on the sandy shore with its great fence of rough poles cut in the jungle, lighted by a few flares, torches dipped in cocoanut oil: and the white man tied to a pole raving, writhing in the flickering light which just showed too Robson's white scared little face? And in the intervals of taking over oysters and settling disputes between Arabs and Somalis and Tamils and Moormen, I sat at the table writing a report (which had to go by runner next morning) on a proposal to introduce the teaching of French in "English schools" in towns. That wasn't a very good report. White gave us the whole history of his life between ten P.M. and four A.M. in the morning. He didn't leave much to the imagination; a parson would have said that in that hour the memory of his sins came upon him – O, I beg your pardon. But really I think they did. I thought I had lived long enough out there to have heard without a shock anything that men can do and do do – especially white men who have "gone under". But I hadn't: I couldn't stomach the story of White's life told by himself. It wasn't only that he had robbed and swindled himself through India up and down for fifteen years. That was bad enough, for there wasn't a station where he hadn't swindled and bamboozled his fellow white men. But it was what he had done when he got away "among the natives" – to men, and women too, away from "civilization", in the jungle villages and high up in the mountains. God! the cold, civilized, corrupted cruelty of it. I told you, I think, that his teeth were pointed and spaced out in his mouth.

'And his remorse was the most horrible thing, tied to that post there, writhing under the flickering light of the flare: the remorse of fear – fear of punishment, of what was coming, of death, of the horrors, real horrors and the phantom horrors of madness.

'Often during the night there was nothing to be heard in the enclosure but his screams, curses, hoarse whispers of fear. We seemed alone there in the vast stillness of the sky: only now and then a little splash from the sea down on the shore. And then would come a confused murmur from the sea and a little later perhaps the wailing voice of one man calling to another from boat to boat across the water "Abdulla! Abdulla!" And I would go out on to the shore. There were boats, ten, fifteen, twenty, perhaps, coming in from the banks, sad, mysterious, in the moonlight, gliding in with the little splashings of the great round oars. Except for the slow moving of the oars one would have thought they were full of the dead, there was not a movement on board, until the boats touched the sand. Then the dark shadows, which lay like dead men about the boats, would leap into life – there would rise a sudden din of hoarse voices, shouting, calling, quarrelling. The boats swarmed with shadows running about, gesticulating, staggering under sacks of oysters, dropping one after the other over the boats' sides into the sea. The sea was full of them and soon the shore too, Arabs, negroes, Tamils, bowed under the weight of the sacks. They came up dripping from the sea. They burst with a roar into the enclosure: they flung down their sacks of oysters with a crash. The place was full of swaying struggling forms: of men calling to one another in their different tongues: of the smell of the sea.

'And above everything one could hear the screams and prayers of the madman writhing at the post. They gathered about him, stared at him. The light of the flares fell on their dark faces, shining and dripping from the sea. They looked calm, impassive, stern. It shone too on the circle of eyes: one saw the whites of them all round him: they seemed to be judging him, weighing him: calm patient eyes of men who watched unastonished the procession of things. The Tamils' squat black figures nearly naked watched him silently, almost carelessly. The Arabs in their long dirty nightshirts, blackbearded, discussed him earnestly together with their guttural voices. Only an enormous negro, towering up to six feet six at least above the crowd, dressed in sacks and an enormous ulster, with ten copper coffee pots slung over his back and a pipe made of a whole cocoanut with an iron tube stuck in it in his hand, stood smiling mysteriously.

'And White thought they weren't real, that they were devils of Hell sent to plague and torture him. He cursed them, whispered at them, howled with fear. I had to explain to them that the Sahib was not well, that the sun had touched him, that they must move away. They understood. They salaamed quietly, and moved away slowly, dignified.

'I don't know how many times this didn't happen during the night. But towards morning White began to grow very weak. He moaned perpetually. Then he began to be troubled by the flesh. As dawn showed grey in the East, he was suddenly shaken by convulsions horrible to see. He screamed for someone to bring him a woman, and, as he screamed, his head fell back: he was dead. I cut the cords quickly in a terror of haste, and covered the horror of the face. Robson was sitting in a heap in his chair: he was sobbing, his face in his hands.

'At that moment I was told I was wanted on the shore. I went quickly. The sea looked cold and grey under the faint light from the East. A cold little wind just ruffled the surface of the water. A solitary boat stood out black against the sky, just throbbing slowly up and down on the water close in shore. They had a dead Arab on board, he had died suddenly while diving, they wanted my permission to bring the body ashore. Four men waded out to the boat: the corpse was lifted out and placed upon their shoulders. They waded back slowly: the feet of the dead man stuck out, toes pointing up, very stark, over the shoulders of the men in front. The body was laid on the sand. The bearded face of the dead man looked very calm, very dignified in the faint light. An Arab, his brother, sat down upon the sand near his head. He covered himself with sackcloth. I heard him weeping. It was very silent, very cold and still on the shore in the early dawn.

'A tall figure stepped forward, it was the Arab sheik, the leader of the boat. He laid his hand on the head of the weeping man and spoke to him calmly, eloquently, compassionately. I didn't understand Arabic, but I could understand what he was saying. The dead man had lived, had worked, had died. He had died working, without suffering, as men should desire to die. He had left a son behind him. The speech went on calmly, eloquently, I heard continually the word Khallas – all is over, finished. I watched the figures outlined against the grey sky – the long lean outline of the corpse with the toes sticking up so straight and stark, the crouching huddled figure of the weeping man and the tall upright sheik standing by his side. They were motionless, sombre, mysterious, part of the grey sea, of the grey sky.

'Suddenly the dawn broke red in the sky. The sheik stopped, motioned silently to the four men. They lifted the dead man on to their shoulders. They moved away down the shore by the side of the sea which began to stir under the cold wind. By their side walked the sheik, his hand laid gently on the brother's arm. I watched them move away, silent, dignified. And over the shoulders of the men I saw the feet of the dead man with the toes sticking up straight and stark.

'Then I moved away too, to make arrangements for White's burial: it had to be done at once.'

There was silence in the smoking-room. I looked round. The Colonel had fallen asleep with his mouth open. The jobber tried to look bored, the Archdeacon was, apparently, rather put out.

'It's too late, I think,' said the Archdeacon, 'to – Dear me, dear me, past one o'clock.' He got up. 'Don't you think you've chosen rather exceptional circumstances, out of the ordinary case?'

The Commissioner was looking into the few red coals that were all that was left of the fire.

'There's another Tamil proverb,' he said: 'When the cat puts his head into a pot, he thinks all is darkness.'

7

Virginia Woolf:
Mrs Dalloway in Bond Street

'Mrs Dalloway in Bond Street' is not an excerpt from Virginia Woolf's
Mrs Dalloway *but a short story about a character from her first novel,*
The Voyage Out. *After finishing the story, Woolf began thinking of a*
series of linked chapters focusing on a party Mrs Dalloway is giving, and
by the time the story was published in 1923, the project had turned into
a novel that was then followed by a series of short stories organized
around the party at the end of the novel. Woolf rewrote elements of the
story for the novel; Clarissa, for instance, sets out to buy flowers not
gloves in the book. Though 'Mrs Dalloway in Bond Street' is explicitly a
post-war story, there is no mention of the shellshocked Septimus Smith,
whose life parallels Clarissa's in Mrs Dalloway. *But the sound of Big*
Ben, the descriptions of London, the allusions to Shelley, Shakespeare,
and others, all are used in the novel, as is the technique of indirect
discourse through which Virginia Woolf renders Mrs Dalloway's
consciousness.

Mrs Dalloway said she would buy the gloves herself.

Big Ben was striking as she stepped out into the street. It was eleven
o'clock and the unused hour was fresh as if issued to children on a beach.
But there was something solemn in the deliberate swing of the repeated
strokes; something stirring in the murmur of wheels and the shuffle of
footsteps.

No doubt they were not all bound on errands of happiness. There is
much more to be said about us than that we walk the streets of Westmin-

ster. Big Ben too is nothing but steel rods consumed by rust were it not for the care of HM's Office of Works. Only for Mrs Dalloway the moment was complete; for Mrs Dalloway June was fresh. A happy childhood – and it was not to his daughters only that Justin Parry had seemed a fine fellow (weak of course on the Bench); flowers at evening, smoke rising; the caw of rooks falling from ever so high, down down through the October air – there is nothing to take the place of childhood. A leaf of mint brings it back: or a cup with a blue ring.

Poor little wretches, she sighed, and pressed forward. Oh, right under the horses' noses, you little demon! and there she was left on the kerb stretching her hand out, while Jimmy Dawes grinned on the further side.

A charming woman, poised, eager, strangely white-haired for her pink cheeks, so Scrope Purvis, CB, saw her as he hurried to his office. She stiffened a little, waiting for Durtnall's van to pass. Big Ben struck the tenth; struck the eleventh stroke. The leaden circles dissolved in the air. Pride held her erect, inheriting, handing on, acquainted with discipline and with suffering. How people suffered, how they suffered, she thought, thinking of Mrs Foxcroft at the Embassy last night decked with jewels, eating her heart out, because that nice boy was dead, and now the old Manor House (Durtnall's van passed) must go to a cousin.

'Good morning to you!' said Hugh Whitbread raising his hat rather extravagantly by the china shop, for they had known each other as children. 'Where are you off to?'

'I love walking in London,' said Mrs Dalloway. 'Really it's better than walking in the country!'

'We've just come up,' said Hugh Whitbread. 'Unfortunately to see doctors.'

'Milly?' said Mrs Dalloway, instantly compassionate.

'Out of sorts,' said Hugh Whitbread. 'That sort of thing. Dick all right?'

'First rate!' said Clarissa.

Of course, she thought, walking on, Milly is about my age – fifty – fifty-two. So it is probably *that*, Hugh's manner had said so, said it perfectly – dear old Hugh, thought Mrs Dalloway, remembering with amusement, with gratitude, with emotion, how shy, like a brother – one would rather die than speak to one's brother – Hugh had always been, when he was at Oxford, and came over, and perhaps one of them (drat the thing!) couldn't ride. How then could women sit in Parliament? How could they do things with men? For there is this extraordinarily deep instinct, something inside one; you can't get over it; it's no use trying; and men like Hugh respect it without our saying it, which is what one loves, thought Clarissa, in dear old Hugh.

She had passed through the Admiralty Arch and saw at the end of the empty road with its thin trees Victoria's white mound, Victoria's billowing motherliness, amplitude and homeliness, always ridiculous, yet how sublime, thought Mrs Dalloway, remembering Kensington Gardens and the old lady in horn spectacles and being told by Nanny to stop dead still and bow to the Queen. The flag flew above the Palace. The King and Queen were back then. Dick had met her at lunch the other day – a thoroughly nice woman. It matters so much to the poor, thought Clarissa, and to the soldiers. A man in bronze stood heroically on a pedestal with a gun on her left hand side – the South African war. It matters, thought Mrs Dalloway walking towards Buckingham Palace. There it stood four-square, in the broad sunshine, uncompromising, plain. But it was character, she thought; something inborn in the race; what Indians respected. The Queen went to hospitals, opened bazaars – the Queen of England, thought Clarissa, looking at the Palace. Already at this hour a motor car passed out at the gates; soldiers saluted; the gates were shut. And Clarissa, crossing the road, entered the Park, holding herself upright.

June had drawn out every leaf on the trees. The mothers of Westminster with mottled breasts gave suck to their young. Quite respectable girls lay stretched on the grass. An elderly man, stooping very stiffly, picked up a crumpled paper, spread it out flat and flung it away. How horrible! Last night at the Embassy Sir Dighton had said, 'If I want a fellow to hold my horse, I have only to put up my hand.' But the religious question is far more serious than the economic, Sir Dighton had said, which she thought extraordinarily interesting, from a man like Sir Dighton. 'Oh, the country will never know what it has lost,' he had said, talking of his own accord, about dear Jack Stewart.

She mounted the little hill lightly. The air stirred with energy. Messages were passing from the Fleet to the Admiralty. Piccadilly and Arlington Street and the Mall seemed to chafe the very air in the Park and lift its leaves hotly, brilliantly, upon waves of that divine vitality which Clarissa loved. To ride; to dance; she had adored all that. Or going long walks in the country, talking, about books, what to do with one's life, for young people were amazingly priggish – oh, the things one had said! But one had conviction. Middle age is the devil. People like Jack'll never know that, she thought; for he never once thought of death, never, they said, knew he was dying. And now can never mourn – how did it go? – a head grown grey . . . From the contagion of the world's slow stain . . . have drunk their cup a round or two before. . . . From the contagion of the world's slow stain! She held herself upright.

But how Jack would have shouted! Quoting Shelley, in Piccadilly!

'You want a pin,' he would have said. He hated frumps. 'My God Clarissa! My God Clarissa!' – she could hear him now at the Devonshire House party, about poor Sylvia Hunt in her amber necklace and that dowdy old silk. Clarissa held herself upright for she had spoken aloud and now she was in Piccadilly, passing the house with the slender green columns, and the balconies; passing club windows full of newspapers; passing old Lady Burdett-Coutts' house where the glazed white parrot used to hang; and Devonshire House, without its gilt leopards; and Claridge's, where she must remember Dick wanted her to leave a card on Mrs Jepson or she would be gone. Rich Americans can be very charming. There was St James's Palace; like a child's game with bricks; and now – she had passed Bond Street – she was by Hatchard's book shop. The stream was endless – endless – endless. Lords, Ascot, Hurlingham – what was it? What a duck, she thought, looking at the frontispiece of some book of memoirs spread wide in the bow window, Sir Joshua perhaps or Romney; arch, bright, demure; the sort of girl – like her own Elizabeth – the only *real* sort of girl. And there was that absurd book, *Soapey Sponge*, which Jim used to quote by the yard; and Shakespeare's Sonnets. She knew them by heart. Phil and she had argued all day about the Dark Lady, and Dick had said straight out at dinner that night that he had never heard of her. Really, she had married him for that! He had never read Shakespeare! There must be some little cheap book she could buy for Milly – *Cranford* of course! Was there ever anything so enchanting as the cow in petticoats? If only people had that sort of humour, that sort of self-respect now, thought Clarissa, for she remembered the broad pages; the sentences ending; the characters – how one talked about them as if they were real. For all the great things one must go to the past, she thought. From the contagion of the world's slow stain . . . Fear no more the heat o' the sun. . . . And now can never mourn, can never mourn, she repeated, her eyes straying over the window; for it ran in her head; the test of great poetry; the moderns had never written anything one wanted to read about death, she thought; and turned.

Omnibuses joined motor cars; motor cars vans; vans taxicabs, taxicabs motor cars – here was an open motor car with a girl, alone. Up till four, her feet tingling, I know, thought Clarissa, for the girl looked washed out, half asleep, in the corner of the car after the dance. And another car came; and another. No! No! No! Clarissa smiled good-naturedly. The fat lady had taken every sort of trouble, but diamonds! orchids! at this hour of the morning! No! No! No! The excellent policeman would, when the time came, hold up his hand. Another motor car passed. How utterly unattractive! Why should a girl of that age paint black round her eyes? And a young man, with a girl, at this hour, when the country – The admirable policeman raised his hand and Clarissa acknowledging his sway, taking her time, crossed, walked towards Bond Street; saw the narrow crooked street, the yellow banners; the thick notched telegraph wires stretched across the sky.

A hundred years ago her great-great-grandfather, Seymour Parry, who ran away with Conway's daughter, had walked down Bond Street. Down Bond Street the Parrys had walked for a hundred years, and might have met the Dalloways (Leighs on the mother's side) going up. Her father got his clothes from Hill's. There was a roll of cloth in the window, and here just one jar on a black table, incredibly expensive; like the thick pink salmon on the ice block at the fishmonger's. The jewels were exquisite – pink and orange stars, paste, Spanish, she thought, and chains of old gold; starry buckles, little brooches which had been worn on sea-green satin by ladies with high head-dresses. But no good looking! One must economize. She must go on past the picture dealer's where one of the odd French pictures hung, as if people had thrown confetti – pink and blue – for a joke. If you had lived with pictures (and it's the same with books and music) thought Clarissa, passing the Aeolian Hall, you can't be taken in by a joke.

The river of Bond Street was clogged. There, like a Queen at a tournament, raised, regal, was Lady Bexborough. She sat in her carriage, upright, alone, looking through her glasses. The white glove was loose at her wrist. She was in black, quite shabby, yet, thought Clarissa, how extraordinarily it tells, breeding, self-respect, never saying a word too much or letting people gossip; an astonishing friend; no one can pick a hole in her after all these years, and now, there she is, thought Clarissa, passing the Countess who waited powdered, perfectly still, and Clarissa would have given anything to be like that, the mistress of Clarefield, talking politics, like a man. But she never goes anywhere, thought Clarissa, and it's quite useless to ask her, and the carriage went on and Lady Bexborough was borne past like a Queen at a tournament, though she had nothing to live for and the old man is failing and they say she is sick of it all, thought Clarissa and the tears actually rose to her eyes as she entered the shop.

'Good morning,' said Clarissa in her charming voice. 'Gloves,' she said with her exquisite friendliness and putting her bag on the counter began, very slowly, to undo the buttons. 'White gloves,' she said. 'Above the elbow,' and she looked straight into the shop-woman's face – but this was not the girl she remembered? She looked quite old. 'These really don't fit,' said Clarissa. The shop-girl looked at them. 'Madame wears bracelets?' Clarissa spread out her fingers. 'Perhaps it's my rings.' And the girl took the grey gloves with her to the end of the counter.

Yes, thought Clarissa, if it's the girl I remember, she's twenty years older. . . . There was only one other customer, sitting sideways at the counter, her elbow poised, her bare hand drooping, vacant; like a figure on a Japanese fan, thought Clarissa, too vacant perhaps, yet some men would adore her. The lady shook her head sadly. Again the gloves were too large. She turned round the glass. 'Above the wrist,' she reproached the grey-headed woman; who looked and agreed.

They waited; a clock ticked; Bond Street hummed, dulled, distant; the woman went away holding gloves. 'Above the wrist,' said the lady, mournfully, raising her voice. And she would have to order chairs, ices, flowers, and cloak-room tickets, thought Clarissa. The people she didn't want would come; the others wouldn't. She would stand by the door. They sold stockings – silk stockings. A lady is known by her gloves and her shoes, old Uncle William used to say. And through the hanging silk stockings quivering silver she looked at the lady, sloping shouldered, her hand drooping, her bag slipping, her eyes vacantly on the floor. It would be intolerable if dowdy women came to her party! Would one have liked Keats if he had worn red socks? Oh, at last – she drew into the counter and it flashed into her mind:

'Do you remember before the war you had gloves with pearl buttons?'

'French gloves, Madame?'

'Yes, they were French,' said Clarissa. The other lady rose very sadly and took her bag, and looked at the gloves on the counter. But they were all too large – always too large at the wrist.

'With pearl buttons,' said the shop-girl, who looked ever so much older. She split the lengths of tissue paper apart on the counter. With pearl buttons, thought Clarissa, perfectly simple – how French!

'Madame's hands are so slender,' said the shop-girl, drawing the glove firmly, smoothly, down over her rings. And Clarissa looked at her arm in the looking-glass. The glove hardly came to the elbow. Were there others half an inch longer? Still it seemed tiresome to bother her – perhaps the one day in the month, thought Clarissa, when it's an agony to stand. 'Oh, don't bother,' she said. But the gloves were brought.

'Don't you get fearfully tired,' she said in her charming voice, 'standing? When d'you get your holiday?'

'In September, Madame, when we're not so busy.'

When we're in the country thought Clarissa. Or shooting. She has a fortnight at Brighton. In some stuffy lodging. The landlady takes the sugar. Nothing would be easier than to send her to Mrs Lumley's right in the country (and it was on the tip of her tongue). But then she remembered how on their honeymoon Dick had shown her the folly of giving impulsively. It was much more important, he said, to get trade with

China. Of course he was right. And she could feel the girl wouldn't like to be given things. There she was in her place. So was Dick. Selling gloves was her job. She had her own sorrows quite separate, 'and now can never mourn, can never mourn,' the words ran in her head. 'From the contagion of the world's slow stain,' thought Clarissa holding her arm stiff, for there are moments when it seems utterly futile (the glove was drawn off leaving her arm flecked with powder) – simply one doesn't believe, thought Clarissa, any more in God.

The traffic suddenly roared; the silk stockings brightened. A customer came in.

'White gloves,' she said, with some ring in her voice that Clarissa remembered.

It used, thought Clarissa, to be so simple. Down down through the air came the caw of the rooks. When Sylvia died, hundreds of years ago, the yew hedges looked so lovely with the diamond webs in the mist before early church. But if Dick were to die tomorrow, as for believing in God – no, she would let the children choose, but for herself, like Lady Bexborough, who opened the bazaar, they say, with the telegram in her hand – Roden, her favourite, killed – she would go on. But why, if one doesn't believe? For the sake of others, she thought, taking the glove in her hand. The girl would be much more unhappy if she didn't believe.

'Thirty shillings,' said the shop-woman. 'No, pardon me Madame, thirty-five. The French gloves are more.'

For one doesn't live for oneself, thought Clarissa.

And then the other customer took a glove, tugged it, and it split.

'There!' she exclaimed.

'A fault of the skin,' said the grey-headed woman hurriedly. 'Sometimes a drop of acid in tanning. Try this pair, Madame.'

'But it's an awful swindle to ask two pound ten!'

Clarissa looked at the lady; the lady looked at Clarissa.

'Gloves have never been quite so reliable since the war,' said the shop-girl, apologizing, to Clarissa.

But where had she seen the other lady? – elderly, with a frill under her chin; wearing a black ribbon for gold eyeglasses; sensual, clever, like a Sargent drawing. How one can tell from a voice when people are in the habit, thought Clarissa, of making other people – 'It's a shade too tight,' she said – obey. The shop-woman went off again. Clarissa was left waiting. Fear no more she repeated, playing her finger on the counter. Fear no more the heat o' the sun. Fear no more she repeated. There were little brown spots on her arm. And the girl crawled like a snail. Thou thy worldly task hast done. Thousands of young men had died that things might go on. At last! Half an inch above the elbow; pearl buttons; five and a quarter. My dear slowcoach, thought Clarissa, do you think I can sit here the whole morning? Now you'll take twenty-five minutes to bring me my change!

There was a violent explosion in the street outside. The shop-women cowered behind the counters. But Clarissa, sitting very upright, smiled at the other lady. 'Miss Anstruther!' she exclaimed.

Part III

Biographies

Biography long and short was a major form of Bloomsbury's writing, and one of their most important legacies. Lytton Strachey, E. M. Forster, and Virginia Woolf all wrote full-length biographies and, along with other Bloomsbury writers, numerous biographical sketches. The 'becoming brevity' that Strachey said was the biographer's first duty (see p. 6) is manifest in Bloomsbury's numerous brief lives, which are not as well known as they should be.

8

E. M. Forster: The Emperor Babur

E. M. Forster's sketch of Babur (1483–1530), the first Moghul emperor, appeared in 1921 as a review of his memoirs (the Leyden and Erskine translation edited by Lucas King). Reprinting it fifteen years later in the collected essays and reviews that he entitled Abinger Harvest *after his Surrey village, Forster made the review into a short biography of Babur. The irreverent tone of the sketch combines with an admiration for Babur's personality and style, and the emperor's love of detail that Forster makes into a motif for his essay.*

At the time that Machiavelli was collecting materials for *The Prince*, a robber boy, sorely in need of advice, was scuttling over the highlands of Central Asia. His problem had already engaged the attention and sympathy of the Florentine; there were too many kings about, and not enough kingdoms. Tamurlane and Gengis Khan (the boy was descended from both) had produced between them so numerous a progeny that a frightful congestion of royalties had resulted along the upper waters of the Jaxartes and the Oxus, and in Afghanistan. One could scarcely travel two miles without being held up by an emperor. The boy had inherited Ferghana, a scrubby domain at the extreme north of the fashionable world; thinking Samarkand a suitable addition, he conquered it from an uncle when he was thirteen. Then Ferghana revolted, and while trying to subdue it he lost Samarkand, too, and was left with nothing at all. His affairs grew worse; steal as he might, others stole quicker, and at eighteen his mother made him marry – a tedious episode. He thought of escaping to China, so hopeless was the block of uncles, and cousins, and aunts;

poisoned coffee and the fire-pencil thinned them out, but only for a moment; up they sprang; again he conquered, lost, conquered and lost for ever Ferghana and Samarkand. Not until he was twenty-one, and had taken to drink, did the true direction of his destiny appear; moving southward, he annexed Kabul. Here the horizon expanded: the waters flow southward again from Kabul, out of the Asian continent into the Indian; he followed them, he took Delhi, he founded the Moghul Empire, and then, not to spoil the perfect outline of his life, he died. Had Machiavelli ever heard of Babur? Probably not. But if the news had come through, how he would have delighted in a career that was not only successful, but artistic! And if Babur had ever heard of Machiavelli, how gladly he would have summoned him and shown him a thing or two! Yes – a thing or two not dreamt of in that philosophy, things of the earth mostly, but Machiavelli didn't know about them, all the same.

These sanguine and successful conquerors generally have defects that would make them intolerable as companions. They are unobservant of all that does not assist them towards glory, and, consequently, vague and pompous about their past; they are so busy; when they have any charm, it is that of our Henry V – the schoolboy unpacking a hamper that doesn't belong to him. But what a happiness to have known Babur! He had all that one seeks in a friend. His energy and ambition were touched with sensitiveness; he could act, feel, observe, and remember; though not critical of his senses, he was aware of their workings, thus fulfilling the whole nature of man. His admirers – and he has many – have called him naïf, because they think it somewhat silly of an emperor to love poetry and swimming for their own sake, and to record many years afterwards that the first time a raft struck, a china cup, a spoon, and a cymbal fell into the water, whereas the second time the raft struck, a nobleman fell in, just as he was cutting up a melon. Charming and quaint (they say), but no more: not realizing that Babur knew what he was about, and that his vitality was so great that all he had experienced rang and glowed, irrespective of its value to historians. It is the temptation of a cultivated man to arrange his experiences, so that they lose their outlines; he, skilled in two languages and all the arts of his day, shunned that false logic, and the sentences in his *Memoirs* jostle against one another like live people in a crowd:

Zulnun Arghun distinguished himself among all the other young warriors in the presence of Sultan Abusaid Mirza by the use of the scimitar, and afterwards, on every occasion on which he went into action, he acquitted himself with distinction. His courage is unimpeached, but certainly he was rather deficient in understanding. . . . He was a pious and orthodox believer, never neglected saying the appointed prayers, and frequently repeated the supererogatory ones. He was madly fond of chess; if a person played at it with one hand he played at it with his two hands. He played without art, just as his fancy suggested. He was the slave of avarice and meanness.

No one of the above sentences accommodates its neighbour. The paragraph is a series of shocks, and this is characteristic of Babur's method, and due to the honesty of his mind. But it is not a naïf paragraph. He desires to describe Zulnun Arghun, and does so with all possible clearness. Similarly, when he is autobiographical. No softening:

When, from the force of youthful imagination and constitutional impulse, I got a desire for wine, I had nobody about my person to invite me to gratify my wishes; nay, there was not one who suspected my secret longing for it. Though I had the appetite, therefore, it was difficult for me, unsolicited as I was, to indulge such unlawful desires. It now came into my head that as they urged me so much, and as, besides, I had come into a refined city like Heri, in which every means of heightening pleasure and gaiety was possessed in perfection, in which all the incentives and apparatus of enjoyment were combined with an invitation to indulgence, if I did not seize the present moment I never could expect such another. I therefore resolved to drink wine.

Here is neither bragging nor remorse; just the recording of conflicting emotions and of the action that finally resulted. On a subsequent page he does feel remorse. On still a subsequent he drinks himself senseless. Fresh, yet mature, the *Memoirs* leave an ambiguous and exquisite impression behind. We are admitted into the writer's inmost confidence, yet that confidence is not, as in most cases, an enervating chamber; it is a mountain stream, arched by the skies of early manhood. And since to his honesty, and energy, and sensitiveness, Babur added a warm heart, since he desired empire chiefly that he might advance his friends, the reader may discover a companion uncommon among the dead and amongst kings. Alexander the Great resembles him a little, but Alexander is mystic and grandiose, whereas there are neither chasms nor fences in Babur, nothing that need hinder the modern man if he cares to come.

Nevertheless . . . old books are troublesome to read, and it is right to indicate the difficulty of this one.

Those awful Oriental names! They welter from start to finish. Sometimes twenty new ones occur on a page and never recur. Among humans there are not only the Turki descendants of Tamurlane and the Moghul descendants of Gengis Khan, all royal, and mostly in motion; long lists of their nobles are given also. Geography is equally trying; as Babur scuttles over the earth a mist of streams, and villages, and mountains arises, from the Jaxartes, in the centre of Asia, to the Nerbudda, in the centre of India. Was this where the man with the melon fell overboard? Or is it the raft where half of us took spirits and the rest *bhang*, and quarrelled in consequence? We can't be sure. Is that an elephant? If so, we must have left Afghanistan. No: we must be in Ferghana again; it's a yak. We never know where we were last, though Agra stands out as the curtain falls, and behind it, as a tomb against the skyline, Kabul. Lists of flowers, fruits, handwritings, headdresses. . . . We who are not scholars may grow tired.

The original manuscript of the *Memoirs* was in Turki, and this brings us to our concluding point, that Babur belongs to the middle of Asia, and does not interpret the mind of India, though he founded a great dynasty there. His description of Hindustan is unfavourable, and has often been quoted with gusto by Anglo-Indians. 'The people', he complains, 'are not handsome, have no idea of the charms of friendly society, of frankly mixing together, or of familiar intercourse . . . no good fruits, no ice or cold water, no good food or bread in their bazaars, no baths or colleges, no candles, no torches, not a candlestick.' Witty and unphilosophic, definite and luxuriant as a Persian miniature, he had small patience with a race which has never found either moral or aesthetic excellence by focusing upon details. He had loved details all his life. Consequently, his great new empire, with its various species of parrots, concerning which he failed to get reliable information, and its myriads of merging gods, was sometimes a nightmare, and he left orders that he was to be buried at Kabul. Nothing in his life was Indian, except, possibly, the leaving of it. Then, indeed, at the supreme moment, a strange ghost visits him, a highly unexpected symptom occurs – renunciation. Humayun, his son, lay sick at Agra, and was not expected to recover. Babur, apprised that some sacrifice was necessary, decided (who told him?) that it must be self-sacrifice. He walked ceremonially three times round the bed, then cried, 'I have borne it away.' From that moment strength ebbed from him into his son, a mystic transfusion of the life-force was accomplished, and the five senses that had felt and discriminated so much blended together, diminished, ceased to exist, like the smoke from the burning ghats that disappears into the sky. Not thus had he faced death in the past. Read what he felt when he was nineteen, and his enemies closed round the upland garden in Ferghana. Then he was rebellious and afraid. But at fifty, by the banks of the sacred Jumna, he no longer desired to continue, discovering, perhaps, that the so-called Supreme Moment is, after all, not supreme, but an additional detail, like a cup that falls into the water, or a game of chess played with both hands, or the plumage of a bird, or the face of a friend.

9

Lytton Strachey:
Madame de Sévigné's Cousin

In much of Strachey's writing, the antipathy for the Victorians is offset by his fondness for seventeenth- and eighteenth-century French culture. The form of 'Madame de Sévigné's Cousin', written in 1924, is described by the book in which it was collected: Portraits in Miniature *(1931). It illustrates again the biographical strategy Strachey set forth in the preface to* Eminent Victorians. *Instead of protraying a major figure of French literature such as the great letter-writer Madame de Sévigné, he chooses her friend and cousin, the minor versifier, Emmanuel de Coulanges (1633–1716), and through him evokes her world. Strachey assumes a familiarity with such figures such as Louis XIV's mistresses or Madame de Grignan, the daughter to whom Madame de Sévigné' was devoted, but his portrait does not depend upon this knowledge for its effects.*

Madame de Sévigné was one of those chosen beings in whom the forces of life are so abundant and so glorious that they overflow in every direction and invest whatever they meet with the virtue of their own vitality. She was the sun of a whole system, which lived in her light – which lives still for us with a kind of reflected immortality. We can watch – with what a marvellous distinctness! – the planets revolving through that radiance – the greater and the less, and the subordinate moons and dimmest asteroids – from Madame de Grignan herself to the dancing gypsies at Vichy. But then, when the central luminary is withdrawn, what an incredible convulsion! All vanish; we are dimly aware for a little of some obscure shapes moving through strange orbits; and after that there is only darkness.

Emmanuel de Coulanges, for instance. He lived a long life, filled his own place in the world, married, travelled, had his failures and his successes ... but all those happenings were mere phenomena; the only reality about him lay in one thing – he was Madame de Sévigné's cousin. He was born when she was seven years old, and he never knew a time when he had not loved her. She had petted the little creature when it was a baby, and she had gone on petting it all her life. He had not been quite an ordinary child: he had had strange fancies. There was a fairy, called *Cafut*, so he declared, to whom he was devoted; this was not approved of – it looked like incipient madness; and several whippings had to be administered before *Cafut* was exorcized. In reality, no one could have been saner than the little Emmanuel; but he had ways of amusing himself which seemed unaccountable to the grandly positive generation into which he had been born. There was something about him which made him no fit contemporary of Bossuet. Madame de Sévigné, so completely, so magnificently, a child of her age, while she loved him, could never take him quite seriously. In her eyes, though he might grow old, he could not grow up. At the age of sixty, white-haired and gouty, he remained for her what, in fact, his tiny pink-cheeked rotundity suggested – an infant still. She found him adorable and unimportant. Even his sins – and in those days sins were serious – might, somehow or other, be disregarded; and besides, she observed that he had only one – it was *gaudeamus*; she scolded him with a smile. It was delightful to have anything to do with him – to talk with him, to laugh at him, to write to him. 'Le style qu'on a en lui écrivant', she said, 'ressemble à la joie et à la santé.' It was true; and some of her most famous, some of her most delicious and life-scattering letters were written to her cousin Coulanges.

He married well – a lady who was related to the great Louvois; but the connection did him little good in the world. For a moment, indeed, an important public office was dangled before his eyes; but it was snapped up by somebody else, and Coulanges, after a few days of disappointment, consoled himself easily enough – with a song. He was very fond of songs, composing them with elegant rapidity to the popular airs of the day; every circumstance of his existence, however grave or however trivial – a journey, a joke, the world's cruelties, his wife's infidelities – he rigged them all out in the bows and ribbons of his little rhymes. His wife was pretty, gay, fashionable, and noted for her epigrams. Her adorers were numerous: there was the Comte de Brancas, famous – immortal, even, as he has his niche in La Bruyère's gallery – for his absentmindedness; there was the Abbé Têtu, remarkable for two things – for remaining the friend both of Madame de Montespan and of Madame de Maintenon, and for being the first person who was ever afflicted by the vapours; and there was the victorious – the scandalously victorious – Marquis de la Trousse. Decidedly the lady was gay – too gay to be quite to the taste of Madame de Sévigné, who declared that she was a leaf fluttering in the wind. 'Cette feuille', she said, 'est la plus frivole et la plus légère marchandise que vous ayez jamais vue.' But Coulanges was indifferent to her lightness; what he did feel was her inordinate success at Court. There she gadded, in a blaze of popularity, launching her epigrams and hobnobbing with Madame de Maintenon; he was out of it; and he was growing old, and the gout attacked him in horrid spasms. At times he was almost sad.

Then, gradually and for no apparent reason, there was a change. What was it? Was the world itself changing? Was one age going out and another coming in? From about the year 1690 onwards, one begins to discern the first signs of the petrifaction, the *rigor mortis* of the great epoch of Louis XIV; one begins to detect, more and more clearly in the circumambient atmosphere, the scent and savour of the eighteenth century. Already there had been symptoms – there had been the fairy *Cafut*, and the Abbé Têtu's vapours. But now there could be no more doubt about it; the new strange tide was flowing steadily in. And upon it was wafted the cockleshell of Coulanges. At fifty-seven, he found that he had come into his own. No longer was he out of it – far from it: his was now the popularity, the inordinate success. He was asked everywhere, and he always fitted in. His songs particularly, his frivolous neat little songs, became the rage; they flew from mouth to mouth; and the young people, at all the fashionable parties, danced as they sang them. At last they were collected by some busybody and printed, to his fury and delight; and his celebrity was redoubled. At the same time a wonderful rejuvenation came upon him; he seemed to grow younger daily; he drank, he guzzled, with astonishing impunity; there must have been a mistake, he said, in his birth certificate – it was ante-dated at least twenty years. As for his gout, it had gone for ever; he had drowned it by bathing, when he was over sixty, all one summer in the Seine. Madame de Sévigné could only be delighted. She had given a great deal of thought to the matter, she told him, and she had come to the conclusion that he was the happiest man in the world. Probably she was right – she almost always was. But, oddly enough, while Coulanges was undergoing this transformation, a precisely contrary one had befallen his wife. She had, in sober truth, grown old – old, and disillusioned, and serious. She could bear the Court no longer – she despised it; she wavered between piety and stoicism; quietly, persistently, she withdrew into herself. Madame de Sévigné, philosophizing and quoting La Fontaine, found – it was surprising – that she admired her – the poor brown leaf; and, on her side, Madame de Coulanges grew more and more devoted to Madame de Sévigné. Her husband mildly amused her. As she watched him flying from country-house to country-house, she suggested that it would save time and trouble if he lived in a swing, so that he might whirl backwards and forwards for the rest of his days, without ever having to touch the earth again. 'C'est toujours son plaisir qui le gouverne,' she observed, with an ironical smile; 'et il est heureux: en faut-il davantage?' Apparently not. Coulanges, adored by beautiful young duchesses, disputed over by enormously wealthy dowagers, had nothing left to wish for. The gorgeous Cardinal de Bouillon took him up – so did the Duc de Bouillon, and the Chevalier – all the Bouillons, in fact; it was a delightful family. The Cardinal carried him off to his country palace, where there was music all day long, and the servants had the air of noblemen, and the *ragouts* reached a height of ecstatic piquancy – *ragouts* from every country in Europe, it seemed – how they understood each other when they came together on his plate, he had no idea – but no matter; he ate them all.

In the midst of this, the inevitable and the unimaginable happened: Madame de Sévigné died. The source of order, light, and heat was no more; the reign of Chaos and Old Night descended. One catches a hurried vision of Madame de Grignan, pale as ashes, elaborating sentences of grief; and then she herself and all her belongings – her husband, her son, her castle, with its terraces and towers, its Canons, its violins, its Mistral, its hundred guests – are utterly abolished. For a little longer, through a dim penumbra, Coulanges and his wife remain just visible. She was struck down – overwhelmed with grief and horror. Was it possible, was it really possible, that Madame de Sévigné was dead? She could hardly believe it. It was a reversal of nature. Surely it could not be. She sat alone, considering life and death, silent, harrowed, and sceptical, while her husband – ah! even her husband felt this blow. The little man wrote a piteous letter to Madame de Grignan's daughter, young Madame de Simiane, and tears blotted the page. He was only a shadow now – all too well he knew it; and yet even shadows must obey the law of their being. In a few weeks he wrote to Madame de Simiane again; he was more cheerful; he was staying with Madame de Louvois in her house at Choisy, a truly delicious abode; but Madame de Simiane must not imagine that he did not pass many moments, in spite of all the company, in sad remembrance of his friend. A few weeks more, and he was dancing; the young people danced, and why should not he, who was as young as the youngest? All the Bouillons were in the house. The jigging vision grows fainter; but a few years later one sees him at the height of his felicity, having been provided by one of his kind friends with a room in the Palace at Versailles. More years pass, he is very old, he is very poor, but what does it matter? –

Je connais de plus en plus
En faisant très-grande chère,
Qu'un estomac qui digère
Vaut plus de cent mille écus.

On his seventy-sixth birthday he sings and dances, and looks forward to being a hundred without any difficulty at all. Then he eats and drinks, and sings and dances again. And so he disappears.

But Madame de Coulanges, ever sadder and more solitary, stayed in her room, thinking, hour after hour, over the fire. The world was nothing to her; success and happiness nothing; heaven itself nothing. She pulled her long fur-trimmed taffeta gown more closely round her, and pushed about the embers, wondering, for the thousandth time, whether it was really possible that Madame de Sévigné was dead.

10

John Maynard Keynes: Newton the Man

In 1933 John Maynard Keynes published a volume of biographical essays on politicians and economists, and he continued to write various types of brief biography. Keynes wrote this portrait of Isaac Newton for his tercentenary in 1942 but left it unrevised. Eventually Geoffrey Keynes read it at the delayed tercentenary celebrations at Trinity College, Cambridge, in July 1946, three months after his brother's death. (Book collecting was one of the accomplishments shared by the Keynes brothers; perhaps the best private collection of Newton's works was owned by Maynard.) Lytton Strachey, who died in 1932, would have delighted in the paradox of Newtonian magic.

It is with some diffidence that I try to speak to you in his own home of Newton *as he was himself*. I have long been a student of the records and had the intention to put my impressions into writing to be ready for Christmas Day 1942, the tercentenary of his birth. The war has deprived me both of leisure to treat adequately so great a theme and of opportunity to consult my library and my papers and to verify my impressions. So if the brief study which I shall lay before you to-day is more perfunctory than it should be, I hope you will excuse me.

One other preliminary matter. I believe that Newton was different from the conventional picture of him. But I do not believe he was less great. He was less ordinary, more extraordinary, than the nineteenth century cared to make him out. Geniuses *are* very peculiar. Let no one here suppose that my object to-day is to lessen, by describing, Cambridge's greatest son. I am trying rather to see him as his own friends and contemporaries saw him. And they without exception regarded him as one of the greatest of men.

In the eighteenth century and since, Newton came to be thought of as the first and greatest of the modern age of scientists, a rationalist, one who taught us to think on the lines of cold and untinctured reason.

I do not see him in this light. I do not think that anyone who has pored over the contents of that box which he packed up when he finally left Cambridge in 1696 and which, though partly dispersed, have come down to us, can see him like that. Newton was not the first of the age of reason. He was the last of the magicians, the last of the Babylonians and Sumerians, the last great mind which looked out on the visible and intellectual world with the same eyes as those who began to build our intellectual inheritance rather less than 10,000 years ago. Isaac Newton, a posthumous child born with no father on Christmas Day, 1642, was the last wonder-child to whom the Magi could do sincere and appropriate homage.

Had there been time, I should have liked to read to you the contemporary record of the child Newton. For, though it is well known to his biographers, it has never been published *in extenso*, without comment, just as it stands. Here, indeed, is the makings of a legend of the young magician, a most joyous picture of the opening mind of genius free from the uneasiness, the melancholy and nervous agitation of the young man and student.

For in vulgar modern terms Newton was profoundly neurotic of a not unfamiliar type, but – I should say from the records – a most extreme example. His deepest instincts were occult, esoteric, semantic – with profound shrinking from the world, a paralysing fear of exposing his thoughts, his beliefs, his discoveries in all nakedness to the inspection and criticism of the world. 'Of the most fearful, cautious and suspicious temper that I ever knew,' said Whiston, his successor in the Lucasian Chair. The too well-known conflicts and ignoble quarrels with Hooke, Flamsteed, Leibnitz are only too clear an evidence of this. Like all his type he was wholly aloof from women. He parted with and published nothing except under the extreme pressure of friends. Until the second phase of his life, he was a wrapt, consecrated solitary, pursuing his studies by intense introspection with a mental endurance perhaps never equalled.

I believe that the clue to his mind is to be found in his unusual powers of continuous concentrated introspection. A case can be made out, as it also can with Descartes, for regarding him as an accomplished experimentalist. Nothing can be more charming that the tales of his mechanical contrivances when he was a boy. There are his telescopes and his optical experiments. These were essential accomplishments, part of his unequalled all-round technique, but not, I am sure, his *peculiar* gift, especially amongst his contemporaries. His peculiar gift was the power of holding continuously in his mind a purely mental problem until he had seen straight through it. I fancy his pre-eminence is due to his muscles of intuition being the strongest and most enduring with which a man has ever been gifted. Anyone who has ever attempted pure scientific or philosophical thought knows how one can hold a problem momentarily in one's mind and apply all one's powers of concentration to piercing through it, and how it will dissolve and escape and you find that what you are surveying is a blank. I believe that Newton could hold a problem in his mind for hours and days and weeks until it surrendered to him its secret. Then being a supreme mathematical technician he could dress it up, how you will, for purposes of exposition, but it was his intuition which was pre-eminently extraordinary – 'so happy in his conjectures,' said de Morgan, 'as to seem to know more than he could possibly have any means of proving.' The proofs, for what they are worth, were, as I have said, dressed up afterwards – they were not the instrument of discovery.

There is the story of how he informed Halley of one of his most fundamental discoveries of planetary motion. 'Yes,' replied Halley, 'but how do you know that? Have you proved it?' Newton was taken aback – 'Why, I've known it for years,' he replied. 'If you'll give me a few days, I'll certainly find you a proof of it' – as in due course he did.

Again, there is some evidence that Newton in preparing the *Principia* was held up almost to the last moment by lack of proof that you could treat a solid sphere as though all its mass was concentrated at the centre, and only hit on the proof a year before publication. But this was a truth which he had known for certain and had always assumed for many years.

Certainly there can be no doubt that the peculiar geometrical form in which the exposition of the *Principia* is dressed up bears no resemblance at all to the mental processes by which Newton actually arrived at his conclusions.

His experiments were always, I suspect, a means, not of discovery, but always of verifying what he knew already.

Why do I call him a magician? Because he looked on the whole universe and all that is in it *as a riddle*, as a secret which could be read by applying pure thought to certain evidence, certain mystic clues which God had laid about the world to allow a sort of philosopher's treasure hunt to the esoteric brotherhood. He believed that these clues were to be found partly in the evidence of the heavens and in the constitution of elements (and that is what gives the false suggestion of his being an experimental natural philosopher), but also partly in certain papers and traditions handed down by the brethren in an unbroken chain back to the original cryptic revelation in Babylonia. He regarded the universe as a cryptogram set by the Almighty – just as he himself wrapt the discovery of the calculus in a cryptogram when he communicated with Leibnitz. By pure thought, by concentration of mind, the riddle, he believed, would be revealed to the initiate.

He *did* read the riddle of the heavens. And he believed that by the same powers of his introspective imagination he would read the riddle of the Godhead, the riddle of past and future events divinely fore-ordained, the riddle of the elements and their constitution from an original undifferentiated first matter, the riddle of health and of immortality. All would be revealed to him if only he could persevere to the end, uninterrrupted, by himself, no one coming into the room, reading, copying, testing – all by himself, no interruption for God's sake, no disclosure, no discordant breakings in or criticism, with fear and shrinking as he assailed these half-ordained, half-forbidden things, creeping back into the bosom of the Godhead as into his mother's womb. 'Voyaging through strange seas of thought *alone*', not as Charles Lamb 'a fellow who believed nothing unless it was as clear as the three sides of a triangle'.

And so he continued for some twenty-five years. In 1687, when he was forty-five years old, the *Principia* was published.

Here in Trinity it is right that I should give you an account of how he lived amongst you during these years of his greatest achievement. The east end of the Chapel projects farther eastwards than the Great Gate. In the second half of the seventeenth century there was a walled garden in the free space between Trinity Street and the building which joins the Great Gate to the Chapel. The south wall ran out from the turret of the Gate to a distance overlapping the Chapel by at least the width of the present pavement. Thus the garden was of modest but reasonable size, as is well shown in Loggan's print of the College in 1690. This was Newton's garden. He had the Fellow's set of rooms between the Porter's Lodge and the Chapel – that, I suppose, now occupied by Professor Broad. The graden was reached by a stairway which was attached to a veranda raised on wooden pillars projecting into the garden from the range of buildings. At the top of this stairway stood his telescope – not to be confused with the observatory erected on the top of the Great Gate during Newton's lifetime (but after he had left Cambridge) for the use of Roger Cotes and Newton's successor, Whiston. This wooden erection was, I think, demolished by Whewell in 1856 and replaced by the stone bay of Professor Broad's bedroom. At the Chapel end of the garden was a small two-storied building, also of wood, which was his laboratory. When he decided to prepare the *Principia* for publication he engaged a young kinsman, Humphrey Newton, to act as his amanuensis (the MS of the *Principia*, as it went to the press, is clearly in the hand of Humphrey). Humphrey remained with him for five years – from 1684 to 1689. When Newton died his nephew-in-law Conduitt wrote to Humphrey for his reminiscences, and among the papers I have is Humphrey's reply.

During these twenty-five years of intense study mathematics and astronomy were only a part, and perhaps not the most absorbing, of his occupations. Our record of these is almost wholly confined to the papers which he kept and put in his box when he left Trinity for London.

Let me give some brief indications of their subject. They are enormously voluminous – I should say that upwards of 1,000,000 words in his handwriting still survive. They have, beyond doubt, no substantial value whatever except as a fascinating sidelight on the mind of our greatest genius.

Let me not exaggerate through reaction against the other Newton myth which has been so sedulously created for the last two hundred years. There was extreme method in his madness. All his unpublished works on esoteric and theological matters are marked by careful learning, accurate method and extreme sobriety of statement. They are just as *sane* as the *Principia*, if their whole matter and purpose were not magical. They were nearly all composed during the same twenty-five years of his mathematical studies. They fall into several groups.

Very early in life Newton abandoned orthodox belief in the Trinity. At this time the Socinians were an important Arian sect amongst intellectual circles. It may be that Newton fell under Socinian influences, but I think not. He was rather a Judaic monotheist of the school of Maimonides. He arrived at this conclusion, not on so-to-speak rational or sceptical grounds, but entirely on the interpretation of ancient authority. He was persuaded that the revealed documents give no support to the Trinitarian doctrines which were due to late falsifications. The revealed God was one God.

But this was a dreadful secret which Newton was at desperate pains to conceal all his life. It was the reason why he refused Holy Orders, and therefore had to obtain a special dispensation to hold his Fellowship and Lucasian Chair and could not be Master of Trinity. Even the Toleration Act of 1689 excepted anti-Trinitarians. Some rumours there were, but not at the dangerous dates when he was a young Fellow of Trinity. In the main the secret died with him. But it was revealed in many writings in his big box. After his death Bishop Horsley was asked to inspect the box with a view to publication. He saw the contents with horror and slammed the lid. A hundred years later Sir David Brewster looked into the box. He covered up the traces with carefully selected extracts and some straight fibbing. His latest biographer, Mr More, has been more candid. Newton's extensive anti-Trinitarian pamphlets are, in my judgement, the most interesting of his unpublished papers. Apart from his more serious affirmation of belief, I have a completed pamphlet showing up what Newton thought of the extreme dishonesty and falsification of records for which St Athanasius was responsible, in particular for his putting about the false calumny that Arius died in a privy. The victory of the Trinitarians in England in the latter half of the seventeenth century was not only as complete, but also as extraordinary, as St Athanasius's original triumph. There is good reason for thinking that Locke was a Unitarian. I have seen it argued that Milton was. It is a blot on Newton's record that he did not murmur a word when Whiston, his successor in the Lucasian Chair, was thrown out of his professorship and out of the University for publicly avowing opinions which Newton himself had secretly held for upwards of fifty years past.

That he held this heresy was a further aggravation of his silence and secrecy and inwardness of disposition.

Another large section is concerned with all branches of apocalyptic writings from which he sought to deduce the secret truths of the Universe – the measurements of Solomon's Temple, the Book of Daniel, the Book of Revelations, an enormous volume of work of which some part was published in his later days. Along with this are hundreds of pages of Church History and the like, designed to discover the truth of tradition.

A large section, judging by the handwriting amongst the earliest, relates to alchemy – transmutation, the philosopher's stone, the elixir of life. The scope and character of these papers have been hushed up, or at least minimized, by nearly all those who have inspected them. About 1650 there was a considerable group in London, round the publisher Cooper, who during the next twenty years revived interest not only in the English alchemists of the fifteenth century, but also in translations of the medieval and post-medieval alchemists.

There is an unusual number of manuscripts of the early English alchemists in the libraries of Cambridge. It may be that there was some continuous esoteric tradition within the University which sprang into activity again in the twenty years from 1650 to 1670. At any rate, Newton was clearly an unbridled addict. It is this with which he was occupied 'about 6 weeks at spring and 6 at the fall when the fire in the elaboratory scarcely went out' at the very years when he was composing the *Principia* – and about this he told Humphrey Newton not a word. Moreover, he was almost entirely concerned, not in serious experiment, but in trying to read the riddle of tradition, to find meaning in cryptic verses, to imitate the alleged but largely imaginary experiments of the initiates of past centuries. Newton has left behind him a vast mass of records of these studies. I believe that the greater part are translations and copies made by him of existing books and manuscripts. But there are also extensive records of experiments. I have glanced through a great quantity of this – at least 100,000 words, I should say. It is utterly impossible to deny that it is wholly magical and wholly devoid of scientific value; and also impossible not to admit that Newton devoted years of work to it. Some time it might be interesting, but not useful, for some student better equipped and more idle than I to work out Newton's exact relationship to the tradition and MSS of his time.

In these mixed and extraordinary studies, with one foot in the Middle Ages and one foot treading a path for modern science, Newton spent the first phase of his life, the period of life in Trinity when he did all his real work. Now let me pass to the second phase.

After the publication of the *Principia* there is a complete change in his habit and way of life. I believe that his friends, above all Halifax, came to the conclusion that he must be rooted out of the life he was leading at Trinity which must soon lead to decay of mind and health. Broadly speaking, of his own motion or under persuasion, he abandons his studies. He takes up University business, represents the University in Parliament; his friends are busy trying to get a dignified and remunerative job for him – the Provostship of King's, the Mastership of Charterhouse, the Controllership of the Mint.

Newton could not be Master of Trinity because he was a Unitarian and so not in Holy Orders. He was rejected as Provost of King's for the more prosaic reason that he was not an Etonian. Newton took this rejection very ill and prepared a long legalistic brief, which I possess, giving reasons why it was not unlawful for him to be accepted as Provost. But, as ill-luck had it, Newton's nomination for the Provostship came at the moment when King's had decided to fight against the right of Crown nomination, a struggle in which the College was successful.

Newton was well qualified for any of these offices. It must not be inferred from his introspection, his absentmindedness, his secrecy and his solitude that he lacked aptitude for affairs when he chose to exercise it. There are many records to prove his very great capacity. Read, for example, his correspondence with Dr Covell, the Vice-Chancellor, when, as the University's representative in Parliament, he had to deal with the delicate question of the oaths after the revolution of 1688. With Pepys and Lowndes he became one of the greatest and most efficient of our civil servants. He was a very successful investor of funds, surmounting the crisis of the South Sea Bubble, and died a rich man. He possessed in exceptional degree almost every kind of intellectual aptitude – lawyer, historian, theologian, not less than mathematician, physicist, astronomer.

And when the turn of his life came and he put his books of magic back into the box, it was easy for him to drop the seventeenth century behind him and to evolve into the eighteenth-century figure which is the traditional Newton.

Nevertheless, the move on the part of his friends to change his life came almost too late. In 1689 his mother, to whom he was deeply attached, died. Somewhere about his fiftieth brithday on Christmas Day 1692, he suffered what we should now term a severe nervous breakdown. Melancholia, sleeplessness, fears of persecution – he writes to Pepys and to Locke and no doubt to others letters which lead them to think that his mind is deranged. He lost, in his own words, the 'former consistency of his mind'. He never again concentrated after the old fashion or did any fresh work. The breakdown probably lasted nearly two years, and from it emerged, slightly 'gaga', but still, no doubt, with one of the most powerful minds of England, the Sir Isaac Newton of tradition.

In 1696 his friends were finally successful in digging him out of Cambridge, and for more than another twenty years he reigned in London as the most famous man of his age, of Europe, and – as his powers gradually waned and his affability increased – perhaps of all time, so it seemed to his contemporaries.

He set up house with his niece Catharine Barton, who was beyond reasonable doubt the mistress of his old and loyal friend Charles Montague, Earl of Halifax and Chancellor of the Exchequer, who had been one of Newton's intimate friends when he was an undergraduate at Trinity. Catharine was reputed to be one of the most brilliant and charming women in the London of Congreve, Swift and Pope. She is celebrated not least for the broadness of her stories, in Swift's *Journal to Stella*. Newton puts on rather too much weight for his moderate height. 'When he rode in his coach one arm would be out of his coach on one side and the other on the other.' His pink face, beneath a mass of snow-white hair, which 'when his peruke was off was a venerable sight', is increasingly both benevolent and majestic. One night in Trinity after Hall he is knighted by Queen Anne. For nearly twenty-four years he reigns as President of the Royal Society. He becomes one of the principal sights of London for all visiting intellectual foreigners, whom he entertains handsomely. He liked to have clever young men about him to edit new editions of the *Principia* – and sometimes merely plausible ones as in the case of Fatio de Duillier.

Magic was quite forgotten. He has become the Sage and Monarch of the Age of Reason. The Sir Isaac Newton of orthodox tradition – the eighteenth-century Sir Isaac, so remote from the child magician born in the first half of the seventeenth century – was being built up. Voltaire returning from his trip to London was able to report of Sir Isaac – "twas his peculiar felicity, not only to be born in a country of liberty, but in an Age when all scholastic impertinences were banished from the World. Reason alone was cultivated and Mankind cou'd only be his Pupil, not his Enemy.' Newton, whose secret heresies and scholastic superstitions it had been the study of a lifetime to conceal!

But he never concentrated, never recovered 'the former consistency of his mind'. 'He spoke very little in company.' 'He had something rather languid in his look and manner.'

And he looked very seldom, I expect, into the chest where, when he left Cambridge, he had packed all the evidences of what had occupied and so absorbed his intense and flaming spirit in his rooms and his garden and his elaboratory between the Great Gate and Chapel.

But he did not destroy them. They remained in the box to shock profoundly any eighteenth- or nineteenth-century prying eyes. They became the possession of Catharine Barton and then of her daughter, Lady Lymington. So Newton's chest, with many hundreds and thousands of words of his unpublished writings, came to contain the 'Portsmouth Papers'.

In 1888 the mathematical portion was given to the University Library at Cambridge. They have been indexed, but they have never been edited. The rest, a very large collection, were dispersed in the auction room in 1936 by Catharine Barton's descendant, the present Lord Lymington. Disturbed by this impiety, I managed gradually to reassemble about half of them, including nearly the whole of the biographical portion, that is, the 'Conduitt Papers', in order to bring them to Cambridge which I hope they will never leave. The greater part of the rest were snatched out of my reach by a syndicate which hoped to sell them at a high price, probably in America, on the occasion of the recent tercentenary.

As one broods over these queer collections, it seems easier to understand – with an understanding which is not, I hope, distorted in the other direction – this strange spirit, who was tempted by the Devil to believe, at the time when within these walls he was solving so much, that he could reach *all* the secrets of God and Nature by the pure power of mind – Copernicus and Faustus in one.

11

Desmond MacCarthy: Disraeli

For years Desmond MacCarthy intended to write a life of John Donne,
but his talents, as he finally realized, were those of a literary journalist.
Although MacCarthy was a Liberal, his sketch of Disraeli – collected
along with one of Gladstone in Portraits *(1931) – shows his preference*
for Disraeli's 'power of self-orientation' over Gladstone's 'powers of self-
deception'. MacCarthy's anecdotal account illustrates his own charm
that was so prized by Bloomsbury friends and others.

I

The statues in Parliament Square are ridiculous; there is no doubt about
that. Next time you are passing just look at Lord Palmerston with his
coat over his arm, stretching out his hand for his hat to an invisible
lavatory attendant; glance at the legs of Sir Robert Peel or turn your eyes
to the figure of Mr Canning habited as a Roman, with, perhaps, a pigeon
perched on his black bald head, and you will be amazed and tempted to
murmur: 'There is no other country that can show anything like this!'
The only statesman on that celebrated spot who does not appear a figure
of fun is Disraeli. I have thought, as I passed that slightly stooping figure
in Garter robes, with head decorously inclined and a long hand laid a
trifle coyly on the Order of St George, 'O Dizzy! Dizzy! Your lucky star!
You made fools of men when you were alive, and when dead even an
official sculptor could not make a fool of you!'

II

Men love ritual, and modern life starves their appetite for it. They will seize upon the most incongruous opportunities of satisfying their craving. Once every spring the woods and hedgerows are robbed of their little pale flowers in order to lay a heaped tribute at the feet of – Disraeli. And what absurd inscriptions accompany these tributes! One huge wreath composed of hundreds of packed flowers was labelled: 'To a great Englishman!' I recalled Carlyle's indignant query: 'How long will John Bull allow this Jew to dance on his belly?' The answer is – many a long year yet.

In Mr Buckle's last volume of his life of Disraeli we have the full story of the origin of this custom. It was started by Queen Victoria, and we know the tone of Disraeli's response. He regarded primroses as 'the gems and jewels of Nature', as 'the ambassadors of spring'; and in using these phrases he was bestowing on their beauty the highest praise, the most extravagant praise he knew how to give, for nothing on earth was so beautiful to him as objects possessing a high prestige value, such as gems and ambassadors. My thoughts began to turn in the direction of prestige: how prestige was deserting the holders of high offices of State and public life, and how, after all, it was the faculty of creating 'prestige' for himself and for others which had been the master gift of this old comedian, half popular tribune, half courtier, whose bronze effigy seemed now to be bowing discreetly and ironically over the wreaths at his feet.

III

I do not often wish I was older, but I sometimes regret that I am not old enough to have seen Dizzy making his way very slowly up the celebrated slope of St James on the arm of Montagu Corry. Happily however he is so picturesque that he is easy to see in imagination.

Once I was present at a discussion between two men, both so famous in their own day and in their own way, that it was naural that they should wonder, perhaps a little wistfully sometimes, how long they would be talked about after they were dead. Ingratiating little books, such as pass during a celebrity's lifetime for biographies, had been written about both of them. The man of letters argued that writers were remembered most clearly; the statesman, that the surest fame was linked to important events in history. And as I listened to instances that each in turn brought forward in support of his view, the idea occurred to me that, as far as this kind of personal fame was concerned, it was not *in proportion* to the importance either of a man's deeds or his books that he became the object of it, but rather according to the degree in which he appealed himself to the imaginations of those who live after him. I instanced small authors who were thought about more often than the great ones. And, if it came to men of action, was not Sir Robert Peel probably the greatest Prime Minister of the nineteenth century? Yet how seldom we recalled him. The suggestion had the effect of changing the conversation, for neither of the two candidates for fame present was, as a human being, likely himself to excite much posthumous curiosity. Now, the peculiarity of Disraeli was that he possessed in an unusual degree that qualification for fame.

One of the scenes in which he figures most often before me in the theatre beneath my hat, is a scene very near the drop of the curtain: a carriage is drawn up at the front door of Hughenden; a bent old man, with glistening raven locks, befurred and befrogged, and of a somnolent saturnine countenance, is already seated within it, and already, it seems, asleep; a footman comes running down the steps carrying one of those circular air-cushions on which lean invalids delight to sit; a flicker animates for a moment the extinct heavy face; the old man waves gently the back of his hand and murmurs, 'Take away that emblem of mortality.' All that I like best in Dizzy is in that story. His unconquerable hatred of the ugly prosaic; his readiness to accept anything at the hands of life except humiliation; his quick fantastic imagination which made him recognize instantly in that india-rubber object an emblem of mortality more sinister than a skull.

One more scene. This time the background is the House of Commons, and the principal figure would hardly be recognized as the same. Two traits the young Disraeli has, however, in common with the old – coal-black glossy ringlets, and a face which at this moment also is an immovable mask. Although his dress is altogether different from that of the befrogged old man in the carriage, it, too, has an extravagance which announces to all beholders that 'good taste' is a quality which the owner of such clothes either despises, or has failed altogether to understand. The impassive young man who is addressing a simmering House (for this is not his first attack upon his respected leader) is as exotic and noticeable as a flamingo in a farm-yard. He would strike one as rather ridiculous, if his affected coolness did not set off a deadly animosity. A few days before he had been apparently rolled out flat by this same respected and respectworthy chief on whom all eyes are now turned; he had been crushed, demolished, as might be expected when practical Integrity deigns at last to turn on a venomous Theatricality. Peel had quoted Canning's lines a few days before; Canning, who had once been Peel's own friend and whom, so Peel's enemies delighted to think, he had afterwards badgered to death. The quotation was apt enough, for Disraeli had kept up hitherto a pretence of being Peel's friendly critic:

> Give me the avowed, erect and manly foe;
> Firm I can meet, perhaps return the blow;
> But of all plagues, good Heaven, thy wrath can send,
> Save me, oh, save me from the candid friend.

One can imagine the effect: the clear, ringing tones with which Peel delivered those lines; the slight emphasis with which such a practised orator would linger on the wood 'manly'; his smooth triumphant air. Now listen to Disraeli's reply: 'If the right honourable gentleman may find it sometimes convenient to reprove a supporter on his right flank, perhaps we deserve it. I, for one, am quite prepared to bow to the rod; but really, if the right honourable gentleman, instead of having recourse to obloquy, would only stick to quotation, he may rely upon it – it would be a safer weapon. It is one he always wields with the hand of a master; and when he does appeal to any authority, in prose or verse, he is sure to be successful, partly because he seldom quotes a passage that has not previously received the meed of Parliamentary approbation, and partly and principally because his quotations are so – happy. The right honourable gentleman knows what the introduction of a great name does in debate – how important is its effect, and occasionally how electrical. He never refers to any author who is not great, and sometimes who is not loved – Canning, for example. That is a name never to be mentioned, I am sure, in the House of Commons without emotion. We all admire his genius; we all – at least most of us – deplore his untimely end; and we all sympathize with him in his fierce struggle with supreme prejudice and sublime mediocrity, with inveterate foes, and with 'candid' friends. The right honourable gentleman may be sure that a quotation from such an authority will always tell – some lines, for example, upon friendship, written by Mr Canning, and quoted by the right honourable gentleman. The theme – the poet – the speaker: what a felicitous combination! Its effect in debate must be overwhelming; and I am sure, were it addressed to me, all that would remain for me would be thus publicly to congratulate the right honourable gentleman, not only on his ready memory, but on his courageous conscience.'

One more peep through the peep-show. This time, let us use Mr Asquith's eyes. The scene is now laid in the autumn of 1864. Disraeli, then leader of the Opposition in the House of Commons, had attended a clerical meeting at Oxford, where Bishop Wilberforce was in the chair:

'The appointed day (it was in the month of November) arrived; the theatre was packed; the Bishop was in the chair. Mr Disraeli, attired, we are told, in a black velvet jacket and a light-coloured waistcoat, with a billy-cock hat in his hands, sauntered in, as if he were paying a surprise visit to a farmers' ordinary. At the request of the Chairman, he got to his feet, and proceeded to deliver, with that superb nonchalance in which he was unrivalled among the orators of the day, one of his most carefully prepared and most effective speeches. Indeed, among all his speeches, leaving aside his prolonged duel with Sir Robert Peel in the 'forties, I myself should select it as the one which best displays his characteristic powers, and their equally effective characteristic limitations: irony, invective, boundless audacity of thought and phrase, the thrill of the shock when least expected, a brooding impression of something which is neither exactly sentiment nor exactly imagination, but has a touch of both, a glittering rhetoric, constantly hovering over the thin boundary line which divides eloquence and bombast. First he pulverized, to the complete satisfaction of the supporters of better endowed small livings, the Broad Church party of the day and its leaders – Stanley, Jowett, Maurice, and the rest. Then came the magniloquent epigram: 'Man, my lord, is a being born to believe.' And, finally, he proceeded to dispose of Darwin and his school. 'What', he asked, 'is the question now being placed before society with glib assurance the most astounding? The question is this: Is man an ape or an angel? My lord, I am on the side of the angels.' There was nothing more to be said. The meeting broke up, their faith reassured, their enthusiasm unrestrained. There had been no victory so complete since 'Coxcombs vanquished Berkeley with a grin.'

IV

'A brooding impression of something which is neither exactly sentiment nor exactly imagination, but has a touch of both, a glittering rhetoric, constantly hovering over the thin boundary line which divides eloquence and bombast' – how admirably that describes Dizzy's style at its best! His writing – I am thinking of his novels – is often so grossly lush and vamped that no writing could possibly be worse. Bret Harte's parody is only a shade more absurd than what it ridicules: 'This simple, yet first-class conversation existed in the morning-room of Plusham, where the mistress of the palatial mansion sat involved in the sacred privacy of a circle of her married daughters. . . . Beautiful forms leaned over frames glowing with embroidery, and beautiful frames leaned over forms inlaid with mother-of-pearl.'

There was a time when the novels themselves were considered, in spite of being crammed with intellect, gaudy and vulgar. Lush in language, unduly profuse in description, often absurd in sentiment they certainly are; yet though Disraeli wrote of splendours and fashion with the gusto of a Ouida he somehow combined with it something not unlike the detachment of a Diogenes. He loved pyramids of strawberries on golden dishes; he revelled in what he was capable of calling 'palatial saloons'; in balustrades, proud profiles, terraces, fountains, marble, tapestries, feasts, and precious stones. ('Good things,' by the bye, 'like the wind on the heath, brother.') His taste was not refined, his sense of beauty deeply committed to prestige values; but how much that is ridiculous and over-rich in his writing is redeemed by the vitality of his preferences and the fearless candour of his romantic buoyancy. 'Think of me,' he wrote after the smashing fiasco of his *Revolutionary Epic*, 'as of some exotic bird which for a moment lost its way in thy cold heaven, but has now regained its course and wings its flight to a more brilliant earth and a brighter sky.' I am afraid, however, when he soars, whether in prose or verse, the effects attained correspond too closely to that unfortunate definition of poetry itself in *Contarini Fleming*, 'The art of poetry is to express natural feelings in unnatural language.' Yet how genuinely romantic he was; and his style even at its worst is a style. The words and sentences, however gaudy and ludicrous – and they often are both, whenever he rhapsodizes or attempts to convey his sense of beauty or of what is noble – do bear a genuine relation to what the writer has really felt. This is also most certainly true of the stories themselves with all their exaggerations and absurdities. It is most perplexing and intriguing. One moment you find yourself exclaiming – 'This is the most impudent paste that ever pretended to be precious,' and the next – 'This is the writing of a man singularly direct, no writer could be more free from the disgusting fear-of-giving-himself-away disease which corrupts insidiously so many imaginations.' One moment he seems like a man who apparently does not know that there is such a thing as ridicule in the world; the next, one discovers that he is not only the greatest master of ridicule himself, but is under no delusion whatever respecting the private opinions which people hold about the pretensions even of their friends – in short, that he is the last man to live in a fool's paradise.

And as a public figure and a politician he perplexes and intrigues us in the same way. Compare him with his great rival Gladstone. At first glance no one can hesitate in deciding which of the two is genuine. Gladstone is in an incandescent state of conviction; whereas Dizzy has charlatan written all over him – 'Peace with Honour', 'Our Young Queen and our old institutions', 'I am on the side of the angels', etc. He makes no concealment of his intention to feed people on phrases; it is the only diet they can digest. Think, too, of the coolness of his retort to Sir Charles Wood, who had made some unanswerable criticisms upon his ridiculous budget, 'I am not a born Chancellor of the Exchequer.' And again, who, Gladstone or Disraeli, treated Queen Victoria with the more genuine respect – there is no doubt which of the two she imagined did so? Gladstone, with all the force of his natural veneration, pleading, ex-postulating before her in the politest of long sentences, or Disraeli, who said of his relations with 'The Fairy', as he called her, 'I never contradict, but I sometimes forget'; who after the publication of *Leaves from my Journal in the Highlands*, referred to 'we authors'; whose dictum on flattery was that it could hardly ever be over-done, and in the case of Royalty must be laid on with a trowel? Do you remember that story of his encounter with a simple, conscientious, high-Tory magnate, whom it was necessary to propitiate? Afterwards the magnate confided to another that though he did not think Mr Disraeli was a very clever man, he was certainly a very good one! I think it was Browning who told Gladstone the story of Dizzy saying at a private view of the Academy that what struck him most, when he looked round, was the appalling absence of imagination, and declaring that very evening in his speech at the Acad-emy dinner that what had impressed him was the imagination shown in the pictures. The story was not a success, the G.O.M. glared at the teller as though he had been the hero of it himself, 'Do you call that funny? I call it *devilish*.' Dizzy was constantly doing 'devilish' things – and with relish. It would be ludicrous to describe him as 'honest'.

And yet when you look deeper into the two men a doubt creeps over you whether after all Disraeli's sincerity was not of a finer, purer quality. Sincerity is a vague word; it means different things in different connec-tions. The sincerity in which Disraeli excelled was the kind which is all-important in an artist and in intimate personal relations. Part of that sincerity consists of a natural incapacity for telling lies to yourself, at any rate gross ones; part of it is courage to refrain, when truth is really essential, from telling lies to other people, and part of it is the power of self-orientation. It is extremely difficult to discover what one really loves and understands best. Human nature is so impressible and imitative. We meet people, read books, and unconsciously propose to ourselves to like what they like, feel as they feel. Many do not discover to their dying day even what gives them pleasure. Dizzy knew himself extremely well. Gladstone's enemies professed to be astounded at his powers of self-deception, and even his admirers were inclined to admit that it was his danger; Labouchere said he did not mind the G.O.M. keeping a card up his sleeve, but he did object to his always believing that the Almighty had put it there. With regard to sincerity in personal relations, Disraeli's marriage is at once proof of its supreme importance and the fact that he possessed that virtue. When Mrs Disraeli was an old lady she once triumphantly exclaimed, 'My Dizzy married me for my money, but I am certain that he would marry me *now* without it.' His marriage had in the course of years turned at last into a perfect relation. It would have been a shabby enough marriage had he told lies to himself and to her. And again, Dizzy never scrupled to admit either to himself or the world that he was actuated by intense personal ambition. In his early books, *Vivian Grey* and *Contarini Fleming*, ambition is the one passion which finds really passionate expression. When he wants to convey a young man's love he instantly compares it with ambition: 'We feel', he exclaims, 'our flaunty ambition fade away like a shrivelled gourd before her vision.' He cannot conceive any stronger way of asserting the power of love than to say that it triumphed for a moment over ambition. His early books are full of genuine groans and ecstasies, but these do not spring from love. The groans and cries in *Henrietta Temple*, his only love story, are hollow and falsetto. On the other hand, Vivian's exclamation 'Curse my lot! that the want of a few rascal counters, and the possession of a little rascal blood, should mar my fortunes,' rings true. So does this: 'View the obscure Napoleon starving in the streets of Paris! What was St Helena to the bitterness of such existence? The visions of past glory might illumine even that dark imprisonment; but to be conscious that his supernatural energies might die away without creating their miracles: can the wheel or the rack rival the torture of such a suspicion?'

V

Personal ambition is not the noblest motive which can actuate a public man, but it is usually one of them, and it is a source of strength to recognize it in oneself and others. I always enjoy, when I think of it, the picture of Dizzy helping Bright on with his coat in the lobby after one of the latter's lofty orations, and whispering as he did so, 'We both know that what brings us here is – ambition.'

Lastly, with regard to that power of self-orientation, which is the power of instantly recognizing how things subtend towards what we value most; in that faculty (it is a part of sincerity) I am inclined to think he was Gladstone's superior. It was often as hard for Gladstone himself as it was for others to discover whether his sympathies were with the old order or not. Disraeli knew with the certainty of an artist what kind of a world he was fighting for. It was one in which the imaginative adventurers would be at home. There must be inequality or there would be no joy – man being a competitive, admiring animal. There must be variety and colour, institutions and customs linking the present with the past, and prizes for youth to struggle for. It must be a world with heaps of luck in it (never mind the injustice, think of the fun), and one which would stimulate dreams and dreamers. A vague ideal for a statesman? Yes, certainly – and much too vague. It was streaked, too, with a fantastic, materialistic, not over-refined, Solomon-in-all-his-glory, messianic mysticism. Certainly it was much too vague a faith for a statesman. But it is almost impossible for a reader of political history to think Disraeli a great practical statesman. He was an imaginative man, an artist. He thought imagination was the greatest power in the world, and he believed that it was only through their imaginations that men could be ruled and guided – and, for matter of that, made happy. It is not the whole truth; but his own career shows how much truth there is in it. 'Even Mormon counts more votaries than Bentham' – that reflection did not fill him with misgivings; on the contrary, it was his supreme consolation.

VI

And it is the old Disraeli who fascinates the imagination most. We have plenty of disillusioned romantics, and we are sick of listening to their wailings. Give us a still blazing fire, though the wind is howling dismally in the chimney!

He despised those who had no sense of the romance of their own lives. No wonder he detested the Whig noblemen, apart from their exclusiveness, who merely used their position as a practical asset; no wonder he adored the young who, having the adventure of an uncommitted life before them, are apt to be most conscious of that romance.

12

Virginia Woolf: Julia Margaret Cameron

Virginia Woolf's hilarious brief life of her mother's aunt, the famous Victorian photographer Julia Margaret Cameron (1815–1879) was written as an introduction to a collection of her photographs published by the Hogarth Press in 1926. A second introduction by Roger Fry discussed the pictures. The volume was entitled Victorian Photographs of Famous Men & Fair Women, *and consists of formidable, hirsute men of genius, such as Carlyle, followed by vacuously beautiful women, such as Virginia Woolf's mother. Woolf's fantastic version of Pattle family history is taken partly from the autobiography of her later friend, Ethel Smyth. Mrs Cameron's eccentric world was also evoked by her great-niece in her private play* Freshwater, *where members of Bloomsbury played the Camerons, G. F. Watts, Ellen Terry, Alfred Tennyson, and others.*

Julia Margaret Cameron, the third daughter of James Pattle of the Bengal Civil Service, was born on June 11, 1815. Her father was a gentleman of marked, but doubtful, reputation, who after living a riotous life and earning the title of 'the biggest liar in India', finally drank himself to death and was consigned to a cask of rum to await shipment to England. The cask was stood outside the widow's bedroom door. In the middle of the night she heard a violent explosion, rushed out, and found her husband, having burst the lid off his coffin, bolt upright menacing her in death as he had menaced her in life. 'The shock sent her off her head then and there, poor thing, and she died raving.' It is the father of Miss Ethel

Smyth who tells the story (*Impressions that Remained*), and he goes on to say that, after 'Jim Blazes' had been nailed down again and shipped off, the sailors drank the liquor in which the body was preserved, 'and, by Jove, the rum ran out and got alight and set the ship on fire! And while they were trying to extinguish the flames she ran on a rock, blew up, and drifted ashore just below Hooghly. And what do you think the sailors said? "That Pattle had been such a scamp that the devil wouldn't let him go out of India!" '

His daughter inherited a strain of that indomitable vitality. If her father was famous for his lies, Mrs Cameron had a gift of ardent speech and picturesque behaviour which has impressed itself upon the calm pages of Victorian biography. But it was from her mother, presumably, that she inherited her love of beauty and her distaste for the cold and formal conventions of English society. For the sensitive lady whom the sight of her husband's body had killed was a Frenchwoman by birth. She was the daughter of Chevalier Antoine de l'Étang, one of Marie Antoinette's pages, who had been with the Queen in prison till her death, and was only saved by his own youth from the guillotine. With his wife, who had been one of the Queen's ladies, he was exiled to India, and it is at Ghazipur, with the miniature that Marie Antoinette gave him laid upon his breast, that he lies buried.

But the de l'Étangs brought from France a gift of greater value than the miniature of the unhappy Queen. Old Madame de l'Étang was extremely handsome. Her daughter, Mrs Pattle, was lovely. Six of Mrs Pattle's seven daughters were even more lovely than she was. 'Lady Eastnor is one of the handsomest women I ever saw in any country,' wrote Henry Greville of the youngest, Virginia. She underwent the usual fate of early Victorian beauty: was mobbed in the streets, celebrated in odes, and even made the subject of a paper in *Punch* by Thackeray, 'On a good-looking young lady'. It did not matter that the sisters had been brought up by their French grandmother in household lore rather than in book learning. 'They were artistic to their finger tips, with an appreciation – almost to be called a culte – for beauty.' In India their conquests were many, and when they married and settled in England, they had the art of making round them, whether at Freshwater or at Little Holland House, a society of their own ('Pattledom' it was christened by Sir Henry Taylor), where they could drape and arrange, pull down and build up, and carry on life in a high-handed and adventurous way which painters and writers and even serious men of affairs found much to their liking. 'Little Holland House, where Mr Watts lived, seemed to me a paradise,' wrote Ellen Terry, 'where only beautiful things were allowed to come. All the women were graceful, and all the men were gifted.' There, in the many rooms of the old Dower House, Mrs Prinsep lodged Watts and Burne Jones, and entertained innumerable friends among lawns and trees which seemed deep in the country, though the traffic of Hyde Park Corner was only two miles distant. Whatever they did, whether in the cause of religion or of friendship, was done enthusiastically.

Was a room too dark for a friend? Mrs Cameron would have a window built instantly to catch the sun. Was the surplice of the Rev. C. Beanlands only passably clean? Mrs Prinsep would set up a laundry in her own house and wash the entire linen of the clergy of St Michael's at her own expense. Then when relations interfered, and begged her to control her extravagance, she nodded her head with its coquettish white curls obediently, heaved a sigh of relief as her counsellors left her, and flew to the writing-table to despatch telegram after telegram to her sisters describing the visit. 'Certainly no one could restrain the Pattles but themselves,' says Lady Troubridge. Once indeed the gentle Mr Watts was known to lose his temper. He found two little girls, the granddaughters of Mrs Prinsep, shouting at each other with their ears stopped so that they could hear no voices but their own. Then he delivered a lecture upon self-will, the vice, he said, which they had inherited from their French ancestress, Madame de l'Étang. 'You will grow up imperious women,' he told them, 'if you are not careful.' Had they not into the bargain an ancestor who blew the lid off his coffin?

Certainly Julia Margaret Cameron had grown up an imperious woman; but she was without her sisters' beauty. In the trio where, as they said, Lady Somers was Beauty, and Mrs Prinsep Dash, Mrs Cameron was undoubtedly Talent.

'She seemed in herself to epitomize all the qualities of a remarkable family,' wrote Mrs Watts, 'presenting them in a doubly distilled form. She doubled the generosity of the most generous of the sisters, and the impulsiveness of the most impulsive. If they were enthusiastic, she was so twice over; if they were persuasive, she was invincible. She had remarkably fine eyes, that flashed like her sayings, and grew soft and tender if she was moved. . . .' But to a child[1] she was a terrifying apparition, 'short and squat, with none of the Pattle grace and beauty about her, though more than her share of their passionate energy and wilfulness. Dressed in dark clothes, stained with chemicals from her photography (and smelling of them too), with a plump eager face and a voice husky, and a little harsh, yet in some way compelling and even charming', she dashed out of the studio at Dimbola, attached heavy swans' wings to the

---

[1] *Memories and Reflections* by Lady Troubridge, p. 34.

children's shoulders, and bade them 'Stand there' and play the part of the
Angels of the Nativity leaning over the ramparts of Heaven.

But the photography and the swans' wings were still in the far future.
For many years her energy and her creative powers poured themselves
into family life and social duties. She had married, in 1838, a very
distinguished man, Charles Hay Cameron, 'a Benthamite jurist and
philosopher of great learning and ability', who held the place, previously
filled by Lord Macaulay, of fourth Member of Council at Calcutta. In the
absence of the Governor-General's wife, Mrs Cameron was at the head
of European society in India, and it was this, in Sir Henry Taylor's
opinion, that encouraged her in her contempt for the ways of the world
when they returned to England. She had little respect, at any rate, for the
conventions of Putney. She called her butler peremptorily 'Man'. Dressed
in robes of flowing red velvet, she walked with her friends, stirring a cup
of tea as she walked, half-way to the railway station in hot summer
weather. There was no eccentricity that she would not have dared on
their behalf, no sacrifice that she would not have made to procure a few
more minutes of their society. Sir Henry and Lady Taylor suffered the
extreme fury of her affection. Indian shawls, turquoise bracelets, inlaid
portfolios, ivory elephants, 'etc.', showered on their heads. She lavished
upon them letters six sheets long 'all about ourselves'. Rebuffed for a
moment, 'she told Alice [Lady Taylor] that before the year was out she
would love her like a sister,' and before the year was out Lady Taylor
could hardly imagine what life had been without Mrs Cameron. The
Taylors loved her; Aubrey de Vere loved her; Lady Monteagle loved her;
and 'even Lord Monteagle, who likes eccentricity in no other form, likes
her.' It was impossible, they found, not to love that 'genial, ardent, and
generous' woman, who had 'a power of loving which I have never seen
exceeded, and an equal determination to be loved'. If it was impossible to
reject her affection, it was even dangerous to reject her shawls. Either she
would burn them, she threatened, then and there, or, if the gift were
returned, she would sell it, buy with the proceeds a very expensive invalid
sofa, and present it to the Putney Hospital for Incurables with an inscription which said, much to the surprise of Lady Taylor, when she
chanced upon it, that it was the gift of Lady Taylor herself. It was better,
on the whole, to bow the shoulder and submit to the shawl.

Meanwhile she was seeking some more permanent expression of her
abundant energies in literature. She translated from the German, wrote
poetry, and finished enough of a novel to make Sir Henry Taylor very
nervous lest he should be called upon to read the whole of it. Volume
after volume was despatched through the penny post. She wrote letters
till the postman left, and then she began her postscripts. She sent the

gardener after the postman, the gardener's boy after the gardener, the donkey galloping all the way to Yarmouth after the gardener's boy. Sitting at Wandsworth Station she wrote page after page to Alfred Tennyson until 'as I was folding your letter came the screams of the train, and then the yells of the porters with the threat that the train would not wait for me', so that she had to thrust the document into strange hands and run down the steps. Every day she wrote to Henry Taylor, and every day he answered her.

Very little remains of this enormous daily volubility. The Victorian age killed the art of letter writing by kindness: it was only too easy to catch the post. A lady sitting down at her desk a hundred years before had not only certain ideals of logic and restraint before her, but the knowledge that a letter which cost so much money to send and excited so much interest to receive was worth time and trouble. With Ruskin and Carlyle in power, a penny post to stimulate, a gardener, a gardener's boy, and a galloping donkey to catch up the overflow of inspiration, restraint was unnecessary and emotion more to a lady's credit, perhaps, than common sense. Thus to dip into the private letters of the Victorian age is to be immersed in the joys and sorrows of enormous families, to share their whooping coughs and colds and misadventures, day by day, indeed hour by hour. The standard of family affection was very high. Illness elicited showers of enquiries and kindnesses. The weather was watched anxiously to see whether Richard would be wet at Cheltenham, or Jane catch cold at Broadstairs. Grave misdemeanours on the part of governesses, cooks, and doctors ('he is guilty of culpable carelessness, profound ignorance' Mrs Cameron would say of the family physician), were detailed profusely, and the least departure from family morality was vigilantly pounced upon and volubly imparted.

Mrs Cameron's letters were formed upon this model; she counselled and exhorted and enquired after the health of dearest Emily with the best; but her correspondents were often men of exalted genius to whom she could express the more romantic side of her nature. To Tennyson she dwelt upon the beauty of Mrs Hambro, 'frolicsome and graceful as a kitten and having the form and eye of an antelope. . . . Then her complexion (or rather her skin) is faultless – it is like the leaf of "that consummate flower" the Magnolia – a flower which is, I think, so mysterious in its beauty as if it were the only thing left unsoiled and unspoiled from the garden of Eden. . . . We had a standard Magnolia tree in our garden at Sheen, and on a still summer night the moon would beam down upon those ripe rich vases, and they used to send forth a scent which made the soul faint with a sense of the luxury of the world of flowers.' From such sentences it is easy to see why Sir Henry Taylor looked forward to reading her novel with dread. 'Her genius (of which she has a great deal) is too profuse and redundant, not distinguishing between felicitous and infelicitous,' he wrote. 'She lives upon superlatives as upon her daily bread.'

But the zenith of Mrs Cameron's career was at hand. In 1860 the Camerons bought two or three rose-covered cottages at Freshwater, ran them together, and supplemented them with outhouses to receive the overflow of their hospitality. For at Dimbola – the name was taken from Mr Cameron's estate in Ceylon – everybody was welcome. 'Convention-alities had no place in it.' Mrs Cameron would invite a family met on the steamer to lunch without asking their names, would ask a hatless tourist met on the cliff to come in and choose himself a hat, would adopt an Irish beggar woman and send her child to school with her own children. 'What will become of her?' Henry Taylor asked, but comforted himself with the reflection that though Julia Cameron and her sisters 'have more of hope than of reason', still 'the humanities are stronger in them than the sentimentalities', and they generally brought their eccentric undertakings to a successful end. In fact the Irish beggar child grew up into a beautiful woman, became Mrs Cameron's parlour-maid, sat for her portrait, was sought in marriage by a rich man's son, filled the position with dignity and competence, and in 1878 enjoyed an income of two thousand four hundred pounds a year. Gradually the cottages took colour and shape under Mrs Cameron's hands. A little theatre was built where the young people acted. On fine nights they trapesed up to the Tennysons and danced; if it were stormy, and Mrs Cameron preferred the storm to the calm, she paced the beach and sent for Tennyson to come and pace by her side. The colour of the clothes she wore, the glitter and hospitality of the household she ruled reminded visitors of the East. But if there was an element of 'feudal familiarity', there was also a sense of 'feudal disci-pline'. Mrs Cameron was extremely outspoken. She could be highly despotic. 'If ever you fall into temptation,' she said to a cousin, 'down on your knees and think of Aunt Julia.' She was caustic and candid of tongue. She chased Tennyson into his tower vociferating 'Coward! Coward!' and thus forced him to be vaccinated. She had her hates as well as her loves, and alternated in spirits 'between the seventh heaven and the bottomless pit'. There were visitors who found her company agitating, so odd and bold were her methods of conversation, while the variety and brilliance of the society she collected round her caused a certain 'poor Miss Stephen' to lament: 'Is there *nobody* commonplace?' as she saw Jowett's four young men drinking brandy and water, heard Tennyson reciting 'Maud', while Mr Cameron wearing a coned hat, a veil, and several coats paced the lawn which his wife in a fit of enthusiasm had created during the night.

In 1865, when she was fifty, her son's gift of a camera gave her at last an outlet for the energies which she had dissipated in poetry and fiction and doing up houses and concocting curries and entertaining her friends. Now she became a photographer. All her sensibility was expressed, and, what was perhaps more to the purpose, controlled in the newborn art. The coal-house was turned into a dark room; the fowl-house was turned into a glass-house. Boatmen were turned into King Arthur; village girls into Queen Guenevere. Tennyson was wrapped in rugs: Sir Henry Taylor was crowned with tinsel. The parlour-maid sat for her portrait and the guest had to answer the bell. 'I worked fruitlessly but not hopelessly,' Mrs Cameron wrote of this time. Indeed, she was indefatigable. 'She used to say that in her photography a hundred negatives were destroyed before she achieved one good result; her object being to overcome realism by diminishing just in the least degree the precision of the focus.' Like a tigress where her children were concerned, she was as magnificently uncompromising about her art. Brown stains appeared on her hands, and the smell of chemicals mixed with the scent of the sweet briar in the road outside her house. She cared nothing for the miseries of her sitters nor for their rank. The carpenter and the Crown Prince of Prussia alike must sit as still as stones in the attitudes she chose, in the draperies she arranged, for as long as she wished. She cared nothing for her own labours and failures and exhaustion. 'I longed to arrest all the beauty that came before me, and at length the longing was satisfied,' she wrote. Painters praised her art; writers marvelled at the character her portraits revealed. She herself blazed up at length into satisfaction with her own creations. 'It is a sacred blessing which has attended my photography,' she wrote. 'It gives pleasure to millions.' She lavished her photographs upon her friends and relations, hung them in railway waiting-rooms, and offered them, it is said, to porters in default of small change.

Old Mr Cameron meanwhile retired more and more frequently to the comparative privacy of his bedroom. He had no taste for society himself, but endured it, as he endured all his wife's vagaries, with philosophy and affection. 'Julia is slicing up Ceylon,' he would say, when she embarked on another adventure or extravagance. Her hospitalities and the failure of the coffee crop ('Charles speaks to me of the flower of the coffee plant. I tell him that the eyes of the first grandchild should be more beautiful than any flowers,' she said) had brought his affairs into a precarious state. But it was not business anxieties alone that made Mr Cameron wish to visit Ceylon. The old philosopher became more and more obsessed with the desire to return to the East. There was peace; there was warmth; there were the monkeys and the elephants whom he had once lived among 'as a friend and a brother'. Suddenly, for the secret had been kept from their friends, the Camerons announced that they were going to visit their sons in Ceylon. Their preparations were made and friends went to say good-bye to them at Southampton. Two coffins preceded them on board packed with glass and china, in case coffins should be unprocurable in the East; the old philosopher with his bright fixed eyes and his beard 'dipt in moonlight' held in one hand his ivory staff and in the other Lady Tennyson's parting gift of a pink rose; while Mrs Cameron, 'grave and valiant', vociferated her final injunctions and controlled not only innumerable packages but a cow.

They reached Ceylon safely, and in her gratitude Mrs Cameron raised a subscription to present the Captain with a harmonium. Their house at Kalutara was so surrounded by trees that rabbits and squirrels and minah birds passed in and out while a beautiful tame stag kept guard at the open door. Marianne North, the traveller, visited them there and found old Mr Cameron in a state of perfect happiness, reciting poetry, walking up and down the verandah, with his long white hair flowing over his shoulders, and his ivory staff held in his hand. Within doors Mrs Cameron still photographed. The walls were covered with magnificent pictures which tumbled over the tables and chairs and mixed in picturesque confusion with books and draperies. Mrs Cameron at once made up her mind that she would photograph her visitor and for three days was in a fever of excitement. 'She made me stand with spiky coconut branches running into my head . . . and told me to look perfectly natural,' Miss North remarked. The same methods and ideals ruled in Ceylon that had once ruled in Freshwater. A gardener was kept, though there was no garden and the man had never heard of the existence of such a thing, for the excellent reason that Mrs Cameron thought his back 'absolutely superb'. And when Miss North incautiously admired a wonderful grass green shawl that Mrs Cameron was wearing, she seized a pair of scissors, and saying: 'Yes, that would just suit you', cut it in half from corner to corner and made her share it. At length, it was time for Miss North to go. But still Mrs Cameron could not bear that her friends should leave her. As at Putney she had gone with them stirring her tea as she walked, so now at Kalutara she and her whole household must escort her guest down the hill to wait for the coach at midnight. Two years later (in 1879) she died. The birds were fluttering in and out of the open door; the photographs were tumbling over the tables; and, lying before a large open window Mrs Cameron saw the stars shining, breathed the one word 'Beautiful', and so died.

13

Leonard Woolf: Herbert Spencer

Another eminent Victorian eccentric is sketched by Leonard Woolf in a review that he reprinted in his Essays *(1927). The once widely discussed evolutionary philosophy of Herbert Spencer (1820–1903) is now a curiosity of intellectual history. Woolf's portrait of the philosopher displays the influence of Lytton Strachey's methods, not just in the ironic depiction of Spencer but also in the biographer's affection for his subject. The tying together of Spencer's personality and thought is quite typical, however, of Leonard Woolf's own philosophy.*

Some thirty years ago it was possible, if you were lucky, to witness a curious spectacle occasionally at Paddington Station. A tall, vigorous red-faced, old gentleman stood in a first-class compartment superintending the operations of four porters. Round the old gentleman's waist was wound a thick piece of string, which 'issued like a tail from underneath the back of his coat', and to the end of the string was attached a brown-paper parcel, which the old gentleman held in his hand. The operations of the porters consisted in slinging a large hammock in the railway carriage, and, when this had been satisfactorily achieved in accordance with his minute directions, the old gentleman was with considerable difficulty hoisted into the hammock. He continued to hold the brown-paper parcel; the blinds were drawn down, and the train steamed out of the station. The old gentleman was Mr Herbert Spencer, and the brown-paper parcel contained that part of the MS of *The Synthetic Philosophy* which he was then writing. And it is worth recalling that upon one of these occasions a porter, who, like a true Englishman, seems to have argued that only rank could warrant and explain such eccentricity, turned to the lady who had been seeing Mr Spencer off, and, with a jerk of the head towards the departing train, said, 'Beg pardon, miss, but is he Earl Spencer?'

A man who attaches himself by a piece of string to his MSS, and who insists upon being slung up in a hammock when he goes by train on his summer holidays, will always to English porters appear eccentric. But the real interest of eccentricities consists in what causes them, and in trying to trace how they arise in the deeper recesses of the mind with sufficient strength to break through the tremendous atmospheric pressure of social convention into which the ordinary man is helplessly born, and out of which he helplessly escapes only by death. In Spencer's case his eccentricities are of more than usual interest, because they sprang from exactly the same mental recesses as the philosophy which made him famous. The string, the hammock, and the ten volumes of *Synthetic Philosophy* are all manifestations of precisely the same mental characteristics. Earls are eccentric because, being earls, they can afford to be independent; Spencer was eccentric because, being the son of an aggressive nonconformist schoolmaster who refused to take off his hat to anyone, he combined a passion for freedom with a passion for ratiocination. Hence when ratiocination 'taught him that by travelling in a hammock when going a long journey he avoided the evil consequences which usually followed the shaking of the train', his passion for liberty caused him immediately to sling his hammock regardless of the fact that more illogical and conventional people sit upon the seats. And hence his *Philosophy* is one vast argumentative paean in praise of ratiocination and individuality and liberty.

It is a great merit in Mr Hugh Eliot's book on Spencer that its author insists upon this connection between the character of the philosopher and the content of his philosophy. I have only one quarrel with Mr Eliot. His exposition and summaries of the eighteen volumes of philosophy are admirable, his judgement of the value and effect of Spencer's thought is sound, his account of his life and character is very amusing. But Mr Eliot's Spencer remains too much the eccentric, the bloodless and passionless philosopher of *Punch*, one of those super-terrestrial thinkers whom one can imagine only *avec de grandes robes de pédants*. No one would imagine from Mr Eliot's pages that Spencer was even in crotchety age a very lovable old man, or that he, when well over three-score years and ten, chased a pretty young lady round the drawing-room and gave her 'a resounding kiss' on the lips. Mr Eliot neither in his text nor his bibliography makes any mention of a singularly fascinating book, *Home*

Life with Herbert Spencer, which was written by the ladies with whom he lived for some eight years near Regent's Park, and which reveals a side of his mind and character that does not receive full justice in the more official biographies.

It is a great mistake in psychology to think that Spencer's emotions and feelings were weak. They were abnormally strong. Great individuality of character springs not from the reasoning part of the mind, but from the emotional, and logic alone never made any man eccentric. The most modern psychology teaches us that the more obvious manifestations of the emotions are no clue to their real nature or strength, that it is what we do with our emotions in the inner recesses of our minds that is most important. As soon as you regard Spencer from this point of view, you get new light upon his mind and character.

Spencer, it is admitted by everyone, had an intense 'individuality' – that is to say, a passion for doing and thinking what he, Spencer, wanted to do and think. 'Few people', he once remarked, 'can say what I can say. I have thought what I liked, done what I liked, been where I liked.' Now one of the things which Spencer liked – nearly everyone in the world does – was to find reasons for proving that what he liked to think was true and what he liked to do was good. And his passion for finding these reasons was as intense as his passion for doing and thinking what he liked, and the two passions continually interacted upon and fanned one another. For instance, he did not like French art, and the reason which he found for it was that 'French art, if not sanguinary, is usually obscene.' The truth was that he had a violent dislike of anything which was either sanguinary or obscene. Now he did not like the sanguinary simply because he had a passion for freedom. The passion for freedom made him an anti-militarist and an anti-Socialist, and a large part of his philosophy is directed to finding reasons for believing in the badness of a militarist and Socialist society. He was very fond of a game of billiards, and therefore when we arrive at the very Holy of Holies of *The Synthetic Philosophy*, Ethics, we find that among other things it provides us with reasons for approving of billiards. Again Spencer's natural inclination was not to philosophy at all, but to science, to tracing the *scientific* causes of all kinds of different phenomena. He had no aptitude and less taste for metaphysics. At the same time he had a strong taste for idleness and a strong distaste for reading books. The results of these likes and dislikes, when combined with an indomitable individuality, are truly amazing. For a quarter of a century he turned philosophy into science. He wrote eighteen volumes on scientific subjects in the most scientific period of history without reading a single book. Those eighteen volumes revolutionized human thought, for they taught us to regard everything in the universe, whether material or mental, whether history, or biology, or psychology, or sociology, or politics, as not static but dynamic. He liked science, and so he thought scientifically. 'I have thought what I liked,' he said, and he might have added, 'I have liked what I thought.' And so finally, when he comes to write about education, he finds a vast number of reasons for believing that science is pre-eminently the best subject for the education of children.

When Spencer was thirty-five he had a curious nervous breakdown, which affected the whole of the rest of his life and his character. The only symptom of this illness seems to have been 'a peculiar sensation in the head'. There can be no doubt that it was one of those nervous disorders which result in the patients becoming ill because they imagine themselves to be ill. Spencer became a permanent valetudinarian of this sort. His individuality naturally came out strongly in his symptoms. For instance, he could not write, talk, or read for more than a few minutes at a time. When writing the *Philosophy*, he and his secretary used to get into a boat on the Serpentine. Spencer would dictate for a quarter of an hour, then row hard for five minutes in order 'to relieve the congestion of blood in the brain', then dictate for another quarter of an hour, and so on. But there is a pathetically comic story which throws some light upon this valetudinarianism. Once, when an old man, he had a particularly severe attack of this symptomless disorder. It was a November day of impenetrable fog, and all day long the old man lay in bed while a maiden lady sat watching in a chair by the fireside. All day long there was complete silence in the room except for a groan from the bed which accompanied the ceaseless raising and dropping of the old man's hand. The fog grew blacker and blacker, the gloom of the room heavier and heavier, when suddenly towards evening a belated bluebottle rose out of a corner and began to buzz drearily about the room. The lady, looking at the bluebottle, said half to herself and half out aloud, 'You ought to be dead.' 'Wh-what! What did you say?' came in feeble surprise from the bed. The lady explained that she had said that the bluebottle ought to be dead at that time of the year. 'I saw no bluebottle,' said Spencer; 'but you suddenly looked straight at me and emphatically cried, "*You* ought to be dead."' The invalid then broke into low, irresistible laughter and promptly began to recover.

Imaginary illnesses are more serious than real ones and more difficult to cure. Spencer devoted to his valetudinarianism the same originality and vigour which produced *The Synthetic Philosophy*. It obsessed him, it attracted and turned in upon himself nearly all the very strong emotions which he had naturally towards ordinary human things like women and children. It threw over the last part of his life a veil of petty and irritable tragedy. 'The average colour of the whole consciousness', he wrote to Mrs Sidney Webb, describing his own mind, 'is grey.' And hence this self-willed, passionate, lovable man appeared to the majority of his contemporaries an embodiment of grey, unemotional, inhuman logic. His last words seem to me a curious allegorical commentary upon his life. When he lay dying, he called his secretary to him and said: 'Now I take this step for the benefit of those who are to be my executors; my intention being that after death this my body shall be conveyed by sea to Portsmouth.' The words, as his secretary remarked, are characteristic in syntactical expression, but meaningless.

Part IV

Essays

The scope of the Bloomsbury essay extends considerably beyond the informal, tentative, personal writing that is often identified with that form. Many of the selections in this reader are essays of various kinds – biographical and autobiographical essays, lecture essays, review essays, travel essays. The pieces collected as essays here have largely to do with aesthetic and political concerns of the Bloomsbury Group.

14

Desmond MacCarthy:
The Post-Impressionists

Though he was a literary and drama critic, MacCarthy was persuaded by his old Cambridge friend Roger Fry to be the Secretary of the famous, controversial Post-Impressionist Exhibition of 1910–11. That meant, among other things, writing up Fry's notes for the unsigned preface to the exhibition's catalogue. 'This work of mine was far more widely quoted than anything I was ever destined to write,' MacCarthy reminisced later, 'and phrases from it like "A good rocking-horse is more like a horse than the snapshot of a Derby winner" were quoted and re-quoted with laughter.' The exhibition was entitled 'Manet and the Post-Impressionists'. (For Fry's account of the exhibition see pp. 400–2.)

The pictures collected together in the present exhibition are the work of a group of artists who cannot be defined by any single term. The term 'Synthesists', which has been applied to them by learned criticism, does indeed express a quality underlying their diversity; and it is the principal business of this introduction to expand the meaning of that word, which sounds too like the hiss of an angry gander to be a happy appellation. As a definition it has the drawback that this quality, common to all, is not always the one most impressive in each artist. In no school does individual temperament count for more. In fact, it is the boast of those who believe in this school, that its methods enable the individuality of the artist to find completer self-expression in his work than is possible to those who have committed themselves to representing objects more literally. This, indeed, is the first source of their quarred with the

Impressionists: the Post-Impressionists consider the Impressionists too naturalistic.

Yet their own connection with Impressionism is extremely close; Cézanne, Gauguin and Van Gogh all learnt in the Impressionist school. There are pictures on the walls by these three artists, painted in their earlier years, which at first strike the eye as being more impressionist than anything else; but, nevertheless, the connection of these artists with the Impressionists is accidental rather than intrinsic.

By the year 1880 the Impressionists had practically won their battle; nor is it likely any group of artists will ever have to fight so hard a one again. They have conquered for future originality, if not the right of a respectful hearing, at least of a dubious attention. By 1880 they had convinced practically everybody whose opinion counted, that their methods and ideas were at any rate those of artists, not those of cranks and charlatans. About this date the reaction against Impressionism, which this exhibition represents, began to be distinctly felt. The two groups had one characteristic in common: the resolve of each artist to express his own temperament, and never to permit contemporary ideals to dictate to him what was beautiful, significant, and worthy to be painted. But the main current of Impressionism lay along the line of recording hitherto unrecognized aspects of objects; they were interested in analysing the play of light and shadow into a multiplicity of distinct colours; they refined upon what was already illusive in nature. In the pictures of Seurat, Cross, and Signac here exhibited, this scientific interest in the representation of colour is still uppermost; what is new in these pictures is simply the method of representing the vibration of light by painting objects in dots and squares. The Post-Impressionists on the other hand were not concerned with recording impressions of colour or light. They were interested in the discoveries of the Impressionists only so far as these discoveries helped them to express emotions which the objects themselves evoked; their attitude towards nature was far more independent, not to say rebellious. It is true that from the earliest times artists have regarded nature as 'the mistress of the masters'; but it is only in the nineteenth century that the close imitation of nature, without any conscious modification by the artist, has been proclaimed as a dogma. The Impressionists were artists, and their imitations of appearances were modified, consciously and unconsciously, in the direction of unity and harmony; being artists they were forced to select and arrange. But the receptive, passive attitude towards the appearances of things often hindered them from rendering their real significance. Impressionism encouraged an artist to paint a tree as it appeared to him at the moment under particular circumstances. It insisted so much upon the importance of his rendering this exact impression that his work often completely failed to express a tree at all; as transferred to canvas it was just so much shimmer and colour. The 'treeness' of the tree was not rendered at all; all the emotion and associations such as trees may be made to convey in poetry were omitted.

This is the fundamental cause of difference between the Impressionists and the group of painters whose pictures hang on these walls. They said in effect to the Impressionists: 'You have explored nature in every direction, and all honour to you; but your methods and principles have hindered artists from exploring and expressing that emotional significance which lies in things, and is the most important subject matter of art. There is much more of that significance in the work of earlier artists who had not a tenth part of your skill in representing appearance. We will aim at that; though by our simplification of nature we shock and disconcert our contemporaries, whose eyes are now accustomed to your revelations, as much as you originally disconcerted your contemporaries by your subtleties and complications.' And there is no denying that the work of the Post-Impressionists is sufficiently disconcerting. It may even appear ridiculous to those who do not recall the fact that a good rocking-horse often has more of the true horse about it than an instantaneous photograph of a Derby winner.

The artists who felt most the restraints which the Impressionist attitude towards nature imposed upon them, naturally looked to the mysterious and isolated figure of Cézanne as their deliverer. Cézanne himself had come in contact with Manet and his art is derived directly from him. Manet, it is true, is also regarded as the father of Impressionism. To him Impressionism owes much of its power, interest and importance. He was a revolutionary in the sense that he refused to accept the pictorial convention of his time. He went back to seventeenth-century Spain for his inspiration. Instead of accepting the convention of light and shade falling upon objects from the side, he chose what seemed an impossibly difficult method of painting, that of representing them with light falling full upon them. This led to a very great change in the method of modelling, and to a simplification of planes in his pictures which resulted in something closely akin to simple linear designs. He adopted, too, hitherto unknown oppositions of colour. In fact he endeavoured to get rid of chiaroscuro.

Regarded as a hopeless revolutionary, he was naturally drawn to other young artists, who found themselves in the same predicament; and through his connection with them and with Monet he gradually changed his severe, closely constructed style for one in which the shifting, elusive aspects of nature were accentuated. In this way he became one of the

Impressionists and in his turn influenced them. Cézanne, however, seized upon precisely that side of Manet which Monet and the other Impressionists ignored. Cézanne, when rendering the novel aspects of nature to which Impressionism was drawing attention, aimed first at a design which should produce the coherent, architectural effect of the masterpieces of primitive art. Because Cézanne thus showed how it was possible to pass from the complexity of the appearance of things to the geometrical simplicity which design demands, his art has appealed enormously to later designers. They recognize in him a guide capable of leading them out of the *cul de sac* into which naturalism had led them. Cézanne himself did not use consciously his new-found method of expression to convey ideas and emotions. He appealed first and foremost to the eye, and to the eye alone. But the path he indicated was followed by two younger artists, Van Gogh and Gauguin with surprising results. Van Gogh's morbid temperament forced him to express in paint his strongest emotions, and in the methods of Cézanne he found a means of conveying the wildest and strangest visions conceived by any artist of our time. Yet he, too, accepts in the main the general appearance of nature; only before every scene and every object he searches first for the quality which originally made it appeal so strangely to him: *that* he is determined to record at any sacrifice.

Gauguin is more of a theorist. He felt that while modern art had opened up undiscovered aspects of nature, it had to a great extent neglected the fundamental laws of abstract form, and above all had failed to realize the power which abstract form and colour can exercise over the imagination of the spectator. He deliberately chose, therefore, to become a decorative painter, believing that this was the most direct way of impressing upon the imagination the emotion he wished to perpetuate. In his Tahitian pictures by extreme simplification he endeavoured to bring back into modern painting the significance of gesture and movement characteristic of primitive art.

The followers of these men are pushing their ideas further and further. In the work of Matisse, especially, this search for an abstract harmony of line, for rhythm, has been carried to lengths which often deprive the figure of all appearance of nature. The general effect of his pictures is that of a return to primitive, even perhaps of a return to barbaric, art. This is inevitably disconcerting; but before dismissing such pictures as violently absurd, it is fair to consider the nature of the problem which the artist who would use abstract design as his principle of expression, has to face. His relation to a modern public is peculiar. In the earliest ages of art the artist's public were able to share in each successive triumph of his skill, for every advance he made was also an advance towards a more obvious representation of things as they appeared to everybody. Primitive art, like the art of children, consists not so much in an attempt to represent what the eye perceives, as to put a line round a mental conception of the object. Like the work of the primitive artist, the pictures children draw are often extraordinarily expressive. But what delights them is to find they are acquiring more and more skill in producing a deceptive likeness of the object itself. Give them a year of drawing lessons and they will probably produce results which will give the greatest satisfaction to them and their relations; but to the critical eye the original expressiveness will have vanished completely from their work.

The development of primitive art (for here we are dealing with men and not children) is the gradual absorption of each newly observed detail into an already established system of design. Each new detail is hailed with delight by their public. But there comes a point when the accumulations of an increasing skill in mere representation begin to destroy the expressiveness of the design, and then, though a large section of the public continue to applaud, the artist grows uneasy. He begins to try to unload, to simplify the drawing and painting, by which natural objects are evoked, in order to recover the lost expressiveness and life. He aims at *synthesis* in design; that is to say, he is prepared to subordinate consciously his power of representing the parts of his picture as plausibly as possible, to the expressiveness of his whole design. But in this retrogressive movement he has the public, who have become accustomed to extremely plausible imitations of nature, against him at every step; and what is more, his own self-consciousness hampers him as well.

The movement in art represented in this exhibition is widely spread. Although, with the exception of the Dutchman, Van Gogh, all the artists exhibited are Frenchmen, the school has ceased to be specifically a French one. It has found disciples in Germany, Belgium, Russia, Holland, Sweden. There are Americans, Englishmen and Scotchmen in Paris who are working and experimenting along the same lines. But the works of the Post-Impressionists are hardly known in England, although so much discussed upon the Continent. The exhibition organized by Mr Robert Dell at Brighton last year has been our only chance of seeing them. The promoters of this exhibition have therefore thought it would be interesting to provide an opportunity for a greater number to judge these artists. The ladies and gentlemen on the Honorary Committee, though they are not responsible for the choice of the pictures, by lending their names have been kind enough to give this project their general support.

15

Clive Bell: The Artistic Problem

Clive Bell polemicized Fry's post-impressionist aesthetics in his book Art
(1914). 'The Artistic Problem', which was written for the Athenaeum *in
1919 and reprinted in* Since Cézanne *three years later, takes up again his
influential ideas of significant form and aesthetic emotion. With the same
stylistic vigour, Bell suggests how these principles constitute the problem
for literary as well as visual artists. Bell's criticism of realism would be
amplified by Virginia Woolf in 'Mr Bennett and Mrs Brown' (see p. 233).*

We all agree now – by 'we' I mean intelligent people under sixty – that
a work of art is like a rose. A rose is not beautiful because it is like
something else. Neither is a work of art. Roses and works of art are
beautiful in themselves. Unluckily, the matter does not end there: a rose
is the visible result of an infinitude of complicated goings on in the bosom
of the earth and in the air above, and similarly a work of art is the
product of strange activities in the human mind. In so far as we are mere
spectators and connoisseurs we need not bother about these; all we are
concerned with is the finished product, the work of art. To produce the
best eggs it may be that hens should be fed on hot meal mash. That is a
question for the farmer. For us what matters is the quality of the eggs,
since it is them and not hot meal mash that we propose to eat for
breakfast. Few, however, can take quite so lordly an attitude towards art.
We contemplate the object, we experience the appropriate emotion, and
then we begin asking 'Why?' and 'How?' Personally, I am so conscious
of these insistent questions that, at the risk of some misunderstanding, I

habitually describe works of art as 'significant' rather than 'beautiful' forms. For works of art, unlike roses, are the creations and expressions of conscious minds. I beg that no theological red herring may here be drawn across the scent.

A work of art is an object beautiful, or significant, in itself, nowise dependent for its value on the outside world, capable by itself of provoking in us that emotion which we call aesthetic. Agreed. But men do not create such things unconsciously and without effort, as they breathe in their sleep. On the contrary, for their production are required special energies and a peculiar state of mind. A work of art, like a rose, is the result of a string of causes: and some of us are so vain as to take more interest in the operations of the human mind than in fertilizers and watering-pots.

In the pre-natal history of a work of art I seem to detect at any rate three factors – a state of peculiar and intense sensibility, the creative impulse, and the artistic problem. An artist, I imagine, is one who often and easily is thrown into that state of acute and sympathetic agitation which most of us, once or twice in our lives, have had the happiness of experiencing. And have you noticed that many men and most boys, when genuinely in love, find themselves, the moment the object of their emotion is withdrawn, driven by their feelings into scribbling verses? An artist, I imagine, is always falling in love with everything. Always he is being thrown into a 'state of mind'. The sight of a tree or an omnibus, the screaming of whistles or the whistling of birds, the smell of roast pig, a gesture, a look, any trivial event may provoke a crisis, filling him with an intolerable desire to express himself. The artist cannot embrace the object of his emotion. He does not even wish to. Once, perhaps, that was his desire; if so, like the pointer and the setter, he has converted the barbarous pouncing instinct into the civilized pleasure of tremulous contemplation. Be that as it may, the contemplative moment is short. Simultaneously almost with the emotion arises the longing to express, to create a form that shall match the feeling, that shall commemorate the moment of ecstasy.

This moment of passionate apprehension is, unless I mistake, the source of the creative impulse; indeed, the latter seems to follow so promptly on the former that one is often tempted to regard them as a single movement. The next step is longer. The creative impulse is one thing; creation another. If the artist's form is to be the equivalent of an experience, if it is to be significant in fact, every scrap of it has got to be fused and fashioned in the white heat of his emotion. And how is his emotion to be kept at white heat through the long, cold days of formal construction? Emotions seem to grow cold and set like glue. The intense power and energy called forth by the first thrilling vision grow slack for want of incentive. What engine is to generate the heat and make taut the energies by which alone significant form can be created? That is where the artistic problem comes in.

The artistic problem is the problem of making a match between an emotional experience and a form that has been conceived but not created. Evidently the conception of some sort of form accompanies, or closely follows, the creative impulse. The artist says, or rather feels, to himself: I should like to express that in words, or in lines and colours, or in notes. But to make anything out of his impulse he will need something more than this vague desire to express or to create. He will need a definite, fully conceived form into which his experience can be made to fit. And this fitting, this matching of his experience with his form, will be his problem. It will serve the double purpose of concentrating his energies and stimulating his intellect. It will be at once a canal and a goad. And his energy and intellect between them will have to keep warm his emotion. Shakespeare kept tense the muscle of his mind and boiling and racing his blood by struggling to confine his turbulent spirit within the trim mould of the sonnet. Pindar, the most passionate of poets, drove and pressed his feelings through the convolutions of the ode. Bach wrote fugues. The master of St Vitale found an equivalent for his disquieting ecstasies in severely stylistic portraits wrought in an intractable medium. Giotto expressed himself through a series of pictured legends. El Greco seems to have achieved his stupendous designs by labouring to make significant the fustian of theatrical piety.

There is apparently nothing that an artist cannot vivify. He can create a work of art out of some riddle in engineering or harmonics, an anecdote, or the frank representation of a natural object. Only, to be satisfactory, the problem must be for him who employs it a goad and a limitation. A goad that calls forth all his energies; a limitation that focuses them on some object far more precise and comprehensible than the expression of a vague sensibility, or, to say the same thing in another way, the creation of indefinite beauty. However much an artist may have felt, he cannot just sit down and express it; he cannot create form in the vague. He must sit down to write a play or a poem, to paint a portrait or a still life.

Almost everyone has had his moment of ecstasy, and the creative impulse is not uncommon; but those only who have a pretty strong sense of art understand the necessity for the artistic problem. What is known of it by the public is not much liked; it has a bad name and is reckoned unsympathetic. For the artistic problem, which limits the artist's freedom, fixes his attention on a point, and drives his emotion through narrow tubes, is what imports the conventional element into art. It seems to come between the spontaneous thrill of the artist and the receptive enthusiasm of his public with an air of artificiality. Thus, a generation brought up on Wordsworth could hardly believe in the genuineness of Racine. Our fathers and grandfathers felt, and felt rightly, that art was something that came from and spoke to the depths of the human soul. But how, said they, should deep call to deep in Alexandrines and a pseudo-classical convention, to say nothing of full-bottomed wigs? They forgot to reckon with the artistic problem, and made the mistake that people make who fancy that nothing looking so unlike a Raphael or a Titian as a Matisse or a Picasso can be a work of art. They thought that because the stuff of art comes from the depths of human nature it can be expressed only in terms of naturalism. They did not realize that the creating of an equivalent for an aesthetic experience out of natural speech or the common forms of nature is only one amongst an infinite number of possible problems. There are still ladies who feel sure that had they been in Laura's shoes Petrarch might have experienced something more vivid than what comes through his mellifluous but elaborate *rime*. To them he would have expressed himself otherwise. Possibly: but whatever he experienced could not have become art – significant form – till it had been withdrawn from the world of experience and converted into poetry by some such exacting problem.

One problem in itself is as good as another, just as one kind of nib is as good as another, since problems are valuable only as means. That problem is best for any particular artist that serves that particular artist best. The ideal problem will be the one that raises his power most while limiting his fancy least. The incessant recourse of European writers to dramatic form suggests that here is a problem which to them is peculiarly favourable. Its conventions, I suppose, are sufficiently strict to compel the artist to exert himself to the utmost, yet not so strict as to present those appalling technical difficulties – the sort presented by a sestina or a chant royal – that make self-expression impossible to any but a consummate master. The novel, on the other hand, as we are just beginning to suspect, affords for most writers an unsatisfactory, because insufficiently rigorous, problem. Each age has its favourites. Indeed, the history of art is very much the history of the problem. The stuff of art is always the same, and always it must be converted into form before it can become art; it is in their choice of converting-machines that the ages differ conspicuously.

Two tasks that painters and writers sometimes set themselves are often mistaken for artistic problems, but are, in fact, nothing of the sort. One is literal representation: the other the supply of genius direct from the cask. To match a realistic form with an aesthetic experience is a problem that has served well many great artists: Chardin and Tolstoy will do as examples. To make a realistic form and match it with nothing is no problem at all. Though to say just what the camera would say is beyond the skill and science of most of us, it is a task that will never raise an artist's temperature above boiling-point. A painter may go into the woods, get his thrill, go home and fetch his panel-box, and proceed to set down in cold blood what he finds before him. No good can come of it, as the gloomy walls of any official exhibition will show. Realistic novels fail for the same reason: with all their gifts, neither Zola, nor Edmond de Goncourt, nor Mr Arnold Bennett ever produced a work of art. Also, a thorough anarchist will never be an artist, though many artists have believed that they were thorough anarchists. One man cannot pour an aesthetic experience straight into another, leaving out the problem. He cannot exude form: he must set himself to create a particular form. Automatic writing will never be poetry, nor automatic scrabbling design. The artist must submit his creative impulse to the conditions of a problem. Often great artists set their own problems; always they are bound by them. That would be a shallow critic who supposed that Mallarmé wrote down what words he chose in what order he pleased, unbound by any sense of a definite form to be created and a most definite conception to be realized. Mallarmé was as severely bound by his problem as was Racine by his. It was as definite – for all that it was unformulated – as absolute, and as necessary. The same may be said of Picasso in his most abstract works: but not of all his followers, nor of all Mallarmé's either.

16

Roger Fry: Art and Socialism

Several months before the second Post-Impressionist Exhibition in 1912 Roger Fry contributed an essay on the artist to Socialism and the Great State: Essays in Construction, *edited by H. G. Wells and others. (Among the other contributors mentioned by Fry is L. G. Chiozza Money, a Member of Parliament who wrote an essay on work.) No socialist, Fry had experienced the effect of plutocracy on art while working for J. P. Morgan. The year after his essay Fry put into practice his ideas about how the applied arts could be made more rational and useful by founding the Omega Workshops, which he ran until 1920. The year the Omega closed, Fry retitled and expanded his essay for inclusion in* Vision and Design.

I am not a Socialist, as I understand that word, nor can I pretend to have worked out those complex estimates of economic possibility which are needed before one can endorse the hopeful forecasts of Lady Warwick, Mr Money, and Mr Wells. What I propose to do here is first to discuss what effect plutocracy, such as it is to-day, has had of late, and is likely to have in the near future, upon one of the things which I should like to imagine continuing upon our planet – namely, art. And then briefly to prognosticate its chances under such a regime as my colleagues have sketched.

As I understand it, art is one of the chief organs of what, for want of a better word, I must call the spiritual life. It both stimulates and controls those indefinable overtones of the material life of man which all of us at moments feel to have a quality of permanence and reality that does not belong to the rest of our experience. Nature demands with no uncertain voice that the physical needs of the body shall be satisfied first; but we feel that our real human life only begins at the point where that is accomplished, that the man who works at some uncreative and uncongenial toil merely to earn enough food to enable him to continue to work has not, properly speaking, a human life at all.

It is the argument of commercialism, as it once was of aristocracy, that the accumulation of surplus wealth in a few hands enables this spiritual life to maintain its existence, that no really valuable or useless work (for from this point of view only useless work has value) could exist in the community without such accumulations of wealth. The argument has been employed for the disinterested work of scientific research. A doctor of naturally liberal and generous impulses told me that he was becoming a reactionary simply because he feared that public bodies would never give the money necessary for research with anything like the same generosity as is now shown by the great plutocrats. But Sir Ray Lankester does not find that generosity sufficient, and is prepared at least to consider a State more ample-spirited.

The situation as regards art and as regards the disinterested love of truth is so similar that we might expect this argument in favour of a plutocratic social order to hold equally well for both art and science, and that the artist would be a fervent upholder of the present system. As a matter of fact, the more representative artists have rarely been such, and not a few, though working their life long for the plutocracy, have been vehement Socialists.

Despairing of the conditions due to modern commercialism, it is not unnatural that lovers of beauty should look back with nostalgia to the age when society was controlled by a landed aristocracy. I believe, however, that from the point of view of the encouragement of great creative art there is not much difference between an aristocracy and a plutocracy. The aristocrat usually had taste, the plutocrat frequently has not. Now taste is of two kinds, the first consisting in the negative avoidance of all that is ill-considered and discordant, the other positive and a by-product; it is that harmony which always results from the expression of intense and disinterested emotion. The aristocrat, by means of his good taste of the negative kind, was able to come to terms with the artist; the plutocrat has not. But both alike desire to buy something which is incommensurate with money. Both want art to be a background to their radiant self-consciousness. They want to buy beauty as they want to buy love; and the painter, picture-dealer, and the pander try perennially to persuade them that it is possible. But living beauty cannot be bought; it must be won. I have said that the aristocrat, by his taste, by his feeling for the accidentals of beauty, did manage to get on to some kind of terms with the artist. Hence the art of the eighteenth century, an art that is prone before the distinguished patron, subtly and deliciously flattering and yet always fine. In contrast to that the art of the nineteenth century is coarse, turbulent, clumsy. It marks the beginning of a revolt. The artist just managed to let himself be coaxed and cajoled by the aristocrat, but when the aristocratic was succeeded by the plutocratic patron with less conciliatory manners and no taste, the artist rebelled; and the history of art in the nineteenth century is the history of a band of heroic Ishmaelites, with no secure place in the social system, with nothing to support them in the unequal struggle but a dim sense of a new idea, the idea of the freedom of art from all trammels and tyrannies.

The place that the artists left vacant at the plutocrat's table had to be filled, and it was filled by a race new in the history of the world, a race for whom no name has yet been found, a race of pseudo-artists. As the prostitute professes to sell love, so these gentlemen professed to sell beauty, and they and their patrons rollicked good-humouredly through the Victorian era. They adopted the name and something of the manner of artists; they intercepted not only the money, but the titles and fame and glory which were intended for those whom they had supplanted. But, while they were yet feasting, there came an event which seemed at the time of no importance, but which was destined to change ultimately the face of things, the exhibition of ancient art at Manchester in 1857. And with this came Ruskin's address on the Political Economy of Art, a work which surprises by its prophetic foresight when we read it half a century later. These two things were the Mene Tekel of the orgy of Victorian Philistinism. The plutocrat saw through the deception; it was not beauty the pseudo-artist sold him, any more than it was love which the prostitute gave. He turned from it in disgust and decided that the only beauty he could buy was the dead beauty of the past. Thereupon set in the worship of *patine* and the age of forgery and the detection of forgery. I once remarked to a rich man that a statue by Rodin might be worthy even of his collection. He replied, 'Show me a Rodin with the *patine* of the fifteenth century, and I will buy it.'

Patine, then, the adventitious material beauty which age alone can give, has come to be the object of a reverence greater than that devoted to the idea which is enshrined within the work of art. People are right to admire *patine*. Nothing is more beautiful than gilded bronze of which time has taken toll until it is nothing but a faded shimmering splendour over depths of inscrutable gloom; nothing finer than the dull glow which Pentelic marble has gathered from past centuries of sunlight and warm

Mediterranean breezes. *Patine* is good, but it is a surface charm added to the essential beauty of expression; its beauty is literally skin-deep. It can never come into being or exist in or for itself; no *patine* can make a bad work good, or the forgers would be justified. It is an adjectival and ancillary beauty scarcely worthy of our prolonged contemplation.

There is to the philosopher something pathetic in the plutocrat's worship of *patine*. It is, as it were, a compensation for his own want of it. On himself all the rough thumb and chisel marks of his maker – and he is self-made – stand as yet unpolished and raw; but his furniture, at least, shall have the distinction of age-long acquaintance with good manners.

But the net result of all this is that the artist has nothing to hope from the plutocrat. To him we must be grateful indeed for that brusque disillusionment of the real artist, the real artist who might have rubbed along uneasily for yet another century with his predecessor, the aristocrat. Let us be grateful to him for this; but we need not look to him for further benefits, and if we decide to keep him the artist must be content to be paid after he is dead and vicariously in the person of an art-dealer. The artist must be content to look on while sums are given for dead beauty, the tenth part of which, properly directed, would irrigate whole nations and stimulate once more the production of vital artistic expression.

I would not wish to appear to blame the plutocrat. He has often honestly done his best for art; the trouble is not of his making more than of the artist's, and the misunderstanding between art and commerce is bound to be complete. The artist, however mean and avaricious he may appear, knows that he cannot really sell himself for money any more than the philosopher or the scientific investigator can sell himself for money. He takes money in the hope that he may secure the opportunity for the free functioning of his creative power. If the patron could give him that instead of money he would bless him; but he cannot, and so he tries to get him to work not quite freely for money; and in revenge the artist indulges in all manner of insolences, even perhaps in sharp practices, which make the patron feel, with some justification, that he is the victim of ingratitude and wanton caprice. It is impossible that the artist should work for the plutocrat; he must work for himself, because it is only by so doing that he can perform the function for which he exists; it is only by working for himself that he can work for mankind.

If, then, the particular kind of accumulation of surplus wealth which we call plutocracy has failed, as surely it has signally failed, to stimulate the creative power of the imagination, what disposition of wealth might be conceived that would succeed better? First of all, a greater distribution of wealth, with a lower standard of ostentation, would, I think, do a great deal to improve things without any great change in other conditions. It is not enough known that the patronage which really counts today is exercised by quite small and humble people. These people with a few hundreds a year exercise a genuine patronage by buying pictures at ten, twenty, or occasionally thirty pounds, with real insight and understanding, thereby enabling the young Ishmaelite to live and function from the age of twenty to thirty or so, when perhaps he becomes known to richer buyers, those experienced spenders of money who are always more cautious, more anxious to buy an investment than a picture. These poor, intelligent first patrons to whom I allude belong mainly to the professional classes; they have none of the pretensions of the plutocrat and none of his ambitions. The work of art is not for them, as for him, a decorative backcloth to his stage, but an idol and an inspiration. Merely to increase the number and potency of these people would already accomplish much; and this is to be noticed, that if wealth were more evenly distributed, if no one had a great deal of wealth, those who really cared for art would become the sole patrons, since for all it would be an appreciable sacrifice, and for none an impossibility. The man who only buys pictures when he has as many motor-cars as he can conceivably want would drop out as a patron altogether.

But even this would only foster the minor and private arts; and what the history of art definitely elucidates is that the greatest art has always been communal, the expression – in highly individualized ways, no doubt – of common aspirations and ideals.

Let us suppose, then, that society were so arranged that considerable surplus wealth lay in the hands of public bodies, both national and local; can we have any reasonable hope that they would show more skill in carrying out the delicate task of stimulating and using the creative power of the artist?

The immediate prospect is certainly not encouraging. Nothing, for instance, is more deplorable than to watch the patronage of our provincial museums. The gentlemen who administer these public funds naturally have not realized so acutely as private buyers the lesson so admirably taught at Christie's, that pseudo or Royal-Academic art is a bad investment. Nor is it better if we turn to national patronage. In Great Britain, at least, we cannot get a postage stamp or a penny even respectably designed, much less a public monument. Indeed, the tradition that all public British art shall be crassly mediocre and inexpressive is so firmly rooted that it seems to have almost the prestige of constitutional precedent. Nor will anyone who has watched a committee commissioning a presentation portrait, or even buying an old master, be in danger of taking too optimistic a view. With rare and shining exceptions, committees seem to be at the mercy of the lowest common denominator of their individual natures, which is dominated by fear of criticism; and fear and its attendant, compromise, are bad masters of the arts.

Speaking recently at Liverpool, Mr Bernard Shaw placed the present situation as regards public art in its true light. He declared that the corruption of taste and the emotional insincerity of the mass of the people had gone so far that any picture which pleased more than ten per cent of the population should be immediately burned. . . .

This, then, is the fundamental fact we have to face. And it is this that gives us pause when we try to construct any conceivable system of public patronage.

For the modern artist puts the question of any socialistic – or, indeed, of any completely ordered – state in its acutest form. He demands as an essential to the proper use of his powers a freedom from restraint such as no other workman expects. He must work when he feels inclined; he cannot work to order. Hence his frequent quarrels with the burgher who knows he has to work when he is disinclined, and cannot conceive why the artist should not do likewise. The burgher watches the artist's wayward and apparently quite unmethodical activity, and envies his job. Now, in any socialistic state, if certain men are licensed to pursue the artistic calling, they are likely to be regarded by the other workers with some envy. There may be a competition for such soft jobs among those who are naturally work-shy, since it will be evident that the artist is not called to account in the same way as other workers.

If we suppose, as seems not unlikely, in view of the immense numbers who become artists in our present social state, that there would be this competition for the artistic work of the community, what methods would be devised to select those required to fill the coveted posts? Frankly, the history of art in the nineteenth century makes us shudder at the results that would follow. One scarcely knows whether they would be worse if Bumble or the Academy were judge. We only know that under any such conditions *none* of the artists whose work has ultimately counted in the spiritual development of the race would have been allowed to practise the coveted profession.

There is in truth, as Ruskin pointed out in his 'Political Economy of Art', a gross and wanton waste under the present system. We have thousands of artists who are only so by accident and by name, on the one hand, and certainly many – one cannot tell how many – who have the special gift but have never had the peculiar opportunities which are to-day necessary to allow it to expand and function. But there is, what in an odd way consoles us, a blind chance that the gift and the opportunity

may coincide; that Shelley and Browning may have a competence, and
Cézanne a farm-house he could retire to. Bureaucratic Socialism would,
it seems, take away even this blind chance that mankind may benefit by
its least appreciable, most elusive treasures, and would carefully organize
the complete suppression of original creative power; would organize into
a universal and all-embracing tyranny the already overweening and
disastrous power of endowed official art. For we must face the fact that
the average man has two qualities which would make the proper selection of the artist almost impossible. He has, first of all, a touching
proclivity to awe-struck admiration of whatever is presented to him as
noble by a constituted authority; and, secondly, a complete absence of
any immediate reaction to a work of art until his judgement has thus
been hypnotized by the voice of authority. Then, and not till then, he
sees, or swears he sees, those adorable Emperor's clothes that he is
always agape for.

I am speaking, of course, of present conditions, of a populace whose
emotional life has been drugged by the sugared poison of pseudo-art, a
populace saturated with snobbishness, and regarding art chiefly for its
value as a symbol of social distinctions. There have been times when such
a system of public patronage as we are discussing might not have been
altogether disastrous. Times when the guilds represented more or less
adequately the genuine artistic intelligence of the time; but the creation,
first of all, of aristocratic art, and finally of pseudo-art, have brought it
about that almost any officially organized system would at the present
moment stereotype all the worst features of modern art.

Now, in thus putting forward the extreme difficulties of any system of
publicly controlled art, we are emphasizing perhaps too much the idea of
the artist as a creator of purely ideal and abstract works, as the medium
of inspiration and the source of revelation. It is the artist as prophet and
priest that we have been considering, the artist who is the articulate soul
of mankind. Now, in the present commercial State, at a time when such
handiwork as is not admirably fitted to some purely utilitarian purpose
has become inanely fatuous and grotesque, the artist in this sense has
undoubtedly become of supreme importance as a protestant, as one who
proclaims that art is a reasonable function, and one that proceeds by a
nice adjustment of means to ends. But if we suppose a state in which all
the ordinary objects of daily life – our chairs and tables, our carpets and
pottery – expressed something of this reasonableness instead of a crazy
and vapid fantasy, the artist as a pure creator might become, not indeed
of less importance – rather more – but a less acute necessity to our
general living than he is to-day. Something of the sanity and purpose-
fulness of his attitude might conceivably become infused into the work of

the ordinary craftsman, something, too, of his creative energy and delight in work. We must, therefore, turn for a moment from the abstractly creative artist to the applied arts and those who practise them.

We are so far obliged to protect ourselves from the implications of modern life that without a special effort it is hard to conceive the enormous quantity of 'art' that is annually produced and consumed. For the special purpose of realizing it I take the pains to write the succeeding paragraphs in a railway refreshment-room, where I am actually looking at those terribly familiar but fortunately fleeting images which such places afford. And one must remember that public places of this kind merely reflect the average citizen's soul, as expressed in his home.

The space my eye travels over is a small one, but I am appalled at the amount of 'art' that it harbours. The window towards which I look is filled in its lower part by stained glass; within a highly elaborate border, designed by someone who knew the conventions of thirteenth-century glass, is a pattern of yellow and purple vine leaves with bunches of grapes, and flitting about among these many small birds. In front is a lace curtain with patterns taken from at least four centuries and as many countries. On the walls, up to a height of four feet, is a covering of lincrusta walton stamped with a complicated pattern in two colours, with sham silver medallions. Above that a moulding but an inch wide, and yet creeping throughout its whole with a degenerate descendant of a Graeco-Roman carved guilloche pattern; this has evidently been cut out of the wood by machine or stamped out of some composition – its nature is so perfectly concealed that it is hard to say which. Above this is a wall-paper in which an effect of eighteenth-century satin brocade is imitated by shaded staining of the paper. Each of the little refreshment-tables has two cloths, one arranged symmetrically with the table, the other a highly ornate printed cotton arranged 'artistically' in a diagonal position. In the centre of each table is a large pot in which every beautiful quality in the material and making of pots has been carefully obliterated by methods each of which implies profound scientific knowledge and great inventive talent. Within each pot is a plant with large dark-green leaves, apparently made of india-rubber. This painful catalogue makes up only a small part of the inventory of the 'art' of the restaurant. If I were to go on to tell of the legs of the tables, of the electric-light fittings, of the chairs into the wooden seats of which some tremendous mechanical force has deeply impressed a large distorted anthemion – if I were to tell of all these things, my reader and I might both begin to realize with painful acuteness something of the horrible toil involved in all this display. Display is indeed the end and explanation of it all. Not one of these things has been made because the maker enjoyed the making; not one has been bought because its contemplation would give any one any pleasure, but solely because each of these things is accepted as a symbol of a particular social status. I say their contemplation can give no one pleasure; they are there because their absence would be resented by the average man who regards a large amount of futile display as in some way inseparable from the conditions of that well-to-do life to which he belongs or aspires to belong. If everything were merely clean and serviceable he would proclaim the place bare and uncomfortable.

The doctor who lines his waiting-room with bad photogravures and worse etchings is acting on exactly the same principle; in short, nearly all our 'art' is made, bought, and sold merely for its value as an indication of social status.

Now consider the case of those men whose life-work it is to stimulate this eczematous eruption of pattern on the surface of modern manufactures. They are by far the most numerous 'artists' in the country. Each of them has not only learned to draw but has learned by sheer application to put forms together with a similitude of that coherence which creative impulse gives. Probably each of them has somewhere within him something of that creative impulse which is the inspiration and delight of every savage and primitive craftsman; but in these manufacturer's designers the pressure of commercial life has crushed and atrophied that creative impulse completely. Their business is to produce, not expressive design, but dead patterns. They are compelled, therefore, to spend their lives behaving in an entirely idiotic and senseless manner, and that with the certainty that no one will ever get positive pleasure from the result; for one may hazard the statement that until I made the effort just now, no one of the thousands who use the refreshment-rooms ever really *looked* at the designs.

This question of the creation and consumption of art tends to become more and more pressing. I have shown just now what an immense mass of art is consumed, but this is not the same art as that which the genuine artist produces. The work of the truly creative artist is not merely useless to the social man – it appears to be noxious and inassimilable. Before art can be 'consumed' the artistic idea must undergo a process of disinfection. It must have extracted and removed from it all, or nearly all, that makes it aesthetically valuable. What occurs when a great artist creates a new idea is somewhat as follows: We know the process well enough, since it has taken place in the last fifty years. An artist attains to a new vision. He grasps this with such conviction that he is able to express it in his work. Those few people in his immediate surroundings who have the faculty of aesthetic perception become very much excited by the new vision. The average man, on the other hand, lacks this faculty and, moreover, instinctively protects the rounded perfection of his universe of thought and feeling from the intrusion of new experience; in consequence he becomes extremely irritated by the sight of works which appear to him completely unintelligible. The misunderstanding between this small minority and the public becomes violent. Then some of the more intelligent writers on art recognize that the new idea is really related to past aesthetic expressions which have become recognized. Then a clever artist, without any individual vision of his own, sees the possibility of using a modification of the new idea, makes an ingenious compromise between it and the old, generally accepted notions of art. The public, which has been irritated by its incomprehension of the new idea, finding the compromise just intelligible, and delighted to find itself cleverer than it thought, acclaims the compromising intermediary as a genius. The process of disinfection thus begun goes on with increasing energy and rapidity, and before long the travesty of the new idea is completely assimilable by the social organism. The public, after swallowing innumerable imitations of the new idea, may even at last reluctantly accept the original creator as a great man, but generally not until he has been dead for some time and has become a vague and mythical figure.

It is literally true to say that the imitations of works of art are more assimilable by the public than originals, and therefore always tend to fetch a higher price in the market at the moment of their production.

The fact is that the average man uses art entirely for its symbolic value. Art is in fact the symbolic currency of the world. The possession of rare and much coveted works of art is regarded as a sign of national greatness. The growth and development of the Kaiser Friedrich museum was due to the active support of the late Emperor, a man whose distaste for genuine art is notorious, but whose sense of the symbolic was highly developed. Large and expensively ornamented buildings become symbols of municipal greatness. The amount of useless ornaments on façades of their offices is a valuable symbol of the financial exuberance of big commercial undertakings; and, finally, the social status of the individual is expressed to the admiring or envious outer world by the streamlines of an aristocratic motor-car, or the superfluity of lace curtains in the front windows of a genteel suburban villa.

The social man, then, lives in a world of symbols, and though he presses other things into his service, such, for instance, as kings, footmen, dogs, women, he finds in art his richest reservoir of symbolic currency. But in a world of symbolists the creative artist and the creative man of science appear in strange isolation as the only people who are not symbolists. They alone are up against certain relations which do not stand for something else, but appear to have ultimate value, to be real.

Art as a symbolic currency is an important means of the instinctive life of man, but art as created by the artist is in violent revolt against the instinctive life, is an expression of the reflective and fully conscious life. It is natural enough, then, that before it can be used by the instinctive life it must be deprived by travesty of its too violent assertion of its own reality. Travesty is necessary at first to make it assimilable, but in the end long familiarity may rob even original works of art of their insistence, so that, finally, even the great masterpieces may become the most cherished symbols of the lords of the instinctive life, may, as in fact they frequently do, become the property of millionaires.

A great deal of misunderstanding and ill-feeling between the artist and the public comes from a failure to realize the necessity of this process of assimilation of the work of art to the needs of the instinctive life.

I suspect that a very similar process takes place with regard to truth. In order that truth may not outrage too violently the passions and egoisms of the instinctive life it, too, must undergo a process of deformation.

Society, for example, accepts as much of the ascertainable truth as it can stand at a given period in the form of the doctrine of its organized religion.

Now what effect would the development of the Great State which this book anticipates have upon all this? First, I suppose that the fact that everyone had to work might produce a new reverence, especially in the governing body, for work, a new sense of disgust and horror at wasteful and purposeless work. Mr Money has written of waste of work; here in unwanted pseudo-art is another colossal waste. Add to this ideal of economy in work the presumption that the workers in every craft would be more thoroughly organized and would have a more decisive voice in the nature and quality of their productions. Under the present system of commercialism the one object, and the complete justification, of producing any article is, that it can be made either by its intrinsic value, or by the fictitious value put upon it by advertisement, to sell with a sufficient profit to the manufacturer. In any socialistic state, I imagine – and to a large extent the Great State will be socialistic at least – there would not be this same automatic justification for manufacture; people would not be induced artificially to buy what they did not want, and in this way a more genuine scale of values would be developed. Moreover, the workman would be in a better position to say how things should be made. After years of a purely commercial standard, there is left even now, in the average workman, a certain bias in favour of sound and reasonable workmanship as opposed to the ingenious manufacture of fatuous and fraudulent objects; and, if we suppose the immediate pressure of sheer necessity to be removed, it is probable that the craftsman, acting through his guild organizations, would determine to some extent the methods of manufacture. Guilds might, indeed, regain something of the political influence that gave us the Gothic cathedrals of the Middle Ages. It is quite probable that this guild influence would act as a check on some innovations in manufacture which, though bringing in a profit, are really disastrous to the community at large. Of such a nature are all the so-called improvements whereby decoration, the whole value of which consists in its expressive power, is multiplied indefinitely by machinery. When once the question of the desirability of any and every production came to be discussed, as it would be in the Great State, it would inevitably follow that some reasonable and scientific classifications would be undertaken with regard to machinery. That is to say, it would be considered in what processes and to what degree machinery ought to replace handiwork, both from the point of view of the community as a whole and from that of the producer. So far as I know, this has never been undertaken even with regard to mere economy, no one having calculated with precision how far the longer life of certain hand-made articles does not more than compensate for increased cost of production. And I suppose that in the Great State other things besides mere economy would come into the calculation. The Great State will live, not hoard.

It is probable that in many directions we should extend mechanical operations immensely, that such things as the actual construction of buildings, the mere laying and placing of the walls might become increasingly mechanical. Such methods, if confined to purely structural elements, are capable of beauty of a special kind, since they can express the ordered ideas of proportion, balance, and interval as conceived by the creative mind of the architect. But in process of time one might hope to see a sharp line of division between work of this kind and such purely expressive and non-utilitarian design as we call ornament; and it would be felt clearly that into this field no mechanical device should intrude, that, while ornament might be dispensed with, it could never be imitated, since its only reason for being is that it conveys the vital expressive power of a human mind acting constantly and directly upon matter.

Finally, I suppose that in the Great State we might hope to see such a considerable levelling of social conditions that the false values put upon art by its symbolizing of social status would be largely destroyed and, the pressure of mere opinion being relieved, people would develop some more immediate reaction to the work of art than they can at present achieve.

Supposing, then, that under the Great State it was found impossible, at all events at first, to stimulate and organize the abstract creative power of the pure artist, the balance might after all be in favour of the new order if the whole practice of applied art could once more become rational and purposeful. In a world where the objects of daily use and ornament were made with practical common sense, the aesthetic sense would need far less to seek consolation and repose in works of pure art.

Nevertheless, in the long run mankind will not allow this function, which is necessary to its spiritual life, to lapse entirely. I imagine, however, that it would be much safer to penalize rather than to stimulate such activity, and that simply in order to sift out those with a genuine passion from those who are merely attracted by the apparent ease of the pursuit. I imagine that the artist would naturally turn to one of the applied arts as his means of livelihood; and we should get the artist coming out of the *bottega*, as he did in fifteenth-century Florence. There are, moreover, innumerable crafts, even besides those that are definitely artistic, which, if pursued for short hours (Sir Leo Money has shown how short these hours might be), would leave a man free to pursue other callings in his leisure.

The majority of poets to-day are artists in this position. It is comparatively rare for anyone to make of poetry his actual means of livelihood. Our poets are, first of all, clerks, critics, civil servants, or postmen. I very much doubt if it would be a serious loss to the community if the pure graphic artist were in the same position. That is to say, that all our pictures would be made by amateurs. It is quite possible to suppose that this would be not a loss, but a great gain. The painter's means of livelihood would probably be some craft in which his artistic powers would be constantly occupied, though at a lower tension and in a humbler way. The Great State aims at human freedom; essentially, it is an organization for leisure – out of which art grows; it is only a purely bureaucratic Socialism that would attempt to control the aesthetic lives of men.

So I conceive that those in whom the instinct for abstract creative art was strongest would find ample opportunities for its exercise, and that the temptation to simulate this particular activity would be easily resisted by those who had no powerful inner compulsion.

In the Great State, moreover, and in any sane Socialism, there would be opportunity for a large amount of purely private buying and selling. Mr Wells's Modern Utopia, for example, hypothecates a vast superstructure of private trading. A painter might sell his pictures to those who were engaged in more lucrative employment, though one supposes that with the much more equal distribution of wealth the sums available for this would be incomparably smaller than at present; a picture would not be a speculation, but a pleasure, and no one would become an artist in the hope of making a fortune.

Ultimately, of course, when art had been purified of its present unreality by a prolonged contact with the crafts, society would gain a new confidence in its collective artistic judgement, and might even boldly assume the responsibility which at present it knows it is unable to face. It might choose its poets and painters and philosophers and deep investigators, and make of such men and women a new kind of kings.

17

Lytton Strachey:
Avons-Nous Changé Tout Cela?

Lytton Strachey's essay takes its title from Molière's Le Médecin malgré
lui, *in which the doctor explains that the heart used to be on the left and
the liver on the right, 'mais nous avons changé tout cela' thanks to a new
medical method. The essay appeared in the* New Statesman *in 1913,
following a controversy over Roger Fry's ridicule of the late Alma
Tadema's work exhibited at the Royal Academy's Burlington House. Fry
said his antique paintings suggested the furniture, clothes, and marble
villas of the Roman Empire were composed of 'highly scented soap'; Sir
William Richmond, RA, urged a boycott of Fry because of his criticism.*

There is a certain house in Rome which deserves, perhaps, in its way, as
much attention as the more famous monuments of that famous city. It is
an old building, with a slab let into the wall, on which is engraved the
following inscription: 'Here Galileo was imprisoned for saying that the
earth goes round the sun.' That is all, and it is enough. The sentence
stands there, summing up in its laconic irony a long chapter of human
folly and human cruelty – a chapter which possibly even now has not
quite been closed. Passers-by look up, read, and, as the humour takes
them, smile or frown over the old story. But I have seen a band of
seminarists go down that street – twenty slow-stepping, black-robed,
pious youths – and somehow it happened, as they passed the building,
that they . . . did not look upward. Perhaps it was as wise; for such as
these there is something decidedly inconvenient about that inscription. I
wanted to run up to them and cry out, 'Tell me, O ye youthful votaries

of the Church Infallible, when was it that the earth *did* begin to go round the sun?' Certainly, so far as the Holy Father was concerned, no efforts were spared to put off that awkward moment for as long as possible. For more than a century after Galileo's death no whisper of his heretical doctrines was heard in Italy. The profane pages of Casanova show us that even in Venice, half-way through the enlightened eighteenth century, educated gentlemen regarded the theory of Copernicus not merely as a questionable error, but as a downright absurdity. However, at last, in 1835, the works of the great Florentine were removed from the Index.

Reflecting on these things – on that age-long struggle between light and darkness, on the martyrdoms and the triumph of human reason, on the humbled pride of religious persecution – one is almost persuaded to be an optimist. Where shall men look for the thumbscrews of the Inquisition? *Où sont les neiges d'antan?* Here, surely, is an achievement for history to point to. One horror, it seems, has been actually abolished from the earth. The fires of Smithfield are out for ever, and the *Origin of Species* can be bought for a shilling at every bookstall. One is tempted to rejoice with Professor Bury, who in his pleasant little book on *The History of Freedom of Thought*, lately published for a shilling too, has painted the picture of Toleration Victorious all *couleur de rose*. Freedom of Thought, he tells us, was established once and for all in the nineteenth century, and we may go on our way congratulating ourselves. Well, that is very nice, very nice indeed – if it is true. But, after all, can we be quite so sure that it *is* true? Is it really credible that the human race should have got along so far as that? That such deeply rooted instincts as the love of persecution and the hatred of heterodoxies should have been dissipated into thin air by the charms of philosophers and the common-sense of that remarkable period the nineteenth century? Perhaps it is worth while looking a little closer to make sure that some mistake has not been made. Optimists like Professor Bury point triumphantly to the undoubted fact that religious persecution has come to an end; and thus, they argue, it follows that the principles of toleration are established. But does it follow? May not there be other causes for the cessation of religious persecution besides the triumph of tolerance? For instance, if religious questions came to be taken less seriously by people in general, would not that lead to the same result? And is not this precisely what has happened? In the sixteenth century the question of Transubstantiation was indeed a burning one: it seemed well worth while sending other people to the stake about it, or even, if it came to a pinch, going to the stake oneself. But to-day we somehow take less interest in the subject; most of us don't know what Transubstantiation is; and so, naturally enough, we are perfectly tolerant, whatever views may be held upon it. But it is not the principles of toleration that make us so – it is mere indifference. We really have no right to pride ourselves upon our love of free thought because, when a man informs us that he believes (or disbelieves) in the Procession of the Holy Ghost, we refrain from forthwith tearing out his tongue with red-hot pincers; or because, when Dr McTaggart writes a book on Religion and Dogma in which his subtle and exquisite arguments leave the Trinity not a leg to stand on, we make no attempt to have him put upon the rack.

If we do want to test the strength of our convictions in the matter of tolerance, we must choose some opinion or some state of mind the very thought of which seriously disturbs us – something which makes the blood rush to our heads in such an access of fury as, no doubt, attacked the men of the sixteenth century whenever they thought of anyone believing (or disbelieving) in the Procession of the Holy Ghost. For instance, when some deplorable working-man blurts out the very propositions that Dr McTaggart has so elegantly propounded, but blurts them out with no sign of elegance – in fact, with every sign of vulgarity and coarseness, with a rough directness that unutterably shocks our sense of propriety and ribald commentaries that make our middle-class ears tingle and turn red – what do we do then? Well, then, we discover that, after all, there are Blasphemy Laws upon the Statute Book and, to show our open-mindedness, we send the working-man to prison for six months.

It seems clear that the change that has come over us is not so much a change in our attitude towards persecution in general as a change in the class of subjects which raise our zeal to persecute. What is known as 'bad taste', for instance, is certainly persecuted at the present day. The milder transgressions of this nature are punished by private society with extreme severity; the more serious are rigorously dealt with by the State. Again, the conventions connected with apparel fill our minds with feelings of awe and sanctity which our ancestors of the Middle Ages reserved for the articles of their Faith. If a man wears unusual clothes, we hate him with the hatred of a Franciscan for a Dominican in the fourteenth century. If he goes so far as not to wear black clothes at dinner, we are quite certain that he is doomed to eternal perdition; while if he actually ventures to wear no clothes when he bathes, we can stand it no longer and punish him by law. But, of course, the region of thought which, in England at any rate, arouses feelings of intolerance in their acutest and most mediaeval forms is that which is concerned with sexual questions. It is in this direction particularly that the expression of opinion is interfered with both by private conventions and public authority to a degree which makes the happy theory that free thought and free speech came to their own once for all in the golden years of the nineteenth century peculiarly absurd. Our machinery for the suppression of inquiry upon this subject is varied and highly successful. We have an official censorship of the stage directed solely to that end; we have police regulations to prevent the dissemination of such literature – either scientific or artistic – as may appear to the authorities to savour of this taint; we have our unofficial, but none the less extremely effective, Library censorship; and we have the elaborate conspiracy of 'respectable' society, not only to taboo the discussion of such questions, but actually to deny that they exist. Here, indeed, we seem to have managed to go one better even than the Middle Ages. Innocent III himself did not forbid heresy as a topic of conversation. But that is just what our modern Innocents have succeeded in doing.

The revenges of Time in the matter of what may and what may not be mentioned are curious to contemplate. Three centuries ago Rabelais, wishing to put forward his unorthodox religious and philosophical opinions, only ventured to do so under a veil of licentious stories and loose jests. If his book were published to-day in England (not as an expensive classic, but as a cheap new work), its philosophy would hardly arouse the faintest interest, but it would certainly be suppressed as an obscene libel. One can imagine a modern Rabelais reversing the process, and palming off his revolutionary views on the relations between the sexes under cover of an exquisitely refined attack on the doctrines of Christianity. If he were clever enough, the book would cause a little flutter in religious circles, which would sufficiently distract the attention of the guardians of our conventions to allow the powder, so to speak, to go down with the jam. On the whole, it seems as if the modern characteristic of intolerance was its concern with ethics rather than with metaphysics. Whether this is a change for the better or not it is difficult to say. Perhaps, if we must try to suppress our neighbour's opinions in one way or another, we had better do so over questions of actual conduct in the actual world than over the subtleties of metaphysical speculation; for at least it shows a more practical spirit. Yet there is something attractive, something elevated and transcendental, about the bloodthirsty, uncompromising ferocity with which past ages have attempted to unravel the profoundest and the strangest mysteries. Who cannot help, in the bottom of his heart, admiring those ancient Fathers who plunged Europe into civil war and anarchy in order to reject a single mystic letter from the creed? After that our own wrangling over such questions as, let us say, whether a play in which an illegal operation is referred to should or should not be publicly performed, strikes one as a trifle *terre-à-terre*. The transition from the metaphysical to the ethical species of persecution may be observed in the case of Shelley. The public of the time was uncertain whether it hated Shelley because he was an Atheist or because he deserted his wife. Nowadays no one would dream of troubling to call the most abandoned scoundrel an Atheist. Will the time ever come when it will seem no less futile to accuse a man of immorality? The spirit of intolerance may be hunted out of ethics as it has been from metaphysics; and then where will it take refuge? Obviously, in aesthetics; and, indeed, after the late fulminations of Sir William Richmond against Post-Impressionism, nobody could be very much surprised if a stake were set up to-morrow for Mr Roger Fry in the courtyard of Burlington House.

18

John Maynard Keynes:
Economic Possibilities for
Our Grandchildren

---

*Keynes's essay on our grandchildren's economic possibilities was pub-
lished a year after the great stock market crash of October 1929. Unfortunately its assumptions on which the solution of 'the economic
problem' depends have not been granted in the sixty years since the essay
appeared, for there have been both serious wars and important increases
in population. Yet the piece is an excellent, light-hearted illustration of
Bloomsbury values, particularly the fundamental distinction between
things good in themselves and things valuable as means to these good
ends. (Keynes's quotation is from* Sylvie and Bruno *by Lewis Carroll.)*

I

We are suffering just now from a bad attack of economic pessimism. It
is common to hear people say that the epoch of enormous economic
progress which characterized the nineteenth century is over; that the
rapid improvement in the standard of life is now going to slow down –
at any rate in Great Britain; that a decline in prosperity is more likely
than an improvement in the decade which lies ahead of us.

I believe that this is a wildly mistaken interpretation of what is
happening to us. We are suffering, not from the rheumatics of old age,
but from the growing-pains of over-rapid changes, from the painfulness
of readjustment between one economic period and another. The increase
of technical efficiency has been taking place faster than we can deal with
the problem of labour absorption; the improvement in the standard of

life has been a little too quick; the banking and monetary system of the world has been preventing the rate of interest from falling as fast as equilibrium requires. And even so, the waste and confusion which ensue relate to not more than $7\frac{1}{2}$ per cent of the national income; we are muddling away one and sixpence in the £, and have only 18s 6d, when we might, if we were more sensible, have £1; yet, nevertheless, the 18s 6d mounts up to as much as the £1 would have been five or six years ago. We forget that in 1929 the physical output of the industry of Great Britain was greater than ever before, and that the net surplus of our foreign balance available for new foreign investment, after paying for all our imports, was greater last year than that of any other country, being indeed 50 per cent greater than the corresponding surplus of the United States. Or again – if it is to be a matter of comparisons – suppose that we were to reduce our wages by a half, repudiate four-fifths of the national debt, and hoard our surplus wealth in barren gold instead of lending it at 6 per cent or more, we should resemble the now much-envied France. But would it be an improvement?

The prevailing world depression, the enormous anomaly of unemployment in a world full of wants, the disastrous mistakes we have made, blind us to what is going on under the surface – to the true interpretation of the trend of things. For I predict that both of the two opposed errors of pessimism which now make so much noise in the world will be proved wrong in our own time – the pessimism of the revolutionaries who think that things are so bad that nothing can save us but violent change, and the pessimism of the reactionaries who consider the balance of our economic and social life so precarious that we must risk no experiments.

My purpose in this essay, however, is not to examine the present or the near future, but to disembarrass myself of short views and take wings into the future. What can we reasonably expect the level of our economic life to be a hundred years hence? What are the economic possibilities for our grandchildren?

From the earliest times of which we have record – back, say to two thousand years before Christ – down to the beginning of the eighteenth century, there was no very great change in the standard of life of the average man living in the civilized centres of the earth. Ups and downs certainly. Visitations of plague, famine, and war. Golden intervals. But no progressive, violent change. Some periods perhaps 50 per cent better than others – at the utmost 100 per cent better – in the four thousand years which ended (say) in AD 1700.

This slow rate of progress, or lack of progress, was due to two reasons – to the remarkable absence of important technical improvements and to the failure of capital to accumulate.

The absence of important technical inventions between the prehistoric age and comparatively modern times is truly remarkable. Almost everything which really matters and which the world possessed at the commencement of the modern age was already known to man at the dawn of history. Language, fire, the same domestic animals which we have today, wheat, barley, the vine and the olive, the plough, the wheel, the oar, the sail, leather, linen and cloth, bricks and pots, gold and silver, copper, tin, and lead – and iron was added to the list before 1000 BC – banking, statecraft, mathematics, astronomy, and religion. There is no record of when we first possessed these things.

At some epoch before the dawn of history – perhaps even in one of the comfortable intervals before the last ice age – there must have been an era of progress and invention comparable to that in which we live today. But through the greater part of recorded history there was nothing of the kind.

The modern age opened, I think, with the accumulation of capital which began in the sixteenth century. I believe – for reasons with which I must not encumber the present argument – that this was initially due to the rise of prices, and the profits to which that led, which resulted from the treasure of gold and silver which Spain brought from the New World into the Old. From that time until today the power of accumulation by compound interest, which seems to have been sleeping for many generations, was reborn and renewed its strength. And the power of compound interest over two hundred years is such as to stagger the imagination.

Let me give in illustration of this a sum which I have worked out. The value of Great Britain's foreign investments today is estimated at about £4,000 million. This yields us an income at the rate of about $6\frac{1}{2}$ per cent. Half of this we bring home and enjoy; the other half, namely, $3\frac{1}{4}$ per cent, we leave to accumulate abroad at compound interest. Something of this sort has now been going on for about 250 years.

For I trace the beginnings of British foreign investment to the treasure which Drake stole from Spain in 1580. In that year he returned to England bringing with him the prodigious spoils of the *Golden Hind*. Queen Elizabeth was a considerable shareholder in the syndicate which had financed the expedition. Out of her share she paid off the whole of England's foreign debt, balanced her budget, and found herself with about £40,000 in hand. This she invested in the Levant Company – which prospered. Out of the profits of the Levant Company, the East India Company was founded; and the profits of this great enterprise were the foundation of England's subsequent foreign investment. Now it happens that £40,000 accumulating at $3\frac{1}{4}$ per cent compound interest approximately corresponds to the actual volume of England's foreign investments at various dates, and would actually amount today to the total of £4,000 million which I have already quoted as being what our foreign investments now are. Thus, every £1 which Drake brought home in 1580 has now become £100,000. Such is the power of compound interest!

From the sixteenth century, with a cumulative crescendo after the eighteenth, the great age of science and technical inventions began, which since the beginning of the nineteenth century has been in full flood – coal, steam, electricity, petrol, steel, rubber, cotton, the chemical industries, automatic machinery and the methods of mass production, wireless, printing, Newton, Darwin, and Einstein, and thousands of other things and men too famous and familiar to catalogue.

What is the result? In spite of an enormous growth in the population of the world, which it has been necessary to equip with houses and machines, the average standard of life in Europe and the United States has been raised, I think, about fourfold. The growth of capital has been on a scale which is far beyond a hundred-fold of what any previous age had known. And from now on we need not expect so great an increase of population.

If capital increases, say, 2 per cent per annum, the capital equipment of the world will have increased by a half in twenty years, and seven and a half times in a hundred years. Think of this in terms of material things – houses, transport, and the like.

At the same time technical improvements in manufacture and transport have been proceeding at a greater rate in the last ten years than ever before in history. In the United States factory output per head was 40 per cent greater in 1925 than in 1919. In Europe we are held back by temporary obstacles, but even so it is safe to say that technical efficiency is increasing by more than 1 per cent per annum compound. There is evidence that the revolutionary technical changes, which have so far chiefly affected industry, may soon be attacking agriculture. We may be on the eve of improvements in the efficiency of food production as great as those which have already taken place in mining, manufacture, and transport. In quite a few years – in our own lifetimes I mean – we may be able to perform all the operations of agriculture, mining, and manufacture with a quarter of the human effort to which we have been accustomed.

For the moment the very rapidity of these changes is hurting us and bringing difficult problems to solve. Those countries are suffering relatively which are not in the vanguard of progress. We are being afflicted with a new disease of which some readers may not yet have heard the

name, but of which they will hear a great deal in the years to come –
namely, *technological unemployment*. This means unemployment due to
our discovery of means of economizing the use of labour outrunning the
pace at which we can find new uses for labour.

But this is only a temporary phase of maladjustment. All this means in
the long run *that mankind is solving its economic problem.* I would
predict that the standard of life in progressive countries one hundred
years hence will be between four and eight times as high as it is today.
There would be nothing surprising in this even in the light of our present
knowledge. It would not be foolish to contemplate the possibility of a far
greater progress still.

II

Let us, for the sake of argument, suppose that a hundred years hence we
are all of us, on the average, eight times better off in the economic sense
than we are today. Assuredly there need be nothing here to surprise us.

Now it is true that the needs of human begins may seem to be
insatiable. But they fall into two classes – those needs which are absolute
in the sense that we feel them whatever the situation of our fellow human
beings may be, and those which are relative in the sense that we feel them
only if their satisfaction lifts us above, makes us feel superior to, our
fellows. Needs of the second class, those which satisfy the desire for
superiority, may indeed be insatiable; for the higher the general level, the
higher still are they. But this is not so true of the absolute needs – a point
may soon be reached, much sooner perhaps than we all of us are aware
of, when these needs are satisfied in the sense that we prefer to devote our
further energies to non-economic purposes.

Now for my conclusion, which you will find, I think, to become more
and more startling to the imagination the longer you think about it.

I draw the conclusion that, assuming no important wars and no
important increase in population, the *economic problem* may be solved,
or be at least within sight of solution, within a hundred years. This means
that the economic problem is not – if we look into the future – *the permanent problem of the human race.*

Why, you may ask, is this so startling? It is startling because – if,
instead of looking into the future, we look into the past – we find that the
economic problem, the struggle for subsistence, always has been hitherto
the primary, most pressing problem of the human race – not only of the
human race, but of the whole of the biological kingdom from the beginnings of life in its most primitive forms.

Thus we have been expressly evolved by nature – with all our impulses and deepest instincts – for the purpose of solving the economic problem. If the economic problem is solved, mankind will be deprived of its traditional purpose.

Will this be a benefit? If one believes at all in the real values of life, the prospect at least opens up the possibility of benefit. Yet I think with dread of the readjustment of the habits and instincts of the ordinary man, bred into him for countless generations, which he may be asked to discard within a few decades.

To use the language of today – must we not expect a general 'nervous breakdown'? We already have a little experience of what I mean – a nervous breakdown of the sort which is already common enough in England and the United States amongst the wives of the well-to-do classes, unfortunate women, many of them, who have been deprived by their wealth of their traditional tasks and occupations – who cannot find it sufficiently amusing, when deprived of the spur of economic necessity, to cook and clean and mend, yet are quite unable to find anything more amusing.

To those who sweat for their daily bread leisure is a longed-for sweet – until they get it.

There is the traditional epitaph written for herself by the old char-woman:

> Don't mourn for me, friends, don't weep for me never,
> For I'm going to do nothing for ever and ever.

This was her heaven. Like others who look forward to leisure, she conceived how nice it would be to spend her time listening-in – for there was another couplet which occurred in her poem:

> With psalms and sweet music the heavens'll be ringing,
> But I shall have nothing to do with the singing.

Yet it will only be for those who have to do with the singing that life will be tolerable – and how few of us can sing!

Thus for the first time since his creation man will be faced with his real, his permanent problem – how to use his freedom from pressing economic cares, how to occupy the leisure, which science and compound interest will have won for him, to live wisely and agreeably and well.

The strenuous purposeful money-makers may carry all of us along with them into the lap of economic abundance. But it will be those peoples, who can keep alive, and cultivate into a fuller perfection, the art of life itself and do not sell themselves for the means of life, who will be able to enjoy the abundance when it comes.

Yet there is no country and no people, I think, who can look forward to the age of leisure and of abundance without a dread. For we have been trained too long to strive and not to enjoy. It is a fearful problem for the ordinary person, with no special talents, to occupy himself, especially if he no longer has roots in the soil or in custom or in the beloved conventions of a traditional society. To judge from the behaviour and the achievements of the wealthy classes today in any quarter of the world, the outlook is very depressing! For these are, so to speak, our advance guard – those who are spying out the promised land for the rest of us and pitching their camp there. For they have most of them failed disastrously, so it seems to me – those who have an independent income but no associations or duties or ties – to solve the problem which has been set them.

I feel sure that with a little more experience we shall use the new-found bounty of nature quite differently from the way in which the rich use it today, and will map out for ourselves a plan of life quite otherwise than theirs.

For many ages to come the old Adam will be so strong in us that everybody will need to do *some* work if he is to be contented. We shall do more things for ourselves than is usual with the rich today, only too glad to have small duties and tasks and routines. But beyond this, we shall endeavour to spread the bread thin on the butter – to make what work there is still to be done to be as widely shared as possible. Three-hour shifts or a fifteen-hour week may put off the problem for a great while. For three hours a day is quite enough to satisfy the old Adam in most of us!

There are changes in other spheres too which we must expect to come. When the accumulation of wealth is no longer of high social importance, there will be great changes in the code of morals. We shall be able to rid ourselves of many of the pseudo-moral principles which have hag-ridden us for two hundred years, by which we have exalted some of the most distasteful of human qualities into the position of the highest virtues. We shall be able to afford to dare to assess the money-motive at its true value. The love of money as a possession – as distinguished from the love of money as a means to the enjoyments and realities of life – will be recognized for what it is, a somewhat disgusting morbidity, one of those semi-criminal, semi-pathological propensities which one hands over with a shudder to the specialists in mental disease. All kinds of social customs and economic practices, affecting the distribution of wealth and of economic rewards and penalties, which we now maintain at all costs, however distasteful and unjust they may be in themselves, because they are tremendously useful in promoting the accumulation of capital, we shall then be free, at last, to discard.

Of course there will still be many people with intense, unsatisfied purposiveness who will blindly pursue wealth – unless they can find some plausible substitute. But the rest of us will no longer be under any obligation to applaud and encourage them. For we shall inquire more curiously than is safe today into the true character of this 'purposiveness' with which in varying degrees Nature has endowed almost all of us. For purposiveness means that we are more concerned with the remote future results of our actions than with their own quality or their immediate effects on our own environment. The 'purposive' man is always trying to secure a spurious and delusive immortality for his acts by pushing his interest in them forward into time. He does not love his cat, but his cat's kittens; nor, in truth, the kittens, but only the kittens' kittens, and so on forward for ever to the end of catdom. For him jam is not jam unless it is a case of jam tomorrow and never jam today. Thus by pushing his jam always forward into the future, he strives to secure for his act of boiling it an immortality.

Let me remind you of the Professor in *Sylvie and Bruno*:

'Only the tailor, sir, with your little bill,' said a meek voice outside the door.

'Ah, well, I can soon settle *his* business,' the Professor said to the children, 'if you'll just wait a minute. How much is it, this year, my man?' The tailor had come in while he was speaking.

'Well, it's been a-doubling so many years, you see,' the tailor replied, a little gruffly, 'and I think I'd like the money now. It's two thousand pound, it is!'

'Oh, that's nothing!' the Professor carelessly remarked, feeling in his pocket, as if he always carried at least *that* amount about with him. 'But wouldn't you like to wait just another year and make it *four* thousand? Just think how rich you'd be! Why, you might be a *king*, if you liked!'

'I don't know as I'd care about being a king,' the man said thoughtfully. 'But it *dew* sound a powerful sight o' money! Well, I think I'll wait –'

'Of course you will!' said the Professor. 'There's good sense in *you*, I see. Good-day to you, my man!'

'Will you ever have to pay him that four thousand pounds?' Sylvie asked as the door closed on the departing creditor.

'*Never*, my child!' the Professor replied emphatically. 'He'll go on doubling it till he dies. You see, it's *always* worth while waiting another year to get twice as much money!'

Perhaps it is not an accident that the race which did most to bring the promise of immortality into the heart and essence of our religions has also done most for the principle of compound interest and particularly loves this most purposive of human institutions.

I see us free, therefore, to return to some of the most sure and certain principles of religion and traditional virtue – that avarice is a vice, that the exaction of usury is a misdemeanour, and the love of money is detestable, that those walk most truly in the paths of virtue and sane wisdom who take least thought for the morrow. We shall once more value ends above means and prefer the good to the useful. We shall honour those who can teach us how to pluck the hour and the day virtuously and well, the delightful people who are capable of taking direct enjoyment in things, the lilies of the field who toil not, neither do they spin.

But beware! The time for all this is not yet. For a least another hundred years we must pretend to ourselves and to everyone that fair is foul and foul is fair; for foul is useful and fair is not. Avarice and usury and precaution must be our gods for a little longer still. For only they can lead us out of the tunnel of economic necessity into daylight.

I look forward, therefore, in days not so very remote, to the greatest change which has ever occurred in the material environment of life for human beings in the aggregate. But, of course, it will all happen gradually, not as a catastrophe. Indeed, it has already begun. The course of affairs will simply be that there will be ever larger and larger classes and groups of people from whom problems of economic necessity have been practically removed. The critical difference will be realized when this condition has become so general that the nature of one's duty to one's neighbour is changed. For it will remain reasonable to be economically purposive for others after it has ceased to be reasonable for oneself.

The *pace* at which we can reach our destination of economic bliss will be governed by four things – our power to control population, our determination to avoid wars and civil dissensions, our willingness to entrust to science the direction of those matters which are properly the concern of science, and the rate of accumulation as fixed by the margin between our production and our consumption; of which the last will easily look after itself, given the first three.

Meanwhile, there will be no harm in making mild preparations for our destiny, in encouraging, and experimenting in, the arts of life as well as the activities of purpose.

But, chiefly, do not let us overestimate the importance of the economic problem, or sacrifice to its supposed necessities other matters of greater and more permanent significance. It should be a matter for specialists – like dentistry. If economists could manage to get themselves thought of as humble, competent people, on a level with dentists, that would be splendid!

19

Leonard Woolf: Fear and Politics

*Leonard Woolf certainly was a socialist, though no Marxist. Fear and
Politics, subtitled 'A Debate at the Zoo', was published as a pamphlet in
the Hogarth Essays series in 1925, and there are various topical allusions
to Prime Minister Stanley Baldwin, Bertrand Russell, the deposed anti-
Bolshevik leaders Kolchak and Denikin, and others. The positions of the
reactionary rhinoceros, the Bolshevik mandrill (a favourite animal name
of Leonard's for Virginia), the fearful owl, and the captivity-loving
elephant are all ironic reflections of Woolf's internationalism. The beast-
fable debate also expresses Woolf's lifelong fascination with animals, and
anticipates, especially in the rhino's emphasis on the political wisdom of
pigs, George Orwell's Animal Farm.*

It is a well established fact that to confine living creatures, to put them
under lock and key or behind iron bars, is one of the most effective
methods of taming and civilizing them. It has been, and is, the universal
practice in civilized countries to imprison the criminal, who will not act,
and the lunatic, who will not think, like his neighbours. Thus is the
criminal tamed, the hooligan civilized, and the lunatic either learns to
think like those outside the asylum – in which case he is discharged with
a certificate of sanity – or he continues, until removed by the great tamer,
death, to think like his immediate neighbours, his fellow lunatics.

Civilization consists in acting and thinking like the ordinary man – the
ordinary man being, in this connection, obviously an ordinary man or
woman of the upper middle classes. The more people there are who act

and think like the ordinary man or woman who is born in Onslow Square or Cadogan Gardens, the more civilization; and if people persist in behaving as if they had been born in the jungle, in utopia, or in the Kingdom of Heaven, they must be shut up under sentence by a judge or magistrate or under a certificate signed by a doctor and a Justice of the Peace. Our judges, magistrates, prison authorities, and Lunacy Commissioners can give innumerable instances in which a few weeks or months confinement have so changed some fellow who had been behaving like a savage that you could not have known that he had not lived all his life in South Kensington.

The object of putting wild animals in cages and of exhibiting them behind iron bars in Zoological Gardens is not primarily to tame and civilize them. The main laudable object of the Zoological Society is to provide a place where civilized children (half price) and civilized adults (one shilling) may spend an afternoon of pleasure combined with instruction and deposit the paper bags in wire receptacles specially constructed for the purpose. But the civilizing power of solitary confinement and imprisonment cannot be confined to the vertebrate bipeds called human beings, and the Zoo has a profound effect upon its permanent inhabitants. Those who have seen the leopard glide swiftly and savagely through the jungle, or an elephant go crashing brutally through the undergrowth, will hardly recognize as the same creatures that great, immobile, meditative cat in the Lion House and that great swaying mass stretching out its trunk through the wooden bars of the Elephant House for a penny bun. Indeed, the observant visitor to the Lion House may notice that it and its inhabitants have acquired something of that sombre melancholy and dingy respectability which is so overpowering in Cromwell Road and Onslow Square, and, without being too fanciful, he may even detect in the eye of the lion staring into space a gleam of the same look which one sometimes sees through a South Kensington window in the eye of an old gentleman pretending to read the Sunday paper behind a white lace curtain.

So civilized have the animals become that, after the Gardens have closed for the night, many of them contrive to meet together in a kind of debating society, the object of which is mutual instruction and improvement. Only those are admitted to membership whose spirits are completely tamed by confinement and civilization: experience has shown the necessity of excluding, for instance, those animals, natives of Asia and Africa, who are not yet able to stand by themselves under the strenuous conditions of the modern world and whose personal habits are offensive, and also the lower classes of even European animals whose smell is naturally unpleasant. It has been regretfully decided also to exclude all the larger carnivora, although, as the aristocratic antelope admitted, they are nearly all 'gentlemen and white men'; but the sombre, meditative melancholy which affects these animals in captivity is liable occasionally to turn into homicidal irascibility, just as in South Kensington occasionally the old gentlemen 'go mad and kill their wives'.

The discussions among the animals admitted to membership almost always come back to one subject, Man. The existence, nature, and mysterious ways of Man have always been, and still are, a source of difficulty and dispute among the animals. At first it was universally believed that men were a kind of spirit, or as we might almost say, gods, who were responsible for all the inexplicable events which happened so regularly in the Zoo. Obviously the keepers were the givers and withholders of food and drink, meted out rewards and punishments, and, by opening and shutting the doors, were the creators of day and night. Then one of the zebras suddenly began to believe that the many men were only an illusion, and that really there was only one omnipotent Man, sitting in a large building invisible in the Zoo and appearing to the animals in the form of keepers and visitors. This belief spread like wildfire, and eventually one of the warthogs announced that he had actually discovered the name of this Man, and that he was called Mitchell; that Mitchell was, however, too sacred a name ever to be uttered, and that in conversation or prayer he had to be addressed as 'Secretary to the Zoological Society'. For a long time after this all the animals believed that there was only one Man, who had created the universe and the Zoo and whose name was 'Secretary to the Zoological Society'.

The snakes are, however, temperamentally agnostic, and one of the Russell's Vipers (*Daboia elegans*) known familiarly as Bertie, some time ago put forward the theory that there was no one omnipotent Man, but only men, and he supported his opinion in such a brilliant speech and with such coldly conclusive logic that he convinced all the more advanced animals who were members of the debating society. This trend of thought was carried a step further by the Orang-outang, a cynical and savage pessimist, who, after hanging upside down on the bars of his cage for the better part of an afternoon and staring fixedly and ferociously at the female visitors, at the next meeting stated his opinion that men and women were animals just like themselves, and that, after careful study, he could see little difference, except in hair and clothes, between a female orang-outang and the women who came into the Apes House, and personally he preferred the female to be both hairy and naked.

The Orang-outang's theory was the cause of violent controversy, the discussion turning almost exclusively upon the resemblance of women to the females of the various species. The monkeys, deer, bears, and pigs were on the side of the Orang-outang, but the male tortoise and male elephant remained for a long time unconvinced, passionately protesting that they could not conceive how a woman, hairy or not hairy, could perform the functions of a female tortoise or a female elephant. The Orang-outang sardonically asked the Elephant whether he could conceive of a female tortoise performing the functions of a female elephant, and would he therefore deny that tortoises were full members, however curiously formed (he intended no offence), of the great animal community and Zoo Society? The Elephant made a dignified and angry reply in which he did not meet the Orang-outang's point. Such nervous exaltation and irritability manifested itself among the members that all the females were asked to withdraw, but even this did not produce calm or relaxation of feeling, and the discussion was adjourned *sine die*.

At the next meeting it was unanimously agreed that the subject of sex should in future be absolutely barred from discussion. There followed many debates upon the Orang-outang's theory. It rapidly gained ground, and one result of the new doctrine was an intensive study of the history, habits, and customs of human beings. The Secretary Bird and the Long-Eared Owl were the first animals who taught themselves to read. Visitors to the Zoo are often careless or absent-minded, and any book or newspaper dropped in one of the houses was eagerly seized upon and added to the public library. The monkeys often succeeded in purloining volumes from the pockets of visitors. Communication was opened with the sparrows who frequent the gardens in great numbers and yet have free access to the outside world, and an agreement was easily reached by which a news service was organized under the direction of the Secretary Bird, the sparrows collecting current information in Fleet Street, in the West End among the clubs, and in Whitehall, and bringing it to the Zoo in return for a fixed share of the animals' food. A precis of the day's news was made under the direction of the Secretary Bird and read out at the beginning of each meeting.

All the animals were greatly interested in the war; it affected their food supply and so brought home to them its immense importance as a struggle between right and wrong, between the ideals of militarist tyranny and democratic freedom. They studied and discussed its deeper cause and effects, and in the process acquired a considerable amount of historical knowledge. Later Bolshevism took the place of the war as a subject of debate, and the General Election of 1924 caused the keenest discussions. I propose to give here a somewhat curtailed account of the debate which was held immediately after the final results of the election became known.

The Rhinoceros, a slow and deliberate speaker, who is almost invariably supported by the Hippopotamus, opened the discussion:

'I rejoice', he said, 'that this Baldwin and his species have won so overwhelming a victory, and I am sure that things will rapidly go back – the only direction in which rapid progress is either safe or desirable – to the state of things which existed before the war and even earlier. Protection, as I have frequently explained, would be meaningless unless it meant, when combined with a tariff and taxes upon imported food, the protection of food, i.e., a cheaper and more abundant food supply. The logical result of the Conservative victory will be a high tariff all round, and I am sure that you will find in the next year that all tariffs in these Gardens, whether of the restaurants or of our Houses, will share in the increase.'

There was a murmur of dissent from the orang-outang and several monkeys, whereupon the Hippopotamus opened his eyes and said in a loud voice, 'Hear, hear!'

'But,' continued the Rhinoceros, who, being extremely short-sighted and even more hard of hearing, was rarely conscious of interruptions or indeed of what was going on about him, 'but I do not wish to discuss the subject of protection, about which we are all agreed. What I wish to talk about is these Russians or Bolsheviks. The appearance of this new species of animal in the world, like the appearance of everything new, is terrifying and spells disaster, and all I can say is that I thoroughly agree with the King, the Baldwins, the Northumberlands, the Banburys, the Poincarés, the ever-to-be-lamented Tsars, and all the other Conservative species of human animal which refuse to have anything to do with, or to recognize the existence of, these appalling creatures . . .'

'I do not wish to appear to boast,' said the Ostrich in a genteel voice, 'but, if you will allow me to say so, does not that show the hereditary wisdom of my race which has taught us that the surest way of conquering fear and destroying evil is to shut our eyes to it?'

The Hippopotamus, who woke up as soon as the Ostrich began to speak, roared her interruption several times into the Rhinoceros's ear and eventually succeeded in making him understand it.

'There is undoubtedly something in what you say,' he allowed. 'To every species of God's creatures' – there was a loud laugh from the monkeys – 'its own peculiar, proper, and hereditary wisdom. It is well-known that my own race is one of the oldest, and has always enjoyed the distinction of being short-sighted and rather deaf. We have learnt by age-long experience – I had an ancestor in the Pliocene Age who was an intimate friend of one of the greatest of the Pteropods – that on the appearance of anything new and terrible, one should stand still for a moment, look fixedly in the direction in which the evil appears to be – or if you are not sure in which direction, then more fixedly in any direction – and finally run away with a blind and magnificent rush. In this manner you may, quite possibly run over and destroy the evil, while, if it does not happen to get in your way, you will at least get out of its way. Simply to shut one's eyes, or, as I understand it, to bury one's head in sand, is no doubt another method of attaining the same end. It is a very ancient method, and therefore has much to recommend it, but it happens not to have been adopted by the race of rhinoceros. However, I have nothing whatever to say against it.

'But let me return to the Bolsheviks. It is clear, I think, from our study of human beings that their species is suffering from a kind of malignant disease of mutability, which for the last century and more the monarchical, aristocratic, and conservative sub-species have unsuccessfully attempted to hold in check. It all began, I understand from our friend the Long-Eared Owl, in 1789. A new and terrible human species, the French revolutionaries, terrorists, or democrats, then suddenly sprang into existence. Human beings do not appear to possess that instinctive and hereditary wisdom that enables other animals to deal effectively, in one way or another, with things new and terrifying. The blind, magnificent rush is not theirs, nor have any of us observed any man or woman effectively bury its head in the sand. When they are afraid, instead of *doing* something, they all start talking at once, and they quarrel and fight among themselves as to the best way of destroying the new phenomenon. That is precisely what happened, I understand, at the time of the French Revolution: instead of destroying the new species, or running away from it, or at least ignoring it, they tried to do all these things at the same time, and in addition, to talk and argue and philosophize over the nature of the new phenomenon.

'The consequence was that this abominable revolution and democracy were never extirpated; the revolutionaries and democrats have continued to propagate their species and to infect every nation of the world. But the root of the evil is this accursed habit of change among human beings. It is about 50 years ago that another new and malignant species of human animal, the German, sprang into existence. Everyone, particularly the people of this country and the French, were immediately, and rightly, terrified of him. But the incredible behaviour of man is shown by the fact that, instead of trampling the Germans out of existence at once, they went on arguing for 44 years about the "German menace", living for the better part of half a century in terror of their lives, spending immense sums of money on guns for shooting Germans, disputing whether one ought to shoot Germans or whether they had enough guns for shooting Germans, but never in all those long years shooting a single German. In fact, when the Chinese species, who do seem to have some hereditary wisdom, being terrified by the sudden appearance of two Germans talk-

ing about Jesus Christ at the other side of Asia, had the sense promptly
to cut their throats, the rest of the world began shooting the Chinese until
they compelled the survivors to give the Germans one of the richest
provinces of China, pay them a large sum of money, and set up the statue
of a German General in one of their chief towns.

'Well, they lived in terror of these accursed Germans for 44 years,
doing nothing at all, beyond shooting a few Chinamen and niggers in
order to keep their courage up. And they would have continued to do
nothing unless a Serbian had shot an Austrian prince – which caused all
the guns to go off everywhere. In the panic which followed they began at
last to shoot Germans, and, in the process, they seemed to learn some of
the hereditary wisdom of my own race, making magnificent blind rushes
up and down the face of the earth for the better part of four years. But
the mutability and changeability of the human animal are most distressing. After shooting Germans happily and contentedly for four years,
they suddenly seem to have grown tired of it and, instead of completing
the job satisfactorily when they had the chance, they allowed a large
number of Germans to survive in Germany, and even to come to this
country. The result is that people, particularly in France, are becoming as
frightened of the Germans whom they have not killed as they were
previously frightened of the Germans whom they have killed.

'To crown all, even before they had stopped killing Germans, there
sprang into existence, in Russia this time, another new species of human
animal, the most terrible and horrible that the world has ever known.
The fundamental evil in the world is change. I cannot understand this
senseless habit of change among man, of continually breeding new species or sub-species. Why, the rhinoceros race has come and gone upon
the face of the earth for hundreds and thousands of years – I had an
ancestor who was famous in the Pliocene Age – and who ever heard of a
rhinoceros changing its hereditary wisdom or breeding a new kind of
rhinoceros? Seven or eight years ago one would have said that in Russia
men were as wise as the Rhinoceros; for hundreds of years they had
altered nothing, the lower classes obeying and working for the upper
classes and worshipping their Little Father, the Tsar. Then unexpectedly
there springs up this obscene species of Bolshevik who want to change
everything, to make the upper classes work for the lower classes, to take
all our possessions away from us, and who have killed the Little Father,
the Tsar.

'Obviously the appearance of this new species in Russia is the greatest
menace which has threatened the world since the glacial period (which
very nearly extinguished the race of rhinoceros, for large numbers of my
ancestors were, at that time, caught in the ice and frozen to death in

Europe). The terror which they inspire in this country is extremely sagacious, for fear is the beginning and the better part of wisdom. But the problem remains: what should the human animals in this country do? They might make a magnificent rush and trample the Russians out of existence, but I admit there are difficulties in the way of doing this, owing to the sea and other things. Personally I should like to see them shoot the Bolsheviks, and all the workers and strikers here who support and copy them. (One of the few useful things which this human animal has invented is the gun, if he would only use it more often against his own sub-species and not so often against other animals.) The difficulty, however, as I understand it, is that the upper classes here are only too ready to shoot the lower classes in Russia who have already shot their own upper classes, while the lower classes here have not yet been sufficiently frightened of the lower classes in Russia to agree to go and shoot them there. Pending the time, then, when the upper classes here shall have instilled into their lower classes that amount of fear of the Bolsheviks which is the beginning of political wisdom, and will induce them to shoot Russians, I do not see that there is a better course to pursue than that adopted by this Baldwin and his Conservative species.

'I hope I may be pardoned a short digression at this point. The sparrows tell us that this Baldwin has a passion for pigs. Now you may have observed that the pig is the only animal native to this country which remotely resembles a rhinoceros. The resemblance is exceedingly remote, but, stretching a point, I would not object if anyone said that the pig does resemble a minute and very inferior rhinoceros, if such a thing could exist. This being the case, it is not improbable that the brain of the English pig, of which we have, unfortunately, no specimen among us, resembles the brain of a minute and very inferior rhinoceros. You will follow my argument when I now suggest that this Baldwin, and through him the Conservatives, have learnt a good deal of their political wisdom from the pigs.

'The policy of Baldwin and his species is a simple one. They are waiting for a time when the newspapers shall have made the lower classes sufficiently afraid and when it will be possible to use them to exterminate the Bolsheviks by shooting. Meanwhile, they keep up their own fear as well as they can; they refuse to have anything to do with the Bolsheviks and, as far as possible, pretend that they do not exist. It is the only thing they can do. For political wisdom may be summed up in the following precepts: "Fear the new and destroy it; if you cannot destroy it, run away; if you cannot run away, shut your eyes and your ears." In other words the highest wisdom consists in a judicious mixture of fear, blindness, and deafness – a mixture which, if I may say so, has distinguished the race of rhinoceros ever since the Pliocene Age.'

The Hippoptamus woke up and roared approval. The Tapir, Camel, Giant Sloth, marmots, and most of the deer applauded. A large number of monkeys leapt to their feet gesticulating and all speaking at the same time. When order was restored, it was agreed that the Mandrill should speak on behalf of the monkeys. He then delivered the following oration, during which he continued, slowly and deliberately, to eat shrimps out of a paper bag:

'I am myself', he said, 'a Bolshevik. It is true that I belong to the intelligentsia among the races and tribes of apes and monkeys, but I have deliberately thrown in my lot with the proletariate. The lower classes eat shrimps, and that is why I eat shrimps out of this paper bag, even while I am speaking in public. If the Rhinoceros would forget his ancestors for a moment and eat shrimps, he would acquire a little more political wisdom.

'The only true thing which the Rhinoceros said was that fear is the beginning and end of political wisdom. But if the upper classes are afraid of the lower classes, the lower classes are even more afraid of the upper classes. The more fear, the more wisdom. That is why true political wisdom is found only among the common monkeys or common people. God is fear – and *vox populi, vox Dei*. If only all the workers of the world would unite – under the leadership of the Mandrill – what terror they would inspire, what terror they would feel! It would be a universal Reign of Terror, a new Holy Roman Empire, a union of the British Empire and League of Nations, a universal socialized Soviet republic – in a word, the millennium.

'For two thousand years or more the human proletariate has lived in terror of the upper classes, and with good reason. Our friend the Long-Eared Owl has taught us all a little history. Freemen and slaves, feudal lords and serfs, aristocrats and peasants, landowners and agricultural labourers, masters and men, employers and employed – it is all the same old story told and retold over again. "The good things of the earth," say the first, "and art and literature and music, by some divine dispensation, are for us, for we are the spirit which makes the wheels of the world go round; and you," they say to the second, "are the cogs and wheels; by some divine dispensation, it is your duty under our direction to go round; in the sweat of your brow shall you eat your bread. Did not Almighty God tell you so? Go round, go round, go round! We may regret that the world has been made in this way; but it is God or Nature or the Logic of Facts; it is not our fault. Go round!"

'And they have been going round for two thousand years and more. Do you think they would have done so except through fear? And they have good cause for fear, for truly your Baldwins and Conservatives, your Kings, Tsars, and capitalists, your aristocrats and landowners and feudal lords know that God is fear and the rich man His prophet. We know what Luther and the upper classes of his time did when the proletariate stopped going round. "Slaughter and stab them," cried Luther, "openly or in secret; kill them as you would a mad dog." And they did; they slaughtered some hundred thousand and only stopped when the survivors began to go round once more. The Russian peasants have just learnt from Kolchak and Denikin that they can expect in the 20th century from the upper classes only what their ancestors got in the 16th.

'And the capitalist? What does the capitalist and behind him the capitalist Government say to the town worker? Work or starve! Work on our terms or starve on your own! There are the machines – our machines and our government and our police and our soldiers and our machine guns. God is fear and we are His prophets. Work – or strike and starve.

'The proletariate learnt its lesson during the war. It learnt that guns can go off in more than one direction. If God is fear, the poor man with a gun in his hand can become a better prophet of God than the rich man without one. That is what has happened in Russia. The cogs and the wheels began to go round, but in the opposite direction; the guns went off, again in the opposite direction. For the first time in history the upper classes became more afraid of the lower classes than the lower of the upper. "Work," said the proletariate to the Tsar and his capitalists, "work – or strike and starve." It is a new and most divine dispensation.

'This Baldwin and his Conservatives and capitalists do well to be afraid. A little wind has begun to blow in Russia which will shake the very bars of our cages before the hurricane is laid. But you cannot trample the wind out of existence, however magnificently blind is your rush, and the storm will not spare your back-side because you have buried the other end of you in the sand. Woe, I say, upon the back-sides of the Baldwins and the capitalists and Conservatives! They are shutting their eyes not to evil, but to a hurricane of good. The day of the Rhinoceros and Hippopotamus and Kings, Tsars, landowners, and capitalists, is over; the day of the common monkey and common people has dawned. It is true that I am not a common monkey; you have only to observe the colouration of my face and back-side to see this. I belong to the intelligentsia. But I have thrown in my lot with the proletariate and I shall rejoice to be their leader now that their day has dawned.

'One word more – on the subject of change. I agree that most things which are new are terrifying. But all change is good. The race of monkeys has always been on the side of change. The Rhinoceros, no doubt, has not changed since he had a distinguished ancestor in the Pliocene Age;

but that is not true of my race. We have always been breeding new races of monkeys. Why, you would hardly be able to tell from his appearance that the little brown monkey who resides in the third cage on the right in the monkey-house – I have a bad memory for names – belongs to the same race as myself. If the Pliocene ancestor of the Rhinoceros had but given a little more attention to the great and beneficent principle of change, the foundation of revolutions, his descendant to-day might have had blue wrinkles on his nose and a sky-blue rump. One of the most reliable of the sparrows told me that both Lenin and Trotsky have that distinguished scheme of colouration.'

When the Mandrill had finished, the monkeys screamed approval, waving their arms and all chattering together (they thought they were singing the 'Red Flag'). Several animals rose to continue the debate, but the Elephant pointed out that the hour was late and called upon the Long-Eared Owl to make the last speech before he himself summed up the discussion. The Owl then spoke as follows:

'It is our custom in these discussions, after hearing the partisan opinion of animals who have taken one side or the other in the controversy under consideration, finally to refer the matter to one of the race of birds whose wings have enabled them to acquire the habit of rising "above the battle" and of obtaining, from a safe distance, an impartial, bird's-eye-view of the situation. I do not pretend myself to understand the extraordinary behaviour of the human race, whether of the Conservatives and capitalists or of the Bolsheviks and proletariate. From the point of view of a bird, Man appears to be a most dangerous animal, so clever that he would have destroyed every living thing on the earth, including himself, if he had not been repeatedly saved by long lucid moments of extreme stupidity. For races and species of animals like ourselves, whose minds and habits have a natural stability, fully to understand this savage and unbalanced creature Man, is, I believe, impossible; but it is occasionally possible to discover some partial explanation of his conduct if you examine his history.

'In political questions, such as the one which we have been discussing, Man appears to be more irrational and unstable than in any others, and to know something of his history is therefore of the greatest importance. By a fortunate accident an absent-minded visitor dropped near my cage the eight volumes of Sorel's *L'Europe et la Révolution Française*, and I have therefore been able to study the history of that revolution which took place in France over 100 years ago, and which throws much light upon the Russian Revolution.

'Now a study of Man's history shows, I think, that our friends the Rhinoceros and the Mandrill, though right in some of their judgements, have made not unnatural errors regarding the irrational conduct of the human race. It is true that the human political organization is founded upon fear, and that when men talk about justice and reason and patriotism, they often really mean panic and terror. For instance, it is only when the majority are sufficiently frightened of a minority that they begin to call the latter criminals and to make laws against them, and then it becomes just to imprison or hang them. You can see this in their treatment of two of their sub-species, the bore and the murderer, both of whom they dislike. But they are frightened of the murderer and not of the bore – consequently they apply justice to the murderer by hanging him, while, as they are not afraid of bores, justice is not applicable to them. Again it has been found absolutely impossible to keep any of their nations patriotic unless it is kept terrified of some other nation, and they have invented a special class of men, called statesmen and diplomatists, who are paid very large salaries in each country and whose duty it is to make the rest of the people afraid of some other nation (or preferably nations) and so keep up their patriotism. In fact one of the gravest charges against the Socialists and Bolsheviks has been that they started a doctrine called internationalism, maintaining that it was unnecessary for any nation or race to be afraid of any other. If this monstrous doctrine were accepted, the whole of the political organization of human beings would collapse and the common people would cease to be patriotic. The Conservatives at the last election saw this danger, and it was only in the nick of time that one of their most intelligent diplomatists invented the "Zinovieff Letter", as it was called, and succeeded in making the common people once more afraid of the Russians, and so patriotic. France is, in fact, the only country in Europe where the political organization is in an absolutely sound state and patriotism permanent and unassailable. The reason is that every Frenchman is innately and permanently terrified of the Germans, and therefore he has in his own heart a perpetual spring of pure and undefiled patriotism. Some foolish people after the war thought that Frenchmen might lose their fear and with it their patriotism, because the Germans had been beaten so soundly that it would be impossible for anyone to be afraid of them. Events proved that dead and unborn Germans can be just as terrifying as live ones. If there has ever been the slightest sign of fear and patriotic fervour flagging in France, it has only been necessary for the statesmen to recall the acts of dead Germans, or to refer to the fact that 50 years hence 500,000 more German babies than French babies will be born every year into the world, and immediately the French people, roused to the highest pitch of terror and enthusiasm, have decided to conscript another 100,000 African negroes into the French Army.

'The Rhinoceros and Mandrill are, therefore, correct in giving to fear a great importance in human politics, but they are both wrong, I think, in the view which they take of what is happening with regard to the Bolsheviks. A study of human history reveals the fact that politically Man is an animal which never learns from experience. He himself is accustomed to say that there is nothing new under the sun, or that *plus ça change plus c'est la même chose*, or that history repeats itself. In this, at any rate, Man shows some understanding of himself. You know that, with his extraordinary love of malignant cruelty, he has invented a small cage with a wheel in it, and that he is accustomed to confine in it one of the most beautiful and cheerful of all animals, the squirrel, and that, apparently, it gives him pleasure to see the squirrel go round and round without making any progress in any direction. The squirrel in the cage is the epitome of Man's history. He is always setting out with drums and trumpets in order to reach the place from which he started, and when he has devastated half the earth in order to get back to his starting point, he complacently remarks that there is no new thing under the sun and that history repeats itself.

'Both the Rhinoceros and Mandrill are wrong in believing that the Russians or Bolsheviks are a new species. They have existed for hundreds of years. They existed in France at the time of the French Revolution, and they performed the same antics there, one hundred and thirty years ago, as they have just been performing in Petrograd and Moscow. The revolutionary wheel goes round, and it makes not a pin's difference whether Mirabeau and Danton and Robespierre are in it or Lenin and Trotsky and some fanatical Russian. And it is precisely the same with the reactionaries and Conservatives: the Tsar and Tsarina, the Allies and Denikin and Kolchak, Mr Baldwin and the Conservatives have copied in every minute particular the antics of Louis XVI and Marie Antoinette, of the Allies of 1791 and the Comte de Provence and the *émigrés*, of Mr Pitt and the Conservatives of 1793.

'In order to prove my point, I should have to read to you the eight volumes of Sorel's *History*. I can now only give you one or two instances which will show you how the human species is revolving in its wheel. The people who made the French Revolution were pacifists and internationalists just like the Russians who made their revolution. In 1789 there was to be universal brotherhood and perpetual peace and "no annexations and no indemnities". At first all the "Liberals" everywhere welcomed the revolution with tears in their eyes, just as they did in 1917. But then fear began. As soon as the revolutionaries in France touched "legal rights" – of the King and the aristocracy and the clergy and, above all, of property – people began to grow afraid – "it may be our turn next," they said. Emigration started at once; there were French Princes, Dukes, Counts, and gentlemen in every country of Europe, already talking of and plotting "intervention". Then it was the turn of the revolutionaries to become afraid; they struck at the *émigrés* and their property or at all who might be suspected of wanting to emigrate. The King and Queen were afraid, and plotted with Austria and Prussia and Russia and the *émigrés*; the revolutionaries were afraid of the King and Queen, of Austria and Prussia and Russia and intervention; they began a "revolutionary propaganda" outside France. Then the English became afraid of the propaganda; they demanded that the French Government should cease its propaganda which was directed against the institutions of other countries. Austria, Prussia, France, and England mobilized their armies or fleets; the *émigrés* mobilized their corps of "volunteers" on the frontiers; and when everyone was sufficiently afraid of everyone else, war. And when the Allies appeared to have been victorious and Fox demanded that peace should be made, "Pitt declared" – I quote M. Sorel – "that England could never negotiate with France as long as she claimed to impose the so-called principles of the Rights of Man, principles of conquest without and disturbance within. Moreover, negotiate with whom? Factions rise and fall one after the other; every post brings the tale of new crimes. If we were to negotiate with Marat, before the end of the negotiations he would have sunk again into the dregs of the people from which he rose and would have left in his place a more atrocious criminal than himself?"

'You will see that poor Mr Baldwin, who believes that he believes in the Rights of Man, is as regards the Rights of the Proletariate precisely at the same point in the wheel where Mr Pitt was revolving in 1793. Now let us turn to Mr MacDonald . . .'

But the Elephant interrupted:

'I do not wish to cut short this discussion, but the hour is late, the night is short, and history and M. Sorel appear to be long. I propose to wind up and sum up this debate. I am too old to be anything but impartial, so that I think you will find me upon the side neither of the Rhinoceros and Mr Baldwin nor of the Mandrill and the Bolsheviks.

'One indisputable and important fact has been established by our discussion. Human beings live in mortal fear the one of the other. Everyone is terrified that his neighbour will cut his throat or shoot him in the back or blow him up with high explosive shells or drop a bomb on his head or destroy his lungs with poison gas or steal his wife or conquer a bit of his native land or a bit of land that he has conquered, or filch his watch or his money, or get better pay than he does, or climb over his head in society.

'It has been pointed out to-night that among human beings justice and patriotism and wisdom and truth are only other names for fear. I agree, but I do not agree that fear is the beginning and end of political wisdom. I want to recall certain facts which some of us naturally have forgotten or have ignored.

'Some of us in these gardens have never been free. Two thousand years ago one of these human animals, I understand, wrote a poem which says: "Of all things not to be born into the world is best, nor to see the beams of the keen sun; but being born, as swiftly as may be to pass the gates of Death, and lie under a great load of earth." And I say to you: "Of all things never to have known freedom is best; but being born free, as swiftly as may be to pass the gates of a Zoological Gardens, and to live behind strong bars and mighty locks."

'Those happy animals among us who have never known what it was to be free, whose tickets upon their cages bear the fortunate inscription BORN IN CAPTIVITY, may not understand what I am going to say. I was born in the jungle. Do you remember the jungle?'

The Elephant trumpeted the words so that they boomed out over the cages and the Mappin Terraces, and a curious hush fell upon the animals. The Elephant trumpeted again: 'Do you remember the jungle?' and every animal felt the note of fear in the sound.

'Some of you, I see,' he went on, 'remember the jungle, but for those of us who do not understand, I will explain. We were free in the jungle, and very pleasant it was on a fresh cool morning to shoulder your way through the undergrowth, the heavy dew dripping from the leaves, and to bring down the saplings with a crash and to feed on the young leaves. I remember the great herds of deer running free on the great plains; I remember how the monkeys laughed and chattered in the flowers, and how the peacocks on the tree-tops screamed their greetings to the rising sun.

'Yes, it was sometimes very pleasant to be free in the jungle. But only for a moment, because the jungle was a place of perpetual fear. We were all, like these human animals, perpetually afraid of one another. It was a continual struggle, a continual killing of one by the other. The deer were perpetually fleeing from the leopard and the tiger, and the leopard and the tiger from their own shadows. Fear ruled us and the beginning and the end of jungle wisdom was fear. We Elephants are old and wise and peaceful, but I can remember how some faint whisper or a little creaking or a faint scent coming from the shadows of the trees would strike a sudden fear into me and I would charge, panic stricken, away through the undergrowth in what, I have no doubt, the Rhinoceros would describe as a magnificent blind rush. It may have been wisdom, but it was not pleasure.

'It is clear from our discussion to-night that men are still living in the jungle. They should learn a lesson from us. Here we are in captivity, peaceful, happy, unafraid, civilized. Here each of us, locked up securely in his or her separate cage, neither harms nor is harmed by, neither fears nor is feared by, any other animal. Is it not clear that Man will never be happy and civilized and unafraid until he has done for himself precisely what he has done for us? These human beings delude themselves that a League of Nations or Protection or armies and navies are going to give them security and civilization in their jungle. But they are the savagest race of carnivora known in the jungle, and they will never be happy and civilized, and the world will never be safe for democracy or for any other animal, until each human animal is confined in a separate cage.'

The Elephant then declared the meeting closed amid applause.

20

Virginia Woolf:
Memories of a Working Women's Guild

'Memories of a Working Women's Guild' was first published as an article and then revised as a preface entitled 'Introductory Letter to Margaret Llewelyn Davies' for Life as We Have Known It *by Co-operative Working Women, which Davies edited and the Hogarth Press published in 1931. Except for its title, Virginia Woolf's text used here is the revised one. The feminist Women's Co-operative Guild was founded in 1883 as part of the consumers' co-operative movement with the additional aim of forwarding the interests of working women; it had some 67,000 members by 1930, according to a note on the guild by Davies. The remarkable evocation of working women's lives by an upper-middle-class writer acutely and regretfully aware of the present impassable barrier between their experience and hers reveals the inanity of calling Virginia Woolf's work snobbish.*

When you asked me to write a preface to a book which you had collected of papers by working women I replied that I would be drowned rather than write a preface to any book whatsoever. Books should stand on their own feet, my argument was (and I think it is a sound one). If they need shoring up by a preface here, an introduction there, they have no more right to exist than a table that needs a wad of paper under one leg in order to stand steady. But you left me the papers, and, turning them over, I saw that on this occasion the argument did not apply; this book is not a book. Turning the pages, I began to ask myself what is this book then, if it is not a book? What quality has it? What ideas does it suggest?

What old arguments and memories does it rouse in me? And as all this had nothing to do with an introduction or a preface, but brought you to mind and certain pictures from the past, I stretched my hand for a sheet of notepaper and wrote the following letter addressed not to the public but to you.

You have forgotten (I wrote) a hot June morning in Newcastle in the year 1913, or at least you will not remember what I remember, because you were otherwise engaged. Your attention was entirely absorbed by a green table, several sheets of paper, and a bell. Moreover you were frequently interrupted. There was a woman wearing something like a Lord Mayor's chain round her shoulders; she took her seat perhaps at your right; there were other women without ornament save fountain pens and despatch boxes – they sat perhaps at your left. Soon a row had been formed up there on the platform, with tables and inkstands and tumblers of water; while we, many hundreds of us, scraped and shuffled and filled the entire body of some vast municipal building beneath. The proceedings somehow opened. Perhaps an organ played. Perhaps songs were sung. Then the talking and the laughing suddenly subsided. A bell struck; a figure rose; a woman took her way from among us; she mounted a platform; she spoke for precisely five minutes; she descended. Directly she sat down another woman rose; mounted the platform; spoke for precisely five minutes and descended; then a third rose, then a fourth – and so it went on, speaker following speaker, one from the right, one from the left, one from the middle, one from the background – each took her way to the stand, said what she had to say, and gave place to her successor. There was something military in the regularity of the proceeding. They were like marksmen, I thought, standing up in turn with rifle raised to aim at a target. Sometimes they missed, and there was a roar of laughter; sometimes they hit, and there was a roar of applause. But whether the particular shot hit or missed there was no doubt about the carefulness of the aim. There was no beating the bush; there were no phrases of easy eloquence. The speaker made her way to the stand primed with her subject. Determination and resolution were stamped on her face. There was so much to be said between the strokes of the bell that she could not waste one second. The moment had come for which she had been waiting, perhaps for many months. The moment had come for which she had stored hat, shoes and dress – there was an air of discreet novelty about her clothing. But above all the moment had come when she was going to speak her mind, the mind of her constituency, the mind of the women who had sent her from Devonshire, perhaps, or Sussex, or some black mining village in Yorkshire to speak their mind for them in Newcastle.

It soon became obvious that the mind which lay spread over so wide a stretch of England was a vigorous mind working with great activity. It was thinking in June 1913 of the reform of the Divorce Laws; of the taxation of land values; of the Minimum Wage. It was concerned with the care of maternity; with the Trades Board Act; with the education of children over fourteen; it was unanimously of opinion that Adult Suffrage should become a Government measure – it was thinking in short about every sort of public question, and it was thinking constructively and pugnaciously. Accrington did not see eye to eye with Halifax, nor Middlesbrough with Plymouth. There was argument and opposition; resolutions were lost and amendments won. Hands shot up stiff as swords, or were pressed as stiffly to the side. Speaker followed speaker; the morning was cut up into precise lengths of five minutes by the bell.

Meanwhile – let me try after seventeen years to sum up the thoughts that passed through the minds of your guests, who had come from London and elsewhere, not to take part, but to listen – meanwhile what was it all about? What was the meaning of it? These women were demanding divorce, education, the vote – all good things. They were demanding higher wages and shorter hours – what could be more reasonable? And yet, though it was all so reasonable, much of it so forcible, some of it so humorous, a weight of discomfort was settling and shifting itself uneasily from side to side in your visitors' minds. All these questions – perhaps this was at the bottom of it – which matter so intensely to the people here, questions of sanitation and education and wages, this demand for an extra shilling, for another year at school, for eight hours instead of nine behind a counter or in a mill, leave me, in my own blood and bones, untouched. If every reform they demand was granted this very instant it would not touch one hair of my comfortable capitalistic head. Hence my interest is merely altruistic. It is thin spread and moon coloured. There is no life blood or urgency about it. However hard I clap my hands or stamp my feet there is a hollowness in the sound which betrays me. I am a benevolent spectator. I am irretrievably cut off from the actors. I sit here hypocritically clapping and stamping, an outcast from the flock. On top of this too, my reason (it was in 1913, remember) could not help assuring me that even if the resolution, whatever it was, were carried unanimously the stamping and the clapping was an empty noise. It would pass out of the open window and become part of the clamour of the lorries and the striving of the hooves on the cobbles of Newcastle beneath – an inarticulate uproar. The mind might be active; the mind might be aggressive; but the mind was without a body; it had no legs or arms with which to enforce its will. In all that audience, among all those women who worked, who bore children, who scrubbed and cooked and bargained, there was not a single woman with a vote. Let them fire off their rifles if they liked, but they would hit no target; there were only blank cartridges inside. The thought was irritating and depressing in the extreme.

The clock had now struck half-past eleven. Thus there were still then many hours to come. And if one had reached this stage of irritation and depression by half-past eleven in the morning, into what depths of boredom and despair would one not be plunged by half-past five in the evening? How could one sit out another day of speechifying? How could one, above all, face you, our hostess, with the information that your Congress had proved so insupportably exacerbating that one was going back to London by the very first train? The only chance lay in some happy conjuring trick, some change of attitude by which the mist and blankness of the speeches could be turned to blood and bone. Otherwise they remained intolerable. But suppose one played a childish game; suppose one said, as a child says, 'Let's pretend.' 'Let's pretend,' one said to oneself, looking at the speaker, 'that I am Mrs Giles of Durham City.' A woman of that name had just turned to address us. 'I am the wife of a miner. He comes back thick with grime. First he must have his bath. Then he must have his supper. But there is only a copper. My range is crowded with saucepans. There is no getting on with the work. All my crocks are covered with dust again. Why in the Lord's name have I not hot water and electric light laid on when middle-class women . . .' So up I jump and demand passionately 'labour saving appliances and housing reform'. Up I jump in the person of Mrs Giles of Durham; in the person of Mrs Phillips of Bacup; in the person of Mrs Edwards of Wolverton. But after all the imagination is largely the child of the flesh. One could not be Mrs Giles of Durham because one's body had never stood at the wash-tub; one's hands had never wrung and scrubbed and chopped up whatever the meat may be that makes a miner's supper. The picture therefore was always letting in irrelevancies. One sat in an armchair or read a book. One saw landscapes and seascapes, perhaps Greece or Italy, where Mrs Giles or Mrs Edwards must have seen slag heaps and rows upon rows of slate-roofed houses. Something was always creeping in from a world that was not their world and making the picture false and the game too much of a game to be worth playing.

It was true that one could always correct these fancy portraits by taking a look at the actual person – at Mrs Thomas, or Mrs Langrish, or Miss Bolt of Hebden Bridge. They were worth looking at. Certainly, there were no armchairs, or electric light, or hot water laid on in their lives; no Greek hills or Mediterranean bays in their dreams. Bakers and butchers did not call for orders. They did not sign a cheque to pay the weekly bills, or order, over the telephone, a cheap but quite adequate seat at the Opera. If they travelled it was on excursion day, with food in string bags and babies in their arms. They did not stroll through the house and say, that cover must go to the wash, or those sheets need changing. They plunged their arms in hot water and scrubbed the clothes themselves. In consequence their bodies were thick-set and muscular, their hands were large, and they had the slow emphatic gestures of people who are often stiff and fall tired in a heap on hard-backed chairs. They touched nothing lightly. They gripped papers and pencils as if they were brooms. Their faces were firm and heavily folded and lined with deep lines. It seemed as if their muscles were always taut and on the stretch. Their eyes looked as if they were always set on something actual – on saucepans that were boiling over, on children who were getting into mischief. Their lips never expressed the lighter and more detached emotions that come into play when the mind is perfectly at ease about the present. No, they were not in the least detached and easy and cosmopolitan. They were indigenous and rooted to one spot. Their very names were like the stones of the fields – common, grey, worn, obscure, docked of all splendours of association and romance. Of course they wanted baths and ovens and education and seventeen shillings instead of sixteen, and freedom and air and . . . 'And,' said Mrs Winthrop of Spennymoor, breaking into these thoughts with words that sounded like a refrain, 'we can wait.' . . . 'Yes,' she repeated, as if she had waited so long that the last lap of that immense vigil meant nothing for the end was in sight, 'we can wait.' And she got down rather stiffly from her perch and made her way back to her seat, an elderly woman dressed in her best clothes.

Then Mrs Potter spoke. Then Mrs Elphick. Then Mrs Holmes of Edgbaston. So it went on, and at last after innumerable speeches, after many communal meals at long tables and many arguments – the world was to be reformed, from top to bottom, in a variety of ways – after seeing Co-operative jams bottled and Co-operative biscuits made, after some song singing and ceremonies with banners, the new President received the chain of office with a kiss from the old President; the Congress dispersed; and the separate members who had stood up so valiantly and spoken out so boldly while the clock ticked its five minutes went back to Yorkshire and Wales and Sussex and Devonshire, and hung their clothes in the wardrobe and plunged their hands in the wash-tub again.

Later that summer the thoughts here so inadequately described, were again discussed, but not in a public hall hung with banners and loud with voices. The head office of the Guild, the centre from which speakers, papers, inkstands and tumblers, as I suppose, issued, was then

in Hampstead. There, if I may remind you again of what you may well
have forgotten, you invited us to come; you asked us to tell you how the
Congress had impressed us. But I must pause on the threshold of that
very dignified old house, with its eighteenth-century carvings and panelling, as we paused then in truth, for one could not enter and go upstairs
without encountering Miss Kidd. Miss Kidd sat at her typewriter in the
outer office. Miss Kidd, one felt, had set herself as a kind of watch-dog
to ward off the meddlesome middle-class wasters of time who come
prying into other people's business. Whether it was for this reason that
she was dressed in a peculiar shade of deep purple I do not know. The
colour seemed somehow symbolical. She was very short, but, owing to
the weight which sat on her brow and the gloom which seemed to issue
from her dress, she was also very heavy. An extra share of the world's
grievances seemed to press upon her shoulders. When she clicked her
typewriter one felt that she was making that instrument transmit messages of foreboding and ill-omen to an unheeding universe. But she
relented, and like all relentings after gloom hers came with a sudden
charm. Then we went upstairs, and upstairs we came upon a very
different figure – upon Miss Lilian Harris, indeed, who, whether it was
due to her dress which was coffee coloured, or to her smile which was
serene, or to the ash-tray in which many cigarettes had come amiably to
an end, seemed the image of detachment and equanimity. Had one not
known that Miss Harris was to the Congress what the heart is to the
remoter veins – that the great engine at Newcastle would not have
thumped and throbbed without her – that she had collected and sorted
and summoned and arranged that very intricate but orderly assembly of
women – she would never have enlightened one. She had nothing whatever to do; she licked a few stamps and addressed a few envelopes – it
was a fad of hers – that was what her manner conveyed. It was Miss
Harris who moved the papers off the chairs and got the tea-cups out of
the cupboard. It was she who answered questions about figures and put
her hand on the right file of letters infallibly and sat listening, without
saying very much, but with calm comprehension, to whatever was said.

Again let me telescope into a few sentences, and into one scene many
random discussions on various occasions at various places. We said
then – for you now emerged from an inner room, and if Miss Kidd was
purple and Miss Harris was coffee coloured, you, speaking pictorially
(and I dare not speak more explicitly) were kingfisher blue and as arrowy
and decisive as that quick bird – we said then that the Congress had
roused thoughts and ideas of the most diverse nature. It had been a
revelation and a disillusionment. We had been humiliated and enraged.
To begin with, all their talk, we said, or the greater part of it, was of

matters of fact. They want baths and money. To expect us, whose minds, such as they are, fly free at the end of a short length of capital to tie ourselves down again to that narrow plot of acquisitiveness and desire is impossible. We have baths and we have money. Therefore, however much we had sympathized our sympathy was largely fictitious. It was aesthetic sympathy, the sympathy of the eye and of the imagination, not of the heart and of the nerves; and such sympathy is always physically uncomfortable. Let us explain what we mean, we said. The Guild's women are magnificent to look at. Ladies in evening dress are lovelier far, but they lack the sculpturesque quality that these working women have. And though the range of expression is narrower in working women, their few expressions have a force and an emphasis, of tragedy or humour, which the faces of ladies lack. But, at the same time, it is much better to be a lady; ladies desire Mozart and Einstein – that is, they desire things that are ends, not things that are means. Therefore to deride ladies and to imitate, as some of the speakers did, their mincing speech and little knowledge of what it pleases them to call 'reality' is, so it seems to us, not merely foolish but gives away the whole purpose of the Congress, for if it is better to be working women by all means let them remain so and not undergo the contamination which wealth and comfort bring. In spite of this, we went on, apart from prejudice and bandying compliments, undoubtedly the women at the Congress possess something which ladies lack, and something which is desirable, which is stimulating, and yet very difficult to define. One does not want to slip easily into fine phrases about 'contact with life', about 'facing facts' and 'the teaching of experience', for they invariably alienate the hearer, and moreover no working man or woman works harder or is in closer touch with reality than a painter with his brush or a writer with his pen. But the quality that they have, judging from a phrase caught here and there, from a laugh, or a gesture seen in passing, is precisely the quality that Shakespeare would have enjoyed. One can fancy him slipping away from the brilliant salons of educated people to crack a joke in Mrs Robson's back kitchen. Indeed, we said, one of our most curious impressions at your Congress was that the 'poor', 'the working classes', or by whatever name you choose to call them, are not downtrodden, envious and exhausted; they are humorous and vigorous and thoroughly independent. Thus if it were possible to meet them not as masters or mistresses or customers with a counter between us, but over the wash-tub or in the parlour casually and con- genially as fellow-beings with the same wishes and ends in view, a great liberation would follow, and perhaps friendship and sympathy would supervene. How many words must lurk in those women's vocabularies that have faded from ours! How many scenes must lie dormant in their

eye which are unseen by ours! What images and saws and proverbial
sayings must still be current with them that have never reached the
surface of print, and very likely they still keep the power which we
have lost of making new ones. There were many shrewd sayings in the
speeches at Congress which even the weight of a public meeting could not
flatten out entirely. But, we said, and here perhaps fiddled with a paper
knife, or poked the fire impatiently by way of expressing our discontent,
what is the use of it all? Our sympathy is fictitious, not real. Because the
baker calls and we pay our bills with cheques, and our clothes are washed
for us and we do not know the liver from the lights we are condemned
to remain forever shut up in the confines of the middle classes, wearing
tail coats and silk stockings, and called Sir or Madam as the case may be,
when we are all, in truth, simply Johns and Susans. And they remain
equally deprived. For we have as much to give them as they to give us –
wit and detachment, learning and poetry, and all those good gifts which
those who have never answered bells or minded machines enjoy by right.
But the barrier is impassable. And nothing perhaps exacerbated us more
at the Congress (you must have noticed at times a certain irritability)
than the thought that this force of theirs, this smouldering heat which
broke the crust now and then and licked the surface with a hot and
fearless flame, is about to break through and melt us together so that life
will be richer and books more complex and society will pool its possessions instead of segregating them – all this is going to happen inevitably,
thanks to you, very largely, and to Miss Harris and to Miss Kidd – but
only when we are dead.

It was thus that we tried in the Guild Office that afternoon to explain
the nature of fictitious sympathy and how it differs from real sympathy
and how defective it is because it is not based upon sharing the same
important emotions unconsciously. It was thus that we tried to describe
the contradictory and complex feelings which beset the middle-class
visitor when forced to sit out a Congress of working women in silence.

Perhaps it was at this point that you unlocked a drawer and took out
a packet of papers. You did not at once untie the string that fastened
them. Sometimes, you said, you got a letter which you could not bring
yourself to burn; once or twice a Guildswoman had at your suggestion written a few pages about her life. It might be that we should find
these papers interesting; that if we read them the women would cease to
be symbols and would become instead individuals. But they were very
fragmentary and ungrammatical; they had been jotted down in the
intervals of housework. Indeed you could not at once bring yourself to
give them up, as if to expose them to other eyes were a breach of
confidence. It might be that their crudity would only perplex, that the

writing of people who do not know how to write – but at this point we burst in. In the first place, every Englishwoman knows how to write; in the second, even if she does not she has only to take her own life for subject and write the truth about that and not fiction or poetry for our interest to be so keenly roused that – that in short we cannot wait but must read the packet at once.

Thus pressed you did by degrees and with many delays – there was the war for example, and Miss Kidd died, and you and Lilian Harris retired from the Guild, and a testimonial was given you in a casket, and many thousands of working women tried to say how you had changed their lives – tried to say what they will feel for you to their dying day – after all these interruptions you did at last gather the papers together and finally put them in my hands early this May. There they were, typed and docketed with a few snapshots and rather faded photographs stuck between the pages. And when at last I began to read, there started up in my mind's eye the figures that I had seen all those years ago at Newcastle with such bewilderment and curiosity. But they were no longer address-ing a large meeting in Newcastle from a platform, dressed in their best clothes. The hot June day with its banners and its ceremonies had vanished, and instead one looked back into the past of the women who had stood there; into the four-roomed houses of miners, into the homes of small shopkeepers and agricultural labourers, into the fields and factories of fifty or sixty years ago. Mrs Burrows, for example, had worked in the Lincolnshire fens when she was eight with forty or fifty other children, and an old man had followed the gang with a long whip in his hand 'which he did not forget to use'. That was a strange reflection. Most of the women had started work at seven or eight, earning a penny on Saturday for washing a doorstep, or twopence a week for carrying suppers to the men at the iron foundry. They had gone into factories when they were fourteen. They had worked from seven in the morning till eight or nine at night and had made thirteen or fifteen shillings a week. Out of this money they had saved some pence with which to buy their mother gin – she was often very tired in the evening and had borne perhaps thirteen children in as many years; or they fetched opium to assuage some miserable old woman's ague in the fens. Old Betty Rollett killed herself when she could get no more. They had seen half-starved women standing in rows to be paid for their match-boxes while they snuffed the roast meat of their employer's dinner cooking within. The smallpox had raged in Bethnal Green and they had known that the boxes went on being made in the sick-room and were sold to the public with the infection still thick on them. They had been so cold working in the wintry fields that they could not run when the ganger gave them leave. They had waded through floods when the Wash overflowed its banks. Kind old ladies had given them parcels of food which had turned out to contain only crusts of bread and rancid bacon rind. All this they had done and seen and known when other children were still dabbling in seaside pools and spelling out fairy tales by the nursery fire. Naturally their faces had a different look on them. But they were, one remembered, firm faces, faces with something indomitable in their expression. Astonishing though it seems, human nature is so tough that it will take such wounds, even at the tenderest age, and survive them. Keep a child mewed in Bethnal Green and she will somehow snuff the country air from seeing the yellow dust on her brother's boots, and nothing will serve her but she must go there and see the 'clean ground', as she calls it, for herself. It was true that at first the 'bees were very frightening', but all the same she got to the country and the blue smoke and the cows came up to her expectation. Put girls, after a childhood of minding smaller brothers and washing doorsteps, into a factory when they are fourteen and their eyes will turn to the window and they will be happy because, as the work-room is six storeys high, the sun can be seen breaking over the hills, 'and that was always such a comfort and help.' Still stranger, if one needs additional proof of the strength of the human instinct to escape from bondage and attach itself whether to a country road or to a sunrise over the hills, is the fact that the highest ideals of duty flourish in an obscure hat factory as surely as on a battlefield. There were women in Christies' felt hat factory, for example, who worked for 'honour'. They gave their lives to the cause of putting straight stitches into the bindings of men's hat brims. Felt is hard and thick; it is difficult to push the needle through; there are no rewards or glory to be won; but such is the incorrigible idealism of the human mind that there were 'trimmers' in those obscure places who would never put a crooked stitch in their work and ruthlessly tore out the crooked stitches of others. And as they drove in their straight stitches they reverenced Queen Victoria and thanked God, drawing up to the fire, that they were all married to good Conservative working men.

Certainly that story explained something of the force, of the obstinacy, which one had seen in the faces of the speakers at Newcastle. And then, if one went on reading these papers, one came upon other signs of the extraordinary vitality of the human spirit. That inborn energy which no amount of childbirth and washing up can quench had reached out, it seemed, and seized upon old copies of magazines; had attached itself to Dickens; had propped the poems of Burns against a dish cover to read while cooking. They read at meals; they read before going to the mill. They read Dickens and Scott and Henry George and Bulwer Lytton and Ella Wheeler Wilcox and Alice Meynell and would like 'to get hold of any good history of the French Revolution, not Carlyle's, please', and B. Russell on China, and William Morris and Shelley and Florence Barclay and Samuel Butler's Note Books – they read with the indiscriminate greed of a hungry appetite, that crams itself with toffee and beef and tarts and vinegar and champagne all in one gulp. Naturally such reading led to argument. The younger generation had the audacity to say that Queen Victoria was no better than an honest charwoman who had brought up her children respectably. They had the temerity to doubt whether to sew straight stitches into men's hat brims should be the sole aim and end of a woman's life. They started arguments and even held rudimentary debating societies on the floor of the factory. In time the old trimmers even were shaken in their beliefs and came to think that there might be other ideals in the world besides straight stitches and Queen Victoria. Strange ideas indeed were seething in their brain. A girl, for instance, would reason, as she walked along the streets of a factory town, that she had no right to bring a child into the world if that child must earn its living in a mill. A chance saying in a book would fire her imagination to dream of future cities where there were to be baths and kitchens and washhouses and art galleries and museums and parks. The minds of working women were humming and their imaginations were awake. But how were they to realize their ideals? How were they to express their needs? It was hard enough for middle-class women with some amount of money and some degree of education behind them. But how could women whose hands were full of work, whose kitchens were thick with steam, who had neither education nor encouragement nor leisure remodel the world according to the ideas of working women? It was then, I suppose, sometime in the eighties, that the Women's Guild crept modestly and tentatively into existence. For a time it occupied an inch or two of space in the *Co-operative News* which called itself The Women's Corner. It was there that Mrs Acland asked, 'Why should we not hold our Co-operative mothers' meetings, when we may bring our work and sit together, one of us reading some Co-operative work aloud, which may afterwards be discussed?' And on April 18th, 1883, she announced that the Women's Guild now numbered seven members. It was the Guild then that drew to itself all that restless wishing and dreaming. It was the Guild that made a central meeting place where formed and solidified all that was else so scattered and incoherent. The Guild must have given the older women, with their husbands and children, what 'clean ground' had given to the little girl in Bethnal Green, or the view of day breaking over the hills had given the girls in the hat factory. It gave them in the first place the rarest of all possessions – a room where they could sit down and think remote from boiling saucepans and crying children; and then that room became not merely a sitting-room and a meeting place, but a workshop where, laying their heads together, they could remodel their houses, could remodel their lives, could beat out this reform and that. And, as the membership grew, and twenty or thirty women made a practice of meeting weekly, so their ideas increased, and their interests widened. Instead of discussing merely their own taps and their own sinks and their own long hours and little pay, they began to discuss education and taxation and the conditions of work in the country at large. The women who had crept modestly in 1883 into Mrs Acland's sitting-room to sew and 'read some Co-operative work aloud', learnt to speak out, boldly and authoritatively, about every question of civic life. Thus it came about that Mrs Robson and Mrs Potter and Mrs Wright at Newcastle in 1913 were asking not only for baths and wages and electric light, but also for adult suffrage and the taxation of land values and divorce law reform. Thus in a year or two they were to demand peace and disarmament and the spread of Co-operative principles, not only among the working people of Great Britain, but among the nations of the world. And the force that lay behind their speeches and drove them home beyond the reach of eloquence was compact of many things – of men with whips, of sick rooms where match-boxes were made, of hunger and cold, of many and difficult childbirths, of much scrubbing and washing up, of reading Shelley and William Morris and Samuel Butler over the kitchen table, of weekly meetings of the Women's Guild, of Committees and Congresses at Manchester and elsewhere. All this lay behind the speeches of Mrs Robson and Mrs Potter and Mrs Wright. The papers which you sent me certainly threw some light upon the old curiosities and bewilderments which had made that Congress so memorable, and so thick with unanswered questions.

But that the pages here printed should mean all this to those who cannot supplement the written word with the memory of faces and the sound of voices is perhaps unlikely. It cannot be denied that the chapters here put together do not make a book – that as literature they have many limitations. The writing, a literary critic might say, lacks detachment and imaginative breadth, even as the women themselves lacked variety and play of feature. Here are no reflections, he might object, no view of life as a whole, and no attempt to enter into the lives of other people. Poetry and fiction seem far beyond their horizon. Indeed, we are reminded of those obscure writers before the birth of Shakespeare who never travelled beyond the borders of their own parishes, who read no language but their own, and wrote with difficulty, finding few words and those awkwardly. And yet since writing is a complex art, much infected by life, these pages have some qualities even as literature that the literate and instructed might envy. Listen, for instance, to Mrs Scott, the felt hat worker: 'I have been over the hill-tops when the snow drifts were over three feet high, and six feet in some places. I was in a blizzard in Hayfield and thought I should never get round the corners. But it was life on the moors; I seemed to know every blade of grass and where the flowers grew and all the little streams were my companions.' Could she have said that better if Oxford had made her a Doctor of Letters? Or take Mrs Layton's description of a match-box factory in Bethnal Green and how she looked through the fence and saw three ladies 'sitting in the shade doing some kind of fancy work'. It has something of the accuracy and clarity of a description by Defoe. And when Mrs Burrows brings to mind that bitter day when the children were about to eat their cold dinner and drink their cold tea under the hedge and the ugly woman asked them into her parlour saying, 'Bring these children into my house and let them eat their dinner there,' the words are simple, but it is difficult to see how they could say more. And then there is a fragment of a letter from Miss Kidd – the sombre purple figure who typed as if the weight of the world were on her shoulders. 'When I was a girl of seventeen,' she writes, 'my then employer, a gentleman of good position and high standing in the town, sent me to his home one night, ostensibly to take a parcel of books, but really with a very different object. When I arrived at the house all the family were away, and before he would allow me to leave he forced me to yield to him. At eighteen I was a mother.' Whether that is literature or not literature I do not presume to say, but that it explains much and reveals much is certain. Such then was the burden that rested on that sombre figure as she sat typing your letters, such were the memories she brooded as she guarded your door with her grim and indomitable fidelity.

But I will quote no more. These pages are only fragments. These voices are beginning only now to emerge from silence into half articulate speech. These lives are still half hidden in profound obscurity. To express even what is expressed here has been a work of labour and difficulty. The writing has been done in kitchens, at odds and ends of leisure, in the midst of distractions and obstacles – but really there is no need for me, in a letter addressed to you, to lay stress upon the hardship of working women's lives. Have not you and Lilian Harris given your best years – but hush! you will not let me finish that sentence and therefore, with the old messages of friendship and admiration, I will make an end.

21

E. M. Forster: What I Believe

E. M. Forster's famous – some would say notorious – essay on his beliefs is also a declaration of Bloomsbury values. The emphasis is on personal relations; only 'love the beloved Republic', in Swinburne's words, gets three cheers. Originally entitled 'Two Cheers for Democracy' and reprinted as 'Credo', the essay then was published in slightly revised form as a pamphlet for the Hogarth Press in 1939 under the title What I Believe. *Forster later included it in the collection of essays to which he gave the title* Two Cheers for Democracy *in 1951. As Forster's remarks about betraying his country rather than betraying his friend continue to be widely quoted out of their context, it is worth rereading them in context here. It should also be noted that Forster's credo was written on the verge of the Second World War.*

I do not believe in Belief. But this is an Age of Faith, and there are so many militant creeds that, in self-defence, one has to formulate a creed of one's own. Tolerance, good temper and sympathy are no longer enough in a world which is rent by religious and racial persecution, in a world where ignorance rules, and Science, who ought to have ruled, plays the subservient pimp. Tolerance, good temper and sympathy – they are what matter really, and if the human race is not to collapse they must come to the front before long. But for the moment they are not enough, their action is no stronger than a flower, battered beneath a military jackboot. They want stiffening, even if the process coarsens them. Faith, to my mind, is a stiffening process, a sort of mental starch, which ought to be applied as sparingly as possible. I dislike the stuff. I do not believe in it, for its own sake, at all. Herein I probably differ from most people, who believe in Belief, and are only sorry they cannot swallow even more than they do. My law-givers are Erasmus and Montaigne, not Moses and St Paul. My temple stands not upon Mount Moriah but in that Elysian Field where even the immoral are admitted. My motto is: 'Lord, I disbelieve – help thou my unbelief.'

I have, however, to live in an Age of Faith – the sort of epoch I used to hear praised when I was a boy. It is extremely unpleasant really. It is bloody in every sense of the word. And I have to keep my end up in it. Where do I start?

With personal relationships. Here is something comparatively solid in a world full of violence and cruelty. Not absolutely solid, for Psychology has split and shattered the idea of a 'Person', and has shown that there is something incalculable in each of us, which may at any moment rise to the surface and destroy our normal balance. We don't know what we are like. We can't know what other people are like. How, then, can we put any trust in personal relationships, or cling to them in the gathering political storm? In theory we cannot. But in practice we can and do. Though A is not unchangeably A, or B unchangeably B, there can still be love and loyalty between the two. For the purpose of living one has to assume that the personality is solid, and the 'self' is an entity, and to ignore all contrary evidence. And since to ignore evidence is one of the characteristics of faith, I certainly can proclaim that I believe in personal relationships.

Starting from them, I get a little order into the contemporary chaos. One must be fond of people and trust them if one is not to make a mess of life, and it is therefore essential that they should not let one down. They often do. The moral of which is that I must, myself, be as reliable as possible, and this I try to be. But reliability is not a matter of contract – that is the main difference between the world of personal relationships and the world of business relationships. It is a matter for the heart, which signs no documents. In other words, reliability is impossible unless there is a natural warmth. Most men possess this warmth, though they often have bad luck and get chilled. Most of them, even when they are politicians, *want* to keep faith. And one can, at all events, show one's own little light here, one's own poor little trembling flame, with the knowledge that it is not the only light that is shining in the darkness, and not the only one which the darkness does not comprehend. Personal relations are despised today. They are regarded as bourgeois luxuries, as products of a time of fair weather which is now past, and we are urged to get rid of them, and to dedicate ourselves to some movement or cause instead. I hate the idea of causes, and if I had to choose between betraying my country and betraying my friend I hope I should have the guts to betray my country. Such a choice may scandalize the modern reader, and he may stretch out his patriotic hand to the telephone at once and ring up the police. It would not have shocked Dante, though. Dante places Brutus and Cassius in the lowest circle of Hell because they had chosen to betray their friend Julius Caesar rather than their country Rome. Probably one will not be asked to make such an agonizing choice. Still, there lies at the back of every creed something terrible and hard for which the worshipper may one day be required to suffer, and there is even a terror and a hardness in this creed of personal relationships, urbane and mild though it sounds. Love and loyalty to an individual can run counter to the claims of the State. When they do – down with the State, say I, which means that the State would down me.

This brings me along to Democracy, 'Even love, the beloved Republic, That feeds upon freedom and lives'. Democracy is not a beloved Republic really, and never will be. But it is less hateful than other contemporary forms of government, and to that extent it deserves our support. It does start from the assumption that the individual is important, and that all types are needed to make a civilization. It does not divide its citizens into the bossers and the bossed – as an efficiency-regime tends to do. The people I admire most are those who are sensitive and want to create something or discover something, and do not see life in terms of power, and such people get more of a chance under a democracy than elsewhere. They found religions, great or small, or they produce literature and art, or they do disinterested scientific research, or they may be what is called 'ordinary people', who are creative in their private lives, bring up their children decently, for instance, or help their neighbours. All these people need to express themselves; they cannot do so unless society allows them liberty to do so, and the society which allows them most liberty is a democracy.

Democracy has another merit. It allows criticism, and if there is not public criticism there are bound to be hushed-up scandals. That is why I believe in the press, despite all its lies and vulgarity, and why I believe in Parliament. Parliament is often sneered at because it is a Talking Shop. I believe in it *because* it is a talking shop. I believe in the Private Member who makes himself a nuisance. He gets snubbed and is told that he is cranky or ill-informed, but he does expose abuses which would otherwise never have been mentioned, and very often an abuse gets put right just by being mentioned. Occasionally, too, a well-meaning public official starts losing his head in the cause of efficiency, and thinks himself God Almighty. Such officials are particularly frequent in the Home Office.

Well, there will be questions about them in Parliament sooner or later, and then they will have to mind their steps. Whether Parliament is either a representative body or an efficient one is questionable, but I value it because it criticizes and talks, and because its chatter gets widely reported.

So two cheers for Democracy: one because it admits variety and two because it permits criticism. Two cheers are quite enough: there is no occasion to give three. Only love the beloved Republic deserves that.

What about Force, though? While we are trying to be sensitive and advanced and affectionate and tolerant, an unpleasant question pops up: does not all society rest upon force? If a government cannot count upon the police and the army, how can it hope to rule? And if an individual gets knocked on the head or sent to a labour camp, of what significance are his opinions?

This dilemma does not worry me as much as it does some. I realize that all society rests upon force. But all the great creative actions, all the decent human relations, occur during the intervals when force has not managed to come to the front. These intervals are what matter. I want them to be as frequent and as lengthy as possible, and I call them 'civilization'. Some people idealize force and pull it into the foreground and worship it, instead of keeping it in the background as long as possible. I think they make a mistake, and I think that their opposites, the mystics, err even more when they declare that force does not exist. I believe that it exists, and that one of our jobs is to prevent it from getting out of its box. It gets out sooner or later, and then it destroys us and all the lovely things which we have made. But it is not out all the time, for the fortunate reason that the strong are so stupid. Consider their conduct for a moment in *The Nibelung's Ring*. The giants there have the guns, or in other words the gold; but they do nothing with it, they do not realize that they are all-powerful, with the result that the catastrophe is delayed and the castle of Valhalla, insecure but glorious, fronts the storms. Fafnir, coiled round his hoard, grumbles and grunts; we can hear him under Europe today; the leaves of the wood already tremble, and the Bird calls its warnings uselessly. Fafnir will destroy us, but by a blessed dispensation he is stupid and slow, and creation goes on just outside the poisonous blast of his breath. The Nietzschean would hurry the monster up, the mystic would say he did not exist, but Wotan, wiser than either, hastens to create warriors before doom declares itself. The Valkyries are symbols not only of courage but of intelligence; they represent the human spirit snatching its opportunity while the going is good, and one of them even finds time to love. Brünnhilde's last song hymns the recurrence of love, and since it is the privilege of art to exaggerate she goes even further, and proclaims the love which is eternally triumphant, and feeds upon freedom and lives.

So that is what I feel about force and violence. It is, alas! the ultimate reality on this earth, but it does not always get to the front. Some people call its absences 'decadence'; I call them 'civilization' and find in such interludes the chief justification for the human experiment. I look the other way until fate strikes me. Whether this is due to courage or to cowardice in my own case I cannot be sure. But I know that, if men had not looked the other way in the past, nothing of any value would survive. The people I respect most behave as if they were immortal and as if society was eternal. Both assumptions are false: both of them must be accepted as true if we are to go on eating and working and loving, and are to keep open a few breathing-holes for the human spirit. No millennium seems likely to descend upon humanity; no better and stronger League of Nations will be instituted; no form of Christianity and no alternative to Christianity will bring peace to the world or integrity to the individual; no 'change of heart' will occur. And yet we need not despair, indeed, we cannot despair; the evidence of history shows us that men have always insisted on behaving creatively under the shadow of the sword; that they have done their artistic and scientific and domestic stuff for the sake of doing it, and that we had better follow their example under the shadow of the aeroplanes. Others, with more vision or courage than myself, see the salvation of humanity ahead, and will dismiss my conception of civilization as paltry, a sort of tip-and-run game. Certainly it is presumptuous to say that we *cannot* improve, and that Man, who has only been in power for a few thousand years, will never learn to make use of his power. All I mean is that, if people continue to kill one another as they do, the world cannot get better than it is, and that, since there are more people than formerly, and their means for destroying one another superior, the world may well get worse. What is good in people – and consequently in the world – is their insistence on creation, their belief in friendship and loyalty for their own sakes; and, though Violence remains and is, indeed, the major partner in this muddled establishment, I believe that creativeness remains too, and will always assume direction when violence sleeps. So, though I am not an optimist, I cannot agree with Sophocles that it were better never to have been born. And although, like Horace, I see no evidence that each batch of births is superior to the last, I leave the field open for the more complacent view. This is such a difficult moment to live in, one cannot help getting gloomy and also a bit rattled, and perhaps short-sighted.

In search of a refuge, we may perhaps turn to hero-worship. But here we shall get no help, in my opinion. Hero-worship is a dangerous vice, and one of the minor merits of a democracy is that it does not encourage it, or produce that unmanageable type of citizen known as the Great Man. It produces instead different kinds of small men – a much finer achievement. But people who cannot get interested in the variety of life, and cannot make up their own minds, get discontented over this, and they long for a hero to bow down before and to follow blindly. It is significant that a hero is an integral part of the authoritarian stock-in-trade today. An efficiency-regime cannot be run without a few heroes stuck about it to carry off the dullness – much as plums have to be put into a bad pudding to make it palatable. One hero at the top and a smaller one each side of him is a favourite arrangement, and the timid and the bored are comforted by the trinity, and, bowing down, feel exalted and strengthened.

No, I distrust Great Men. They produce a desert of uniformity around them and often a pool of blood too, and I always feel a little man's pleasure when they come a cropper. Every now and then one reads in the newspapers some such statement as: 'The *coup d'état* appears to have failed, and Admiral Toma's whereabouts is at present unknown.' Admiral Toma had probably every qualification for being a Great Man – an iron will, personal magnetism, dash, flair, sexlessness – but fate was against him, so he retires to unknown whereabouts instead of parading history with his peers. He fails with a completeness which no artist and no lover can experience, because with them the process of creation is itself an achievement, whereas with him the only possible achievement is success.

I believe in aristocracy, though – if that is the right word, and if a democrat may use it. Not an aristocracy of power, based upon rank and influence, but an aristocracy of the sensitive, the considerate and the plucky. Its members are to be found in all nations and classes, and all through the ages, and there is a secret understanding between them when they meet. They represent the true human tradition, the one permanent victory of our queer race over cruelty and chaos. Thousands of them perish in obscurity, a few are great names. They are sensitive for others as well as for themselves, they are considerate without being fussy, their pluck is not swankiness but the power to endure, and they can take a joke. I give no examples – it is risky to do that – but the reader may as well consider whether this is the type of person he would like to meet and to be, and whether (going further with me) he would prefer that this type should *not* be an ascetic one. I am against asceticism myself. I am with the old Scotsman who wanted less chastity and more delicacy. I do not feel that my aristocrats are a real aristocracy if they thwart their bodies, since bodies are the instruments through which we register and enjoy the world. Still, I do not insist. This is not a major point. It is clearly possible to be sensitive, considerate and plucky and yet be an ascetic too, and if anyone possesses the first three qualities I will let him in! On they go – an invincible army, yet not a victorious one. The aristocrats, the elect, the chosen, the Best People – all the words that describe them are false, and all attempts to organize them fail. Again and again Authority, seeing their value, has tried to net them and to utilize them as the Egyptian Priesthood or the Christian Church or the Chinese Civil Service or the Group Movement, or some other worthy stunt. But they slip through the net and are gone; when the door is shut, they are no longer in the room; their temple, as one of them remarked, is the holiness of the Heart's affections, and their kingdom, though they never possess it, is the wide-open world.

With this type of person knocking about, and constantly crossing one's path if one has eyes to see or hands to feel, the experiment of earthly life cannot be dismissed as a failure. But it may well be hailed as a tragedy, the tragedy being that no device has been found by which these private decencies can be transmitted to public affairs. As soon as people have power they go crooked and sometimes dotty as well, because the possession of power lifts them into a region where normal honesty never pays. For instance, the man who is selling newspapers outside the Houses of Parliament can safely leave his papers to go for a drink, and his cap beside them: anyone who takes a paper is sure to drop a copper into the cap. But the men who are inside the Houses of Parliament – they cannot trust one another like that, still less can the Government they compose trust other governments. No caps upon the pavement here, but suspicion, treachery and armaments. The more highly public life is organized the lower does its morality sink; the nations of today behave to each other worse than they ever did in the past, they cheat, rob, bully and bluff, make war without notice, and kill as many women and children as possible; whereas primitive tribes were at all events restrained by taboos. It is a humiliating outlook – though the greater the darkness, the brighter shine the little lights, reassuring one another, signalling: 'Well, at all events, I'm still here. I don't like it very much, but how are you?' Unquenchable lights of my aristocracy! Signals of the invincible army! 'Come along – anyway, let's have a good time while we can.' I think they signal that too.

The Saviour of the future – if ever he comes – will not preach a new Gospel. He will merely utilize my aristocracy, he will make effective the goodwill and the good temper which are already existing. In other words, he will introduce a new technique. In economics, we are told that if there was a new technique of distribution there need be no poverty, and people would not starve in one place while crops were being ploughed under in another. A similar change is needed in the sphere of morals and politics.

The desire for it is by no means new; it was expressed, for example, in theological terms by Jacopone da Todi over six hundred years ago. 'Ordena questo amore, tu che m'ami,' he said; 'O thou who lovest me – set this love in order.' His prayer was not granted, and I do not myself believe that it ever will be, but here, and not through a change of heart, is our probable route. Not by becoming better, but by ordering and distributing his native goodness, will Man shut up Force into its box, and so gain time to explore the universe and to set his mark upon it worthily. At present he only explores it at odd moments, when Force is looking the other way, and his divine creativeness appears as a trivial by-product, to be scrapped as soon as the drums beat and the bombers hum.

Such a change, claim the orthodox, can only be made by Christianity, and will be made by it in God's good time: man always has failed and always will fail to organize his own goodness, and it is presumptuous of him to try. This claim – solemn as it is – leaves me cold. I cannot believe that Christianity will ever cope with the present world-wide mess, and I think that such influence as it retains in modern society is due to the money behind it, rather than to its spiritual appeal. It was a spiritual force once, but the indwelling spirit will have to be restated if it is to calm the waters again, and probably restated in a non-Christian form. Naturally a lot of people, and people who are not only good but able and intelligent, will disagree here; they will vehemently deny that Christianity has failed, or they will argue that its failure proceeds from the wickedness of men, and really proves its ultimate success. They have Faith, with a large F. My faith has a very small one, and I only intrude it because these are strenuous and serious days, and one likes to say what one thinks while speech is comparatively free; it may not be free much longer.

The above are the reflections of an individualist and a liberal who has found liberalism crumbling beneath him and at first felt ashamed. Then, looking around, he decided there was no special reason for shame, since other people, whatever they felt, were equally insecure. And as for individualism – there seems no way of getting off this, even if one wanted to. The dictator-hero can grind down his citizens till they are all alike, but he cannot melt them into a single man. That is beyond his power. He can order them to merge, he can incite them to mass-antics, but they are obliged to be born separately, and to die separately, and, owing to these unavoidable termini, will always be running off the totalitarian rails. The memory of birth and the expectation of death always lurk within the human being, making him separate from his fellows and consequently capable of intercourse with them. Naked I came into the world, naked I shall go out of it! And a very good thing too, for it reminds me that I am naked under my shirt, whatever its colour.

Part V

Reviews

The Bloomsbury Group all began to write professionally as reviewers, and various members, including those represented in this section, spent at least some part of their careers earning money by regular reviewing. Bloomsbury reviewers were versatile critics who wrote well on a variety of subjects. The Group reviewed for an assortment of periodicals, but by the nineteen-thirties much of their reviewing was concentrated in the *New Statesman and Nation*.

22

Desmond MacCarthy:
The New St Bernard

Desmond MacCarthy began his critical career as a reviewer of the Edwardian theatre. In the 1920s under the apt pseudonym of 'Affable Hawk' he was columnist and literary editor of the New Statesman. *MacCarthy edited* Life and Letters *in the 1930s and ended his reviewing career as the principal literary columnist for the* Sunday Times. *MacCarthy is chiefly read now for his criticism of George Bernard Shaw's plays. Shaw himself said MacCarthy was closer to the mark in his early reviews than anyone else.* Man and Superman *was the subject of MacCarthy's first Shaw review in November 1903, and it reveals how Bloomsbury's emerging values were to differ from Shaw's. The review was published in the Cambridge-sponsored* Independent Review, *which also published the early work of Forster and Strachey.*

Mr Bernard Shaw always supplies his own criticism. In this book[1] we have a dedicatory epistle of 37 pages; a pamphlet, supposed to have been written by the principal character, of some 64 pages; and, in the middle of the play itself, a dream-dialogue in Hell, between Don Juan, the Devil, Doña Ana and the Statue, more than half as long as the four Acts taken together. These are occasions which the author takes of explaining his theory of life, his religion in fact, his politics, and his views on the relations of the sexes. He has always been 'anxiously explanatory'. In his

---

[1] *Man and Superman.* By Bernard Shaw. Constable. 6s.

journalist days, when the plays or publications of the week gave him no purchase, he used frankly to divert the topic to himself. There is no objection on earth to this method. All criticism which is not purely technical cannot help being an exposition of the writer's philosophy, and there is no reason why a man should not take his own work or himself for a text, provided he uses himself as a diagram of the species and what he says is sensible.

Mr Shaw is both an artist and a critic; that is to say, there is no escape for him. He must aspire to be an artist-philosopher, or for ever hold his peace; and he is perfectly aware of the disabilities which this position implies. He cannot be content with any representation of life, however beautiful it may be, or however natural, that is not co-ordinated into some view of the world and the general aim of man. This is the real ground of his quarrel with Shakespeare; that Shakespeare has 'two loves of comfort and despair', or rather many loves and no religion. This quarrel Mr Shaw has characteristically used as part of a constant system of self-advertisement, to which he confesses with much relish of his own frankness. He has always made unscrupulous use of the Press as a confessional. It refreshes his self-respect to say: 'I am a natural born mountebank.' After that, he feels justified in considering everybody else equally bad, and only inferior to himself in honesty. In the same way, people who have a dim inkling that they are a little mad, sometimes pretend that they are more mad than they are; for then they have the comfort of feeling that the difference between themselves and others, of which they are conscious, is under their control, and can be shaken off at will. Similarly, too, those who are haunted by the feeling that they are not as single-hearted as they have assured themselves, may recover their self-respect and a sense of ironical superiority at the same time, by puzzling others, and making believe that they are more frivolous than they really are. The confessional is only a method of keeping uppermost a healthy-minded attitude towards your own shortcomings, by coming to feel that you stand in a sense more outside them than is really the case.

No one indeed, who has his wits about him when he reads, considers Mr Shaw a 'mountebank'. But it is possible that Mr Shaw would take a truer view of the world, if he allowed these self-doubts to rankle a little more, instead of airing them in the confessional. Perhaps, if he were not at bottom so certain that he was always in earnest himself, he would not be so certain that men are liars to the backbone of their souls. This is a suggestion of the Devil's Advocate, which should be after his own heart.

In the dedicatory epistle Mr Shaw complains that 'instead of exclaiming – "send this inconceivable Satanist to the stake," the respectable newspapers pith me by announcing – "another book by this brilliant and thoughtful author." ' It is entirely his own fault. If a man has used his convictions as a means to draw attention to himself, he will never get those he addresses to believe that his ideas are as genuinely held, or as important, as may really be the case. If Mr Shaw wishes to be listened to by a 'pit of philosophers', or howled at by the thoughtless, he must cease to think it worth while to print cheap smart sayings, such as the Revolutionist's Handbook at the end of this play contains. Some of these are true enough, but expressed in a way which suggests that the writer wishes to shock or be admired more than he wishes to convince; others would be worth saying in conversation; while others such as – 'The vilest abortionist is he who attempts to mould a child's character,' or – but it is not worth while to quote them.

The play itself is a tragic-comic love chase of a man by a woman; the subject is sexual attraction, not in its secondary effects in the social order, or as a motive modifying or intensifying other emotions, but in itself, as the 'Life Force'. The peculiarity of the author's view of the relations of the sexes is, that he believes Woman, to whom, according to him, the fulfilment of her sex is *the* function of her life, to be always in reality the pursuer. This truth he thinks has been disguised from the sane man, by the fact that those who have written the most impressive books, in which mankind look to see themselves reflected, instead of keeping their eyes on their own experience, are the only kind of men who are *not* helpless in the presence of sexual attraction. Partly also in self-defence men have adopted the feeble convention that it is the part of Man to woo, and of Woman to wait. But in fact it is the artist alone who is not in danger of capture and absorption by woman, and therefore his account of the matter is bad evidence. This is an astonishing assertion; it is not borne out by the life of most men of genius, and it is extravagant to suppose that a picture of life, so unlike the ordinary man's experience, would have been docilely accepted by him for so long.

However, Mr Shaw gives his theory for what it is worth, and makes an interesting play out of it. *Ann* is 'Everywoman'. As a living character in the play she is excellent, and the scene between her and *Tanner* in the first Act is about as good as it can be. Her instinct leads her to mark him down as the father for her children. He knows that marriage means loss of liberty, and therefore of efficiency and happiness; for he has no respect for Ann's character, and only admires her for the completeness with which all her impulses, actions, and thoughts are subordinated to nature's purpose; though, as a matter of fact, it is her fearlessness, ingenuity, and sense of fun, which make her attractive. The first two Acts are mainly concerned with the wiles she employs to draw him closer, in the third he dashes off in his motor-car to escape her, and, in the fourth, he is run down and surrenders. The incidents and arrangement of the play recall the musical farces of the Gaiety. Representatives of all the latest up-to-date types figure in the story. There is an Irish American millionaire talking his jargon, and his typical American son (who is very well described) talking his; a comic anarchist, a comic chauffeur, a band of comic brigands; and all the principal characters motor across Europe, and meet at the end in the garden of a villa in Granada.

But what does the machinery matter, if the author has succeeded in expressing his idea? Jack Tanner, with his explosions of nervous force and exasperated eloquence, is as well done as Ann. The contrasting male character is the poetical, chivalrous, romantic *Octavius. He* woos Ann, who would only be willing to take him as a *pis-aller*; for the poetic temperament is barren, 'the Life Force passes it by.' Marriage, if he only knew, would be equally fatal to him; for his goddess, his inspiration, would vanish in the real 'flesh and blood' woman and mother, who is not lovable in herself and *in so far as she is 'woman' (and Ann is little else) can only really care for her children.* It is a blemish in the play that Octavius is made such a muff; the contrast loses a possible extra impressiveness. Tanner in the end, as Don Juan explains of himself in the dream, yields because he cannot help it. He despises Ann, she is bully and liar, 'and unscrupulously uses her personal fascinations to make men give her what she wants, which makes her something for which there is no polite name'. She will think his aspirations and efforts to reform society absurd, and thwart him as much as she dares; and, above all, she is a hypocrite. But Tanner surrenders with a good conscience after all; for Ann and he, in submitting to their attraction for each other, become the servants of 'the Life Force', or will of the world. Henceforth they are instruments to the creation of the Superman, which is the only aim worth working for in this world; and they are both right to sacrifice, she her happiness and perhaps her life, he his happiness and aims and generous ambitions, for such things cannot compare in importance with the bringing into the world of children, born of mutual attraction. But the institution which compels two people who have nothing in common, saving this impulse towards each other, to spend their two lives together, is iniquitous. The conclusion logically follows from the assertion that the child is the sole end of marriage, that it is absurd to make marriage binding. Moreover, the consideration that the rest of life will have to be spent together induces men and women to marry for irrelevant reasons, such as affection or self-interest, to the detriment of the next generation.

This book then is significant as an attack on marriage, but it is also significant as the despairing cry of a reformer. Mr Shaw has always been a social reformer, and his ideas are what he cares about; for Art's sake he would never have penned a line, although he is the ablest of imaginative prose-writers who have not already almost said their say. *Mrs Warren's Profession* and the first part of the preface to *Plays for Puritans*, both attempts at social sanitation, were most satisfactory compositions. But in this book the author despairs of all methods of improving society, save one – breeding by selection a better race of men: this is the last hencoop to which he clings in the universal wreckage of his hopes. The fact is, he has at last found out that he never had any faith in men, his heroes included. He cannot believe in the individual, so he believes in the perfectibility of the race by artful contrivance. This is the aim to which he calls on all who are worth anything to devote their lives, the idea which is to stiffen craven backs, and for which he tries to believe men will give up most of the things they care about – their romances and pleasures, as Mr Shaw calls them. But if a man love not his brother whom he hath seen, how shall he love the Superman whom he hath not seen?

As Mr Shaw very seriously urges the selective breeding of citizens by the State as the only rational aim of a man who has the interests of his fellows at heart, it is worth while recalling the fact that the present state of our knowledge of the subject is not even sufficient to produce a male or female as required. And how incomparably more difficult would be the production of Goethes, Shelleys, Caesars, and Cromwells, who alone satisfy Mr Shaw, or a race of athlete philosophers. Until our knowledge is completer, it is hardly sane to work for a reform which would create havoc and loss and misery in the lives of the best among the living, for the sake of those who, after all, may never be born.

But there is a peculiarity in Mr Shaw's vision, which enables him to contemplate such misery and loss with indifference. It underlies his wit, and his hilarity, which are often so delightful, and determines what is most characteristic in his attitude towards death, marriage, art and heaven – or the ideal, as it is indicated in the dream in the third Act of this play. He cannot see that men and women are lovable, and therefore he cannot value for their own sakes the emotions which they rouse in each other, or rather, he simply does not believe in them. The utterances and actions of the characters in each play and story he has written, who are represented as having a clear view of themselves and the nature of things, agree with the impression which each work as a whole leaves behind.

All his plays and novels, even those parts written more strictly in his Bumbledonian capacity, though in a less degree than the others, are vitiated by this one fatal defect in his vision. He cannot see that human beings are lovable, and therefore that they can be anything but humbugs or fools, when they speak or behave as though they loved each other. There is indeed a third alternative; they may be poets.

In this loveless world of Mr Shaw's imagination, death is not a matter to make any outcry about, and regret, after a short period, if it is not a sham, is a bad habit. For if men are not lovable or loved, Don Juan is right in saying that, if we only knew it, 'a funeral is a festival in black.' In the *Unsocial Socialist*, Trefusis, when he finds himself crying as he stands by the bedside of his dead wife, says: 'This is a fraud I never dreamt of, tears and no sorrow.' And he goes on, after thinking over his life and his own insignificance: 'Here I am, moralising over her as though I were God Almighty, and she a baby. The more you remind a man of what he is, the more conceited he becomes.' The reader not infrequently gets an impression of a man reflecting himself in a glass, and admiring the ugliness of his own grin. But in a world where there is no beauty, honesty is the most admirable thing; and if men and women are not lovable, Trefusis is right in admiring his own honesty, though it should not console him so much for what it reveals.

If men and women are not lovable, then the state of 'being in love', when they are completely satisfied with each other, is of all states the most asinine and contemptible. So much so, that Mr Shaw believes that any two people with a spark of sense must know that they are deceiving, and any rational person that he is deceived into the bargain. 'Each worshipper knows that his love is a transient sham, or a copy from his favourite poem; but he believes honestly in the love of others for him.' Trefusis declares: 'My own belief is, that no latter-day man has any faith in the thoroughness or permanence of his affection for his mate.' Don Juan, arguing against marriage, says, that no man is lovable when he is known intimately. These are the author's opinions; at any rate, those which determine his judgements on the importance of emotions and events described in his imaginative writings. It is impossible to *prove* that men or women are lovable, or that sex may help them, as it does apparently in most cases of the strongest affection, to realize that the one deserves all that the other feels. It is certainly true that many people believe it, and the fact that Mr Shaw does not, is for them a *defect* which underlies his whole picture of life. These will find consolation in an assertion in the Dedicatory Epistle at the beginning of this book: that love, as the great writers represent it, is a piece of barren special pleading, either in favour of pleasure if written when they were young, or of asceticism if written when they were old. Any one who has overlooked so many distinctions in literature may well have missed as many in his observation of life.

Heaven and Hell in the dream-dialogue are the two rival ways of regarding the world. Heaven is the contemplation of *things as they are to Mr Shaw*, and the helping of the world forward to something better – the

Superman; Hell the preoccupation with personal affections and beauty, for which Mr Shaw can find so little place on earth.

It would be rash to promise him the pain and triumph of the stake, which he claims as his right. But there is another and very real way in which artists and thinkers, who feel they have something important to teach, more commonly have to suffer: namely, the discovery that their sense of proportion is not so profound as they supposed, and that a great many of the ideas to which they have devoted their lives are not 'worth a dump as a philosophy of life'.

23

Clive Bell: Ibsen

As MacCarthy could introduce post-impressionism when the occasion arose, so Clive Bell could review drama. Bell began his writing career in 1909 as a literary reviewer for the distinguished Athenaeum. *Only after the first Post-Impressionist Exhibition did he begin to write art criticism. Bell's 1912 review of a critical study of Henrik Ibsen shows the transition he was to make. Bell remained uncertain as to whether the significant form of great visual art could be found in literature. He has no doubts in this early review, however, that Ibsen's expression of 'essential reality' comes through his dramatic form. Bell included his Ibsen review in a selection of* Athenaeum *reviews that he reprinted in* Pot-Boilers *in 1918.*

Was it chance made Mr Ellis Roberts mention Cézanne on the fourth page of a book about Ibsen?[1] One cannot think so. Similarities in the work and circumstances of the two men can hardly have escaped him. Born within a dozen years of each other (Ibsen was born in 1828), both matured in a period when the professions of writing and painting were laboriously cultivated at the expense of art. Each, unguided except by his own sense of dissatisfaction with his surroundings, found a way through the sloughs of romance and the deserts of realism, to the high country beyond them. Both sought and both found the same thing – the thing above literature and painting, the stuff out of which great literature and painting are made.

[1] 'Henrik Ibsen: a Critical Study.' By R. Ellis Roberts. (Secker.)

The Romantics and Realists were like people coming to cuffs about which is the more important thing in an orange, the history of Spain or the number of pips. The instinct of the romantic, invited to say what he felt about anything, was to recall its associations. A rose made him think of quaint gardens and gracious ladies and Edmund Waller and sundials, and a thousand pleasant things that, at one time or another, had befallen him or someone else. A rose touched life at a hundred pretty points. A rose was interesting because it had a past. On this the realist's comment was 'Mush!' or words to that effect. In like predicament, he would give a detailed account of the properties of *Rosa setigera*, not forgetting to mention the urn-shaped calyx-tube, the five imbricated lobes, or the open corolla of five obovate petals. To an Ibsen or a Cézanne one account would appear as irrelevant as the other, since both omitted the thing that mattered, what philosophers used to call 'the thing in itself', what now they would call 'the essential reality':

SOLNESS. . . . Do you read much?
HILDA. No, never! I have given it up. For it all seems so irrelevant.
SOLNESS. That is just my feeling.

It was just what the books left out that Ibsen wanted to express.

He soon worked through the romantic tradition. It hampered him long enough to prevent *Peer Gynt* from becoming a great poem; after that he found himself on the threshold of a world where everything mattered too much in itself for its associations to be of consequence. Attempting to analyse Ibsen's characters used to be a pastime for fools; to-day, we all know that they come from that world where everything has been reduced to an essence that defies analysis. There Ibsen was never so completely at home as Cézanne; he lacked the imagination by which alone one arrives and remains in the world of reality. His vision was more uncertain and so his faith was weaker. He was a less ferociously sincere artist. When vision began to fail he took refuge in a catalogue of facts or in unconvincing symbolism: Cézanne tossed his picture into a bush. Perhaps that is why a new generation, hungry for great contemporary art, turns more hopefully to painting than to literature.

Thirty years ago it would have been misleading to say, what is undoubtedly true, that it is as an artist that Ibsen is great. To call a man a good artist came to much the same thing as calling him a good ping-pong player: it implied that he was proficient in his own business; it did not imply that he was a great man who affected life greatly. Therefore many people who understood Ibsen and were moved by his plays preferred to call him a political thinker or a social reformer; while their enemies, the aesthetes, were very willing to call him a great artist, since by doing so they excused themselves from paying the least attention to anything that he said. Ibsen was a reformer in the sense that all great artists are reformers; it is impossible to speak of reality without criticizing civiliza- tion. In the same way he was a politician; it is impossible to care passionately about art without caring about the fate of mankind. But Mr Roberts is certainly right in holding that to appreciate Ibsen we must consider him as an artist.

Ibsen approached humanity in the spirit of an artist. He sought that essential thing in men and women by which we should know them if the devil came one night and stole away their bodies; we may call it character if we choose. He imagined situations in which character would be re- vealed clearly. The subjects of his plays are often 'problems', because he was interested in people who only when 'problems' arise are seen to be essentially different from one another, or, indeed, from the furniture with which they live. There is no reason to suppose that Ibsen had any love for 'problems' as such; and we are tempted to believe that some modern 'problems' are nothing more than situations from Ibsen's plays. Ibsen's method is the true artist's method. The realist writing about people tends to give an inventory of personal peculiarities, and a faithful report of all that is said and done. The romantic hopes, somehow, to 'create an atmosphere' by suggesting what he once felt for something not altogether unlike the matter in hand. Ibsen sets himself to discover the halfpenny- worth of significance in all this intolerable deal of irrelevance. Which is the word, which the gesture, that, springing directly from the depths of one character, penetrates to the depths of another? What is the true cause of this hubbub of inconsequent words and contradictory actions? Nothing less remote than the true cause will serve, nothing else is firmly rooted in reality. Is that man expressing what he feels or is he paying out what he thinks he is expected to feel? Have I pushed simplification as far as it will go? Are there no trappings, no overtones, nothing but what is essential to express my vision of reality? And, above all, is my vision absolutely sharp and sure? These were the questions Ibsen had to answer. When he succeeded he was a great artist, not, as Mr Roberts suggests, in the manner of Shakespeare, but in the manner of Aeschylus.

There is no more obvious proof of the greatness of Ibsen's art than the perfection of its form. To assert that fine form always enfolds fine thought and feeling would imply a knowledge of literature to which it would be effrontery in a critic to pretend. He may be allowed, however, to advise any one who is ready with an instance of great form enclos- ing a void to verify his impressions: it was thus that one critic at any rate came to appreciate Goldoni and Alfieri. Be that as it may, this is certain: a perfectly conceived idea never fails to express itself in perfect form. Ibsen did not shirk the labour of making his conceptions as hard, and definite, and self-supporting as possible. No matter how auto-biographical some of his best plays may be, he is too good an artist to allow them to lean on his personal experience; they have to stand firmly on their own feet. Ibsen, therefore, worked his conceptions to such a degree of hardness and self-consistency that he could detach them from himself and study them impersonally. That is why his plays are models of form. And if there be an Academy of Letters that takes its duties seriously, *Rosmersholm* and *Ghosts* are, we presume, in the hands of every young person within its sphere of influence. The students are shown, we hope, that Ibsen's form is superb, not because Ibsen paid any particular attention to the precepts of Aristotle, but because, like Sophocles, who had the misfortune to pre-decease the Stagirite, he knew precisely what he wanted to say, and addressed himself exclusively to the task of saying it. To achieve great form is needed neither science nor tradition, but intense feeling, vigorous thinking, and imagination. Formlessness is not a sign of spirited revolt against superstition; it is a mere indication of muddle-headedness.

The subject-matter of Ibsen's plays is reality; unfortunately, his imagination was not always strong enough to keep a sure hold on it. When the vision faded he took refuge in symbolism or literality. There was a commonplace background to his mind, of which we see too much in such plays as *An Enemy of the People* and *Pillars of Society*. It is this commonplace and rather suburban quality that tempts us occasionally to explain Ibsen's popularity by the fact that he represented the revolt of the supremely unimportant, of whom there happen to be quite a number in the world. With the symbolism of *The Master-Builder* no fault can be found. It is a legitimate and effective means of expressing a sense of reality. The theme is never lost. The artist who sacrifices his human relations, but dare not give all, dare not give his vanity or his life to the ideal, moves steadily to his inevitable doom. Whether he move in the form of Halvard Solness, the cowardly architect of genius, fearless of ideas but fearful of action, or in the form of the symbolical master-builder, the artist who tries to have the best of both worlds, matters not a straw. The medium of expression changes, but the theme is constant: the conception is whole. That is more than can be said of *The Lady from the Sea*, where the symbolism comes perilously near padding; or of *When We Dead Awaken*, where it often expresses nothing relevant, merely standing picturesquely for commonplaces, and filling gaps.

To read one of Ibsen's great plays is always thrilling; to read one for the first time is an event. If a savage who took locomotives and motor-cars for granted, as inexplicable creatures of whim and fancy, suddenly were shown, not by vague adumbration, but by straightforward exposition, that they were expressions of intelligible laws controlled by comprehensible machinery, he could not be more amazed than was the nineteenth century by Ibsen. For Ibsen took nothing for granted. He saw little on the surface of life that corresponded with reality; but he did not cease to believe in reality. That was where he differed both from the Philistines and from the elect. He saw that the universe was something very different from what it was generally supposed to be: he saw the futility of popular morals and popular metaphysics; but he neither swallowed the conventions nor threw up his hands in despair, declaring the whole thing to be an idiotic farce. He knew that truth and goodness had nothing to do with law and custom; but he never doubted that there were such things; and he went beneath the surface to find them. It was Ibsen's revelation of a new world, in which moral values were real and convincing, that thrilled the nineteenth century, and thrills us yet. Can any one read sedately that scene in *Ghosts* in which Mrs Alving shows with bewildering simplicity that, however respectable the Pastor's morality may be, it is pure wickedness?

PASTOR MANDERS. You call it 'cowardice' to do your plain duty? Have you forgotten that a son ought to love and honour his father and mother?
MRS ALVING. Do not let us talk in such general terms. Let us ask: Ought Oswald to love and honour Chamberlain Alving?
MANDERS. Is there no voice in your mother's heart that forbids you to destroy your son's ideals?
MRS ALVING. But what about the truth?
MANDERS. But what about the ideals?
MRS ALVING. Oh – ideals, ideals! If only I were not such a coward!

Ibsen's social and political ideas follow necessarily from the nature of his art. He knew too much about the depths of character to suppose that people could be improved from without. He agreed with our grandmothers that what men need are new hearts. It is good feeling that makes good men, and the sole check on bad feeling is conscience. Laws, customs, and social conventions he regarded as ineffectual means to good. There is no virtue in one who is restrained from evil by fear. He went further: he regarded external restraints as means to bad, since they come between a man and his conscience and blunt the moral sense. 'So long as I keep to the rules,' says the smug citizen, 'I am of the righteous.' Ibsen loathed the State, with its negative virtues, its mean standards, its mediocrity, and its spiritual squalor. He was a passionate individualist.

Perhaps no one has seen more clearly that the State, at its best, stands for nothing better than the lowest common factor of the human mind. What else can it stand for? State ideals must be ideals that are not beyond the intellect and imagination of 'the average citizen'; also, since average minds are not pervious to reason, the reasoning of statesmen must be rhetoric. State morals – law and custom that is to say – are nothing more than excuses for not bothering about conscience. But Ibsen, being an artist, knew that he who would save his soul must do what he feels to be right, not what is said to be so. Feeling is the only guide, and the man who does what he feels to be wrong does wrong, whatever the State may say.

The plain, though by no means frank, determination of society to suppress the individual conscience lest it should clash with the interests of the community seems positively to have shocked him. To be fine, he believed, men must think and feel for themselves and live by their own sense of truth and beauty, not by collective wisdom or reach-me-down ideals.

> What sort of truths do the majority rally round? Truths so stricken in years that they are sinking into decrepitude. When a truth is so old as that, gentlemen, it's in a fair way to become a lie (*Laughter and jeers*).

How could Ibsen help being something of a politician? He seems really to have wished his fellow-creatures to be fine, and to have been angry with them because they wished to be nothing of the sort. He did not understand that this passionate individualism, this sense of personal responsibility, this claim to private judgement, is what no modern State, be it democratic, bureaucratic or autocratic, can tolerate. Men long for the ease and assurance of conformity and so soon as they are sufficiently organized enforce it. Truth is the enemy – *écrasez l'infâme*! Poor, silly old Stockmann in *An Enemy of the People* blurts it out, blurts out that the water-supply is contaminated and his native health-resort no better than a death-trap, for no better reason than that he feels it is what he ought to do. He fails to consider the feelings and, what is even more important, the financial interests of his neighbours, and the neighbours make short work of him, as they generally do of people who think and feel and act for themselves – of saints and artists in fact. Thus it comes about that the prophets are stoned and the best plays censored, while people such as Ibsen loathe the State with its herd-instincts, now decently baptized however, and known as Morality and Idealism.

Whether Ibsen was in the right is not for a reviewer to decide. Mr Roberts has strong views on the subject, which he is at no pains to conceal. For this we are far from blaming him. Indeed, we feel that the personal note imported by the author's intellectual bias gives some flavour to a book which, owing to the complete absence of charm or distinction, would be otherwise insipid. It is a competent, but woefully uninspiring, piece of work. Above all things, Mr Roberts lacks humour – a quality indispensable in a writer on Ibsen. For Ibsen, like other men of genius, is slightly ridiculous. Undeniably, there is something comic about the picture of the Norwegian dramatist, spectacled and frock-coated, 'looking', Mr Archer tells us, 'like a distinguished diplomat', at work amongst the orange-groves of Sorrento on *Ghosts*.

> Ibsen was keenly sensitive to place, and if we would get the utmost feeling out of his plays we must remember how large a part was played by fortunate or unfortunate position and circumstances in contributing to the wonderful 'atmosphere' of the dramas.

That is what Mr Roberts thinks. A sense of humour would also have saved him from the one black note of sentimentality in the book:

> Ellida might be Solveig analysed – but analysed with how loving a touch, how unerring a kindness; it is as if a great surgeon were operating on a woman he loved.

Such things, we had imagined, could only be written by members of the Académie française.

24

Leonard Woolf: Freud's
Psychopathology of Everyday Life

Leonard Woolf was proud of his early Freud review, which the New Weekly *published in June 1914. It was the first notice of Freud's work to appear in a non-medical English journal. Freud originally wrote the* Psychopathology of Everyday Life *in 1901; the authorized English translation by A. A. Brill was done in 1914. To prepare for the review, Woolf read* The Interpretation of Dreams *and recognized in these two books the substantial truth of Freud's theories as well as his imaginative power as a writer. A decade later the Woolfs' Hogarth Press became Freud's English publisher.*

Dr Brill, who has already translated Freud's greatest and most difficult work, *Die Traumdeutung* (*The Interpretation of Dreams*), now makes available for the English reader the far easier and more popular *Zur Psychopathologie des Alltagsleben. Psychopathology of Everyday Life* is a book which naturally would have a wider appeal than Freud's other writings. In the first place, for the serious student of psychology and of the strange application of that science to the art of medicine through Psychoanalysis, this book will serve as the best 'introduction' to Freud's peculiar theories. To such students one word of warning is necessary. Freud is a most difficult and elusive writer and thinker. One is tempted to say that he suffers from all the most brilliant defects of genius. Whether one believes in his theories or not, one is forced to admit that he writes with great subtlety of mind, a broad and sweeping imagination more characteristic of the poet than the scientist or the medical practitioner. This wide imaginative power accounts for his power of grasping in the midst of intricate analysis of details the bearing of those details upon a much wider and quite other field of details. The result is that he rarely gives, as one of his American disciples has said, a 'complete or systematic exposition' of any subject: his works are often a series of brilliant and suggestive hints. And yet from another point of view this series of hints is subtly knit together into a whole in such a way that the full meaning of a passage in one book is often only to be obtained by reference to some passage in another book. No one is really competent to give a final judgement upon even the *Psychology of Everyday Life* who has not studied the *Interpretation of Dreams*, and Freud's more distinctly pathological writings.

But even to that curious product of civilization, 'the ordinary reader', the *Psychology of Everyday Life* should be full of interest.

It is an eminently readable book. It deals with subjects which to most people are peculiarly fascinating; in the first place, one's self, the working of one's own mind as one goes about the occupations of one's everyday life, lighting a pipe, writing a letter, forgetting a name, or misquoting a line of poetry. Then, as with most of Freud's works, it deals particularly with the more mysterious workings of the human mind, those 'recesses' of our own hearts in which the darkness of our ignorance seems to be greater than almost anywhere else. There are few persons who have not felt the fascination of speculating upon the mysteries of the memories of childhood, the curious way in which the door of forgetfulness seems to have closed for us upon so many important happenings only to open momentarily in a vivid picture of some utterly trivial scene in those dim and earliest years. Or, again, that disturbing and ghostly feeling as one walks into a strange room, that one has been here before precisely in these circumstances, that everything is happening, things done and words spoken, precisely as everything happened in that mysterious 'before', a time and an event, which though it is so insistently real to us, yet seems to belong to a life lived previously or to some forgotten dream.

Many of these subjects the reader will find touched upon in Freud's characteristic way in this book, imaginatively, often humorously, always briefly and suggestively. The ordinary reader will almost certainly pronounce the verdict: 'Very interesting but too far-fetched.' To discuss the justice of that verdict would require a volume of many pages instead of the one or two columns allowed the reviewer. But this may be said categorically and confidently, that there can be no doubt that there is a substantial amount of truth in the main thesis of Freud's book, and that truth is of great value. The thesis is briefly that a large number of the mental acts of our everyday life which we ordinarily believe to be determined by chance, such as forgetting a name or an intention, making a *lapsus linguae*, or a mistake in writing, are really strictly determined by unconscious and often repressed motives of our own minds. Probably everyone would admit the simplest instances of the unconscious working of motives within us; for instance, everyone is aware of how much more frequently we forget to carry out an unpleasant than a pleasant intention. But Freud's real originality consists in his subtle analysis of many other ordinary mental processes, his peculiar methods of interpretation by which he seeks to bring to the light of consciousness the thoughts and motives which otherwise remain buried in the darkness of our unconsciousness. Here it is that the *Psychopathology of Everyday Life* is linked up with his theories of dreams and his theories of insanity, for his methods of interpretation are very often precisely similar to those used in his interpretation of dreams. It is his aim to show that it is the 'dark half' of the mind which in the perfectly normal waking man produces all kinds of trivial errors and slips and forgettings and rememberings, and which under other conditions will, following the same laws, produce the absurd fantasies of sleep or the terrible fantasies of madness.

25

Lytton Strachey:
Mr Hardy's New Poems

Lytton Strachey had been a weekly reviewer for the widely read
Spectator *from 1907 to 1909. After that he did only occasional reviews,*
such as the one of Thomas Hardy's poems written for the New Statesman
in December 1914 – four months into the First World War. Strachey says
nothing about the war directly; he brings out the affecting melancholy
of Hardy's poems instead, by contrasting them with other poetry such
as the remote work of the new Poet Laureate Robert Bridges. Though he
did not like Hardy's novels, Strachey appreciated their influence on
poems that he did admire.

Mr Hardy's new volume of poems[1] is a very interesting, and in some
ways a baffling book, which may be recommended particularly to
aesthetic theorists and to those dogmatic persons who, ever since the
days of Confucius, have laid down definitions upon the function and
nature of poetry. The dictum of Confucius is less well known than it
ought to be. 'Read poetry, oh my children!' he said, 'for it will teach you
the divine truths of filial affection, patriotism, and natural history.' Here
the Chinese sage expressed, with the engaging frankness of his nation, a
view of poetry implicitly held by that long succession of earnest critics for
whom the real justification of any work of art lies in the edifying nature

---

[1] *Satires of Circumstance, Lyrics and Reveries, with Miscellaneous Pieces.* By Thomas
Hardy. Macmillan.

of the lessons which it instils. Such generalizations upon poetry would be more satisfactory if it were not for the poets. One can never make sure of that inconvenient and unreliable race. The remark of Confucius, for instance, which, one feels, must have been written with a prophetic eye upon the works of Wordsworth, seems absurdly inapplicable to the works of Keats. Then there is Milton's famous 'simple, sensuous, and passionate' test – a test which serves admirably for Keats, but which seems in an odd way to exclude the complicated style, the severe temper, and the remote imaginations of Milton himself. Yet another school insists upon the necessity of a certain technical accomplishment; beauty is for them, as it was – in a somewhat different connection – for Herbert Spencer, a '*sine qua non*'. Harmony of sound, mastery of rhythm, the exact and exquisite employment of words – in these things, they declare, lies the very soul of poetry, and without them the noblest thoughts and the finest feelings will never rise above the level of tolerable verse. This is the theory which Mr Hardy's volume seems especially designed to disprove. It is full of poetry; and yet it is also full of ugly and cumbrous expressions, clumsy metres, and flat, prosaic turns of speech. To take a few random examples, in the second of the following lines cacophony is incarnate:

> Dear ghost, in the past did you ever find
> Me one whom consequence influenced much?

A curious mixture of the contorted and the jog-trot appears in such a line as:

> And adumbrates too therewith our unexpected troublous case;

while a line like:

> And the daytime talk of the Roman investigations

trails along in the manner of an undistinguished phrase in prose. Even Mr Hardy's grammar is not impeccable. He speaks of one,

> whom, anon,
> My great deeds done,
> Will be mine alway.

And his vocabulary, though in general it is rich and apt, has occasional significant lapses, as, for instance, in the elegy on Swinburne, where, in the middle of a passage deliberately tuned to a pitch of lyrical resonance not to be found elsewhere in the volume, there occurs the horrid hybrid 'naïvely' – a neologism exactly calculated, one would suppose, to make the classic author of *Atalanta* turn in his grave.

It is important to observe such characteristics, because, in Mr Hardy's case, they are not merely superficial and occasional blemishes; they are in reality an essential ingredient in the very essence of his work. The originality of his poetry lies in the fact that it bears everywhere upon it the impress of a master of prose fiction. Just as the great seventeenth-century writers of prose, such as Sir Thomas Browne and Jeremy Taylor, managed to fill their sentences with the splendour and passion of poetry, while still preserving the texture of an essentially prose style, so Mr Hardy, by a contrary process, has brought the realism and sobriety of prose into the service of his poetry. The result is a product of a kind very difficult to parallel in our literature. Browning, no doubt, in his intimate and reflective moods – in *By the Fireside* or *Any Wife to Any Husband* – sometimes comes near it; but the full-blooded and romantic optimism of Browning's temper offers a singular contrast to the re-pressed melancholy of Mr Hardy's. Browning was too adventurous to be content for long with the plain facts of ordinary existence; he was far more at home with the curiosities and the excitements of life; but what gives Mr Hardy's poems their unique flavour is precisely their utter lack of romanticism, their common, undecorated presentments of things. They are, in fact, modern as no other poems are. The author of *Jude the Obscure* speaks in them, but with the concentration, the intensity, the subtle disturbing force of poetry. And he speaks; he does not sing. Or rather, he talks – in the quiet voice of a modern man or woman, who finds it difficult, as modern men and women do, to put into words exactly what is in the mind. He is incorrect; but then how unreal and artificial a thing is correctness! He fumbles; but it is that very fumbling that brings him so near to ourselves. In that 'me one whom consequence influenced much', does not one seem to catch the very accent of hesitat-ing and half-ironical affection? And in the drab rhythm of that 'daytime talk of the Roman investigations', does not all the dreariness of long hours of boredom lie compressed? And who does not feel the perplexity, the discomfort, and the dim agitation in that clumsy collection of vocables – 'And adumbrates too therewith our unexpected troublous case'? What a relief such uncertainties and inexpressivenesses are after the delicate exactitudes of our more polished poets! And how mysterious and potent are the forces of inspiration and sincerity! All the taste, all the scholarship, all the art of the Poet Laureate seem only to end in something that is admirable, perhaps, something that is wonderful, but something that is irremediably remote and cold; while the flat, undistinguished poetry of Mr Hardy has found out the secret of touching our marrow-bones.

It is not only in its style and feeling that this poetry reveals the novelist; it is also in its subject-matter. Many of the poems – and in particular the remarkable group of 'fifteen glimpses' which gives its title to the volume – consist of compressed dramatic narratives, of central episodes of passion and circumstance, depicted with extraordinary vividness. A flashlight is turned for a moment upon some scene or upon some character, and in that moment the tragedies of whole lives and the long fatalities of human relationships seem to stand revealed:

> My stick! he says, and turns in the lane
> To the house just left, whence a vixen voice
> Comes out with the firelight through the pane,
> And he sees within that the girl of his choice
> Stands rating her mother with eyes aglare
> For something said while he was there.
>
> 'At last I behold her soul undraped!'
> Thinks the man who had loved her more than himself. . . .

It is easy to imagine the scene as the turning-point in a realistic psychological novel; and, indeed, a novelist in want of plots or incidents might well be tempted to appropriate some of the marvellously pregnant suggestions with which this book is crowded. Among these sketches the longest and most elaborate is the *Conversation at Dawn*, which contains in its few pages the matter of an entire novel – a remorseless and terrible novel of modern life. Perhaps the most gruesome is *At the Draper's*, in which a dying man tells his wife how he saw her in a shop, unperceived:

> You were viewing some lovely things. '*Soon required*
> *For a widow, of latest fashion*';
> And I knew 'twould upset you to meet the man
> Who had to be cold and ashen
>
> And screwed in a box before they could dress you
> '*In the last new note of mourning,*'
> As they defined it. So, not to distress you,
> I left you to your adorning.

As these extracts indicate, the prevailing mood in this volume – as in Mr Hardy's later novels – is not a cheerful one. And, in the more reflective and personal pieces, the melancholy is if anything yet more intense. It is the melancholy of regretful recollection, of bitter speculation, of immortal longings unsatisfied; it is the melancholy of one who has suffered in Gibbon's poignant phrase, 'the abridgment of hope'. Mortality, and the cruelties of time, and the ironic irrevocability of things – these are the themes upon which Mr Hardy has chosen to weave his grave and moving variations. If there is joy in these pages, it is joy that is long since dead; and if there are smiles, they are sardonical. The sentimentalist will find very little comfort among them. Sometimes, perhaps, his hopes will rise a little – for the sentimentalist is a hopeful creature; but they will soon be dashed. 'Who is digging on my grave?' asks the dead woman, who has been forgotten by her lover and her kinsfolk and even her enemy; since it is none of these, who can it be?

> O it is I, my mistress dear,
> Your little dog, who still lives near,
> And much I hope my movements here
> Have not disturbed your rest.

'Ah, yes!' murmurs the ghost:

> *You* dig upon my grave . . .
> Why flashed it not on me
> That one true heart was left behind?
> What feeling do we ever find
> To equal among human kind
> A dog's fidelity?

And so, with this comforting conclusion, the poem might have ended. But that is not Mr Hardy's way.

'Mistress,' comes the reply:

> I dug upon your grave
> To bury a bone, in case
> I should be hungry near this spot
> When passing on my daily trot,
> I am sorry, but I quite forgot
> It was your resting-place.

That is all; the desolation is complete. And the gloom is not even relieved by a little elegance of diction.

26

E. M. Forster:
The Complete Poems of C. P. Cavafy

The Alexandrian poet Constantine Cavafy (1863–1933) was E. M. Forster's most important literary discovery during his First World War Red Cross service in Egypt. In an earlier review of his poetry Forster described him as 'a Greek gentleman in a straw hat, standing absolutely motionless at a slight angle to the universe'. There are interesting parallels between the literary personalities of Cavafy and Forster and, as the review brings out, between the modern situation of the Greeks and the English. Forster's review of a translation of Cavafy's poems by John Mavrogordato was originally entitled 'In the Rue Lepsius' when it appeared in The Listener *in July 1951; Forster reprinted it under the present title in* Two Cheers for Democracy.*

The first English translation of Cavafy was made by Cavafy.

The occasion is over thirty years ago now, in his flat, 10 rue Lepsius, Alexandria; his dusky family-furnished flat. He is back from his work in a government office; the Third Circle of the Irrigation employs him as it might have employed many of his heroes. I am back from my work, costumed in khaki; the British Red Cross employs me. We have been introduced by an English friend, our meetings are rather dim, and Cavafy is now saying with his usual gentleness, 'You could never understand my poetry, my dear Forster, never.' A poem is produced – 'The God Abandons Antony' – and I detect some coincidences between its Greek and public-school Greek. Cavafy is amazed. 'Oh, but this is good, my dear Forster, this is very good indeed,' and he raises his hand, takes over, and leads me through. It was not my knowledge that touched him but my desire to know and to receive. He had no idea then that he could be widely desired, even in the stumbling North. To be understood in Alexandria and tolerated in Athens was the extent of his ambition.

Since that distant day, many other translators have had a shot. The shooter most to my taste is George Valassopoulo. He had the advantage of working with the poet and he has brought much magic across; Cavafy is largely magic. But Valassopoulo only translated, and only wished to translate, some of the poems. What was needed, and has been happily found, is a translator for them all, for all the 154 of them: Professor John Mavrogordato. This eminent scholar has done a most valuable piece of work, lucid, faithful, intelligent; he has enabled us to read what Cavafy wanted to say, and to read it in its proper perspective. For Cavafy as a historical poet, or as an erotic poet, or an introspective one, would fail to convey that Mediterranean complexity. We need all of him if we are to understand anything.

All the poems are short. They are learned, sensuous, ironic, civilized, sensitive, witty. Where's their centre? Courage enters, though not in an ordinary nor a reputable form. Cavafy appreciates cowardice also, and likes the little men who can't be consistent or maintain their ideals, and can't know what is happening and have to dodge.

> Be afraid of grandeurs, O my soul;
> And if you cannot conquer your ambitions
> With hesitation always and precautions
> Follow them up.

Be afraid, if you are Caesar, of that obscure person in the crowd; he may be Artemidorus trying to warn you against death. Be afraid lest, into your comfortable flat, Pompey's head is carried on a trencher. Be afraid if, like Nero, you lie asleep, of the obscure tumblings in the cupboard; your little household gods are falling over each other in terror, because they, not you, can hear the approaching footsteps of the Erinyes. And if you are brave your courage is only genuine when, like those who fought at Thermopylae, you know you are certain to perish.

Courage and cowardice are equally interesting to his amoral mind, because he sees in both of them opportunities for sensation. What he envies is the power to snatch sensation, to triumph over the moment even if remorse ensues. Perhaps that physical snatching is courage; it is certainly the seed of exquisite memories and it is possibly the foundations of art. The amours of youth, even when disreputable, are delightful, thinks Cavafy, but the point of them is not that: the point is that they create the future, and may give to an ageing man in a rue Lepsius perceptions he would never have known.

> The years of my youth, my life of pleasure –
> How clearly I see the meaning of them now.
>
> What unnecessary, what vain repentances . . .
>
> But I did not see the meaning then.
>
> Under the dissolute living of my youth
> Were being formed the intentions of my poetry,
> The province of my art was being planned.
>
> And that is why my repentances were never lasting.
> My resolutions to control myself, to change,
> Used to endure for two weeks at most.

The attitude recalls Proust's, but the temperament differs. Cavafy is never embittered, never the invalid. He is thankful to have lived, and

> Young men even now are repeating his verses.
> His visions pass before their lively eyes.
> Their healthy brains enjoying,
> Their welldrawn, tightskinned flesh,
> Even now are moved by his revelations of beauty.

He has something of the antique faith in fame. He is not a super-sensitive Frenchman. He is not English. He is not even British. Alexandria's his home.

> Environment, of house, of city centres, city quarters
> Which I look upon and where I walk; years and years.
>
> I have created you in the midst of joy and in the midst of sorrows;
> With so many circumstances, with so many things.
>
> And you have been made sensation, the whole of you, for me.

Alexandria is the city which he creates and over which he leans, meditative, when sorrows and triumphs recur; the city over which Antony, nearly two thousand years before him, may have leant when the music sounded and the God abandoned him. It is in Alexandria that he died in 1933 at the age of seventy; the Greek Hospital lay close by to receive him.

His material as a poet, then, begins with his own experiences and sensations: his interest in courage and cowardice and bodily pleasure, and so on. He begins from within. But he never makes a cult of himself or of what he feels. All the time he is being beckoned to and being called to by history, particularly by the history of his own race. History, too, is full of courage, cowardice, lust, and is to that extent domestic. But it is something more. It is an external inspiration. And he found in the expanses and recesses of the past, in the clash of great names and the tinkle of small ones, in the certified victories and slurred defeats, in the jewels and the wounds and the vast movements beginning out of nothing and sometimes ending nowhere: he found in them something that transcended his local life and freshened and strengthened his art. Demurely, ironically, he looks into the past, for he knew the answers. Cleopatra did not win Actium. Julian did not reinstate paganism. Anna Comnena took the wrong side. The Senate sit in state to receive the barbarians; news comes that there are no more barbarians, so the Senate have nothing to do. Sometimes there is a double irony; the Prince from western Libya impresses the Alexandrians by his reticence and dignity; he is actually a most ordinary youth, who dare not speak because of his awful Greek accent,

> and he suffered no little discomfort
> Having whole conversations stacked inside him.

'Exactly what I feel in England,' a Greek friend remarked to me. The irony became triple as he spoke, and Cavafy would have appreciated this further turn of the screw.

There is, however, nothing patronizing in his attitude to the past, nor have his cameos the aloofness of Heredia. The warmth of the past enthralls him even more than its blunders, and he can give the sense of human flesh and blood continuing through centuries that are supposed to be unsatisfactory. A tomb here, an inscription there; coloured glass worn by an emperor and empress at their coronation because they have no jewels. Sometimes the supernatural appears, and not always ominously: as in 'One of their Gods', it may enrich voluptuousness:

> When one of them was passing through the market
> Of Seleukeia, about the hour of evenfall,
> Like a tall, a beautiful, a perfect youth,
> With the joy of incorruptibility in his eyes,
> With his black and perfumed hair,
> The passers-by would look at him,

And one would ask another if he knew him,
And if he was a Greek of Syria, or a stranger. But a few
Who observed with greater attention
Would understand and draw aside;
And while he disappeared under the arcades,
In the shadows and in the lights of evening,
Going towards the quarter which at night only
Lives, with orgies and debauchery,
And every kind of drunkenness and lust,
They would wonder which it could be of Them,
And for what disreputable sensuality
He had come down to the streets of Seleukeia
From those Majestical, All-holy Mansions.

The idea that the Divine should descend to misbehave, so shocking to the Christian, comes naturally enough to a paganizing Greek, and the poem (which I first knew in a Valassopoulo translation) sums up for me much that is characteristic. And how admirable is its construction! Only two sentences, and the second one descending and descending until the final abrupt ascent.

His attitude to the past did not commend him to some of his contemporaries, nor is it popular today. He was a loyal Greek, but Greece for him was not territorial. It was rather the influence that has flowed from his race this way and that through the ages, and that (since Alexander the Great) has never disdained to mix with barbarism, has indeed desired to mix; the influence that made Byzantium a secular achievement. Racial purity bored him, so did political idealism. And he could be caustic about the claims of the tight-lipped little peninsula overseas. 'Aristocracy in modern Greece?' he once exclaimed. 'To be an aristocrat there is to have made a corner in coffee in the Peiraeus in 1849.' The civilization he respected was a bastardy in which the Greek strain prevailed, and into which, age after age, outsiders would push, to modify and be modified. If the strain died out – never mind: it had done its work, and it would have left, far away upon some Asian upland, a coin of silver, stamped with the exquisite head of a Hellenizing king. Pericles, Aristides, Themistocles, schoolroom tyrants: what did they know of this extension which is still extending, and which sometimes seemed (while he spoke) to connote the human race?

Half humorously, half seriously, he once compared the Greeks and the English. The two peoples are almost exactly alike, he argued: quick-witted, resourceful, adventurous. 'But there is one unfortunate difference between us, one little difference. We Greeks have lost our capital – and the results are what you see. Pray, my dear Forster, oh pray, that you never lose your capital.'

That was in 1918. British insolvency seemed impossible then. In 1951, when all things are possible, his words make one think – words of a very wise, very civilized man, words of a poet who has caught hold of something that cannot be taken away from him by bankruptcy, or even by death.

27

Virginia Woolf: Ernest Hemingway

A number of Bloomsbury essays and reviews were written for American magazines and newspapers. Virginia Woolf's review of Ernest Hemingway's short stories Men Without Women *was entitled 'An Essay in Criticism' when it appeared as the front page review of the* New York Herald Tribune's *Sunday book section on 9 October 1927. The criticism of Hemingway's modernism resembles in some ways Woolf's dissatisfaction with Edwardian fiction in 'Mr Bennett and Mrs Brown' (p. 233). This was the only review of Hemingway Virginia Woolf wrote. Hemingway found it and the Bloomsbury Group 'damned irritating'.*

Human credulity is indeed wonderful. There may be good reasons for believing in a King or a Judge or a Lord Mayor. When we see them go sweeping by in their robes and their wigs, with their heralds and their outriders, our knees begin to shake and our looks to falter. But what reason there is for believing in critics it is impossible to say. They have neither wigs nor outriders. They differ in no way from other people if one sees them in the flesh. Yet these insignificant fellow creatures have only to shut themselves up in a room, dip a pen in the ink, and call themselves 'we', for the rest of us to believe that they are somehow exalted, inspired, infallible. Wigs grow on their heads. Robes cover their limbs. No greater miracle was ever performed by the power of human credulity. And, like most miracles, this one, too, has had a weakening effect upon the mind of the believer. He begins to think that critics, because they call themselves so, must be right. He begins to suppose that something actually happens to a book when it has been praised or denounced in print. He begins to doubt and conceal his own sensitive, hesitating apprehensions when they conflict with the critics' decrees.

And yet, barring the learned (and learning is chiefly useful in judging the work of the dead), the critic is rather more fallible than the rest of us. He has to give us his opinion of a book that has been published two days, perhaps, with the shell still sticking to its head. He has to get outside that cloud of fertile, but unrealized, sensation which hangs about a reader, to solidify it, to sum it up. The chances are that he does this before the time is ripe; he does it too rapidly and too definitely. He says that it is a great book or a bad book. Yet, as he knows, when he is content to read only, it is neither. He is driven by force of circumstances and some human vanity to hide those hesitations which beset him as he reads, to smooth out all traces of that crab-like and crooked path by which he has reached what he choses to call 'a conclusion'. So the crude trumpet blasts of critical opinion blow loud and shrill, and we, humble readers that we are, bow our submissive heads.

But let us see whether we can do away with these pretences for a season and pull down the imposing curtain which hides the critical process until it is complete. Let us give the mind a new book, as one drops a lump of fish into a cage of fringed and eager sea anemones, and watch it pausing, pondering, considering its attack. Let us see what prejudices affect it; what influences tell upon it. And if the conclusion becomes in the process a little less conclusive, it may, for that very reason, approach nearer to the truth. The first thing that the mind desires is some foothold of fact upon which it can lodge before it takes flight upon its speculative career. Vague rumours attach themselves to people's names. Of Mr Hemingway, we know that he is an American living in France, an 'advanced' writer, we suspect, connected with what is called a movement, though which of the many we own that we do not know. It will be well to make a little more certain of these matters by reading first Mr Hemingway's earlier book, *The Sun Also Rises*, and it soon becomes clear from this that, if Mr Hemingway is 'advanced', it is not in the way that is to us most interesting. A prejudice of which the reader would do well to take account is here exposed; the critic is a modernist. Yes, the excuse would be because the moderns make us aware of what we feel subconsciously; they are truer to our own experience; they even anticipate it, and this gives us a particular excitement. But nothing new is revealed about any of the characters in *The Sun Also Rises*. They come before us shaped, proportioned, weighed, exactly as the characters of Maupassant are shaped and proportioned. They are seen from the old angle; the old reticences, the old relations between author and character are observed.

But the critic has the grace to reflect that this demand for new aspects and new perspectives may well be overdone. It may become whimsical. It may become foolish. For why should not art be traditional as well as original? Are we not attaching too much importance to an excitement which, though agreeable, may not be valuable in itself, so that we are led to make the fatal mistake of overriding the writer's gift?

At any rate, Mr Hemingway is not modern in the sense given; and it would appear from his first novel that this rumour of modernity must have sprung from his subject matter and from his treatment of it rather than from any fundamental novelty in his conception of the art of fiction. It is a bare, abrupt, outspoken book. Life as people live it in Paris in 1927 or even in 1928 is described as we of this age do describe life (it is here that we steal a march upon the Victorians) openly, frankly, without prudery, but also without surprise. The immoralities and moralities of Paris are described as we are apt to hear them spoken of in private life. Such candour is modern and it is admirable. Then, for qualities grow together in art as in life, we find attached to this admirable frankness an equal bareness of style. Nobody speaks for more than a line or two. Half a line is mostly sufficient. If a hill or a town is described (and there is always some reason for its description) there it is, exactly and literally built up of little facts, literal enough, but chosen, as the final sharpness of the outline proves, with the utmost care. Therefore, a few words like these: 'The grain was just beginning to ripen and the fields were full of poppies. The pasture land was green and there were fine trees, and sometimes big rivers and chateaux off in the trees' – which have a curious force. Each word pulls its weight in the sentence. And the prevailing atmosphere is fine and sharp, like that of winter days when the boughs are bare against the sky. (But if we had to choose one sentence with which to describe what Mr Hemingway attempts and sometimes achieves, we should quote a passage from a description of a bullfight: 'Romero never made any contortions, always it was straight and pure and natural in line. The others twisted themselves like corkscrews, their elbows raised and leaned against the flanks of the bull after his horns had passed, to give a faked look of danger. Afterwards, all that was faked turned bad and gave an unpleasant feeling. Romero's bullfighting gave real emotion, because he kept the absolute purity of line in his movements and always quietly and calmly let the horns pass him close each time.') Mr Hemingway's writing, one might paraphrase, gives us now and then a real emotion, because he keeps absolute purity of line in his movements and lets the horns (which are truth, fact, reality) pass him close each time. But there is something faked, too, which turns bad and gives an unpleasant feeling – that also we must face in course of time.

And here, indeed, we may conveniently pause and sum up what point we have reached in our critical progress. Mr Hemingway is not an advanced writer in the sense that he is looking at life from a new angle. What he sees is a tolerably familiar sight. Common objects like beer bottles and journalists figure largely in the foreground. But he is a skilled and conscientious writer. He has an aim and makes for it without fear or circumlocution. We have, therefore, to take his measure against some-body of substance, and not merely line him, for form's sake, beside the indistinct bulk of some ephemeral shape largely stuffed with straw. Reluctantly we reach this decision, for this process of measurement is one of the most difficult of a critic's tasks. He has to decide which are the most salient points of the book he has just read; to distinguish accurately to what kind they belong, and then, holding them against whatever model is chosen for comparison, to bring out their deficiency or their adequacy.

Recalling *The Sun Also Rises*, certain scenes rise in memory: the bullfight, the character of the Englishman, Harris; here a little landscape which seems to grow behind the people naturally; here a long, lean phrase which goes curling round a situation like the lash of a whip. Now and again this phrase evokes a character brilliantly, more often a scene. Of character, there is little that remains firmly and solidly elucidated. Something indeed seems wrong with the people. If we place them (the comparison is bad) against Tchekov's people, they are flat as cardboard. If we place them (the comparison is better) against Maupassant's people they are crude as a photograph. If we place them (the comparison may be illegitimate) against real people, the people we liken them to are of an unreal type. They are people one may have seen showing off at some café; talking a rapid, high-pitched slang, because slang is the speech of the herd, seemingly much at their ease, and yet if we look at them a little from the shadow not at their ease at all, and, indeed, terribly afraid of being themselves, or they would say things simply in their natural voices. So it would seem that the thing that is faked is character; Mr Hemingway leans against the flanks of that particular bull after the horns have passed.

After this preliminary study of Mr Hemingway's first book, we come to the new book, *Men Without Women*, possessed of certain views or prejudices. His talent plainly may develop along different lines. It may broaden and fill out; it may take a little more time and go into things – human beings in particular – rather more deeply. And even if this meant the sacrifice of some energy and point, the exchange would be to our private liking. On the other hand, his is a talent which may contract and harden still further! it may come to depend more and more upon the emphatic moment; make more and more use of dialogue, and cast narrative and description overboard as an encumbrance.

The fact that *Men Without Women* consists of short stories, makes it probable that Mr Hemingway has taken the second line. But, before we explore the new book, a word should be said which is generally left unsaid, about the implications of the title. As the publisher puts it . . . 'the softening feminine influence is absent – either through training, discipline, death, or situation.' Whether we are to understand by this that women are incapable of training, discipline, death, or situation, we do not know. But it is undoubtedly true, if we are going to persevere in our attempt to reveal the processes of the critic's mind, that any emphasis laid upon sex is dangerous. Tell a man that this is a woman's book, or a woman that this is a man's, and you have brought into play sympathies and antipathies which have nothing to do with art. The greatest writers lay no stress upon sex one way or the other. The critic is not reminded as he reads them that he belongs to the masculine or the feminine gender. But in our time, thanks to our sexual perturbations, sex consciousness is strong, and shows itself in literature by an exaggeration, a protest of sexual characteristics which in either case is disagreeable. Thus Mr Lawrence, Mr Douglas, and Mr Joyce partly spoil their books for women readers by their display of self-conscious virility; and Mr Hemingway, but much less violently, follows suit. All we can do, whether we are men or women, is to admit the influence, look the fact in the face, and so hope to stare it out of countenance.

To proceed then – *Men Without Women* consists of short stories in the French rather than in the Russian manner. The great French masters, Mérimée and Maupassant, made their stories as self-conscious and compact as possible. There is never a thread left hanging; indeed, so contracted are they that when the last sentence of the last page flares up, as it so often does, we see by its light the whole circumference and significance of the story revealed. The Tchekov method is, of course, the very opposite of this. Everything is cloudy and vague, loosely trailing rather than tightly furled. The stories move slowly out of sight like clouds in the summer air, leaving a wake of meaning in our minds which gradually fades away. Of the two methods, who shall say which is the better? At any rate, Mr Hemingway, enlisting under the French masters, carries out their teaching up to a point with considerable success.

There are in *Men Without Women* many stories which, if life were longer, one would wish to read again. Most of them indeed are so competent, so efficient, and so bare of superfluity that one wonders why they do not make a deeper dent in the mind than they do. Take the pathetic story of the Major whose wife died – 'In Another Country'; or the sardonic story of a conversation in a railway carriage – 'A Canary for One'; or stories like 'The Undefeated' and 'Fifty Grand' which are full of the sordidness and heroism of bullfighting and boxing – all of these are good trenchant stories, quick, terse, and strong. If one had not summoned the ghosts of Tchekov, Mérimée, and Maupassant, no doubt one would be enthusiastic. As it is, one looks about for something, fails to find something, and so is brought again to the old familiar business of ringing impressions on the counter, and asking what is wrong?

For some reason the book of short stories does not seem to us to go as deep or to promise as much as the novel. Perhaps it is the excessive use of dialogue, for Mr Hemingway's use of it is surely excessive. A writer will always be chary of dialogue because dialogue puts the most violent pressure upon the reader's attention. He has to hear, to see, to supply the right tone, and to fill in the background from what the characters say without any help from the author. Therefore, when fictitious people are allowed to speak it must be because they have something so important to say that it stimulates the reader to do rather more than his share of the work of creation. But, although Mr Hemingway keeps us under the fire of dialogue constantly, his people, half the time, are saying what the author could say much more economically for them. At last we are inclined to cry out with the little girl in 'Hills Like White Elephants': 'Would you please please please please please please please stop talking?'

And probably it is this superfluity of dialogue which leads to that other fault which is always lying in wait for the writer of short stories: the lack of proportion. A paragraph in excess will make these little craft lopsided and will bring about that blurred effect which, when one is out for clarity and point, so baffles the reader. And both these faults, the tendency to flood the page with unnecessary dialogue and the lack of sharp, unmistakable points by which we can take hold of the story, come from the more fundamental fact that, though Mr Hemingway is brilliantly and enormously skilful, he lets his dexterity, like the bullfighter's cloak, get between him and the fact. For in truth story-writing has much in common with bullfighting. One may twist one's self like a corkscrew and go through every sort of contortion so that the public thinks one is running every risk and displaying superb gallantry. But the true writer stands close up to the bull and lets the horns – call them life, truth, reality, whatever you like – pass him close each time.

Mr Hemingway, then, is courageous; he is candid; he is highly skilled; he plants words precisely where he wishes; he has moments of bare and nervous beauty; he is modern in manner but not in vision; he is self-consciously virile; his talent has contracted rather than expanded; compared with his novel his stories are a little dry and sterile. So we sum him up. So we reveal some of the prejudices, the instincts and the fallacies out of which what it pleases us to call criticism is made.

Part VI

Polemics

A number of Bloomsbury's full-length works could be classified as polemics: Clive Bell's *Art*, Lytton Strachey's *Eminent Victorians*, John Maynard Keynes's *The Economic Consequences of the Peace*, Leonard Woolf's *Quack, Quack!*, Virginia Woolf's *Three Guineas*. The genre is a very eclectic one in Bloomsbury's writings. Shorter Bloomsbury polemics represented here have to do with literary, social, and art criticism as well as biography and politics.

28

Lytton Strachey: Matthew Arnold

Lytton Strachey's debunking of Matthew Arnold was written for the
New Statesman *on 1 August 1914, just before the beginning of the First
World War. It was originally entitled 'A Victorian Critic'. Nothing
Strachey wrote so clearly reveals the assumptions behind* Eminent
Victorians, *which he was about to begin writing. Noteworthy, for
example, is the implication that the wrong kind of Victorians became
eminent. Not all Bloomsbury agreed with Strachey's judgement. Virginia
Woolf called Arnold a great critic in* The Common Reader. *As for her
response to the criticism of her father Leslie Stephen, Woolf once wrote
to Strachey that she attached more importance to the man than to
his books.*

To the cold and youthful observer there is a strange fascination about
the Age of Victoria. It has the odd attractiveness of something which is
at once very near and very far off; it is like one of those queer fishes that
one sees behind glass at an aquarium, before whose grotesque proportions and sombre menacing agilities one hardly knows whether to laugh
or to shudder; when once it has caught one's eye, one cannot tear oneself
away. Probably its reputation will always be worse than it deserves.
Reputations, in the case of ages no less than of individuals, depend, in the
long run, upon the judgements of artists; and artists will never be fair to
the Victorian Age. To them its incoherence, its pretentiousness, and its
incurable lack of detachment will always outweigh its genuine qualities
of solidity and force. They will laugh and they will shudder, and the

world will follow suit. The Age of Victoria was, somehow or other, unaesthetic to its marrow-bones; and so we may be sure it will never loom through history with the glamour that hangs about the Age of Pericles or the brilliance that sparkles round the eighteenth century. But if men of science and men of action were not inarticulate, we should hear a different story.

The case of Matthew Arnold is a case in point. And who has not heard of Matthew Arnold? Certainly, out of every hundred who have, you would not find more than forty who could tell you anything of his contemporary, Lyell, for instance, who revolutionized geology, or more than twenty who would attach any meaning whatever to the name of another of his contemporaries, Dalhousie, who laid the foundations of modern India. Yet, compared to the work of such men as these, how feeble, how insignificant was Matthew Arnold's achievement! But he was a literary man; he wrote poetry, and he wrote essays discussing other poets and dabbling in general reflections. And so his fame has gone out to the ends of the earth, and now the Clarendon Press have done him the honour of bringing out a cheap collection of his essays,[1] so that even the working-man may read him and find out the heights that could be reached, in the way of criticism, during the golden years of the 'sixties. Surely, before it is too late, a club should be started – an Old Victorian Club – the business of whose members would be to protect the reputation of their Age and give it a fair chance with the public. Perhaps such a club exists already – in some quiet corner of Pimlico; but if so, it has sadly neglected one of its most pressing duties – the hushing-up of Matthew Arnold.

For here in this collection of essays there lies revealed what was really the essential and fatal weakness of the Victorian Age – its incapability of criticism. If we look at its criticism of literature alone, was there ever a time when the critic's functions were more grievously and shamelessly mishandled? When Dryden or Johnson wrote of literature, they wrote of it as an art; but the Victorian critic had a different notion of his business. To him literature was always an excuse for talking about something else. From Macaulay, who used it as a convenient peg for historical and moral disquisitions, to Leslie Stephen, who frankly despised the whole business, this singular tradition holds good. In what other age would it have been possible for a literary critic to begin an essay on Donne, as Leslie Stephen once did, with the cool observation that, as he was not interested in Donne's poetry, he would merely discuss his biography? An historian

---

[1] *Essays by Matthew Arnold.* Oxford University Press.

might as well preface an account of Columbus with the remark that, as he was not interested in Columbus's geographical discoveries, he would say nothing about that part of his career. It was their ineradicable Victorian instinct for action and utility which drove these unfortunate writers into so strangely self-contradictory a position. 'No one in his senses', they always seem to be saying, 'would discuss anything so impalpable and frivolous as a work of art; and yet it is our painful duty to do so; therefore we shall tell you all we can about the moral lessons we can draw from it, and the period at which it was produced, and the curious adventures of the man who produced it; and so, as you must admit, we shall have done our duty like the Englishmen that we are.'

This was not quite Matthew Arnold's way; he went about his business with more subtlety. He was a man, so he keeps assuring us, of a refined and even fastidious taste; it was his mission to correct and enlighten the barbarism of his age; he introduced the term 'philistine' into England, and laughed at Lord Macaulay. Yet it is curious to observe the flagrant ineptitudes of judgement committed by a writer of his pretensions directly he leaves the broad flat road of traditional appreciation. On that road he is safe enough. He has an unbounded admiration for Shakespeare, Dante, and Sophocles; he considers Virgil a very fine writer, though marred by melancholy; and he has no doubt that Milton was a master of the grand style. But when he begins to wander on to footpaths of his own, how extraordinary are his discoveries! He tells us that Molière was one of the five or six supreme *poets* of the world; that Shelley will be remembered for his essays and letters rather than for his poetry; that Byron was a greater poet than Coleridge or Shelley or Keats; that the French alexandrine is an inefficient poetical instrument; that Heine was an 'incomparably more important figure' in European poetry than Victor Hugo. As to his taste, a remarkable instance of it occurs in his Lectures on translating Homer. Describing the Trojan encampments by night on the plains of Troy, with their blazing watch-fires as numerous as the stars, Homer concludes with one of those astonishingly simple touches which, for some inexplicable reason, seem to evoke an immediate vision of thrilling and magical romance: 'A thousand fires were kindled in the plain; and by each one there sat fifty men in the light of the blazing fire. And the horses, munching white barley and rye, and standing by the chariots, waited for the bright-throned Morning.' Such was Homer's conception – it was the horses who were waiting for the morning. But Matthew Arnold will not have it so. 'I want to show you,' he says, 'that it is possible in a plain passage of this sort to keep Homer's simplicity without being heavy and dull'; and accordingly he renders the passage thus:

By their chariots stood the steeds, and champ'd the white barley,
While their masters sate by the fire and waited for Morning.

'I prefer', he explains, 'to attribute this expectation of Morning to the master and not to the horse.' *I prefer!* Surely, if ever the word 'philistine' were applicable, this is the occasion for it. And, indeed, Arnold himself seems to have felt a twinge of conscience. 'Very likely,' he adds, with a charming ingenuousness, 'in this particular, as in any other particular, I may be wrong.'

One of the surest signs of a man's taste being shaky is his trying to prop it up by artificial supports. Matthew Arnold was always doing this. He had a craving for Academies. He thought that if we could only have a Literary Academy in England we should all be able to tell what was good and what was bad without any difficulty; for, of course, the Academy would tell us. He had a profound reverence for the French Academy – a body which has consistently ignored every manifestation of original genius; and no doubt the annual exhibitions of the Royal Academy gave him exquisite satisfaction. He even had dreams of a vast international Academy; carried away by the vision, he seemed almost to imagine that it was already in existence. 'To be recognised by the verdict of such a confederation', he exclaims, 'is indeed glory; a glory which it would be difficult to rate too highly. For what could be more beneficent, more salutary? The world is forwarded by having its attention fixed on the best things; and here is a tribunal, free from all suspicion of national and provincial partiality, putting a stamp on the best things, and recommending them for general honour and acceptance.' But, failing this, failing the impartial tribunal which shall put 'a stamp on the best things', one can fall back upon other devices. If one is in doubt as to the merit of a writer, the best course one can take is to make him, so to speak, run the gauntlet of 'the great masters'. We must 'lodge well in our minds' lines and expressions of the great masters – 'short passages, even single lines will serve our turn quite sufficiently' – and these we shall find 'an infallible touchstone' for testing the value of all other poetry. The plan is delightfully simple; there is, indeed, only one small difficulty about it: it cannot come into operation until we have decided the very question which it is intended to solve – namely, who 'the great masters' are.

'The world is forwarded by having its attention fixed on the best things.' Yes; *the world is forwarded*. Here, plainly enough, is the tip of the Victorian ear peeping forth from under the hide of the aesthetic lion; the phrase might have come straight from Mr Roebuck or the *Daily Telegraph* – those perpetual targets for Matthew Arnold's raillery. But when he proceeds to suggest yet another test for literature, when he asserts that, in order to decide upon the value of any piece of writing, what we must do is to ask ourselves whether or not it is a 'Criticism of Life' – then, indeed, all concealment is over; the whole head of the animal is out. There is something pathetic about the eager persistence with which Matthew Arnold enunciates this doctrine. How pleased with himself he must have been when he thought of it! How beautifully it fitted in with all his needs! How wonderfully it smoothed away all the difficulties of his situation! For, of course, he was nothing if not a critic, a man whose nature it was to look at literature from the detached and disinterested standpoint of a refined – a fastidious – aesthetic appreciation; and yet ... and yet ... well, after all (but please don't say so), how *could* anyone, at this time of day, in the 'sixties, be expected to take literature seriously, on its own merits, as if it were a thing to be talked about for its own sake? The contradiction was obvious, and it was reconciled by that ingenious godsend, the theory of the Criticism of Life. By means of that theory it became possible to serve God and Mammon at the same time. Life, as everyone knew, was the one serious affair in the world – active, useful life; but then literature, it turned out – or rather, all literature that was worth anything – was a criticism of life; and so, after all, Matthew Arnold was justified in writing about it, and the public were justified in reading what Matthew Arnold wrote, for they were not merely reading about literature – who would do that? – they were reading about the Criticism of Life. And it is singular to see the shifts to which Matthew Arnold was put in order to carry out this theory consistently. He had somehow to bring all 'the great masters' into line with it. Shakespeare was easy enough, for he will fit into any theory; and Sophocles, of course, saw life steadily and saw it whole; but Dante and Milton – a queer kind of criticism of life they give us, surely! But they were so elevated, so extremely elevated, that they would pass; as for Sappho and Catullus, it was convenient not to mention them. Of course Matthew Arnold was careful to give no very exact explanation of his famous phrase, and one is always being puzzled by his use of it. Pope, one would have thought, with those palpitating psychological portraits of his, in which are concentrated the experience and passion of one of the sharpest and most sensitive observers who ever lived – Pope might well be considered a critic of life; but for some reason or other Pope would not do. Byron, on the other hand – not the Byron of *Don Juan*, but the Byron of *Childe Harold* and *Manfred* – did very well indeed. But we must remember that Byron was still fashionable in the 'sixties, and that Pope was not.

Certainly it is a curious and instructive case, that of Matthew Arnold: all the more so since no one could suppose that he was a stupid man. On the contrary, his intelligence was above the average, and he could write lucidly, and he got up his subjects with considerable care. Unfortunately, he mistook his vocation. He might, no doubt, if he had chosen, have done some excellent and lasting work upon the movements of glaciers or the fertilization of plants, or have been quite a satisfactory collector in an up-country district in India. But no; he *would* be a critic.

29

John Maynard Keynes:
Mr Lloyd George

John Maynard Keynes's picture of Lloyd George (1863–1945) was subtitled 'A Fragment' when published finally in Essays in Biography *(1933). It followed there an account of the Council of Four that established the Versailles Treaty at the end of the First World War. In a footnote Keynes explains his fragment's relation to* The Economic Consequences of the Peace – *his famous polemic against the treaty that had been drawn up by President Woodrow Wilson, Premier Georges Clemenceau (known as 'The Tiger') and Prime Minister Lloyd George. Among the issues referred to are Wilson's Fourteen Points for peace and the question of what indemnity Germany should pay. Lloyd George, for his part, later described Keynes as a 'volatile soothsayer' dashing at conclusions 'with acrobatic ease'.*

I should prefer to end this chapter here.[1] But the reader may ask, What part in the result did the British Prime Minister play? What share had England in the final responsibility? The answer to the second question is

---

[1] I wrote the preceding description of the Council of Four in the summer of 1919 immediately after my resignation as Treasury representative at the Peace Conference. Friends, to whom I showed it for criticism, pressed me to add a further passage concerning Mr Lloyd George, and in an attempt to satisfy them I wrote what here follows. But I was not content with it, and I did not print it in *The Economic Consequences of the Peace*, where the chapter on 'The Conference' appeared as it was originally written with no addendum. I was also influenced by a certain compunction. I had been very close to Mr

not clear-cut. And as to the first, who shall paint the chameleon, who can tether a broomstick? The character of Lloyd George is not yet rendered, and I do not aspire to the task.

The selfish, or, if you like, the legitimate interests of England did not, as it happened, conflict with the Fourteen Points as vitally as did those of France. The destruction of the fleet, the expropriation of the marine, the surrender of the colonies, the suzerainty of Mesopotamia – there was not much here for the President to strain at, even in the light of his professions, especially as England, whose diplomatic moderation as always was not hampered by the logical intransigency of the French mind, was ready to concede in point of form whatever might be asked. England did not desire the German fleet for herself, and its destruction was a phase of disarmament. The expropriation of the marine was a legitimate compensation, specifically provided for in the pre-Armistice conditions, for the lawless campaign of submarines which had been the express occasion of America's entering the war. Over the colonies and Mesopotamia England demanded no exclusive sovereignty, and they were covered by the Doctrine of Mandates under the League of Nations.

Thus when the British Delegation left for Paris there seemed no insuperable obstacles to an almost complete understanding between the British and the American negotiators. There were only two clouds on the horizon – the so-called freedom of the seas and the Prime Minister's election pledges on the indemnity. The first, to the general surprise, was never raised by the President, a silence which, presumably, was the price he deemed it judicious to pay for British co-operation on other more vital issues; the second was more important.

The co-operation, which was thus rendered possible, was largely realized in practice. The individual members of the British and American delegations were united by bonds of fraternal feeling and mutual respect, and constantly worked together and stood together for a policy of honest

---

Lloyd George at certain phases of the Conference, and I felt at bottom that this, like almost everything else that one could say about him, was only partial. I did not like to print in the heat of the moment what seemed to me, even in the heat of the moment, to be incomplete.

I feel some compunction still. But nearly fourteen years have passed by. These matters belong now to history. It is easier to explain than it was then, that this is an aspect, a thing seen but not the whole picture and to offer it as a record of how one, who saw the process at close quarters, sincerely felt at the time.

dealing and broad-minded humanity. And the Prime Minister, too, soon established himself as the President's friend and powerful ally against the Latins' alleged rapacity or lack of international idealism. Why then did not the joint forces of these two powerful and enlightened autocrats give us the Good Peace?

The answer is to be sought more in those intimate workings of the heart and character which make the tragedies and comedies of the domestic hearthrug than in the supposed ambitions of empires or philosophies of statesmen. The President, the Tiger, and the Welsh witch were shut up in a room together for six months and the Treaty was what came out. Yes, the Welsh *witch* – for the British Prime Minister contributed the female element to this triangular intrigue. I have called Mr Wilson a non-conformist clergyman. Let the reader figure Mr Lloyd George as a *femme fatale*. An old man of the world, a *femme fatale*, and a non-conformist clergyman – these are the characters of our drama. Even though the lady was very religious at times, the Fourteen Commandments could hardly expect to emerge perfectly intact.

I must try to silhouette the broomstick as it sped through the twilit air of Paris.

Mr Lloyd George's devotion to duty at the Paris Conference was an example to all servants of the public. He took no relaxation, enjoyed no pleasures, had no life and no occupation save that of Prime Minister and England's spokesman. His labours were immense and he spent his vast stores of spirit and of energy without stint on the formidable task he had put his hand to. His advocacy of the League of Nations was sincere; his support of a fair application of the principle of self-determination to Germany's eastern frontiers was disinterested. He had no wish to impose a Carthaginian Peace; the crushing of Germany was no part of his purpose. His hatred of war is real, and the strain of pacifism and radical idealism, which governed him during the Boer War, is a genuine part of his composition. He would have defended a Good Peace before the House of Commons with more heart than he did that which he actually brought back to them.

But in such a test of character and method as Paris provided, the Prime Minister's naturally good instincts, his industry, his inexhaustible nervous vitality were not serviceable. In that furnace other qualities were called for – a policy deeply grounded in permanent principle, tenacity, fierce indignation, honesty, loyal leadership. If Mr Lloyd George had no good qualities, no charms, no fascinations, he would not be dangerous. If he were not a syren, we need not fear the whirlpools.

But it is not appropriate to apply to him the ordinary standards. How can I convey to the reader, who does not know him, any just impression of this extraordinary figure of our time, this syren, this goat-footed bard, this half-human visitor to our age from the hag-ridden magic and enchanted woods of Celtic antiquity? One catches in his company that flavour of final purposelessness, inner irresponsibility, existence outside or away from our Saxon good and evil, mixed with cunning, remorselessness, love of power, that lend fascination, enthralment, and terror to the fair-seeming magicians of North European folklore. Prince Wilson sailing out from the West in his barque *George Washington* sets foot in the enchanted castle of Paris to free from chains and oppression and an ancient curse the maid Europe, of eternal youth and beauty, his mother and his bride in one. There in the castle is the King with yellow parchment face, a million years old, and with him an enchantress with a harp singing the Prince's own words to a magical tune. If only the Prince could cast off the paralysis which creeps on him and, crying to heaven, could make the Sign of the Cross, with a sound of thunder and crashing glass the castle would dissolve, the magicians vanish, and Europe leap to his arms. But in this fairy-tale the forces of the half-world win and the soul of Man is subordinated to the spirits of the earth.

Lloyd George is rooted in nothing; he is void and without content; he lives and feeds on his immediate surroundings; he is an instrument and a player at the same time which plays on the company and is played on by them too; he is a prism, as I have heard him described, which collects light and distorts it and is most brilliant if the light comes from many quarters at once; a vampire and a medium in one.

Whether by chance or by design, the principal British war aims (with the exception of the Indemnity, if this was one of them) were dealt with in the earliest stages of the Conference. Clemenceau was criticized at the time for his tardiness in securing the primary demands of France. But events proved him to be right in not forcing the pace. The French demands, as I have pointed out, were much more controversial than those of the British; and it was essential to get the British well embroiled in a Peace of selfish interests before putting the professions of the Conference to a severer test. The British demands afforded an excellent *hors-d'oeuvre* to accustom the delicate palate of the President to the stronger flavours which were to come. This order of procedure laid the British Prime Minister open to the charge, whenever he seemed too critical of French demands, that, having first secured every conceivable thing that he wanted himself, he was now ready with characteristic treachery to abandon his undertakings to his French comrades. In the atmosphere of Paris this seemed a much more potent taunt than it really was. But it gained its real strength, in its influence on the Prime Minister, from three special attendant circumstances. In two respects the Prime Minister found himself unavoidably and inextricably on Clemenceau's side – in the matters of the Indemnity and of the Secret Treaties. If the President's morale was maintained intact, Mr Lloyd George could not hope to get his way on these issues; he was, therefore, almost equally interested with Clemenceau in gradually breaking down this morale. But, besides, he had Lord Northcliffe and the British Jingoes on his heels, and complaints in the French press were certain to find their echo in a certain section of the British also.

If, therefore, he were to take his stand firmly and effectively on the side of the President, there was needed an act of courage and faith which could only be based on fundamental beliefs and principles. But Mr Lloyd George has none such, and political considerations pointed to a middle path.

Precisely, therefore, as the President had found himself pushed along the path of compromise, so also did the Prime Minister, though for very different reasons. But while the President failed because he was very bad at the game of compromise, the Prime Minister trod the way of ill-doing because he was far too good at it.

The reader will thus apprehend how Mr Lloyd George came to occupy an ostensibly middle position, and how it became his role to explain the President to Clemenceau and Clemenceau to the President and to seduce everybody all round. He was only too well fitted for the task, but much better fitted for dealing with the President than with Clemenceau. Clemenceau was much too cynical, much too experienced, and much too well educated to be taken in, at his age, by the fascinations of the lady from Wales. But for the President it was a wonderful, almost delightful, experience to be taken in hand by such an expert. Mr Lloyd George had soon established himself as the President's only real friend. The President's very masculine characteristics fell a complete victim to the feminine enticements, sharpness, quickness, sympathy of the Prime Minister.

We have Mr Lloyd George, therefore, in his middle position, but exercising more sway over the President than over Clemenceau. Now let the reader's mind recur to the metaphors. Let him remember the Prime Minister's incurable love of a deal; his readiness to surrender the substance for the shadow; his intense desire, as the months dragged on, to get a conclusion and be back to England again. What wonder that in the eventual settlement the real victor was Clemenceau.

Even so, close observers never regarded it as impossible right up to the conclusion of the affair that the Prime Minister's better instincts and truer judgement might yet prevail – he knew in his heart that this Peace would disgrace him and that it might ruin Europe. But he had dug a pit for himself deeper than even he could leap out of; he was caught in his own toils, defeated by his own methods. Besides, it is a characteristic of his inner being, of his kinship with the trolls and soulless simulacra of the earth, that at the great crises of his fortunes it is the lower instincts of the hour that conquer.

These were the personalities of Paris – I forbear to mention other nations or lesser men: Clemenceau, aesthetically the noblest; the President, morally the most admirable; Lloyd George, intellectually the subtlest. Out of their disparities and weaknesses the Treaty was born, child of the least worthy attributes of each of its parents, without nobility, without morality, without intellect.

30

Clive Bell: Wilcoxism

Clive Bell's use of the American poetaster Ella Wheeler Wilcox (1850–1919) to deflate the praise given to a Royal Academy exhibition of modern British art by the Athenaeum *in February 1920 was first published in the* Athenaeum *as well as the* New Republic *in March and then revised for his book* Since Cézanne *(1922). (The month before, Bell had also reviewed a one-man show of Duncan Grant's for the* Athenaeum *and stressed his English artistry.) Wyndham Lewis, who had been quarrelling with Bloomsbury since Omega Workshop days, accepted Bell's provocation and wrote to the* Athenaeum *attacking the dishonesty and effrontery of his provincial attitude towards Parisian art. Bell's reply began 'I should be sorry to quarrel with Mr Wyndham Lewis about anything so insignificant as my character or his art . . .'*

To return from Paris, full of enthusiasm for contemporary art, and find oneself forced immediately into an attitude of querulous hostility is surely a melancholy thing. It is my fate; but it is not my fault. Had I found our native quidnuncs in a slightly less exalted humour, had they gushed a little less over their imperial painters at Burlington House, had they made the least effort to preserve a sense of proportion, I, for my part, had held my peace. But, deafened by the chorus of hearty self-applause with which British art has just been regaling itself, a critic who hopes that his country is not once again going to make itself the laughing-stock of Europe is bound at all risks to say something disagreeable.

In that delightful book *The Worlds and I*, for bringing me acquainted
with which I shall ever be grateful to *The Athenaeum*, nothing is more
delightful than the chapter in which Mrs Wilcox takes us through the list
of the great writers she has known. We are almost as much pleased by the
authoress's confident expectation that we shall be thrilled to learn any
new fact about Miss Aldrich, who wrote 'one of the most exquisite lyrics
in the language'; about Rhoda Hero Dunn, 'a genius' with 'an almost
Shakespearean quality in her verse', or about Elsa Barker, whose poem
'The Frozen Grail', 'dedicated to Peary and his band, is an epic of august
beauty', and whose sonnet 'When I am Dead' 'ranks with the great
sonnets of the world', as she would be surprised to discover that we had
never heard of one of them. Mrs Wilcox believed, in perfect good faith,
that the crowd of magazine-makers with whom she associated were, in
fact, the great figures of the age. She had no reason for supposing that we
should not be as much interested in first-hand personal gossip about
Zona Gale and Ridgeley Torrence, Arthur Grissom (first editor of the
Smart Set), Judge Malone, Theodosia Garrison, and Julie Opp
Faversham ('even to talk with whom over the telephone gives me a sense
of larger horizons') as we should have been in similar gossip about
Swinburne and Hardy, Henry James and Mallarmé, Laforgue, Anatole
France, Tolstoy, Tchekov, or Dostoevsky.

And, as Mrs Wilcox had no reason for supposing that her friends were
not the greatest writers alive, what reason had she for supposing that
they were not the greatest that ever lived? Without the taste, the intelligence, or the knowledge which alone can give some notion of what's
what in art, she was obliged to rely on more accessible criteria. The
circulation of her own works, for instance, must have compared favourably with that of most poets. To be sure there was Shakespeare and the
celebrated Hugo – or was it Gambetta? But what grounds could there
be for thinking that she was not superior to the obscure John Donne or
the obscurer Andrew Marvell, or to Arthur Rimbaud, of whom no one
she had ever heard of had ever heard? Mrs Wilcox was not dishonest in
assuming that the most successful writer in her set was the best in the
world; she was not conceited even; she was merely ridiculous.

It is disquieting to find the same sort of thing going on in England,
where our painters are fiercely disputing with each other the crown of
European painting, and our critics appraising the respective claims of Mr
Augustus John and Mr John Nash as solemnly as if they were comparing
Cézanne with Renoir. It is more than disquieting, it is alarming, to detect
symptoms of the disease – this distressing disease of Wilcoxism – in *The
Athenaeum* itself. Yet I am positive that not long since I read in this very
paper that Mr Wyndham Lewis was more than a match for Matisse and

Derain; and, having said so much, the critic not unnaturally went on to suggest that he was a match for Leonardo da Vinci. Since then I have trembled weekly lest the infection should have spread to our literary parts. Will it be asserted, one of these Fridays, that the appetizing novels of Mr Gilbert Cannan are distinctly better than Hardy's Wessex tales, and comparable rather with the works of Jane Austen?

To save ourselves from absurdity, and still more to save our painters from inspissating that trickle of fatuity which wells from heads swollen with hot air, critics should set themselves to check this nasty malady. Let them make it clear that to talk of modern English painting as though it were the rival of modern French is silly. In old racing days – how matters stand now I know not – it used to be held that French form was about seven pounds below English: the winner of the Derby, that is to say, could generally give the best French colt about that weight and a beating. In painting, English form is normally a stone below French. At any given moment the best painter in England is unlikely to be better than a first-rate man in the French second class. Whistler was never a match for Renoir, Degas, Seurat, and Manet; but Whistler, Steer, and Sickert may profitably be compared with Boudin, Jongkind, and Berthe Morisot. And though Duncan Grant holds his own handsomely with Marchand, Vlaminck, Lhote, de Segonzac, Bracque and Modigliani, I am not yet prepared to class him with Matisse, Picasso, Derain, and Bonnard.

Having bravely recognized this disagreeable truth, let us take as much interest in contemporary British painting as we can. I will try to believe that it merits more enthusiasm than I have been able to show, provided it is not made a point of patriotism to excite oneself about the Imperial War Museum's pictures exhibited at Burlington House. As a matter of fact, the most depressing thing about that show was the absence of the very quality for which British art has been most justly admired – I mean sensibility. Mr Wilson Steer's picture seemed to me the best in the place, just because Mr Steer has eyes with which, not only to see, but to feel. To see is something; Mr Steer also feels for what he sees; and this emotion is the point of departure for his pictures. That he seems almost completely to have lost such power as he ever had of giving to his vision a coherent and self-supporting form is unfortunate; still, he does convey to us some modicum of the thrill provoked in him by his vision of Dover Harbour.

Those thoughtful young men, on the other hand, whose works have been causing such a commotion might almost as well have been blind. They seem to have seen nothing; at any rate, they have not reacted to what they saw in that particular way in which visual artists react. They are not expressing what they feel for something that has moved them as artists, but, rather, what they think about something that has horrified them as men. Their pictures depart, not from a visual sensation, but from a moral conviction. So, naturally enough, what they produce is mere 'arty' anecdote. This, perhaps, is the secret of their success – their success, I mean, with the cultivated public. Those terrible young fellows who were feared to be artists turn out after all to be innocent Pre-Raphaelites. They leave Burlington House without a stain upon their characters.

This is plain speaking; how else should a critic, who believes that he has diagnosed the disease, convince a modern patient of his parlous state? To just hint a fault and hesitate dislike (not Pope, but I split that infinitive) is regarded nowadays merely as a sign of a base, compromising spirit; or not regarded at all. Artists, especially in England, cannot away with qualified praise or blame: and if they insist on all or nothing I can but offer them the latter. Nevertheless, I must assert, for my own satisfaction, that in many even of our most imperial artists, in the brothers Spencer and the brothers Nash, in Mr Lewis, Mr Roberts, Mr Bomberg, and Mr Lamb, I discover plenty of ability; only I cannot help fancying that they may have mistaken the nature of their gifts. Were they really born to be painters? I wonder. But of this I am sure: their friends merely make them look silly by comparing them with contemporary French masters, or even with Leonardo da Vinci.

Wilcoxism is a terrible disease because it slowly but surely eats away our sense of imperfection, our desire for improvement, and our power of self-criticism. Modesty and knowledge are the best antidotes; and a treatment much recommended by the faculty is to take more interest in art and less in one's own prestige. Above all, let us cultivate a sense of proportion. Let us admire, for instance, the admirable, though somewhat negative, qualities in the work of Mr Lewis – the absence of vulgarity and false sentiment, the sobriety of colour, the painstaking search for design – without forgetting that in the Salon d'Automne or the Salon des Indépendants a picture by him would neither merit nor obtain from the most generous critic more than a passing word of perfunctory encouragement; for in Paris there are perhaps five hundred men and women – drawn from the four quarters of the earth – all trying to do what Mr Lewis tries to do, and doing it better.

31

E. M. Forster: Me, Them and You

E. M. Forster's polemic on another Royal Academy exhibition, this time of John Singer Sargent's work, was published in the New Leader *in 1926 and then reprinted in* Abinger Harvest. *(When Virginia Woolf saw Sargent's 'Gassed' at Burlington House several years earlier, she thought the exhibition rooms 'rang like a parrot house with the intolerable vociferations of gaudy and brainless birds'.)*

I have a suit of clothes. It does not fit, but is of stylish cut. I can go anywhere in it and I have been to see the Sargent pictures at the Royal Academy. Underneath the suit was a shirt, beneath the shirt was a vest, and beneath the vest was Me. Me was not exposed much to the public gaze; two hands and a face showed that here was a human being; the rest was swathed in cotton or wool.

Yet Me was what mattered, for it was Me that was going to see Them. Them what? Them persons what governs us, them dukes and duchesses and archbishops and generals and captains of industry. They have had their likenesses done by this famous painter (artists are useful sometimes), and, for the sum of one and six, they were willing to be inspected. I had one and six, otherwise I should have remained in the snow outside. The coins changed hands. I entered the exhibition, and found myself almost immediately in the presence of a respectable family servant.

'Wretched weather,' I remarked civilly. There was no reply, the forehead swelled, the lips contracted haughtily. I had begun my tour with a very serious mistake, and had addressed a portrait of Lord Curzon. His face had misled me into thinking him a family servant. I ought to have looked only at the clothes, which were blue and blazing, and which he clutched with a blue-veined hand. They cost a hundred pounds perhaps. How cheap did my own costume seem now, and how impossible it was to imagine that Lord Curzon continues beneath his clothes, that he, too (if I may venture on the parallel), was a Me.

Murmuring in confusion, I left the radiant effigy and went into the next room. Here my attention was drawn by a young Oriental, subtle and charming and not quite sure of his ground. I complimented him in flowery words. He winced, he disclaimed all knowledge of the East. I had been speaking to Sir Phillip Sassoon. Here again I ought to have looked first at the clothes. They were slightly horsey and wholly English, and they put mine to shame. Why had he come from Tabriz, or wherever it was, and put them on? Why take the long journey from Samarcand for the purpose of denouncing our Socialists? Why not remain where he felt himself Me? But he resented analysis and I left him.

The third figure – to do her justice – felt that she was Me and no one else could be, and looked exactly what she was: namely, the wife of our Ambassador at Berlin. Erect she stood, with a small balustrade and a diplomatic landscape behind her. She was superbly beautiful and incredibly arrogant, and her pearls would have clothed not mere hundreds of human beings but many of her fellow-portraits on the walls. What beat in the heart – if there was a heart – I could not know, but I heard pretty distinctly the voice that proceeded from the bright red lips. It is not a voice that would promote calm in high places, not a voice to promote amity between two nations at a difficult moment in their intercourse. Her theme was precedence, and perhaps it is wiser to allow her to develop it in solitude.

And I drifted from Them to Them, fascinated by the hands and faces which peeped out of the costumes. Lord Roberts upheld with difficulty the rows of trinkets pinned on his uniform; Sir Thomas Sutherland was fat above a fat black tie; a riding costume supported the chinless cranium of a Duke; a Mr John Fife 'who showed conspicuous ability in the development of the granite industry' came from Aberdeen in black; and a Marquess actually did something: he was carrying the Sword of State on the occasion of King Edward's Coronation; while a page carried his train. Sometimes the painter saw through his sitters and was pleasantly mischievous at their expense; sometimes he seemed taken in by them – which happens naturally enough to a man who spends much time dangling after the rich. In spite of the charm of his work, and the lovely colours, and the gracious pictures of Venice, a pall of upholstery hung over the exhibition. The portraits dominated. Gazing at each other over our heads, they said, 'What would the country do without us? We have got the decorations and the pearls, we make fashions and wars, we have the largest houses and eat the best food, and control the most important industries, and breed the most valuable children, and ours is the Kingdom and the Power and the Glory.' And, listening to their chorus, I felt this was so, and my clothes fitted worse and worse, and there seemed in all the universe no gulf wider than the gulf between Them and Me – no wider gulf, until I encountered You.

You had been plentiful enough in the snow outside (your proper place), but I had not expected to find You here in the place of honour, too. Yours was by far the largest picture in the show. You were hung between Lady Cowdray and the Hon. Mrs Langman, and You were entitled 'Gassed'. You were of godlike beauty – for the upper classes only allow the lower classes to appear in art on condition that they wash themselves and have classical features. These conditions you fulfilled. A line of golden-haired Apollos moved along a duck-board from left to right with bandages over their eyes. They had been blinded by mustard gas. Others sat peacefully in the foreground, others approached through the middle distance. The battlefield was sad but tidy. No one complained, no one looked lousy or overtired, and the aeroplanes overhead struck the necessary note of the majesty of England. It was all that a great war picture should be, and it was modern because it managed to tell a new sort of lie. Many ladies and gentlemen fear that Romance is passing out of war with the sabres and the chargers. Sargent's masterpiece reassures them. He shows that it is possible to suffer with a quiet grace under the new conditions, and Lady Cowdray and the Hon. Mrs Langman, as they looked over the twenty feet of canvas that divided them, were still able to say, 'How touching,' instead of 'How obscene.'

Still, there You were, though in modified form, and in mockery of your real misery, and though the gulf between Them and Me was wide, still wider yawned the gulf between us and You. For what could we do without you? What would become of our incomes and activities if you declined to exist? You are the slush and dirt on which our civilization rests, which it treads under foot daily, which it sentimentalizes over now and then, in hours of danger. But you are not only a few selected youths in khaki, you are old men and women and dirty babies also, and dimly and obscurely you used to move through the mind of Carlyle. 'Thou wert our conscript, on Thee the lot fell. . . .' That is as true for the twentieth century as for the nineteenth, though the twentieth century – more cynical – feels that it is merely a true remark, not a useful one, and that economic conditions cannot be bettered by booming on about the brotherhood of man. 'For in Thee also a godlike frame lay hidden, but it was not to be unfolded,' not while the hard self-satisfied faces stare at each other from the walls and say, 'But at all events we founded the Charity Organization Society – and look what we pay in wages, and look what our clothes cost, and clothes mean work.'

The misery goes on, the feeble impulses of good return to the sender, and far away, in some other category, far away from the snobbery and glitter in which our souls and bodies have been entangled, is forged the instrument of the new dawn.

32

Virginia Woolf:
Mr Bennett and Mrs Brown

In 1924 Virginia Woolf read a paper to the Cambridge Heretics Society entitled 'Character in Fiction'. The rather exclusive Heretics Society consisted of men and women associated with the university who met on Sundays and discussed various free-thinking topics. Woolf revised her paper for T. S. Eliot's Criterion *magazine, and then finally published it as a Hogarth Press pamphlet under the new title* Mr Bennett and Mrs Brown. *Like Strachey's preface to* Eminent Victorians, *the essay is a Bloomsbury manifesto, and its polemical criticism of Edwardian fiction is analogous to Strachey's condemnation of Victorian biography. Woolf is speaking as a novelist; her questioning of characterization in Edwardian novels reflects her own efforts to convey the reality of Georgian characters in* Jacob's Room, *which she published two years before, and in* Mrs Dalloway, *the novel she was now writing. Less explicitly, Woolf is also speaking as a woman enraged by Bennett's condescending view of women that she feared might discourage some of them from writing. Arnold Bennett said later he had not read Woolf's critique of him, and he continued to complain that younger writers, including her, were not creating convincing characters.*

It seems to me possible, perhaps desirable, that I may be the only person in this room who has committed the folly of writing, trying to write, or failing to write, a novel. And when I asked myself, as your invitation to speak to you about modern fiction made me ask myself, what demon whispered in my ear and urged me to my doom, a little figure rose before me – the figure of a man, or of a woman, who said, 'My name is Brown. Catch me if you can.'

Most novelists have the same experience. Some Brown, Smith, or Jones comes before them and says in the most seductive and charming way in the world, 'Come and catch me if you can.' And so, led on by this will-o'-the-wisp, they flounder through volume after volume, spending the best years of their lives in the pursuit, and receiving for the most part very little cash in exchange. Few catch the phantom; most have to be content with a scrap of her dress or a wisp of her hair.

My belief that men and women write novels because they are lured on to create some character which has thus imposed itself upon them has the sanction of Mr Arnold Bennett. In an article from which I will quote he says: 'The foundation of good fiction is character-creating and nothing else.... Style counts; plot counts; originality of outlook counts. But none of these counts anything like so much as the convincingness of the characters. If the characters are real the novel will have a chance; if they are not, oblivion will be its portion....' And he goes on to draw the conclusion that we have no young novelists of first-rate importance at the present moment, because they are unable to create characters that are real, true, and convincing.

These are the questions that I want with greater boldness than discretion to discuss to-night. I want to make out what we mean when we talk about 'character' in fiction; to say something about the question of reality which Mr Bennett raises; and to suggest some reasons why the younger novelists fail to create characters, if, as Mr Bennett asserts, it is true that fail they do. This will lead me, I am well aware, to make some very sweeping and some very vague assertions. For the question is an extremely difficult one. Think how little we know about character – think how little we know about art. But, to make a clearance before I begin, I will suggest that we range Edwardians and Georgians into two camps; Mr Wells, Mr Bennett, and Mr Galsworthy I will call the Edwardians; Mr Forster, Mr Lawrence, Mr Strachey, Mr Joyce, and Mr Eliot I will call the Georgians. And if I speak in the first person, with intolerable egotism, I will ask you to excuse me. I do not want to attribute to the world at large the opinions of one solitary, ill-informed, and misguided individual.

My first assertion is one that I think you will grant – that everyone in this room is a judge of character. Indeed it would be impossible to live for a year without disaster unless one practised character-reading and had some skill in the art. Our marriages, our friendships depend on it; our business largely depends on it; every day questions arise which can only be solved by its help. And now I will hazard a second assertion, which is more disputable perhaps, to the effect that on or about December 1910 human character changed.

I am not saying that one went out, as one might into a garden, and there saw that a rose had flowered, or that a hen had laid an egg. The change was not sudden and definite like that. But a change there was, nevertheless; and, since one must be arbitrary, let us date it about the year 1910. The first signs of it are recorded in the books of Samuel Butler, in *The Way of All Flesh* in particular; the plays of Bernard Shaw continue to record it. In life one can see the change, if I may use a homely illustration, in the character of one's cook. The Victorian cook lived like a leviathan in the lower depths, formidable, silent, obscure, inscrutable; the Georgian cook is a creature of sunshine and fresh air; in and out of the drawing-room, now to borrow *The Daily Herald*, now to ask advice about a hat. Do you ask for more solemn instances of the power of the human race to change? Read the *Agamemnon*, and see whether, in process of time, your sympathies are not almost entirely with Clytemnestra. Or consider the married life of the Carlyles, and bewail the waste, the futility, for him and for her, of the horrible domestic tradition which made it seemly for a woman of genius to spend her time chasing beetles, scouring saucepans, instead of writing books. All human relations have shifted – those between masters and servants, husbands and wives, parents and children. And when human relations change there is at the same time a change in religion, conduct, politics, and literature. Let us agree to place one of these changes about the year 1910.

I have said that people have to acquire a good deal of skill in character-reading if they are to live a single year of life without disaster. But it is the art of the young. In middle age and in old age the art is practised mostly for its uses, and friendships and other adventures and experiments in the art of reading character are seldom made. But novelists differ from the rest of the world because they do not cease to be interested in character when they have learnt enough about it for practical purposes. They go a step further; they feel that there is something permanently interesting in character in itself. When all the practical business of life has been discharged, there is something about people which continues to seem to them of overwhelming importance, in spite of the fact that it has no bearing whatever upon their happiness, comfort, or income. The study of character becomes to them an absorbing pursuit; to impart character an obsession. And this I find it very difficult to explain: what novelists mean when they talk about character, what the impulse is that urges them so powerfully every now and then to embody their view in writing.

So, if you will allow me, instead of analysing and abstracting, I will tell you a simple story which, however pointless, has the merit of being true, of a journey from Richmond to Waterloo, in the hope that I may show you what I mean by character in itself; that you may realize the different aspects it can wear; and the hideous perils that beset you directly you try to describe it in words.

One night some weeks ago, then, I was late for the train and jumped into the first carriage I came to. As I sat down I had the strange and uncomfortable feeling that I was interrupting a conversation between two people who were already sitting there. Not that they were young or happy. Far from it. They were both elderly, the woman over sixty, the man well over forty. They were sitting opposite each other, and the man, who had been leaning over and talking emphatically to judge by his attitude and the flush on his face, sat back and became silent. I had disturbed him, and he was annoyed. The elderly lady, however, whom I will call Mrs Brown, seemed rather relieved. She was one of those clean, threadbare old ladies whose extreme tidiness – everything buttoned, fastened, tied together, mended and brushed up – suggests more extreme poverty than rags and dirt. There was something pinched about her – a look of suffering, of apprehension, and, in addition, she was extremely small. Her feet, in their clean little boots, scarcely touched the floor. I felt that she had nobody to support her; that she had to make up her mind for herself; that, having been deserted, or left a widow, years ago, she had led an anxious, harried life, bringing up an only son, perhaps, who, as likely as not, was by this time beginning to go to the bad. All this shot through my mind as I sat down, being uncomfortable, like most people, at travelling with fellow passengers unless I have somehow or other accounted for them. Then I looked at the man. He was no relation of Mrs Brown's I felt sure; he was of a bigger, burlier, less refined type. He was a man of business I imagined, very likely a respectable corn-chandler from the North, dressed in good blue serge with a pocket-knife and a silk handkerchief, and a stout leather bag. Obviously, however, he had an unpleasant business to settle with Mrs Brown; a secret, perhaps sinister business, which they did not intend to discuss in my presence.

'Yes, the Crofts have had very bad luck with their servants,' Mr Smith (as I will call him) said in a considering way, going back to some earlier topic, with a view to keeping up appearances.

'Ah, poor people,' said Mrs Brown, a trifle condescendingly. 'My grandmother had a maid who came when she was fifteen and stayed till she was eighty' (this was said with a kind of hurt and aggressive pride to impress us both perhaps).

'One doesn't often come across that sort of thing nowadays,' said Mr Smith in conciliatory tones.

Then they were silent.

'It's odd they don't start a golf club there – I should have thought one of the young fellows would,' said Mr Smith, for the silence obviously made him uneasy.

Mrs Brown hardly took the trouble to answer.

'What changes they're making in this part of the world,' said Mr Smith looking out of the window, and looking furtively at me as he did so.

It was plain, from Mrs Brown's silence, from the uneasy affability with which Mr Smith spoke, that he had some power over her which he was exerting disagreeably. It might have been her son's downfall, or some painful episode in her past life, or her daughter's. Perhaps she was going to London to sign some document to make over some property. Obviously against her will she was in Mr Smith's hands. I was beginning to feel a great deal of pity for her, when she said, suddenly and inconsequently.

'Can you tell me if an oak-tree dies when the leaves have been eaten for two years in succession by caterpillars?'

She spoke quite brightly, and rather precisely, in a cultivated, inquisitive voice.

Mr Smith was startled, but relieved to have a safe topic of conversation given him. He told her a great deal very quickly about plagues of insects. He told her that he had a brother who kept a fruit farm in Kent. He told her what fruit farmers do every year in Kent, and so on, and so on. While he talked a very odd thing happened. Mrs Brown took out her little white handkerchief and began to dab her eyes. She was crying. But she went on listening quite composedly to what he was saying, and he went on talking, a little louder, a little angrily, as if he had seen her cry often before; as if it were a painful habit. At last it got on his nerves. He stopped abruptly, looked out of the window, then leant towards her as he had been doing when I got in, and said in a bullying, menacing way, as if he would not stand any more nonsense,

'So about that matter we were discussing. It'll be all right? George will be there on Tuesday?'

'We shan't be late,' said Mrs Brown, gathering herself together with superb dignity.

Mr Smith said nothing. He got up, buttoned his coat, reached his bag down, and jumped out of the train before it had stopped at Clapham Junction. He had got what he wanted, but he was ashamed of himself; he was glad to get out of the old lady's sight.

Mrs Brown and I were left alone together. She sat in her corner opposite, very clean, very small, rather queer, and suffering intensely. The impression she made was overwhelming. It came pouring out like a draught, like a smell of burning. What was it composed of – that overwhelming and peculiar impression? Myriads of irrelevant and incongruous ideas crowd into one's head on such occasions; one sees the person, one sees Mrs Brown, in the centre of all sorts of different scenes. I thought of her in a seaside house, among queer ornaments: sea-urchins, models of ships in glass cases. Her husband's medals were on the mantelpiece. She popped in and out of the room, perching on the edges of chairs, picking meals out of saucers, indulging in long, silent stares. The caterpillars and the oak-trees seemed to imply all that. And then, into this fantastic and secluded life, in broke Mr Smith. I saw him blowing in, so to speak, on a windy day. He banged, he slammed. His dripping umbrella made a pool in the hall. They sat closeted together.

And then Mrs Brown faced the dreadful revelation. She took her heroic decision. Early, before dawn, she packed her bag and carried it herself to the station. She would not let Smith touch it. She was wounded in her pride, unmoored from her anchorage; she came of gentlefolks who kept servants – but details could wait. The important thing was to realize her character, to steep oneself in her atmosphere. I had no time to explain why I felt it somewhat tragic, heroic, yet with a dash of the flighty, and fantastic, before the train stopped, and I watched her disappear, carrying her bag, into the vast blazing station. She looked very small, very tenacious; at once very frail and very heroic. And I have never seen her again, and I shall never know what became of her.

The story ends without any point to it. But I have not told you this anecdote to illustrate either my own ingenuity or the pleasure of travelling from Richmond to Waterloo. What I want you to see in it is this. Here is a character imposing itself upon another person. Here is Mrs Brown making someone begin almost automatically to write a novel about her. I believe that all novels begin with an old lady in the corner opposite. I believe that all novels, that is to say, deal with character, and that it is to express character – not to preach doctrines, sing songs, or celebrate the glories of the British Empire, that the form of the novel, so clumsy, verbose, and undramatic, so rich, elastic, and alive, has been evolved. To express character, I have said; but you will at once reflect that the very widest interpretation can be put upon those words. For example, old Mrs Brown's character will strike you very differently according to the age and country in which you happen to be born. It would be easy enough to write three different versions of that incident in the train, an English, a French, and a Russian. The English writer would make the old lady into a 'character'; he would bring out her oddities and mannerisms; her buttons and wrinkles; her ribbons and warts. Her personality would dominate the book. A French writer would rub out all that; he would sacrifice the individual Mrs Brown to give a more general view of human nature; to make a more abstract, proportioned, and harmonious whole. The Russian would pierce through the flesh; would reveal the soul – the soul alone, wandering out into the Waterloo Road, asking of life some tremendous question which would sound on and on in our ears after the book was finished. And then besides age and country there is the writer's temperament to be considered. You see one thing in character, and I another. You say it means this, and I that. And when it comes to writing each makes a further selection on principles of his own. Thus Mrs Brown can be treated in an infinite variety of ways, according to the age, country, and temperament of the writer.

But now I must recall what Mr Arnold Bennett says. He says that it is only if the characters are real that the novel has any chance of surviving. Otherwise, die it must. But, I ask myself, what is reality? And who are the judges of reality? A character may be real to Mr Bennett and quite unreal to me. For instance, in this article he says that Dr Watson in *Sherlock Holmes* is real to him: to me Dr Watson is a sack stuffed with straw, a dummy, a figure of fun. And so it is with character after character – in book after book. There is nothing that people differ about more than the reality of characters, especially in contemporary books. But if you take a larger view I think that Mr Bennett is perfectly right. If, that is, you think of the novels which seem to you great novels – *War and Peace*, *Vanity Fair*, *Tristram Shandy*, *Madame Bovary*, *Pride and Prejudice*, *The Mayor of Casterbridge*, *Villette* – if you think of these books, you do at once think of some character who has seemed to you so real (I do not by that mean so lifelike) that it has the power to make you think not merely of it itself, but of all sorts of things through its eyes – of religion, of love, of war, of peace, of family life, of balls in county towns, of sunsets, moonrises, the immortality of the soul. There is hardly any subject of human experience that is left out of *War and Peace* it seems to me. And in all these novels all these great novelists have brought us to see whatever they wish us to see through some character. Otherwise, they would not be novelists; but poets, historians, or pamphleteers.

But now let us examine what Mr Bennett went on to say – he said that there was no great novelist among the Georgian writers because they cannot create characters who are real, true, and convincing. And there I cannot agree. There are reasons, excuses, possibilities which I think put a different colour upon the case. It seems so to me at least, but I am well aware that this is a matter about which I am likely to be prejudiced, sanguine, and near-sighted. I will put my view before you in the hope that you will make it impartial, judicial, and broad-minded. Why, then, is it so hard for novelists at present to create characters which seem real, not only to Mr Bennett, but to the world at large? Why, when October comes round, do the publishers always fail to supply us with a masterpiece?

Surely one reason is that the men and women who began writing novels in 1910 or thereabouts had this great difficulty to face – that there was no English novelist living from whom they could learn their business. Mr Conrad is a Pole; which sets him apart, and makes him, however admirable, not very helpful. Mr Hardy has written no novel since 1895. The most prominent and successful novelists in the year 1910 were, I suppose, Mr Wells, Mr Bennett, and Mr Galsworthy. Now it seems to me that to go to these men and ask them to teach you how to write a novel – how to create characters that are real – is precisely like going to a bootmaker and asking him to teach you how to make a watch. Do not let me give you the impression that I do not admire and enjoy their books. They seem to me of great value, and indeed of great necessity. There are seasons when it is more important to have boots than to have watches. To drop metaphor, I think that after the creative activity of the Victorian age it was quite necessary, not only for literature but for life, that someone should write the books that Mr Wells, Mr Bennett, and Mr Galsworthy have written. Yet what odd books they are! Sometimes I wonder if we are right to call them books at all. For they leave one with so strange a feeling of incompleteness and dissatisfaction. In order to complete them it seems necessary to do something – to join a society, or, more desperately, to write a cheque. That done, the restlessness is laid, the book finished; it can be put upon the shelf, and need never be read again. But with the work of other novelists it is different. *Tristram Shandy* or *Pride and Prejudice* is complete in itself; it is self-contained; it leaves one with no desire to do anything, except indeed to read the book again, and to understand it better. The difference perhaps is that both Sterne and Jane Austen were interested in things in themselves; in character in itself; in the book in itself. Therefore everything was inside the book, nothing outside. But the Edwardians were never interested in character in itself; or in the book in itself. They were interested in something outside. Their books, then, were incomplete as books, and required that the reader should finish them, actively and practically, for himself.

Perhaps we can make this clearer if we take the liberty of imagining a little party in the railway carriage – Mr Wells, Mr Galsworthy, Mr Bennett are travelling to Waterloo with Mrs Brown. Mrs Brown, I have said, was poorly dressed and very small. She had an anxious, harassed look. I doubt whether she was what you call an educated woman. Seizing upon all these symptoms of the unsatisfactory condition of our primary schools with a rapidity to which I can do no justice, Mr Wells would instantly project upon the window-pane a vision of a better, breezier, jollier, happier, more adventurous and gallant world, where these musty railway carriages and fusty old women do not exist; where miraculous barges bring tropical fruit to Camberwell by eight o'clock in the morning; where there are public nurseries, fountains, and libraries, dining-rooms, drawing-rooms, and marriages; where every citizen is generous and candid, manly and magnificent, and rather like Mr Wells himself. But nobody is in the least like Mrs Brown. There are no Mrs Browns in Utopia. Indeed I do not think that Mr Wells, in his passion to make her what she ought to be, would waste a thought upon her as she is. And what would Mr Galsworthy see? Can we doubt that the walls of Doulton's factory would take his fancy? There are women in that factory who make twenty-five dozen earthenware pots every day. There are mothers in the Mile End Road who depend upon the farthings which those women earn. But there are employers in Surrey who are even now smoking rich cigars while the nightingale sings. Burning with indignation, stuffed with information, arraigning civilization, Mr Galsworthy would only see in Mrs Brown a pot broken on the wheel and thrown into the corner.

Mr Bennett, alone of the Edwardians, would keep his eyes in the carriage. He, indeed, would observe every detail with immense care. He would notice the advertisements; the pictures of Swanage and Portsmouth; the way in which the cushion bulged between the buttons; how Mrs Brown wore a brooch which had cost three-and-ten-three at Whitworth's bazaar; and had mended both gloves – indeed the thumb of the left-hand glove had been replaced. And he would observe, at length, how this was the non-stop train from Windsor which calls at Richmond for the convenience of middle-class residents, who can afford to go to the theatre but have not reached the social rank which can afford motor-cars, though it is true, there are occasions (he would tell us what), when they hire them from a company (he would tell us which). And so he would gradually sidle sedately towards Mrs Brown, and would remark how she had been left a little copyhold, not freehold, property at Datchet, which, however, was mortgaged to Mr Bungay the solicitor – but why should I presume to invent Mr Bennett? Does not Mr Bennett write novels himself? I will open the first book that chance puts in my way – *Hilda Lessways*. Let us see how he makes us feel that Hilda is real, true, and convincing, as a novelist should. She shut the door in a soft, controlled way, which showed the constraint of her relations with her mother. She was fond of reading *Maud*; she was endowed with the power

to feel intensely. So far, so good; in his leisurely, surefooted way Mr
Bennett is trying in these first pages, where every touch is important, to
show us the kind of girl she was.

But then he begins to describe, not Hilda Lessways, but the view from
her bedroom window, the excuse being that Mr Skellorn, the man who
collects rents, is coming along that way. Mr Bennett proceeds:

'The bailiwick of Turnhill lay behind her; and all the murky district of
the Five Towns, of which Turnhill is the northern outpost, lay to the
south. At the foot of Chatterley Wood the canal wound in large curves on
its way towards the undefiled plains of Cheshire and the sea. On the
canal-side, exactly opposite to Hilda's window, was a flour-mill, that
sometimes made nearly as much smoke as the kilns and the chimneys
closing the prospect on either hand. From the flour-mill a bricked path,
which separated a considerable row of new cottages from their appurte-
nant gardens, led straight into Lessways Street, in front of Mrs Lessways'
house. By this path Mr Skellorn should have arrived, for he inhabited the
farthest of the cottages.'

One line of insight would have done more than all those lines of
description; but let them pass as the necessary drudgery of the novelist.
And now – where is Hilda? Alas. Hilda is still looking out of the window.
Passionate and dissatisfied as she was, she was a girl with an eye for
houses. She often compared this old Mr Skellorn with the villas she saw
from her bedroom window. Therefore the villas must be described. Mr
Bennett proceeds:

'The row was called Freehold Villas: a consciously proud name in a
district where much of the land was copyhold and could only change
owners subject to the payment of "fines", and to the feudal consent of a
"court" presided over by the agent of a lord of the manor. Most of the
dwellings were owned by their occupiers, who, each an absolute monarch of the soil, niggled in his sooty garden of an evening amid the flutter
of drying shirts and towels. Freehold Villas symbolised the final triumph
of Victorian economics, the apotheosis of the prudent and industrious
artisan. It corresponded with a Building Society Secretary's dream of
paradise. And indeed it was a very real achievement. Nevertheless,
Hilda's irrational contempt would not admit this.'

Heaven be praised, we cry! At last we are coming to Hilda herself. But
not so fast. Hilda may have been this, that, and the other; but Hilda not
only looked at houses, and thought of houses; Hilda lived in a house.
And what sort of a house did Hilda live in? Mr Bennett proceeds:

'It was one of the two middle houses of a detached terrace of four
houses built by her grandfather Lessways, the teapot manufacturer; it
was the chief of the four, obviously the habitation of the proprietor of the

terrace. One of the corner houses comprised a grocer's shop, and this house had been robbed of its just proportion of garden so that the seigneurial garden-plot might be triflingly larger than the other. The terrace was not a terrace of cottages, but of houses rated at from twenty-six to thirty-six pounds a year; beyond the means of artisans and petty insurance agents and rent-collectors. And further, it was well built, generously built; and its architecture, though debased, showed some faint traces of Georgian amenity. It was admittedly the best row of houses in that newly settled quarter of the town. In coming to it out of Freehold Villas Mr Skellorn obviously came to something superior, wider, more liberal. Suddenly Hilda heard her mother's voice. . . .'

But we cannot hear her mother's voice, or Hilda's voice; we can only hear Mr Bennett's voice telling us facts about rents and freeholds and copyholds and fines. What can Mr Bennett be about? I have formed my own opinion of what Mr Bennett is about – he is trying to make us imagine for him; he is trying to hypnotize us into the belief that, because he has made a house, there must be a person living there. With all his powers of observation, which are marvellous, with all his sympathy and humanity, which are great, Mr Bennett has never once looked at Mrs Brown in her corner. There she sits in the corner of the carriage – that carriage which is travelling, not from Richmond to Waterloo, but from one age of English literature to the next, for Mrs Brown is eternal, Mrs Brown is human nature, Mrs Brown changes only on the surface, it is the novelists who get in and out – there she sits and not one of the Edwardian writers has so much as looked at her. They have looked very powerfully, searchingly, and sympathetically out of the window; at factories, at Utopias, even at the decoration and upholstery of the carriage; but never at her, never at life, never at human nuture. And so they have developed a technique of novel-writing which suits their purpose; they have made tools and established conventions which do their business. But those tools are not our tools, and that business is not our business. For us those conventions are ruin, those tools are death.

You may well complain of the vagueness of my language. What is a convention, a tool, you may ask, and what do you mean by saying that Mr Bennett's and Mr Wells's and Mr Galsworthy's conventions are the wrong conventions for the Georgians? The question is difficult: I will attempt a short cut. A convention in writing is not much different from a convention in manners. Both in life and in literature it is necessary to have some means of bridging the gulf between the hostess and her unknown guest on the one hand, the writer and his unknown reader on the other. The hostess bethinks her of the weather, for generations of hostesses have established the fact that this is a subject of universal interest in which we all believe. She begins by saying that we are having a wretched May, and, having thus got into touch with her unknown guest, proceeds to matters of greater interest. So it is in literature. The writer must get into touch with his reader by putting before him something which he recognizes, which therefore stimulates his imagination, and makes him willing to co-operate in the far more difficult business of intimacy. And it is of the highest importance that this common meeting-place should be reached easily, almost instinctively, in the dark, with one's eyes shut. Here is Mr Bennett making use of this common ground in the passage which I have quoted. The problem before him was to make us believe in the reality of Hilda Lessways. So he began, being an Edwardian, by describing accurately and minutely the sort of house Hilda lived in, and the sort of house she saw from the window. House property was the common ground from which the Edwardians found it easy to proceed to intimacy. Indirect as it seems to us, the convention worked admirably, and thousands of Hilda Lessways were launched upon the world by this means. For that age and generation, the convention was a good one.

But now, if you will allow me to pull my own anecdote to pieces, you will see how keenly I felt the lack of a convention, and how serious a matter it is when the tools of one generation are useless for the next. The incident had made a great impression on me. But how was I to transmit it to you? All I could do was to report as accurately as I could what was said, to describe in detail what was worn, to say, despairingly, that all sorts of scenes rushed into my mind, to proceed to tumble them out pell-mell, and to describe this vivid, this overmastering impression by likening it to a draught or a smell of burning. To tell you the truth, I was also strongly tempted to manufacture a three-volume novel about the old lady's son, and his adventures crossing the Atlantic, and her daughter, and how she kept a milliner's shop in Westminster, the past life of Smith himself, and his house at Sheffield, though such stories seem to me the most dreary, irrelevant, and humbugging affairs in the world.

But if I had done that I should have escaped the appalling effort of saying what I meant. And to have got at what I meant I should have had to go back and back and back; to experiment with one thing and another; to try this sentence and that, referring each word to my vision, matching it as exactly as possible, and knowing that somehow I had to find a common ground between us, a convention which would not seem to you too odd, unreal, and far-fetched to believe in. I admit that I shirked that arduous undertaking. I let my Mrs Brown slip through my fingers. I have told you nothing whatever about her. But that is partly the great Edwardians' fault. I asked them – they are my elders and betters – How shall I begin to describe this woman's character? And they said, 'Begin by saying that her father kept a shop in Harrogate. Ascertain the rent. Ascertain the wages of shop assistants in the year 1878. Discover what her mother died of. Describe cancer. Describe calico. Describe –' But I cried, 'Stop! Stop!' And I regret to say that I threw that ugly, that clumsy, that incongruous tool out of the window, for I knew that if I began describing the cancer and the calico, my Mrs Brown, that vision to which I cling though I know no way of imparting it to you, would have been dulled and tarnished and vanished for ever.

That is what I mean by saying that the Edwardian tools are the wrong ones for us to use. They have laid an enormous stress upon the fabric of things. They have given us a house in the hope that we may be able to deduce the human beings who live there. To give them their due, they have made that house much better worth living in. But if you hold that novels are in the first place about people, and only in the second about the houses they live in, that is the wrong way to set about it. Therefore, you see, the Georgian writer had to begin by throwing away the method that was in use at the moment. He was left alone there facing Mrs Brown without any method of conveying her to the reader. But that is inaccurate. A writer is never alone. There is always the public with him – if not on the same seat, at least in the compartment next door. Now the public is a strange travelling companion. In England it is a very suggestible and docile creature, which, once you get it to attend, will believe implicitly what it is told for a certain number of years. If you say to the public with sufficient conviction, 'All women have tails, and all men humps,' it will actually learn to see women with tails and men with humps, and will think it very revolutionary and probably improper if you say 'Nonsense. Monkeys have tails and camels humps. But men and women have brains, and they have hearts; they think and they feel,' – that will seem to it a bad joke, and an improper one into the bargain.

But to return. Here is the British public sitting by the writer's side and saying in its vast and unanimous way, 'Old women have houses. They have fathers. They have incomes. They have servants. They have hot water bottles. That is how we know that they are old women. Mr Wells and Mr Bennett and Mr Galsworthy have always taught us that this is the way to recognize them. But now with your Mrs Brown – how are we to believe in her? We do not even know whether her villa was called Albert or Balmoral; what she paid for her gloves; or whether her mother died of cancer or of consumption. How can she be alive? No; she is a mere figment of your imagination.'

And old women of course ought to be made of freehold villas and copyhold estates, not of imagination.

The Georgian novelist, therefore, was in an awkward predicament. There was Mrs Brown protesting that she was different, quite different, from what people made out, and luring the novelist to her rescue by the most fascinating if fleeting glimpse of her charms; there were the Edwardians handing out tools appropriate to house building and house breaking; and there was the British public asseverating that they must see the hot water bottle first. Meanwhile the train was rushing to that station where we must all get out.

Such, I think, was the predicament in which the young Georgians found themselves about the year 1910. Many of them – I am thinking of Mr Forster and Mr Lawrence in particular – spoilt their early work because, instead of throwing away those tools, they tried to use them. They tried to compromise. They tried to combine their own direct sense of the oddity and significance of some character with Mr Galsworthy's knowledge of the Factory Acts, and Mr Bennett's knowledge of the Five Towns. They tried it, but they had too keen, too overpowering a sense of Mrs Brown and her peculiarities to go on trying it much longer. Something had to be done. At whatever cost of life, limb, and damage to valuable property Mrs Brown must be rescued, expressed, and set in her high relations to the world before the train stopped and she disappeared for ever. And so the smashing and the crashing began. Thus it is that we hear all round us, in poems and novels and biographies, even in newspaper articles and essays, the sound of breaking and falling, crashing and destruction. It is the prevailing sound of the Georgian age – rather a melancholy one if you think what melodious days there have been in the past, if you think of Shakespeare and Milton and Keats or even of Jane Austen and Thackeray and Dickens; if you think of the language, and the heights to which it can soar when free, and see the same eagle captive, bald, and croaking.

In view of these facts – with these sounds in my ears and these fancies in my brain – I am not going to deny that Mr Bennett has some reason when he complains that our Georgian writers are unable to make us believe that our characters are real. I am forced to agree that they do not pour out three immortal masterpieces with Victorian regularity every autumn. But instead of being gloomy, I am sanguine. For this state of things is, I think, inevitable whenever from hoar old age or callow youth the convention ceases to be a means of communication between writer and reader, and becomes instead an obstacle and an impediment. At the present moment we are suffering, not from decay, but from having no code of manners which writers and readers accept as a prelude to the more exciting intercourse of friendship. The literary convention of the time is so artificial – you have to talk about the weather and nothing but the weather throughout the entire visit – that, naturally, the feeble are tempted to outrage, and the strong are led to destroy the very foundations and rules of literary society. Signs of this are everywhere apparent. Grammar is violated; syntax disintegrated; as a boy staying with an aunt for the week-end rolls in the geranium bed out of sheer desperation as the solemnities of the sabbath wear on. The more adult writers do not, of course, indulge in such wanton exhibitions of spleen. Their sincerity is desperate, and their courage tremendous; it is only that they do not know which to use, a fork or their fingers. Thus, if you read Mr Joyce and Mr Eliot you will be struck by the indecency of the one, and the obscurity of the other. Mr Joyce's indecency in *Ulysses* seems to me the conscious and calculated indecency of a desperate man who feels that in order to breathe he must break the windows. At moments, when the window is broken, he is magnificent. But what a waste of energy! And, after all, how dull indecency is, when it is not the overflowing of a super-abundant energy or savagery, but the determined and public-spirited act of a man who needs fresh air! Again, with the obscurity of Mr Eliot. I think that Mr Eliot has written some of the loveliest single lines in modern poetry. But how intolerant he is of the old usages and politenesses of society – respect for the weak, consideration for the dull! As I sun myself upon the intense and ravishing beauty of one of his lines, and reflect that I must make a dizzy and dangerous leap to the next, and so on from line to line, like an acrobat flying precariously from bar to bar, I cry out, I confess, for the old decorums, and envy the indolence of my ancestors who, instead of spinning madly through mid-air, dreamt quietly in the shade with a book. Again, in Mr Strachey's books, *Eminent Victorians* and *Queen Victoria*, the effort and strain of writing against the grain and current of the times is visible too. It is much less visible, of course, for not only is he dealing with facts, which are stubborn things, but he has fabricated, chiefly from eighteenth-century material, a very discreet code of manners of his own, which allows him to sit at table with the highest in the land and to say a great many things under cover of that exquisite apparel which, had they gone naked, would have been chased by the men-servants from the room. Still, if you compare *Eminent Victorians* with some of Lord Macaulay's essays, though you will feel that Lord Macaulay is always wrong, and Mr Strachey always right, you will also feel a body, a sweep, a richness in Lord Macaulay's essays which show that his age was behind him; all his strength went straight into his work; none was used for purposes of concealment or of conversion. But Mr Strachey has had to open our eyes before he made us see; he has had to search out and sew together a very artful manner of speech; and the effort, beautifully though it is concealed, has robbed his work of some of the force that should have gone into it, and limited his scope.

For these reasons, then, we must reconcile ourselves to a season of failures and fragments. We must reflect that where so much strength is spent on finding a way of telling the truth the truth itself is bound to reach us in rather an exhausted and chaotic condition. Ulysses, Queen Victoria, Mr Prufrock – to give Mrs Brown some of the names she has made famous lately – is a little pale and dishevelled by the time her rescuers reach her. And it is the sound of their axes that we hear – a vigorous and stimulating sound in my ears – unless of course you wish to sleep, when, in the bounty of his concern, Providence has provided a host of writers anxious and able to satisfy your needs.

Thus I have tried, at tedious length, I fear, to answer some of the questions which I began by asking. I have given an account of some of the difficulties which in my view beset the Georgian writer in all his forms. I have sought to excuse him. May I end by venturing to remind you of the duties and responsibilities that are yours as partners in this business of writing books, as companions in the railway carriage, as fellow travellers with Mrs Brown? For she is just as visible to you who remain silent as to us who tell stories about her. In the course of your daily life this past week you have had far stranger and more interesting experiences than the one I have tried to describe. You have overheard scraps of talk that filled you with amazement. You have gone to bed at night bewildered by the complexity of your feelings. In one day thousands of ideas have coursed through your brains; thousands of emotions have met, collided, and disappeared in astonishing disorder. Nevertheless, you allow the writers to palm off upon you a version of all this, an image of Mrs Brown, which has no likeness to that surprising apparition whatsoever. In your modesty you seem to consider that writers are of different blood and bone from yourselves; that they know more of Mrs Brown than you do. Never was there a more fatal mistake. It is this division between reader and writer, this humility on your part, these professional airs and graces on ours, that corrupt and emasculate the books which should be the healthy offspring of a close and equal alliance between us. Hence spring those sleek, smooth novels, those portentous and ridiculous biographies, that milk and watery criticism, those poems melodiously celebrating the innocence of roses and sheep which pass so plausibly for literature at the present time.

Your part is to insist that writers shall come down off their plinths and pedestals, and describe beautifully if possible, truthfully at any rate, our Mrs Brown. You should insist that she is an old lady of unlimited capacity and infinite variety; capable of appearing in any place; wearing any dress; saying anything and doing heaven knows what. But the things she says and the things she does and her eyes and her nose and her speech and her silence have an overwhelming fascination, for she is, of course, the spirit we live by, life itself.

But do not expect just at present a complete and satisfactory present-ment of her. Tolerate the spasmodic, the obscure, the fragmentary, the failure. Your help is invoked in a good cause. For I will make one final and surpassingly rash prediction – we are trembling on the verge of one of the great ages of English literature. But it can only be reached if we are determined never, never to desert Mrs Brown.

Part VII

Talks

Bloomsbury's talks differ from their essays not in subject matter so much as occasion. Each is shaped by the speaker's relation to his or her audience. Of the six talks included here, one was given to a Cambridge discussion society and another to a London women's organization; one was a slide lecture for a general audience, and three were radio broadcasts.

33

Lytton Strachey: Art and Indecency

Three years before Virginia Woolf spoke to the Heretics Society (see p. 233), Lytton Strachey addressed them on the subject of art and indecency. His paper, however, was based on a much earlier one that he read to the famous secret undergraduate society known as the Apostles. Strachey's central idea is developed from the philosopher G. E. Moore's notion of organic wholes in Principia Ethica, *but the illustrations and classifications are purely Stracheyan. The talk was posthumously published in* The Really Interesting Question and Other Papers, *edited by Paul Levy (1972).*

The question that I want to discuss is partly aesthetic and partly moral: exactly how much of one and how much of the other, it is difficult to say. In general, the relation between aesthetics and ethics is apt to be confused. On the one hand, it seems clear that a work of art ought to be judged as a work of art, and as nothing else; that is to say, its value must be determined upon purely aesthetic grounds – just as the value of a dinner must be determined upon culinary grounds, and that of a steam-engine upon considerations of engineering. It would be absurd to praise a locomotive for its virtue, or to condemn a soup as immoral; and it seems no less absurd to discuss the ethics of a symphony. Conversely, it is ridiculous to introduce aesthetic considerations into moral questions; the Kaiser's delinquencies have really nothing to do with his moustaches; and, while it is probable that some at any rate of the 11,000 virgins of Cologne were not good-looking, their holiness remains unimpeachable.

So far, then, 'art for art's sake' appears to be a reasonable proposition. But two provisos must be made. In the first place, it is no doubt true that the *effects produced* by a work of art may be of an ethical nature. It would be unnecessarily sceptical to doubt this; for there does not seem to be any specific quality in works of art which should exempt them from producing results of this kind. If men are capable of being made better or worse by forces outside themselves, there is no reason to exclude from those forces literature, painting, and music. The Bible is fine poetry: but it would be paradoxical to deny that its dissemination has produced moral results (of one kind or another) of the highest importance. It is, however, equally clear that it is impossible to estimate the moral effects of any work of art apart from a great number of particular circumstances. No general rule can be laid down; what is one man's meat is another man's poison; many clergymen who have read Catullus with impunity, have been, it is reported, completely demoralized by Mrs Humphry Ward. Time, place, age, nationality, character, the accidents of mood and temper, all these, together with innumerable other concomitant facts, must be taken into account in every case. And, when the account has been made up and the balance struck, it is important to remember that the resulting judgement is *not* a judgement on the work of art itself, but simply on its effects. The distinction, though it is sometimes overlooked, is really fundamental. In what follows, I shall make no attempt to deal with this side of the question – the question of ethical effects.

But there is another, and a more direct, way in which ethics and aesthetics are related. It is certain that *ethical constituents* are often to be found in works of art. In many tragedies, to take an obvious example, questions of right and wrong, of good and evil, are of very great importance. The wickedness of Iago is a vital part of *Othello*. It is, therefore, impossible to maintain that ethical considerations are necessarily irrelevant to art; and when the phrase 'art for art's sake' is intended to cover such a proposition, it is false. Among the many and varied elements which go to the making of works of art, ethical elements sometimes occur. These ethical elements, however, are parts of an aesthetic whole; and the aesthetic whole must be judged by purely aesthetic standards. In this sense, 'art for art's sake' expresses the true doctrine.

These general remarks may I hope simplify the discussion of the particular question, or group of questions, that I wish to put before you – namely, is there any peculiar relation between the artistic and the indecent, and if there is, what is it? The question is highly controversial, and has been approached from a great many points of view; but the main currents of opinion are fairly easily discernible. There are three classes of persons whose views upon the subject are pronounced and completely incompatible. The first of these classes is an extremely respectable one – the class of prudes. The prudes regard with horror, detestation, and anger any introduction of indecency into works of art. They are not only a respectable, but a busy race. In their time, they have done a great deal. They have affixed fig-leaves to the statues of the Gods of Antiquity, they have draped the posteriors of Michael Angelo's devils, they have bowdlerized Shakespeare, and prohibited the performance of the *Oedipus Rex*. They are, however, diminishing both in numbers and in assurance. They seem never to have recovered from the loss which they sustained on the death of Queen Victoria. Ever since that sad event, they have fallen sick of a grievous malady: they have begun to compromise. Now a prude who compromises is a prude lost. The whole strength of his position lies in its rigidity: (it is like a maidenhead – either all there, or not there at all). Mr Bowdler was inexpugnable. Shakespeare contains indecencies; indecency is bad: the inference is obvious: remove the indecencies, and you will improve Shakespeare. Mr Bowdler did so, and Queen Victoria was satisfied; but her degenerate successors are not. They have quietly abandoned Mr Bowdler, and in so doing they have let the enemy into their citadel. For once admit that there are any exceptions – that there is a single exception – to the golden rule of prudery: – 'all indecency is bad, of whatever kind and in whatever circumstances' – and you will find that you are slipping down an inclined plane which may land you in heaven knows what alarming position. If Shakespeare is really better with his indecencies than without them, may not the same be said of Swift? and if it be true of Swift, then why not of Rabelais? And if Rabelais is tolerated, surely it is straining at a gnat and swallowing a camel to disapprove of the Restoration dramatists. It is possible, no doubt, to refine and to distinguish, to construct whole elaborate casuistries of indecency; but such theorizings seem to be based on no definite principles, and to differ in the most divergent ways according to individual taste. Thus at the present time the party of the prudes presents a spectacle of the utmost confusion. Without the golden rule of Victoria they resemble, in incoherence and multiplicity, the Protestant sects after their rejection of the infallibility of Rome. Among the various groups of prudes that one meets with, there is no criterion for deciding which are the orthodox. There are some who are disgusted by the tittering flippancy of Sterne, but who relish the honest coarseness of Fielding; there are others who find Fielding barbarous, but are edified by the realism of Zola. Some, who put Giorgione's *Concert* over their mantel pieces, turn away in horror from Manet's *Déjeuner sur L'Herbe*; while the authorities, who hang Bronzius's *Venus and Cupid* on the walls of the National Gallery, conceal Michael Angelo's *Leda* in the cellar. One finds a learned divine, who is appalled when Renan writes on the ethics of passion, translating with infinite labour into the purest English the truly shocking Dialogues of Plato. At the same time the official censor of stage plays, while he protects the diluted ineptitudes of Parisian salaciousness, declares in tones of thunder that there are two subjects which may never, never, be referred to in any theatre – Jesus Christ and incest.

It is not surprising that there has been a reaction against this curiously confused and wavering creed; and the form of the reaction was almost inevitable in a scientific generation. The majority of advanced thinkers on the subject fall into my second class, and may be appropriately called the Naturalists. To them, the whole question of indecency is simplified in a fundamental manner, because, in their opinion, there is really no such thing. Indecency does not exist. It is a superstition, a myth – the result of a mixture of barbarous and ignorant tradition and the artificialities of civilization, of erroneous education and a confused association of ideas. The acts which are popularly called indecent – the acts of repro-duction, of excretion, and so forth, are – so the Naturalists affirm – indistinguishable from the other bodily functions. They are necessary, natural acts, and it is as absurd to attach ethical qualities to them as it would be to attach ethical qualities to eating or blowing one's nose – for instance – to the emission of seminal fluid from a penis as it would be to attach them to the emission of mucous fluid from a nose. 'All this fuss about a little bit of flesh!' the Naturalists seem to exclaim; though it is true that the word 'flesh' would be hardly to their liking; they would prefer to speak, less figuratively, of 'the sexual instinct'. For it is a noticeable peculiarity of theirs that they have a great love of latinized locutions; and the reason for this is obvious: there is something detached and scientific in such expressions as 'coitus', 'fellatio', or 'homosexualist' which is lacking in the more coloured phraseology of familiar speech, and which makes them therefore more appropriate to the naturalistic way of thinking. Such being their views, the Naturalists, when asked what in their opinion was the relation between the artistic and the indecent, would reply that the whole question was without significance; that, as the very notion of 'indecency' was a fallacious one, it was absurd to suppose that the merit of a work of art would be affected by the presence or the absence of it; and they would probably add some regrets that a foolish superstition should discourage the artistic presentation of various psychological and medical truths of great importance – such as, for instance, the excretory aberrations of infants, or the unpleasant consequences of venereal infection.

Now there can, I think, be little doubt that the naturalistic view of the case has much to recommend it. It is simple, and it is decidedly advanced; and if one were obliged to choose between it, and the view of the prudes, most thoughtful and unbiased inquirers would probably declare for the Naturalists. But these two opinions are not the only alternatives. There is a third party – a class whose sentiments are apt to be overlooked, for they have no high pretensions and, as a rule, they are without the habit of philosophical disquisition; yet they are a large, and even an influential class – the class of the Bawdy. The superior person, from his moral or intellectual eminence, may affect to look down upon the Bawdy; but are they in reality to be despised? In the first place, it must not be forgotten that among this class are to be reckoned some of the very greatest of the human race – Aristophanes, Rabelais, Voltaire. And then, is it possible to put on one side and treat as of no account the predilections of the multitudes who, through so many ages, have been moved to admiration and delight by the works of those masters, and of many more who belong to the same category? The prim Victorians who were shocked by Charlotte Brontë were no doubt, in one sense, highly respectable; but the loose Elizabethans who shook their sides over the solid lewdnesses of Ben Jonson were, perhaps, respectable in another sense – that is to say they deserved to be respected. At any rate, it is certain that between these two classes – the prudes and the Bawdy – there can be no agreement; they are naturally exclusive. But it is no less certain that the opposition is equally fundamental between the Bawdy and the Naturalists. For, if the Naturalists are right, the whole basis of the bawdy standpoint is destroyed. If indeed there is no such thing as indecency, Aristophanes, Rabelais, Voltaire, are undoubtedly the most futile of the writers, their jests are meaningless, and their admirers are bamboozled fools. This certainly seems a paradoxical conclusion; and the question arises whether the premises of the Naturalists will really support it. Now the naturalistic argument rests, as we have seen, on the contention that the acts usually termed indecent are merely natural acts, and that there is therefore no reason to put them in a special category. Suppose we admit this, what follows? Surely nothing; for is it not clear that, however we describe the acts, the real point at issue is concerned, far less with the acts themselves, than with the feelings accompanying them? It is upon the feelings, and not upon the acts, that we base our judgement when we assert something to be indecent; it is, in short, a state of mind that we are considering, not a state of body. To do otherwise is to commit the fallacy of those amiable educationists who blandly set out to teach their little charges the 'mysteries of sex' by means of diagrams illustrating the secretive properties of glands, or a few short lessons on the functions of stamens and pistils. Alas! the 'mysteries of sex' do not lie there. You might as well try to describe the nature of war by means of the plans of battlefields. It is not at all a question of properties and functions, or of glands and ducts, or of movements of living tissue: it is a question of mental states – of extraordinary agitations, of unexpected and dominating impulses, of intensifying excitements, of unparalleled joys; and the young pupil who has no acquaintance with these sensations knows no more of the 'mysteries of sex' than the young soldier knows of war who has never been in action. And it is for this reason that the latinized vocabulary affected by the Naturalists must be regarded with suspicion. For, in spite of its air of detachment, it is in reality a means of concealing the actual facts. The Saxon words, with their emotional associations, are far more truthful. What could be more unaffecting than the expression 'coitus'? But the reality, which it designates, is not unappetizing at all.

Thus the case of the Naturalists, owing to their failure to realize that indecency depends on feelings and not on acts, appears to break down. Are we then to throw ourselves without more ado into the arms of the Bawdy? Perhaps it would be wise to pause; for they are a reckless, *tête-montée*, and not at all philosophical race. They are apt to defend their doings upon totally incompatible grounds. Nothing is commoner than to find them when they are attacked by the prudes for indecency, exclaiming loudly, and in tones of outraged innocence, that they are *not* indecent, that they have been monstrously misunderstood, it is the prudes who have dirty minds, not they, that *they* have been only anxious to inculcate the highest virtues, if only the prudes would take the trouble to read them aright. A famous instance of this line of defence may be seen in Dryden's and Vanburgh's replies to the attacks of Jeremy Collier. On the other hand, at other moments, their argument is very different. Indecency, they seem to say, is a positive merit in art; we will have just as much of it as we like, and if that is a good deal more than *you* like – well, so much the worse for you. Such is the attitude of the French decadents of the last century. Clearly these views are mutually destructive. But is the bawdy case capable of a more satisfactory defence?

First, it seems certain that the *extreme* bawdy position is untenable. It is surely possible that in some cases the merit of a work of art may be decreased by indecency. It is easy to think of pornographic works which have no artistic merit and of Music Hall revues which would be artistically improved by the deletion of the feeble indecencies which they contain. But, on the other hand, the *extreme* prude position is equally impossible. A work of art which is indecent may be of the highest merit. Between these two extremes, what sort of a middle course can we steer?

The view I suggest is that works of art must be considered as complex wholes, composed of a great number of parts; the value of these wholes cannot be determined merely by a *sum* of the values of the parts, but depends upon their *combination*. That wholes of this kind exist it is easy to see. A whole, for instance, consisting of the pleasurable contemplation of a beautiful object is made up of two parts – the pleasurable contemplation, and the beautiful object. Now a beautiful object, in isolation, is probably almost valueless; and mere pleasurable contemplation, directed towards no particular object is of small value; yet the two together form a whole of very great value indeed. Now, if as I believe, works of art are wholes of this nature, it is obvious that to consider the value of their parts in isolation is futile: it will give no indication of the total value of the whole. A part which, in isolation, might be of purely negative value, might in combination, form a whole of high merit. Remove it, and though it is valueless in itself, its absence will destroy the value of the whole. Indecency, when it appears in works of art, seems to me to be a part of this nature. It is impossible to determine its value apart from the combination of which it forms a part. The value of some wholes may be decreased by its presence; but the value of others may be immeasurably increased; and indeed its presence may be absolutely vital to the value of a work of art. This theory I think affords an explanation of the curiously conflicting views that obtain on the subject. Indecent feelings, indecent acts, when considered in isolation are very liable to appear in an odious light. They strike the cool observer as out of place; they are inappropriate to his surroundings; they are shocking in fact; combined with the rest of his state of mind – the state of mind of the unemotional onlooker – they form a complex whole which is unpleasant and ugly, and he therefore condemns them as bad. But, place these same indecencies in another complex whole – in a work of art – in which they are fitted to their surroundings, in which they are gradually led up to and elaborated, so that the observer, no longer cool, no longer unemotional, feels, sympathizes, and understands – then the case is altered: the dull and horrid image of a sensualist's imagination becomes the vital element of some radiant creation – one of the poems of Catullus, one of the comedies of Congreve, of Tristram Shandy, of Candide.

34

Roger Fry: Impressionism

Roger Fry was celebrated in the 1920s for his slide lectures on exhibitions at Burlington House in London. Virginia Woolf in her biography of Fry has described how the audiences watched him gazing afresh at each picture: 'they could see the sensation strike and form; he could lay bare the very moment of perception.' The last of a series on French art that Fry gave (and published as Characteristics of French Art *in 1932) was devoted to impressionism. Throughout his career Fry remained critical of what he saw as the impressionists' obsessive concern with perception and corresponding lack of form. In his 1920 'Retrospect', he admitted that he had underrated what was the only vital art movement of the time (see p. 399). Fry selected some of his black-and-white slides as illustrations when his lectures were published but they have been omitted here.*

Impressionism began when artists decided to create their imagery by using nothing but the data revealed by vision from a fixed view-point. When they realized that their business was with what things looked like and not with what, as we say, they really are; meaning, of course, by that, all that we can find out by looking from various angles, by touch and, in the figure, by dissection. It was the seventeenth-century Dutch painters who first sat down in one place and painted pictures without moving. When once they did this they discovered quite new aspects of vision, new effects of perspective, new patterns made by the odd juxta-position of things.

And as their whole mind was concentrated on vision they discovered new things about light and shade and colour. They saw how shadows were filled with reflected light and how the different orientations of the different planes of an object led to changes in the local colour, how it became more blue here, more orange or red there.

Impressionism implied, then, two possible changes in art. One the result of looking at things from unfamiliar aspects, the other the result of noting changes in local colour due to different sources of light. And we can divide the French Impressionists into two groups according as they explored mainly one or the other of these two roads. Bazille was perhaps the first to give the new note of colour, but Monet was the most adventurous explorer of such atmospheric effects on local colour, followed by Pissarro and Sisley and to some extent by Renoir. Degas found his opportunity in the unexpected angles of vision.

The whole movement is typical of that French readiness to apprehend the unexpected aspects of actual life, but its data were explored with an almost scientific method and persistence which exemplifies French willingness to trust to logical deductions.

Bazille, whose death in the war of 1870 blighted a brilliant promise, establishes such link as there is between Manet and Impressionism. He was in close touch with Manet and painted with his frank flat statement of planes, but on this basis he had begun just before his death to play with effects of atmospheric colour. One of his pictures at the Luxembourg shows a family group sitting on a garden terrace on a summer evening. Here he took note of the violet lights that strike on the edges of the figures from the cold blue of the sky behind, the amber of the direct sunlight and the golden oranges of reflected light from the sunlit gravel. Here already, in essence, is the new scale of colours which Impressionism exploited.

Monet also in his early works painted with frank oppositions of flat patches of colour, but with him the passion to explore the new effects which Impressionism had suddenly revealed increasingly absorbed his whole energy. His attitude became almost that of a scientific researcher, his pictures demonstrations of what he had discovered. In order to get the full effects of brilliant sunshine he began to break his surfaces into small touches of brilliant colour. Gradually the objects he represented lost their consistency, everything was resolved into the flat mosaic of colour patches which is, of course, a more or less accurate account of what the retina receives or what things would look like if our minds had never learned to interpret it as representing solid objects in space. It is true, no doubt, that from this coloured mosaic of Monet's the eye does reconstruct the objects more or less clearly as it does in nature. Only, since Monet puts the accent so strongly on the atmospheric effects, tending to exaggerate these – as early art had exaggerated the local colour – he loses all possibility of any definite formal design. Monet, indeed, had no interest in that. He cared only to reproduce on his canvas the actual visual sensation as far as that was possible. Perhaps if one had objected to him that this was equivalent to abandoning art, which has always been an interpretation of appearances in relation to certain human values, he would have been unmoved because he aimed almost exclusively at a scientific documentation of appearances. This was characteristic of the period when the greatly increased prestige of science had led to a good deal of rather wild speculation about its relation to art. Monet's attitude was not unlike that of Zola who regarded his novels mainly as scientific records of social life.

At the end of his long life Monet obtained the ideal conditions for such a conception of art as his. He was commissioned to paint the walls of the Orangerie in Paris. Here, in an oval room lit from above, he painted a continuous band of canvas with representations of a pond filled with water-lilies of various kinds and colours. As the eye follows the band round we pass from morning to afternoon and finally to sunset. We get the effect of an imagery with no boundaries, just as we do in an actual scene where we can turn in any direction. There is no attempt to organize the vision in any way, there is no pattern, no apparent rhythm. Such unity as there is depends on the uniform quality of the texture. It lacks, therefore, all those properties of an ordered formal structure which we are wont to expect, even more from a wall painting than an easel picture. But the sheer force of Monet's passionate conviction, his marvellous certainty of observation, have a kind of impressiveness though it is doubtful whether the effect is of the same kind as one gets from a great work of art.

The two other chief artists who explored the same field as Monet were Pissarro and Sisley. They neither of them shared the scientific obsession of Monet, and used the new visual data not as ends in themselves, but as the mode in which their experiences in front of nature could be most fully expressed. Whereas Monet chose those moments when the effects of atmospheric colour were at their intensest or strangest, Pissarro chose, by preference, the quieter effects of grey weather or of veiled sunlight which allowed him to express his gentle meditative mood. Monet succeeds in banishing almost all overtones of feeling from his landscapes, he brings you before the scene without a hint of any meaning that he has discovered, whereas before Pissarro's pictures one is conscious of looking at the scene in the presence of an infinitely discreet but definite personality.

With Sisley the interpretation becomes far more important, and its significance more profound and exhilarating. In his lifetime he was regarded as perhaps the least important of the group, but little by little his work has begun to stand out more and more. His personality reveals itself more clearly as we get to know the work better, and we realize that he was no mere recorder of a new aspect of vision but a great imaginative artist.

There were, at Burlington House, two snow scenes, one by Monet and one by Sisley. The Monet was a miracle of exact observation and notation. It was, indeed, so exact in its tone and colour that it almost literally made one shiver with cold. With that, apart from one's marvel at the artist's skill, the matter ended. Before the Sisley, though this too struck one as intensely true, that judgement seemed unimportant compared with one's delight that the artist had discovered in it, no doubt by imperceptible changes of accent and emphasis due to the unconscious bias of his sensibility, so entrancing a harmony and one that evoked such intense overtones of feeling. Sisley was, I think, the only one of this group who was able to use the intenser, more brilliant colours, which the study of atmospheric effects had revealed, with as perfect a harmonization as Corot had attained in a less extended scale.

He surpassed the others no less in the significance of his design, in his infallible instinct for spacing and proportion. His designs have, to a high degree, that pictorial architecture which Monet's so conspicuously lack.

If one had to choose one artist as the typical representative of the French genius, I for one should choose Degas. More than any other artist I can name, he is unthinkable out of France or even out of Paris. Only there, is the response to life both of eye and mind exasperated to such a pitch of acuity by the friction of other minds all attuned to let nothing slip by unnoticed. Everyone who has often driven across Paris in a taxi-cab must have constated that people's latent period of nervous reaction is shorter than elsewhere, and the intelligence and sensibility of the Parisian population seem correspondingly quickened.

The French then, typified by Degas, are quicker than others at reading the meanings of vision. But if we ask towards what end, to satisfy what purposes, this quick apprehension is set, it is more difficult to give an answer. We can judge, for instance, that the great Italians read nature under the stress of certain rather exalted emotional states, that the Flemish on the whole read it in terms of ordinary life or of rather elementary emotions. But before Degas one is at a loss. It is certainly no mere neutral curiosity, no desire merely to state undigested facts. His reading is consistent and is directed by some intense feeling. One of the commonest motives for which people read the visible hieroglyphics of city life is to gratify their sense of fun. We certainly look at people to laugh at them, whether kindly or unkindly depends on our nature. And some kind of comedic feeling of a rather harsh kind is certainly sensed behind Degas's imagery. But it is not, properly speaking, satirical. That would be far too crude and forced a direction for so complex and subtle a spirit as Degas's: it would imply too superficial and easy a distortion. He penetrates to deeper levels of truth. But I find in him a kind of passion of disillusionment, an intense desire not to be the dupe of appearances.

Thus he loved the theatre and the ballet and the life of the stage, but always a part of his pleasure is the detection of the fraud practised on us by their illusory effects. Even when the ballerina is on the stage, where the illusion is at its highest, he likes to let us into the secret. And, to make more sure, he follows her behind the scenes to the drudgery of the practice-room and the squalor of her private life. But where no illusion is attempted, where people are absorbed in their own affairs and unconscious of a spectator, Degas will find entertainment just in the accidental jumbles of the kaleidoscope of life and will seize on patterns of unfamiliar beauty. And he will pursue his ends of disillusionment and enchantment at the same time, life for him being intricately woven of the two. He will give you the painted face of a *chanteuse* in a *café concert* so that you must guess at what she hides, but at the same time this life of artifice and pretence provides for us harmonies of line and light and colour which, accidental and unintentional though they are, are none the less exquisite and a curious conflicting emotion is aroused by thus realizing both at once.

I am trying, all too clumsily I fear, to give you what I feel to be the specific quality of most of Degas's art in which the psychological and dramatic elements are so curiously compounded with his passion for certain formal patterns. Degas always objected to being called an Impressionist though he was in close touch with the Impressionist group. It is true that he never showed any interest in the new discoveries in atmospheric colour, but he was an Impressionist in so far as he accepted the unusual angles of vision which was one of those results of the Impressionist attitude that had already been explored by the Dutch in the seventeenth century. But Degas pushed this much further and in doing so he owed not a little to the Japanese prints which were becoming known to the Western world for the first time during the seventies of the last century.

Take, for instance, a design like *Les Coulisses*. Such a way of cutting the figures and of placing the two faces in the top corner of the rectangle is unthinkable at any previous period in European art. In all previous pictures the figures were placed more centrally as though they were to some extent awaiting the spectator. Here we get, what exactly suits Degas's detective instinct, the sensation of having stumbled upon the scene unawares, of its being by accident that this peep-hole has let us into the secret. That appearance of a fortuitous and casual apparition increases the illusion that this is life itself only momentarily passing across our field of vision. And yet with that appearance of accident, that dispersal of the centres of interest, see how he has managed to get in all the significant facts. We do not need any more than that profile of the man and the edge of his hat and coat to know all about him, and what intensity of expression is concentrated in the movement of the hands. Degas is one of the most incisively expressive draughtsmen there has ever been. The hands are tremulous with life to the finger-tips and yet though he is so minutely precise he is never tedious or merely descriptive. His contour is so subtly varied in its accent at every point that it does not isolate the form from its surroundings. It suggests, too, the whole inner structure of the volume of a head or arm.

Degas had an almost idolatrous reverence for Ingres, and he owes much to his conception of the contour as vividly evocative of the volume it defines. And yet no two artists are more distinct. Ingres looked always for suavely melodious linear harmonies. He used nature only so far as it gave him suggestions for that. Degas is too much intrigued by life itself to press it into any preconceived scheme. He wants its full complexity and strangeness; so his rhythms are far less evidently melodious, the phrasing has to be varied incessantly in order to miss no shade of meaning, it must be more elastic even at the cost of being less seductive. But Degas does not lose himself in detail however far he pursues it; he always keeps his sense of the volume and of the fundamental character of the form. You can feel that here in the firm drawing of the woman's figure, in the solidity and consistency of the arm.

Degas's drawing is, then, the exact opposite of calligraphic drawing. He never allows himself to adopt a formula of any kind. His alert apprehension is never relaxed for a second. Every tiniest fraction of his line records his nervous tension. His drawing is the very antithesis of superficial facility. No wonder then that he could scarcely afford to be a painter in the special sense of the word. By his drawing he had, as it were, distilled from the dense substance of reality this quintessential expression, and so, even when he paints, he dare not cloy and encumber that with a rich impasto. And he lacked too, I think, the special sensuality of the painter. He was not in love with the material quality of objects but only with an almost intellectual abstract of them. He grasps the solid forms of his figures, but he will not give us their density and resistance or the full complexity of their substance.

His use of a composition based on Oriental rather than European tradition was peculiarly adapted to his conception of drawing. His passion for pursuing expression to the very finger-tips of his figures implied a tendency to centrifugal arrangements which is in contrast to the general tendency of European design in which, with a view to the use of large masses in pictorial architecture, there was always a tendency to avoid sharply marked excrescences. Degas therefore had to find a formal system in which small isolated forms, such as a fully extended arm or leg must occasion, would not break the harmony.

How well he succeeded may be seen by the *Répétition* where the balance of the composition is attained precisely by the placing and directions of these sharply isolated forms. He shows astonishing tact and ingenuity in his solution of this difficult venture. He manages by his special conception of design to allow himself, at any point, those sharp incisive contrasts and silhouettes which all the great European artists had denied themselves in the interest of breadth and unity and yet he never falls into the meanness of a tight and isolating definition.

With such a passionate interest in all the implications of appearances it is natural that, without ever being a portrait painter in the professional sense, he should have painted some of the finest portraits of the century: certainly some of the most intriguing and the most revelatory. For I do not think one can name any one portrait by him which remains in the memory as a great piece of music or poetry does, or as, indeed, a few of Renoir's and Cézanne's do. Here again, it is his intense detective instinct that checks the urge of a single concentrated feeling. He sees so many aspects of the truth; he refuses to choose a single one and bend everything to its complete expression. He must always leave that sense of the casual and transitory which is of the essence of life itself.

Thus in his astonishingly vivid portrait of the *Comte Lepic and his Daughters* we have almost the effect of a snapshot taken, without the subject's knowledge, by some casual passer-by who just got him as he hurried across the field of vision. It requires an effort to fix the attention on the subtle revelations of character in face and pose; Degas refuses to intervene at all. And again, it is only by a fixed attention that one realizes with what a marvellous sensibility for formal significance every line contributes to the design so that what appears accidental is seen to be the result of deliberate intention.

Wherever, then, life revealed by its contingencies those hidden, unintentional significances of psychological meaning and curious arabesque, Degas was to be found. On the race-course, where the jig-saw puzzle of the horses' legs hinted at one of those elusive rhythms of which he was a master; at the ballet, where legs and arms fluttered their signals; in the cafés at night, when the lamplit streets wove extravagant patterns behind jaded faces; at the milliners' shops, where the intriguing complications of fashionable fancy and the intent preoccupation of the clients produced strange combinations, Degas steals in with his detective gaze and that prodigious visual memory which spared him from giving himself away by producing a sketch-book.

As Degas grew older his zest for all these aspects of life declined. He withdrew himself from the world. He was in part the victim of his own dangerously brilliant wit, for he was one of the wittiest men of the day, and had estranged too many acquaintances by such unforgettable phrases as his definition of the painter Besnard as '*Le pompier qui a pris feu!*' In the isolation of his house in Montmartre he reconstructed for himself a little corner of life which he could explore at his leisure. He got models to come in. But merely to pose them in a studio would have prevented that immediate contact with life which was essential to him. So he arranged a bathroom where they could live the life of the toilet before his eyes. This limitation of his field had the happiest results. It coincided with his growing passion for formal as opposed to psychological values. His imaginative grasp of form became broader and more plastic. He no longer found its sharpest meanings in details and extremities, it was the large sequences of the nude figure that began to matter most. In a sense this was a return to the great European tradition, but he still made great use of his odd angles of vision to create new and unexpected situations.

In a small monotype we see him still mainly concerned with the contour to which the *contre-jour* effect gives its full force. But how completely it evokes the whole volume of the figure, and already here he extracts a more flowing rhythm than before from his understanding of the pose.

To this period belong his sculptures. The centrifugal tendencies of his early design were more inconsistent with sculptural than with pictorial unity, and where they persist we tend to feel that the desire for expression interferes too much with the balance and repose necessary to great sculpture. But the little torso reveals his profound plastic apprehension in the richness of its content and the rhythmic continuity of the movement.

But to return to his paintings, or rather his pastels, for in almost all these late works he abandoned oils in favour of that medium. Here at last he found his fullest expression. With pastel he had no temptation to that thinness and dryness of quality, that tendency to sharp definition which marks his early work. In these pastels his quality becomes broader and his rhythms more flowing, he expresses something of that full density and complexity of texture which he had before not been able, as it were, to afford.

Still later and he avoided effects in which all emphasis is laid on the contour. He became more and more fascinated by the sequences of modelling within the contour. As he proceeds his rhythms depend less and less on tone; more and more it is the sequence of planes, the plastic rhythm which becomes the dominant theme. And he discovers therein ever more fascinating and original constructions. But these have a new gravity and impressiveness. We no longer notice his ingenuity and cunning. His imagination works at a higher emotional pitch, his interpretation of the actual touches deeper levels of our feeling. In such works Degas at last revealed his greatest qualities.

In temperament, Renoir makes a striking contrast to Degas. Whilst Degas was fascinated by the factitious and artificial side of city life Renoir loved what was rustic and natural. Whilst Degas looked on life with ironical disillusionment, Renoir loved with a kind of lyrical ecstasy all the simple good things of life, the beauty and force of the young human animal, roses, sunlight and meadows waving in the breeze.

Though for long they both lived and worked in Montmartre, it was typical of them that Degas lived in a narrow street and spent his life in the cafés and behind the scenes of the Opera, whilst Renoir found what had once been a country house and still had a large garden, and it was there that he painted the working girls whom he persuaded to pose. In these surroundings they wore a very different air from the jaded and overworked *danseuses* in the foyer of the music-hall.

La Femme au Chat shows such a model fallen asleep in the studio with the cat on her lap. How utterly different Renoir's attitude is from Degas's. He has no desire to read too deeply; so far from wishing to be disillusioned he gladly accepts the face value of things, though in fact he is no dupe because it is the underlying animal basis of life that stirs his lyrical sensuality. He has no concern with the complications which sophisticated life introduces, with psychological and social intricacies.

That basic animalism of all human life is enough to evoke the tender, sympathetic comprehension which he expresses by the caressing touch of his ample modelling. Therein he rejoins the great Venetians, Titian above all, and to a less extent Rubens. For Renoir is one of the most obvious 'old masters' of the nineteenth century. For, though he painted the life of his time it was not what was specially characteristic of that which he felt most intensely. Wherever there was sunlight and flowers and youth, wherever the sap of life flowed freely enough to provoke the simple joy in living, he had his material, and he communes with past ages in the embracing simplicity of that pagan faith.

It is this generous, receptive, lyrical sensuality which at bottom directs Renoir in almost all his work. He seems scarcely conscious of the problems which modern life poses for an artist, of how to select and how to interpret, he is led so immediately, so irresistibly towards what he loves. And his love conjures all anxieties and fears. He paints with surprising ease and assurance, but without any assertion of his power; he is an utter stranger to virtuosity; one never wonders either at his skill or his pictorial science.

There was, however, a period of his life when this would not be quite true. In the early work of the seventies he was already a great master, but pedantic critics told him he could not draw and he, unfortunately, listened enough to them to endeavour to prove that he could, by painting with a tight unyielding contour to his forms. A great deal of the work of the eighties is marred by this disastrous obsession. Much of his quality, of course, remains, but his feeling for form was most concerned with the sequence of planes within the contour; he never was a great linealist, and his effort to prove himself one set up a hopeless contradiction with his dominant feeling. The hard enamelled surfaces of these pictures, though they declare his technical power, seem to deny the most essential part of his sensibility, his feeling for what one may perhaps call the atmospheric halo of lighted surfaces, especially for the elusive quality which the play of light on flesh creates.

Fortunately from the early nineties on till his death in 1919 he ceased to check this natural bias and progressed always in the direction of greater breadth of design, luminosity and brilliance of colour. To some extent this development was actually accelerated by his infirmity. For years before his death his hand was paralysed by rheumatism, but his immense pictorial science enabled him to work within the limits which this imposed. He could now only paint by the movements of the arm, but his design, by now, scarcely demanded anything but the larger statements of relief. He needed no precision of contour. Indeed he scarcely needed more than the vaguest suggestion of whereabouts the contour lay. He expressed himself solely in the saliences of his main masses. It is marvellous how much he could express with this elliptically pictorial shorthand.

Renoir alone among modern masters insisted on using the full range of expression of oil paint. He could not dispense with the full scale which the Venetians and Rubens had employed. Whereas most nineteenth-century painters had been content to use oils by the opposition of flat patches of opaque colour, Renoir needed the full range. He needed to contrast the staining of transparent colours with the dense opacities of lighted surfaces and the muted radiance and subdued relief of a penumbra.

His feeling for colour was always intense. In conformity with the large simple lines of his emotional life it is in a certain sense obvious, at all events there is no research for strange or unfamiliar, or what one may call, discordant harmonies. In colour as in all things he loved the simplest, most obvious things too well to tire of them, and the older he got the more he revelled in scarlets, oranges and yellows, set off by notes of vivid green and pure blue and rose.

And in this joy in pure positive notes he found the advantage of the new discoveries of his day. Not that he ever became pedantically attached to the strict application of the laws of atmospheric colour, for he plays with them as easily and unconsciously as with all other principles and systems, taking hints for what he wants and leaving the rest, according to the dictates of his happy instinctive judgement.

As may be supposed, Renoir had none of Degas's curiosity about the strange patterns which the juxtaposition of objects might build up. He was primarily interested in the things themselves which he liked in his frank, sensual way. He takes the position from which one would normally look at these and places them in the simplest, often the most obvious way, on his canvas. Not but what at times he could arrive at a complex and clearly articulated design. In the *Mme Charpentier and her Daughters* the placing of the figures in the picture space is as original and personal as it is felicitous, and the figures are built up into a beautifully flowing sequence of forms into which he has amusingly woven the black and white patches of the dog.

Les Parapluies at the Tate Gallery is another ambitious design in which he has found a happy solution of the complicated material. The umbrellas, the midinettes' band-box and the child's hoop are all used as a foil to the fluctuating rhythms of the figures.

Later on again in his often repeated groups of *Baigneuses* he showed his power to contrive the most complicated systems of arabesque without losing rhythmic continuity. But we note that he accepts a more or less traditional method, though he uses it with his effortless mastery. Renoir's composition is easy and harmonious, always adequate to his idea, but not, in itself, a matter of passionate interest or one of his chief means of expression. In this he is again in striking contrast to Degas. Except when he was trying to prove that he could draw, he trusted implicitly to his rich sensibility and his robust good sense. It is not surprising that his favourite, almost his only, author was La Fontaine. Renoir was the great modern master of the commonplace in the sense that he expressed the joys of life of the average, healthy, unsophisticated man – but, of course, to give to that feeling an expression of such radiant gaiety and such lyrical urgency implies anything but a commonplace nature.

I have said so much of Cézanne elsewhere that perhaps you will be glad that I can here give but the briefest hints of his position. One point, however, falls naturally into line with the general theme of these lectures. I have tried to isolate the specific qualities of French art. In my first lecture I had to point out that the great Pietà from Avignon (now in the Louvre) stood out from all other French Primitives in that it had much more the qualities of Italian than of French design and I suggested that the author was typically Mediterranean. Now at the other end of the story I find a similar striking exception in the case of Cézanne. That he was intensely a Provençal is significant, for to me he seems to achieve designs which inevitably recall to us the great Italians. He has something of their amplitude of form, of their simplicity of large co-ordinated masses. His rhythms have that gravity and momentum which was in general foreign to the nimbler, subtler, more insinuating movements typical of French sensibility. Before his great designs we think more readily of Masaccio than of Watteau.

Cézanne was one of the Impressionist group and it was from them that he learned the colour effects which, with great modifications, formed the basis of his colour schemes. But he was always disquieted by their want of structural design. His love of the Old Masters made him believe that there was something of the utmost importance for the mind in that more solid pictorial construction which the Impressionists disregarded. He always said, 'If I could only realize.' Realizing, for him, did not mean verisimilitude, of that he had a horror, but the discovery in appearances of some underlying structural unity which answered a profound demand of the spirit. His problem was how to use the new revelations of Impressionism to give that result. How, without missing the infinity of nature, the complexity and richness of its vibrations, how to build that solidly and articulately co-ordinated unity in which the spirit can rest satisfied. And it was the extent to which he succeeded in solving this problem that gives his work that significance which seems to me to appear more impressive and more profound as it grows more familiar to us. I confess that in the present exhibition, seeing his work alongside of his great contemporaries, I have felt quite unrepentant about the things which I have said in the past.

Two or three pictures are all that I have time to discuss and I choose them to illustrate this aspect of his work. There is something almost paradoxical in the extreme simplicity of the pretext, a few apples on a table in front of a wall-paper and the stateliness, the monumental gravity of the effect. Cézanne has realized the density and solidity of the objects and yet nothing is isolated. There is a continuous movement throughout the picture. With the colour, you would feel this more because you would find as many transitions and variations in the flat wall-paper as in the modelling of the apples.

That is the new unifying element which Cézanne brought into design from the Impressionists. Chardin does sometimes paint objects *and* a background; with Cézanne, every part of the picture is equally functional.

As an example let us take *Landscape*. Here what first strikes us is the strong articulation of the design, the solidity and salience of the house, the architectural building of the mountains. But all is continuous and suggests the infinite complexity out of which those simple forms have, as it were, crystallized. He has used more minute variations and gradations to construct that empty flat piece of foreground than to build his roads and trees.

And at the end of his life Cézanne developed the strangest method in order to express this profound sense of a continuous plastic rhythm penetrating throughout a whole composition. By some mysterious power he was able to give to the mountain, the houses, the trees, all their solid integrity, to articulate them in a clearly felt space and yet to sustain a rhythm of plastic movement almost unbroken from one end of the canvas to another. Only in the very latest of Titian's works can I find something akin to this, a similar short-circuiting, as it were, of all ordinary methods of expressing form.

Like Cézanne, Seurat was dissatisfied with the looseness of Impressionist design. He represents in its extreme form that second and opposite characteristic of the French genius, its desire for an almost mathematical orderliness and precision of relations. It was intolerable to him that we should owe anything to chance, even to the happiest of chances. It appears that at times he dreamed of so clearly grasping the principles of harmony in form and colour that they could be applied by anyone; that it would need no special gift of sensibility and imagination to create a work of art. His own work, so intensely personal, so full of his unique sensibility, would be enough if it were necessary to show the absurdity of this dream. In drawing he aimed at the most precise and at the same time the most rigidly simplified statement of the fundamental character.

And he disposed the forms upon his canvas with such precise understanding of the relative positions which the design demanded that they have a strange fixity. The contours are so firm in their elementary, almost geometrical curves, the intervals are discovered with such mathematical certainty that the notion of anything moving cannot be entertained. Poussin, who had a similar desire for completely ascertained relations, kept in his imagery a long way from life; he dreaded lest any suggestion of the actual might break the illusion of a world of nobler beings than those among whom we live. Yet here is a man who takes everything from the most banal scenes of his time and yet withdraws them into a world of almost religious meditation and detachment. There is a strange tranquillity and repose about Seurat's designs in which everything seems to occupy its predestined situation.

Though, as I say, every single detail has been accepted from the actual facts of everyday life, all life has been withdrawn from them. To begin with, his contours are a kind of concentrated abstract of the complex appearances of nature, they are boiled down and reduced to an almost geometrical simplicity, and within the contours the modelling has been flattened and ironed out. We need not fear that his figures will move and destroy his composition – they cannot move, they are pressed specimens of humanity held for ever isolated and fixed in the pellucid amber of Seurat's space. For here lies the paradox of Seurat's art. His figures tell in the design almost as flat arabesques on the surface of his canvas and yet he used to define painting as *'l'art de creuser une toile'*, 'the art of making a canvas a hollow'. And in fact he does hollow out his picture space and feels so intensely about that that he will not fill it with anything more bulky than his flattened and scarcely modelled figures.

Both Seurat and Cézanne reacted against Impressionism, but they travelled in different directions. Cézanne finally conceived of space as permeated by a continuous plastic rhythm, Seurat suppressed, or rather compressed his plastic relief and his flattened figures merely measure intervals in the all-embracing space.

Space indeed is his real subject, and his feeling for it is so intense that he could make a design of almost nothing else. By his profound understanding of atmospheric colour – the one thing he took from the Impressionists – he was able to make us realize vividly the recession of this unbroken expanse of sand and no less the vaster arching curve of the sky, and by breaking this uniformity just in the right place by his houses and his masts and by those two small posts which are almost the keys to the whole composition he has created a design of singular significance and unity. There is something strangely fascinating about this figure seeking with a kind of religious fervour for abstract perfection in the distracted Parisian world of the eighties and nineties of the last century. I am glad to close my review of French art on a note so unlike the ordinarily received notions of *la vie parisienne*.

35

Virginia Woolf: Professions for Women

Virginia Woolf's talk on women's professions, posthumously published in The Death of the Moth and Other Essays *(1942), is a revised, shortened version of a talk given to the London branch of the National Society for Women's Service in 1931. There are allusions in the text to Coventry Patmore's sequence of poems* The Angel in the House *(1854–63) as well as to Woolf's own* A Room of One's Own *which she published in 1929. 'Professions for Women' became one of the working titles for the novel-essay* The Pargiters *that eventually split into two books:* The Years *(1937) and* Three Guineas *(1938).*

When your secretary invited me to come here, she told me that your Society is concerned with the employment of women and she suggested that I might tell you something about my own professional experiences. It is true I am a woman; it is true I am employed; but what professional experiences have I had? It is difficult to say. My profession is literature; and in that profession there are fewer experiences for women than in any other, with the exception of the stage – fewer, I mean, that are peculiar to women. For the road was cut many years ago – by Fanny Burney, by Aphra Behn, by Harriet Martineau, by Jane Austen, by George Eliot – many famous women, and many more unknown and forgotten, have been before me, making the path smooth, and regulating my steps. Thus, when I came to write, there were very few material obstacles in my way. Writing was a reputable and harmless occupation. The family peace was not broken by the scratching of a pen. No demand was made upon the family purse. For ten and sixpence one can buy paper enough to write all the plays of Shakespeare – if one has a mind that way. Pianos and models, Paris, Vienna and Berlin, masters and mistresses, are not needed by a writer. The cheapness of writing paper is, of course, the reason why women have succeeded as writers before they have succeeded in the other professions.

But to tell you my story – it is a simple one. You have only got to figure to yourselves a girl in a bedroom with a pen in her hand. She had only to move that pen from left to right – from ten o'clock to one. Then it occurred to her to do what is simple and cheap enough after all – to slip a few of those pages into an envelope, fix a penny stamp in the corner, and drop the envelope into the red box at the corner. It was thus that I became a journalist; and my effort was rewarded on the first day of the following month – a very glorious day it was for me – by a letter from an editor containing a cheque for one pound ten shillings and sixpence. But to show you how little I deserve to be called a professional woman, how little I know of the struggles and difficulties of such lives, I have to admit that instead of spending that sum upon bread and butter, rent, shoes and stockings, or butcher's bills, I went out and bought a cat – a beautiful cat, a Persian cat, which very soon involved me in bitter disputes with my neighbours.

What could be easier than to write articles and to buy Persian cats with the profits? But wait a moment. Articles have to be about something. Mine, I seem to remember, was about a novel by a famous man. And while I was writing this review, I discovered that if I were going to review books I should need to do battle with a certain phantom. And the phantom was a woman, and when I came to know her better I called her after the heroine of a famous poem, The Angel in the House. It was she who used to come between me and my paper when I was writing reviews. It was she who bothered me and wasted my time and so tormented me that at last I killed her. You who come of a younger and happier generation may not have heard of her – you may not know what I mean by the Angel in the House. I will describe her as shortly as I can. She was intensely sympathetic. She was immensely charming. She was utterly unselfish. She excelled in the difficult arts of family life. She sacrificed herself daily. If there was chicken, she took the leg; if there was a draught she sat in it – in short she was so constituted that she never had a mind or a wish of her own, but preferred to sympathize always with the minds and wishes of others. Above all – I need not say it – she was pure. Her purity was supposed to be her chief beauty – her blushes, her great grace. In those days – the last of Queen Victoria – every house had its Angel. And when I came to write I encountered her with the very first words. The shadow of her wings fell on my page; I heard the rustling of her skirts in the room. Directly, that is to say, I took my pen in my hand to review that novel by a famous man, she slipped behind me and whispered: 'My dear, you are a young woman. You are writing about a book that has been written by a man. Be sympathetic; be tender; flatter; deceive; use all the arts and wiles of our sex. Never let anybody guess that you have a mind of your own. Above all, be pure.' And she made as if to guide my pen. I now record the one act for which I take some credit to myself, though the credit rightly belongs to some excellent ancestors of mine who left me a certain sum of money – shall we say five hundred pounds a year? – so that it was not necessary for me to depend solely on charm for my living. I turned upon her and caught her by the throat. I did my best to kill her. My excuse, if I were to be had up in a court of law, would be that I acted in self-defence. Had I not killed her she would have killed me. She would have plucked the heart out of my writing. For, as I found, directly I put pen to paper, you cannot review even a novel without having a mind of your own, without expressing what you think to be the truth about human relations, morality, sex. And all these questions, according to the Angel of the House, cannot be dealt with freely and openly by women; they must charm, they must conciliate, they must – to put it bluntly – tell lies if they are to succeed. Thus, whenever I felt the shadow of her wing or the radiance of her halo upon my page, I took up the inkpot and flung it at her. She died hard. Her fictitious nature was of great assistance to her. It is far harder to kill a phantom than a reality. She was always creeping back when I thought I had despatched her. Though I flatter myself that I killed her in the end, the struggle was severe; it took much time that had better have been spent upon learning Greek grammar; or in roaming the world in search of adventures. But it was a real experience; it was an experience that was bound to befall all women writers at that time. Killing the Angel in the House was part of the occupation of a woman writer.

But to continue my story. The Angel was dead; what then remained? You may say that what remained was a simple and common object – a young woman in a bedroom with an inkpot. In other words, now that she had rid herself of falsehood, that young woman had only to be herself. Ah, but what is 'herself'? I mean, what is a woman? I assure you, I do not know. I do not believe that you know. I do not believe that anybody can know until she has expressed herself in all the arts and professions open to human skill. That indeed is one of the reasons why I have come here – out of respect for you, who are in process of showing us by your experiments what a woman is, who are in process of providing us, by your failures and successes, with that extremely important piece of information.

But to continue the story of my professional experiences. I made one pound ten and six by my first review; and I bought a Persian cat with the proceeds. Then I grew ambitious. A Persian cat is all very well, I said; but a Persian cat is not enough. I must have a motor car. And it was thus that I became a novelist – for it is a very strange thing that people will give you a motor car if you will tell them a story. It is a still stranger thing that there is nothing so delightful in the world as telling stories. It is far pleasanter than writing reviews of famous novels. And yet, if I am to obey your secretary and tell you my professional experiences as a novelist, I must tell you about a very strange experience that befell me as a novelist. And to understand it you must try first to imagine a novelist's state of mind. I hope I am not giving away professional secrets if I say that a novelist's chief desire is to be as unconscious as possible. He has to induce in himself a state of perpetual lethargy. He wants life to proceed with the utmost quiet and regularity. He wants to see the same faces, to read the same books, to do the same things day after day, month after month, while he is writing, so that nothing may break the illusion in which he is living – so that nothing may disturb or disquiet the mysterious nosings about, feelings round, darts, dashes and sudden discoveries of that very shy and illusive spirit, the imagination. I suspect that this state is the same both for men and women. Be that as it may, I want you to imagine me writing a novel in a state of trance. I want you to figure to yourselves a girl sitting with a pen in her hand, which for minutes, and indeed for hours, she never dips into the inkpot. The image that comes to my mind when I think of this girl is the image of a fisherman lying sunk in dreams on the verge of a deep lake with a rod held out over the water. She was letting her imagination sweep unchecked round every rock and cranny of the world that lies submerged in the depths of our unconscious being. Now came the experience, the experience that I believe to be far commoner with women writers than with men. The line raced through the girl's fingers. Her imagination had rushed away. It had sought the pools, the depths, the dark places where the largest fish slumber. And then there was a smash. There was an explosion. There was foam and confusion. The imagination had dashed itself against something hard. The girl was roused from her dream. She was indeed in a state of the most acute and difficult distress. To speak without figure she had thought of something, something about the body, about the passions which it was unfitting for her as a woman to say. Men, her reason told her, would be shocked. The consciousness of what men will say of a woman who speaks the truth about her passions had roused her from her artist's state of unconsciousness. She could write no more. The trance was over. Her imagination could work no longer. This I believe to be a very common experience with women writers – they are impeded by the extreme conventionality of the other sex. For though men sensibly allow themselves great freedom in these respects, I doubt that they realize or can control the extreme severity with which they condemn such freedom in women.

These then were two very genuine experiences of my own. These were two of the adventures of my professional life. The first – killing the Angel in the House – I think I solved. She died. But the second, telling the truth about my own experiences as a body, I do not think I solved. I doubt that any woman has solved it yet. The obstacles against her are still immensely powerful – and yet they are very difficult to define. Outwardly, what is simpler than to write books? Outwardly, what obstacles are there for a woman rather than for a man? Inwardly, I think, the case is very different; she has still many ghosts to fight, many prejudices to overcome. Indeed it will be a long time still, I think, before a woman can sit down to write a book without finding a phantom to be slain, a rock to be dashed against. And if this is so in literature, the freest of all professions for women, how is it in the new professions which you are now for the first time entering?

Those are the questions that I should like, had I time, to ask you. And indeed, if I have laid stress upon these professional experiences of mine, it is because I believe that they are, though in different forms, yours also. Even when the path is nominally open – when there is nothing to prevent a woman from being a doctor, a lawyer, a civil servant – there are many phantoms and obstacles, as I believe, looming in her way. To discuss and define them is I think of great value and importance; for thus only can the labour be shared, the difficulties be solved. But besides this, it is necessary also to discuss the ends and the aims for which we are fighting, for which we are doing battle with these formidable obstacles. Those aims cannot be taken for granted; they must be perpetually questioned and examined. The whole position, as I see it – here in this hall surrounded by women practising for the first time in history I know not how many different professions – is one of extraordinary interest and importance. You have won rooms of your own in the house hitherto exclusively owned by men. You are able, though not without great labour and effort, to pay the rent. You are earning your five hundred pounds a year. But this freedom is only a beginning; the room is your own, but it is still bare. It has to be furnished; it has to be decorated; it has to be shared. How are you going to furnish it, how are you going to decorate it? With whom are you going to share it, and upon what terms? These, I think are questions of the utmost importance and interest. For the first time in history you are able to ask them; for the first time you are able to decide for yourselves what the answers should be. Willingly would I stay and discuss those questions and answers – but not to-night. My time is up; and I must cease.

36

Desmond MacCarthy:
The Job of a Dramatic Critic

By the 1930s, various members of the Bloomsbury Group including the Woolfs, Desmond MacCarthy, Roger Fry, E. M. Forster, and John Maynard Keynes were giving radio talks for the British Broadcasting Corporation. The best known of Bloomsbury broadcasters were MacCarthy and Forster. MacCarthy's talk on being a drama critic combines theory with autobiography for the listening audience as he sets forth some of the bases for his criticism. The broadcast was given in May 1939 and published in the BBC's The Listener *the same month.*

Though my subject is a general one – Dramatic Criticism – I think I can treat it best by telling you first something about my own career as a dramatic critic. If not the eldest of those who practise that art today – and why I call it an art will presently appear – I have, I believe, been at it longest.

In a book of cuttings I found the other day the first notice of a play I ever wrote. It was a criticism of *The Taming of the Shrew*, written in August, 1905, for *The Speaker*, that once celebrated liberal weekly which became, while I was on its staff, *The Nation*. The new editor, Massingham, wanted to write about the theatre himself – so I lost my job. Then, in April, 1913, *The New Statesman* started, and engaged me as its dramatic critic. Thus, since *The New Statesman* eventually swallowed *The Nation*, which had already swallowed *The Speaker*, I consider that I have been dramatic critic to the same paper for nearly thirty-four years, which (however the colour of its progressive politics has changed) has continued to keep the same sort of point of view on its literary side. Naturally, in the course of all those years I couldn't well help acquiring some general ideas about dramatic criticism, and those I propose to impart.

Perhaps it may interest you – at least any of you who have ever envied the job of a dramatic critic – to hear how it came my way. It was chance, just chance. *The Speaker*'s articles on the theatre had once enjoyed a considerable reputation (A. B. Walkley had been its critic before he went to *The Times*). But when I began to review occasionally for *The Speaker*, these articles were not giving the editor entire satisfaction. Farrar, his dramatic critic, was a quick-minded man, but he was first and foremost an enthusiastic botanist (he died, I think, flower-hunting in Tibet); and when he was on one of his exploratory expeditions and a stop-gap had to be found, the editor thought of trying young Desmond MacCarthy. Moral: if you want to keep a post on a paper, don't take long holidays.

But why *me*? What were my qualifications? Only that I had loved going to the theatre from childhood and I was, thank goodness, a spoilt child. How far that process had been carried may be inferred from an early recollection which I still cherish of my parents exchanging glances and then of one of them saying in front of me. 'It's *impossible* to spoil that child!' Well, they enjoyed watching my excitement in a theatre so much that they not only took me often, but allowed me to choose the plays, and you can fancy the kind of plays a small boy who had a reassuring hand to clutch during the performances, would choose.

In the 'eighties and early 'nineties melodrama was very popular, and melodrama of a crudity that would be laughed at today. The famous home of such plays in London was, of course, the Adelphi Theatre, and in provincial towns they figured even more prominently. The hoardings were plastered with gigantic pictures of men being stabbed or hurled over waterfalls, or of deep-sea divers striving to cut each other's air-pipes, or of a woman in white lying gagged and bound in front of an on-rushing train, or, as in the case of *The Lights o' London*, of two brave little, kidnapped orphans shivering in a snowstorm. These pictures invariably decided my choice. The first good play I ever saw (age ten) was *Macbeth*, at the Lyceum, with Irving and Ellen Terry in it; that (also) left an overwhelming impression.

But not only were the melodramas I preferred crude, but the audience enjoyed them with a like simplicity. At the end of each act the actors crossed the stage in front of the curtain, bowing. While the hero and the heroine were wildly cheered, the villain was invariably greeted with a storm of boos and hisses; and the louder we howled the wider he grinned, for he had aimed at inspiring loathing, and then he knew he had succeeded. The audience was not applauding the actors so much as the characters they represented – what they stood for. Even the minor hero – say a dauntless sailor who had struck his chest, crying, 'Here are my arms and here's my manly bosom, but where's my Mary?' – he also was sure of applause; and so was Mary, who, though he didn't know it, was at that very moment in most *deadly* peril owing to her devotion to the blameless heroine.

Now, no member of the audience ever cheered and booed with more passion than I did. Only once in the twentieth century have I been again a member of that kind of audience; it was in the East End at a Yiddish theatre.

That such audiences enjoyed themselves hugely you can imagine; but it is also true that their response was the kind that actors want most of all to excite. Of course, actors hope that their skill will be appreciated, and that people will notice *how* they act, but what they want still more is to make an overwhelming, direct, emotional impression; the praise of the connoisseur is precious to them, but their first wish is to make the audience forget the actor in the part.

I said just now that when I began to write dramatic criticism I had no qualifications. But perhaps this habit, acquired during the impressionable years of nine to sixteen, of responding to scenes and characters on the stage as though they were *real*, was a good preparation. Naturally, with experience our insight into human nature deepens and our knowledge of how people really do behave becomes more sure; and consequently plots, situations and characters which once delighted may begin to bore or even disgust by their falsity or absurdity. But unless we have acquired an instinctive habit of responding emotionally to a play as though it were a bit of real life (provided of course it is not a poetic fantasy or parable), the shades of falsity or truth in it may escape our notice. The same is true of acting – the actors' interpretation of human nature. There is only one way of judging a play and its performance: first, to let it flow over you and swamp you – if it can, then to examine the wrinkles which the waves have left, so to speak, in the sand when the tide has gone out.

First yield yourself up to it, then, unmoved, examine what it was that moved you. The ultimate questions which dramatic criticism tries to answer are: (1) What was the dramatist after? (2) How did the actors help or hinder his intentions? (3) What was the value of his aim to any feeling, thinking human being? Has this play and the actors in it left anything with me I shall find myself thinking of again? Except of course when trying to make conversation which doesn't count.

All criticism is, at bottom, an exceedingly highbrow occupation. Though a critic who knows his business will not only make his comments as amusing as possible, but draw like an artist or a creator on his own experience to drive them home. If he is a man of sense he will also keep in mind that to succeed in entertaining our fellow-men for two or three hours and make them forget themselves, is in itself a service and by no means easy; though not comparable to others which Drama can perform. What are these? Let me use a simile I have used before.

I suggest that we should think of the drama as an instrument like an organ which has at least three keyboards. The top manual, so to speak, is the story: that is to say, the sequence of incident and interplay of character and emotion which, if the play in question is to be good, must be absorbing and convincing. We must, while we watch and listen, feel that we are in the presence of real people and that real things are happening to them. To achieve this is by no means easy, yet a play which only succeeds in this respect is still far from being a work of art. Nearly all the playwrights who draw large audiences are more or less expert in playing on this upper manual.

The second keyboard is that of ideas. The dramatist who can play on both the upper manual and the middle one at the same time is in a different class from the one who can play on the upper alone. It has been Bernard Shaw's brilliant execution on the second keyboard, with just sufficient plausibility in his touch upon the first, which has made him the most famous of contemporary playwrights.

But there is a third keyboard, one which he has seldom touched, though he has used it. How am I to suggest what I want it to symbolize? I can do so only in rather vague terms, and must fetch a small circle. The people who have been most reluctant to admit the eminence of Bernard Shaw are those to whom aesthetic emotions are very important, who, if interested in ideas and the criticism of life, do not value a work of art proportionally as such ideas are embodied in it or can be deduced from it. They do not value a play because at the conclusion of it they walk away with a clearer notion of what changes in current morality or society would increase man's happiness. They demand that a work of art should lift them above even such considerations, and inspire a mood in which exultation and detachment are blended. They don't value either a play or a novel in proportion to the extent that it prompts them to rush away and *do* something, or to think out some problem. What they value most – and they seldom get it – is the sense of sharing with a great mind a contemplative attitude towards the world.

Now it is the greatest triumph of the dramatist – and a task of almost insuperable difficulty – to achieve these three ends at once: to compose an interesting story which shall be perfectly logic-tight and convincing; to manage that story so that it will also suggest ideas stimulating to the intellect and of obvious moral importance; and lastly, to leave the spectator feeling that he has shared with a mind, much greater than his own, the thrill of feeling and thinking down into the very roots of life. And when these three ends are achieved another kind of pleasure is also transmitted to those capable of appreciating what is called *form*, namely the constant sense of an exquisite adaptation of means to end throughout the whole work.

By the way, there is one test of a play every playgoer can apply: watch during the intervals how you behave with your friends, or rather how your mind is behaving. If you find yourself talking with interested animation about things in general, the play is probably not worth much. If, again, you find yourself eagerly sharing with others your impressions of the act just over, and you notice that when the first curtain-bell rings everyone chucks away just-lighted cigarettes and makes briskly for their seats, then, probably, the play will be a success and is good of its kind. Everybody has been at least thinking of what he has just seen and is anxious to know what is going to happen next. But if, during the intervals, you find yourself hoping that no one will speak to you, and slinking away with a polite wan smile from anyone you know, then, because those are symptoms that you are still heaving with emotion or want to focus something (perhaps you don't know what), then the play may be one of real consequence. During the intervals of *Mourning Becomes Electra* and the Saint Denis performance of *The Three Sisters* I would have gladly 'cut' any friend.

One more point. Actors on the whole have a lower opinion of dramatic critics than playwrights have. Firstly for a reason which is not the critics' fault. To explain to the public why a passage of acting was particularly excellent may require a closer analysis of the dramatic situation than the space at his disposal permits, so he has to content himself with saying: 'In the scene with her brother Miss X was remarkably good.' And even if right the chances are that he will not impress any actor (except Miss X) with his perspicacity. For acting, like painting, is a technical affair. You know what painters think of art critics? They may think an art critic a good judge of the comparative merits of pictures, but they can't help despising him a little because usually he does not know *how* the effects he admires were attained. Of course the painter likes to be praised for 'the luminosity of his receding planes' or what not, but while *he* knows that this effect was largely due to a dab of brown on a cow's shoulder, the critic seldom does. It is the same with acting. The critic may justly praise some thrilling scene, but he doesn't necessarily know how much its force was due, say, to the actor keeping his face hidden from the audience till a certain precise moment. For the actor, himself, however, and his fellow actors, it may be that *there* lay the proof of his mastery of his art – not in ringing tones or gestures well within the compass of many another actor, and for which the critics praised him. It takes much experience before the playgoer or critic distinguishes between what is difficult and what is easy in acting; between success in what the profession calls 'fool-proof parts', or 'fat-parts', sure of making an effect, and in those which demand the most skilful precision if they are to carry due weight. In the former the actor may deserve commendation; in the latter the highest possible praise. Yet it is not often that this difference is observed by dramatic critics.

37

John Maynard Keynes:
On Reading Books

John Maynard Keynes's 'On Reading Books' was broadcast as part of a Books and Authors series in June 1936 and then published in a cut version by The Listener. *The deleted portions have been restored by the editor of Keynes's collected writings. Keynes manages in the course of his talk to refer to four of his Bloomsbury friends in addition to their friend T. S. Eliot. Keynes's discussion of their book on Russia also suggests Bloomsbury's mixed admiration for Sidney and Beatrice Webb, while the advocacy of 'traditionalism and a careful conservatism . . .' may surprise some of Keynes's critics.*

The first step towards reading – I think you will agree – is to be able to read. Now, according to the law, we are all of us taught to read. Police magistrates are much shocked if a witness cannot read. Yet, in truth, there are very many people, even amongst the highly educated and professional classes, who read with difficulty. I mean by this that they read slowly and with effort, that it tires them – that they do not read as easily as they breathe. On the other hand, I expect that there are many of you, who earn your daily bread in ways for which reading is not important and yet do possess one of the best of all gifts – the eye which can pick up the print effortlessly. At any rate to acquire this – and many of you could acquire it merely by practice – is the first step. I emphasize this, because many people think they can read, but they can't. They do not know how far they fall behind the practised reader. We are inclined to think that of six people living in one house all will be much alike in their ability to read. But it is not so. Compare yourself with your friends and neighbours, and find out, first of all, whether you really know how to read – whether, as I have said, you read as easily as you breathe. Newspapers are good practice in learning how to skip; and, if he is not to lose his time, every serious reader must have this art.

When you can both walk and skip through a book, what next? I am afraid that I can give you very little advice on contemporary novels. I do not much care for them when I am lazy and relaxed; nor yet when I am contemplative and serious. They do not instruct or comfort or uplift me. It is thought almost a virtue in a modern writer to empty on us the slops of his mind just as they come. And their works are not even trash. For trash can be delightful, and, indeed, a necessary part of one's daily diet. I read the newspapers because they're mostly trash. But when I glance into this contemporary stuff, I find such heavy-going, such undigested, unenhanced, unintrinsic, unintuitive, such misunderstood, mishandled, mishapen, such muddled handling of human hopes and life; and without support from the convention and the tradition which in a great age of self-expression can make even the second-rate delightful. So if you want a serious novel, read the old ones – older, at any rate, than the last ten years. This year's novels are not so good, nor such pleasant easy reading, as Jane Austen's *Emma* or Thomas Hardy's *Tess of the D'Urbervilles* or E. M. Forster's *A Room with a View*. It is only commonsense advice to try these and their fellows first.

Nevertheless – to begin on the groundfloor – there is one class of author, unpretending, workmanlike, ingenious, abundant, delightful heaven-sent entertainers, in which our age has greatly excelled. There are several of them and we are each entitled to our favourites. I mean Edgar Wallace, Agatha Christie, P. G. Wodehouse, – to name mine. I need not mention particular examples, you all know them, and each of them has what is a merit in a favourite author, that their different books are all exactly the same. There is a great purity in these writers, a remarkable absence of falsity and fudge, so that they live and move, serene, Olympian and aloof, free from any pretended contact with the realities of life, each in his world of phantasy moving through the heavens according to its own laws. There is no more perfect relaxation than these.

It is the mark of a species of work in which a particular period excels that even the inferior examples of it have some merit. On this test memoirs and biographies are our best speciality to-day. Perhaps we owe it partly to Lytton Strachey that certain repressions and reserves which had a stranglehold on the last generation have sufficiently relaxed to let a little truth and character and the colour of life peep through. Virginia Woolf, who reads *all* of them, tells me that at least nine out of ten can be enjoyed. The memoir or skimming autobiography is something which our generation *en masse* has somehow learned to write. The very old-fashioned are still too anecdotal and regard their autobiographies as no more than a last opportunity to tell once again all the good stories they have told before. But to-day a great many of such writers achieve much more than this. I could mention a number. Laura Knight's *Grease Paint and Oil Paint* and Eleanor Farjeon's *A Nursery in the Nineties*, both out this spring, are excellent examples. Or to go back three or four years, Karsavina's *Theatre Street* is a sweet book. Many even of the lives of public characters, who were distinguished in the War, – books which were unreadable written in the earlier fashion – have much interest and charm. I particularly enjoyed one which did not attract much notice, the Life of Lord Wester Wemyss by his wife. But, as Virginia Woolf says, this is a class in which it is safe to-day to choose almost at random; so much more agreeable and amusing, so much more touching, bringing so much more of the pattern of life, than the daydreams of a housemaid, or, alternatively, the daydreams of a nervous wreck, which is the average modern novel. And in this context it is not out of place to mention Winston Churchill's enthralling history [*The World Crisis*], so largely a memoir, of the World War. Even two out of the few recent novels I have read and enjoyed, J. R. Ackerley's *Hindoo Holiday* and David Garnett's *Beany Eye* are, in fact, fragments of memoirs. It is a mixed lot you see. But they have splinters of truth and life in them. Besides we are just ready to be taken back, as a fair sprinkling of these books do take us, to the high comedy, the charm and security, of the Edwardian age in which most of us grew up. The early Victorian humours have grown a little stale by now, a little artificial, stereotyped and overdone. But the Edwardian age is near enough for us quickly to recognize hints and to know truth from falsehood. We want only to be reminded what it was like, and the research of times past in our own memories will do the rest. Our nostalgia is for the charmed years before the War. We need only a few hints of how we lived then, a few old photographs to bring back the taste of the biscuits we ate and the inner feeling in the whole body of what it was like to be alive in the reign of King Edward and Queen Alexandra.

The explanation of the comparative excellence of this class of writing is to be found, perhaps, in the principle that, if we cannot have art which is rare and particularly rare to-day, the next best is truth and actual experience. There is not much art in any writing to-day. But in the memoirs and autobiographies we seem to have caught the knack of recording quite a fair modicum of truth. And when this can be achieved, the memoirs of any age are delightful. I picked up the other day in a catalogue of remainders (the book was published in 1931, but failed, I suppose, to catch the public) the first English translation of *The Book of My Life* by Jerome Cardan, the Italian physician, philosopher and mathematician who lived in the sixteenth century, one of the earliest known of frank confessions and revealing autobiography, and a remarkable example of it.

There is not much contemporary poetry to recommend. But we have one poet, the Anglo-American, T. S. Eliot, whose name will be spread, I believe, ever more widely as our ears become attuned to him. Two books of his have lately come our way, – *Murder in the Cathedral*, not a thriller as the title teasingly suggests, but a religious drama in verse concerning the murder of Thomas à Becket, and his *Collected Poems 1909–1935*, which between them, Mr Eliot tells us, contain all of his poetry which he wishes to preserve. Here we have, I am sure, the outstanding poetry of our generation, poetry in the great tradition with music and meaning. Mr Eliot's underlying significance and allusion is often obscure; but he has the rarest of possessions, the ear of a poet, and the music of his speech is apparent as soon as the reader becomes a little familiar with it, and the craft with which he freshly echoes older poetry, and the associations of word and meaning.

> What seas what shores what grey rocks and what islands
> What water lapping the bow
> And scent of pine and the woodthrush singing through the firs
> What images return
> O my daughter.

There are many branches of knowledge to-day which are in no condition to be successfully and decently popularized. Much of anthropology and the history of very early civilization is, however, in the stage where strange facts are being collected; and even when some of the facts are disputed by other experts, it is intelligible reading for any of us; – for example *Adam's Ancestors* by Leakey, *The Old Stone Age* by Miles Burkitt and Dr Woolley's account of Sumeria. I advise the common reader to sample the current output of these fascinating subjects to see if they suit his taste. But philosophy and physics, for example, are certainly no food for him just now and most popular books about them are better avoided. They flatter to deceive. I am not quite sure in which class that exciting, dangerous subject, psychology, now falls. But, for the moment, I am afraid, my own subject of political economy is scarcely fit for the general public; though a popular exposition may again be possible when the experts have become clearer amongst themselves. One book there is, however, falling within this field which every serious citizen will do well to look into – the extensive description of *Soviet Communism* by Mr and Mrs Sidney Webb. It is on much too large a scale to be called a popular book, but the reader should have no difficulty in comprehending the picture it conveys. Until recently events in Russia were moving too fast and the gap between paper professions and actual achievements was too wide for a proper account to be possible. But the new system is now sufficiently crystallized to be reviewed. The result is impressive. The Russian innovators have passed, not only from the revolutionary stage, but also from the doctrinaire stage. There is little or nothing left which bears any special relation to Marx and Marxism as distinguished from other systems of socialism. They are engaged in the vast administrative task of making a completely new set of social and economic institutions work smoothly and successfully over a territory so extensive that it covers one sixth of the land surface of the world. Methods are still changing rapidly in response to experience. The largest scale empiricism and experimentalism which has ever been attempted by disinterested administrators is in operation. Meanwhile the Webbs have enabled us to see the direction in which things appear to be moving and how far they have got. It is an enthralling work, because it contains a mass of extra-ordinarily important and interesting information concerning the evolu-tion of the contemporary world. It leaves me with a strong desire and hope that we in this country may discover how to combine an unlimited readiness to experiment with changes in political and economic methods and institutions, whilst preserving traditionalism and a sort of careful conservatism, thrifty of everything which has human experience behind it, in every branch of feeling and of action.

May I conclude with a little general advice from one who can claim to be an experienced reader to those who have learnt to read but have not yet gained experience? A reader should acquire a wide general acquaintance with books *as such*, so to speak. He should approach them with all his senses; he should know their touch and their smell. He should learn how to take them in his hands, rustle their pages and reach in a few seconds a first intuitive impression of what they contain. He should, in the course of time, have touched many thousands, at least ten times as many as he really reads. He should cast an eye over books as a shepherd over sheep, and judge them with the rapid, searching glance with which a cattle-dealer eyes cattle. He should live with more books than he reads, with a penumbra of unread pages, of which he knows the general character and content, fluttering round him. This is the purpose of libraries, one's own and other people's, private and public. It is also the purpose of good bookshops, both new and second hand, of which there are still some, and would that there were more. A bookshop is not like a railway booking-office which one approaches knowing what one wants. One should enter it vaguely, almost in a dream, and allow what is there freely to attract and influence the eye. To walk the rounds of the bookshops, dipping in as curiosity dictates, should be an afternoon's entertainment. Feel no shyness or compunction in taking it. Bookshops exist to provide it, and the booksellers welcome it, well knowing how it will end. It is a habit to acquire in boyhood.

38

E. M. Forster: In My Library

E. M. Forster in his BBC talk on reading thought the book collecting that Keynes so enjoyed was non-adult. There was little unanimity in Bloomsbury in such matters. Forster's broadcast was one of a series on personal libraries that included a contribution by MacCarthy as well. Like Keynes's, Forster's talk was reduced to a single page in The Listener *where it was published in July 1949. Forster restored the cuts when reprinting it in* Two Cheers for Democracy. *Autobiography is again part of the talk; the humour and tone of voice are very characteristic of Forster's writing.*

You are soon in my library and soon out of it, for most of the books are contained in a single room. I keep some more of them in a bedroom and in a little sitting-room and in a bathroom cupboard, but most of them are in what we will politely term the library. This is a commodious apartment – twenty-four feet by eighteen – and a very pleasant one. The ceiling is high, the paint white, the wallpaper ribboned-white, and the sun, when it shines, does so through lofty windows of early Victorian Gothic. Even when it does not shine, the apartment remains warm and bright, for it faces south. Round the walls are a dozen wooden bookcases of various heights and shapes, a couple of them well designed, the others cheap. In the middle of the room stands a curious object: a bookcase which once belonged to my grandfather. It has in its front a little projecting shelf supported on two turned pillars of wood, and it has a highly polished back. Some say it is a converted bedstead. It stood in a similar position in the middle of his study over a hundred years ago – he was a country clergyman. Bedstead or not, it is agreeable and original, and I have tried to fill it with volumes of gravity, appropriate to its past. Here are the theological works of Isaac Barrow, thirteen volumes, full morocco, stamped with college arms. Here are the works of John Milton, five volumes, similarly garbed. Here is Evelyn's Diary in full calf, and Arnold's Thucydides, and Tacitus and Homer. Here are my grandfather's own works, bearing titles such as *One Primeval Language*, *The Apocalypse Its Own Interpreter* and *Mohammedanism Unveiled*. Have you read my grandfather's works? No? Have I read them? No.

My grandfather, then, is one of the influences that I can trace in my little collection. I never knew him in the flesh. He must have been rather alarming. His character was dogmatic and severe, and he would not approve of some of the company which I oblige him to keep today. For close by, in a bookcase between the two windows, lurk works of another sort – Anatole France, Marcel Proust, Heredia, André Gide – the type of Frenchman whose forerunners he denounced in a sermon preached to his village in 1871 on the occasion of the fall of Paris. It is ironical that the book belonging to him which I most cherish should be a French book. This is a great encyclopaedia in fifty-two volumes – the *Biographie Universelle* of 1825. Each volume bears his dignified bookplate with our family arms and also the bookplate of Sir James Mackintosh, its previous owner. It is in bad condition – all the backs off – but it is a useful work of reference of the leisurely type, and makes excellent reading. There is nothing slick about it. It dates from the days before the world broke up, and it is a good thing occasionally to go back to these days. They steady us.

The next influence I have to note is that of his daughter, my aunt. I inherited her possessions, and had to sell or give away most of her books before I could fit into my present quarters. But I kept what I liked best, and enough to remind me of her cultivated and attractive personality. She was a maiden lady of strong character, and a great reader, particularly of good prose. Trollope, Jane Austen, Charlotte Yonge, Malory, sound biographies of sound Victorians – these have come down from her. Books on birds also – Bewick and Morris. The birds remind me of her bookplate. She had a charming personal one of a foliated arabesque round a shield, and from the arabesque peep out birds, dogs and a squirrel – some of the living creatures who surrounded her country home where she led a quiet, happy and extremely useful life. She was interested in crafts – she started classes for leatherwork in the village. She was herself a designer and worker, she designed and executed book-covers which were made up at the binder's, and my shelves (to which we now return) are enriched by several examples of her skill. Here are the Letters of Charles Darwin (whom she had known), and Ruskin's *Praeterita*, and Ruskin's *Giotto* – a fine example in pigskin, introducing the legendary O of Giotto and her own initials. The most ambitious of all her bindings – *The Rubáiyát of Omar Khayyám* – I gave away after her death to an oriental friend. I still miss that lovely book and wish I possessed it. I still see the charming design with which she decorated its cover – polo-players adapted from an ancient Persian miniature – a design for which the contemporary dust-jacket is a poor substitute.

However, I am contemporary myself and I must get on to myself and not linger amongst ancestral influences any longer. What did I bring to my library? Not much deliberately. I have never been a collector, and as for the first-edition craze, I place it next door to stamp-collecting – I can say no less. It is non-adult and exposes the book-lover to all sorts of nonsense at the hands of the book-dealer. One should never tempt book-dealers. I am myself a lover of the interiors of books, of the words in them – an uncut book is about as inspiriting as a corked-up bottle of wine – and much as I enjoy good print and good binding and old volumes they remain subsidiary to the words: words, the wine of life. This view of mine is, I am convinced, the correct one. But even correctness has had its disadvantages, and I am bound to admit that my library, so far as I have created it, is rather a muddle. Here's one sort of book, there's another, and there is not enough of any sort of book to strike a dominant note. Books about India and by Indians, modern poetry, ancient history, American novels, travel books, books on the state of the world, and on the world-state, books on individual liberty, art-albums, Dante and books about him – they tend to swamp each other, not to mention the usual pond of pamphlets which has to be drained off periodically. The absence of the collector's instinct in me, the absence of deliberate choice, have combined with a commendable variety of interests to evolve a library which will not make any definite impression upon visitors.

I have not a bookplate – too diffident or too much bother. I cannot arrange books well either; shall it be by subjects or by heights? Shall a tall old Froissart stand beside *The Times Atlas*, or beside a tiny Philippe de Commines? I do not bang or blow them as much as I should, or oil their leather backs, or align those backs properly. They are unregimented. Only at night, when the curtains are drawn and the fire flickers, and the lights are turned off, do they come into their own, and attain a collective dignity. It is very pleasant to sit with them in the firelight for a couple of minutes, not reading, not even thinking, but aware that they, with their accumulated wisdom and charm, are waiting to be used, and that my library, in its tiny imperfect way, is a successor to the great private libraries of the past. 'Do you ever lend books?' someone may say in a public-spirited tone of voice at this point. Yes, I do, and they are not returned, and still I lend books. Do I ever borrow books? I do, and I can see some of them unreturned around me. I favour reciprocal dishonesty. But the ownership of the things does give me peculiar pleasure, which increases as I get older. It is of the same kind, though not so strong, as the desire to possess land. And, like all possessiveness, it does not go down to the roots of our humanity. Those roots are spiritual. The deepest desire in us is the desire to understand, and that is what I meant just now when I said that the really important thing in books is the words in them – words, the wine of life – not their binding or their print, not their edition value or their bibliomaniac value, or their uncuttability.

One's favourite book is as elusive as one's favourite pudding, but there certainly are three writers whom I would like to have in every room, so that I can stretch out my hand for them at any moment. They are Shakespeare, Gibbon and Jane Austen. There are two Shakespeares in this library of mine and also two outside it, one Gibbon and one outside it, one Jane Austen and two outside it. So I am happily furnished. And, of course, I have some Tolstoy, but one scarcely wants Tolstoy in every room. Shakespeare, Gibbon and Jane Austen are my choice, and in a library one thinks of Gibbon most. Gibbon loved books but was not dominated by them. He knew how to use them. His bust might well stand on my grandfather's bookcase, to my grandfather's indignation.

Part VIII

Travel Writings

Europe and the Mediterranean were the locations of most of the Bloomsbury Group's travelling and travel writing. Forster and Leonard Woolf also knew and wrote about the Indian empire but never ventured further east. Lytton Strachey wrote about India too but never travelled there, and neither Strachey nor Virginia Woolf visited the United States. France, Spain, Italy, Greece were Bloomsbury's favourite countries – after Britain.

39

Leonard Woolf:
The Gentleness of Nature

The title of Leonard Woolf's 'The Gentleness of Nature' is typically ironical. His subject is the pitilessness of nature, as he knew it while serving in the Ceylon civil service from 1904 to 1911; Woolf's subtext is the inability of imperialism to do anything about it. The same concerns are to be found in the novel The Village in the Jungle *that Woolf wrote out of his Ceylon experiences and also in the autobiography* Growing *which he wrote fifty years later. The essay was done for the* New Statesman *in 1917 and reprinted in Leonard Woolf's* Essays *(1927).*

The other day there was a hard frost upon the Sussex downs; a bitter north-east wind raced across the bare, whitened hill-sides. Late in the evening I came upon a green plover sitting on the ground, ceaselessly turning its head from side to side. I picked it up, and found it to be unwounded, its wings unharmed, and not a speck or blemish upon its magnificent plumage. When set down upon the ground, it began again to turn its head from side to side, and so, I imagine, it would have gone on sitting there with closed eyes, dumbly and patiently turning its head from side to side, until, in the bitter cold of the night wind, it as dumbly and patiently died.

In England, even upon the bleakest downlands, it is a rare thing to find a wild animal dying of what the coroner calls 'natural causes'. That is because in this country we have succeeded so amazingly in taming Nature that she hides entirely from us her ruthless ferocity, her dark and gloomy ways. To the Englishman Nature is a thing of spring, of lambs gambolling in snakeless meadows, of wild flowers and the song of larks. In our towns we have covered her over completely with paving-stones, and asphalt, and houses; in the fields we cover her up with corn and turnips and fat sheep and shiny domesticated cows; in the rich man's park we cover her up with ridiculous hand-fed pheasants.

But elsewhere, in the East for example, where Nature rules man and not man Nature, the depth of her melancholy and her iron ruthlessness become apparent. The curious forgotten fact is that even in England not so many generations back she was like that. To-day in our churches we still pray anachronistically to be delivered from the scourge of cattle murrain. Some years ago in Ceylon, I saw what it really was that our forefathers so fervently prayed God for protection against. It was Nature – pitiless, untamed, and all-powerful – appearing in the form not of violets and cowslips, but of pain and destruction and wholesale death. There is a district in the south of Ceylon consisting principally of jungle. The chief population consists of wild pig, deer, buffaloes, leopards, and elephants. But there is also a human population of about 100,000 living in scattered villages. Such wealth as these men have lies in their herds of cattle, in the bulls which draw their carts, and the domesticated buffaloes which, treading the round of the rice-fields in primeval fashion, take the place of ploughs, and treading the grain upon the threshing-floor serve the purpose of the flail and threshing-machine.

Upon this district there descended suddenly murrain or rinderpest. It was the season when the crops were on the ground, and the cattle had therefore been driven out from the villages to graze in the jungles or the great open spaces of dry lagoons. The disease first appeared in a herd of 150 buffaloes grazing in such a lagoon. When I went to the place, the ground was covered with great beasts lying dead or dying, and the flics were swarming over the dead and dying alike. Out of the clouds of far-off Colombo, that mysterious entity, 'the Government', sent down its orders that all cattle should be tethered or impounded, that all 'suspected' beasts should be segregated and 'infected' shot. But it was all useless. The disease had spread already into the jungle, to the wild buffaloes, and the jungle was soon full of death. The carcasses lay thick in the lagoons, and on the game tracks, and around the waterholes. The herds of wild pig came and fed upon the infected bodies, sickened, carried the disease back to the domestic cattle of the villages, and died everywhere in hundreds. In the thickest jungle you came upon even the great sambhur deer dying. And the villager, after the manner of the East, prepared to watch ruin descend upon him silently and patiently. He would do nothing. He had never tethered a buffalo or put his half-wild bulls within fences, and therefore to tether a buffalo now or to impound his cattle was not only useless but impossible. He had never killed his own animals, and therefore nothing on earth would induce him now to kill a plague-stricken beast, though it were a mere living mass of flies and maggots. Even on the few main roads bulls dropped and died, and were left to rot where they had fallen. Herds of two hundred dwindled in a few months to two or three head of cattle, and many a village saw almost its entire wealth swept away in a week.

Around the village the grim cruelty of Nature had full sway. There was a village of some forty huts, a little Government school, a tank, and a stretch of rice-fields, set in the jungle. A villager told me that there was a plague-stricken buffalo near the tank. I went through a little patch of jungle and came out upon the bund of the tank. It was a pleasant sight after the dry, scrubby, barren jungle. Great kumbuk and tamarind trees grew upon the bund, the sheet of water was starred with lotus flowers, a great flight of teal flew whirring round and round high overhead. I sat down for a moment, and then far off across the tank in the water caught sight of a black patch, clearly a wallowing buffalo. And almost immediately it stirred, and, as I sat there, I saw that it was very slowly moving towards me. This in itself was strange, for a buffalo will always move away from you, and I had expected a long, hot chase. As it came nearer, even at 250 yards, you could see from its slow gait that it was plague-stricken, and as I sat there in the sun watching it drag itself towards me I felt as if it was deliberately coming to be killed, to be put out of some intolerable agony. At 100 yards I fired at it with a rifle and missed completely, but it paid no attention and continued to plod straight towards me. I fired again and it fell dead. And when I went up to it I found that the whole of one side of its face, including the eye, had been eaten away by maggots.

But it was in the real, thick jungle that one got the full impression of the pitilessness and melancholy of Nature. That hot season, when the murrain was still in the land, I went one night to sit up and watch the animals at a waterhole. It was many miles from any village, and for miles it was the only hole which had not dried up, so that the wild beasts for a great distance round about had to come nightly to drink at it. When I reached it towards evening, the sight and smell of it were alike appalling. The jungle was dense, and suddenly you came out of it upon a great slope of bare rock raised above the trees. In the centre was an immense deep hole full of water. Upon the rock around the hole were twelve dead buffaloes, three dead sambhur deer, and half a dozen dead pigs. In the water floated three huge swollen carcasses. The jungle round was littered with bodies. The maddening thirst which comes with the disease had brought the wretched creatures to the waterhole, and there they had dropped and died. One carcass had been half-eaten by a leopard at some distance from the hole, so I determined to watch there while my men dragged the bodies from the waterhole, and made as clear a space as possible on the rocks. I made myself a little screen of branches a few yards from the body and sat down to wait. In the jungle there is no kind of joyousness or movement of bird or animal life. Everything slinks by silently, fearfully, almost sadly. As I watched, a small grey mongoose slipped into view, slunk into the belly of the buffalo and began to feed on the flesh. Nothing else moved, no sound came, and then suddenly there stood a few yards in front of me the leopard, quite motionless except for the tip of his tail which moved slowly from side to side. He stood there listening and staring intently for a second or two, and then the mongoose scuttled out of the carcass, and the leopard melted away immediately from before my eyes, just as he had appeared, without any visible movements, like a picture thrown upon a screen by a magic-lantern and then instantly removed.

I went back to the waterhole. For hours there was no sign of life, except once for a few minutes down a track I saw a black object, probably a jackal, leaping about silently in the moonlight, wildly like some mad thing. Nothing came to the hole and no sound broke the stillness until about two in the morning, when a great crashing rose up from below in the jungle. Then an enormous head appeared in the bright moonlight from the deep shadows of the trees, and ponderously an elephant shouldered himself on to the rock. Another and another followed – eleven, one behind the other. Then very slowly and deliberately they lined up in a row at the waterhole, a gigantic bull at one end and two tiny beasts at the other end of the line. They stood there slowly and sadly swaying their trunks and their great heads, and lifting first one foot and then another. The old bull at last put his trunk into the water, but it was too foul to drink. For a few minutes the whole line stood there in the bright light of the moon as if they were part of the rock, but with the same melancholy swaying of the trunks and heads. Then very slowly the old elephant turned away and one behind the other they filed into the jungle. There was no water for them, I knew, within twenty miles.

40

Desmond MacCarthy:
Two Historic Houses

Desmond MacCarthy visited South Africa eight years after the Boer War in 1910. His characterizations of the Boer leader Paul Kruger and the imperialist Cecil Rhodes are done through their houses, which were near Pretoria and Cape Town. The rather abrupt end of the sketch leaves the reader with the impression that Kruger interests MacCarthy more than Rhodes. MacCarthy collected 'Two Historic Houses' in Remnants *(1918), then retitled it 'Oom Paul and Cecil Rhodes: Two Houses' in* Portraits *(1931).*

One is an unlovely little bungalow near Pretoria, with a tin roof and a dark veranda, standing beside a rough road down which a puff of wind sends clouds of tawny dust. The stony ground is cracked and weedy. The landscape has a littered, slovenly look as though it were not virgin soil, but an enormous tract of uncomfortable building land. Near the house lie many years' accumulations of tins; meat tins, sardine tins, fruit tins, biscuit tins, oil cans and broken pots. They have mostly rusted down to kinship with the soil, but here and there the sun, blazing like a white combustion in the sky, still strikes out a flash among the shards and weeds. Four strides take one to the veranda, the steps of which are guarded by two small couchant lions of heraldic type with rueful countenances. Where did they come from? Witnessing to man's power of conventionalizing natural forms, to that freedom of conception and submissiveness to tradition upon which imaginative art depends, they seem on this spot singularly impressive. Amid so much aridity, material and spiritual, they seem unique, beyond criticism, relics of a former world.

Under this veranda old Paul Kruger used to sit, with his pipe, his Bible and his spittoon, gazing across the road at the large proportionless reach-me-down building, half church and half conventicle, where he used to preach on Sundays. It was the site, this tin 'stoop', of historic and cautious colloquies, and of many slow, sly meditations and religious resolves. Looking back it seems to me as though he must have been there himself when I visited it, so strong at the time was the sense of his presence. I seem to *remember* a black ungainly figure – a drayman dressed as an undertaker – with brown, black-nailed hands slackly joined across the creases of an ancient frock-coat, sitting there, hunched and motionless; a heavy yellow mask of a face seen in the shadow, with low forehead, thick eyebrows, neck-beard and saurian eyes, preoccupied and drowsily watchful. Every now and again the wind would lift a cloud of grit from the road and blow it tinkling against the corrugated roof and dry shivering bushes. The loneliness and publicity of the place, its solitude and lack of privacy are appalling to one sensitive to ordered permanence and to that 'tranquillizing stamp of man's affections upon the things around him which gives a sense of home'. Like many a great man, Kruger was an epitome of the characteristics of his race, the flower of its most conservative instincts. The Boer, though physically an immovable sort of man and reluctant to uproot himself, has a trekker's indifference to his immediate surroundings, and he is as content to live for years in his own litter as though he were moving on next month. He loves not possessions, but money and independence, and not money as one who knows its value, its immediate possibilities, but as one who has known the importance of hoarding necessitous resources. Here lived one who, it is said, was very rich. What an effort of imagination to supply here a background of ghostly money-bags! What a contrast between this house and Groote-Schuur where his enemy lived, who also bothered little about luxury, ceremony or show, but liked to have things about him fine, solid and elegant!

To one who arrives at his own sense of rival political ideals in a country more through impressions than through statistics and statements, the contrast between the homes of Cecil Rhodes and Paul Kruger has much to say. Groote-Schuur is built in a fold of the spurs of Table Mountain, one of the most beautiful sites in the world, among bright, green pines and chestnut trees. Its garden is laid out in careless masses of flowers, which mix with the woods and slopes beyond. The house is not what we should consider a large one. It is built in a kind of Italianate Dutch style, with thick white walls, and wide verandas supported by slender columns. Its decorations are akin to the sober, solid exuberance of old Dutch wardrobes and heavy, brass-bound chests. It is cool, spacious yet compact, and superbly comfortable; and it is haunted by a very different presence. A heavy-shouldered, restless man with reddish hair, who talks and talks in a reedy head-voice, and whose prominent formidable eyes are lit with the glare of dreams, visions of vast empty territories, gigantic material possibilities. The Hero as Financier! It was a long time before I could envisage such a character; and I am not sure that I like his fervid followers now. But I realize that he gave them imaginative 'openings' as no one else could, and threw upon their projects and activities the light of larger issues and impersonal aims, just as for his people 'Oom Paul' expressed a biblical ideal. The smoke of our inglorious war has cleared away, but the struggle between those two ideals is still going on, the one with all the faults and virtues of old Scottish Calvinism, the other with all those of a pioneering, commercial civilization.

In the dining-room of the tin bungalow outside Pretoria stands the black coffin case of Kruger. It was strewn when I saw it with withering wreaths; every foot, too, of the walls was covered with laurel trophies, and at the end of the small dark wall hung one of the few genuine specimens I have seen of modern primitive art. The head of the last President of the Republic (life size) was represented as bursting through a hard blue sky, the colour of a sparrow's egg. The collar-stud and tie were carefully painted, and then abruptly cut off by more blue sky. On either side of his head a miniature angel hovered; one, propping a large book against a cloud, was presumably writing in it the deeds of the hero, the other was about to crown him with a little wreath the size of a bracelet; and underneath, far below, was a sea of human hats, diminishing to the horizon; straw hats, felt hats, bowlers, sun hats, caps and waving sticks. The artist had evidently felt uncertain of his power of inventing human faces, and he had relied upon hats to produce the effect of a gigantic acclamation. It was the best his own people could do for Kruger in the way of art, which is not in their line. To the memory of Rhodes his countrymen set up the great bronze horse of Watts, which champs and paws beneath a rider who looks eagerly out under his hand across seas and miles of fertile land; a monument reminiscent in every line of the long inheritance of civilization.

What a subject for an imaginative historian, the struggle between these two and that conflict between ideals! Not for an historian most interested in weighing immediate rights and wrongs in the quarrel between the two nations, but for an historian with a sense of drama, and of the everlasting inevitable clash of new things with old. Kruger is one of the most tragic figures; all the more tragic for his narrownesses and crookednesses. For me the dusty, dark room and tin 'stoop' was full of echoes of those Cromwellian speeches of his, with their dry references of Peter v., verses 7 and 8, or Revelation xiv. 9, 10, 12 and 13, as the case might be, and their closings, 'I have spoken', 'I have done.' I remembered his flight that night in September 1900, when his country was swarming with the enemy, and the fighting Boers were making their way north through an uninhabitable country to reorganize there and begin the struggle again. I remembered the opening words of his final Proclamation: 'Whereas the great age of His Honour the State President renders it impossible for His Honour to continue to accompany the Commandoes,' and imagined his parting from his grey-haired wife that evening, to see whom as a boy of sixteen he once swam a river in spate, which the ferry-man refused to cross.

41

E. M. Forster: Cnidus

'Cnidus' was Forster's third publication after he left college, and it indicates how soon he found his voice as a writer. The essay appeared in the Independent Review *in 1904 and Forster reprinted it, slightly revised, in* Abinger Harvest *some thirty years later. The comic travelogue is about not being able to see much of the ancient Greek city of Cnidus, home of the famous Demeter that Forster would use again as a central symbol in his novel* The Longest Journey. *The essay ends in fantasy with the appearance of a figure resembling Hermes, god of travellers and conductor of the dead, whom Forster also invokes in the preface to his collection of short stories (see pp. 10–12).*

Cnidus is not yet a seaside resort, nor am I afraid of making it one by describing my visit to it. There are some places that are safe from popularity – for example, the peninsula in Southern Asia Minor, townless, roadless, three miles across and fifty miles long, at the end of which lies Cnidus.

Greek captains never will use a chart. They sometimes have one, but it is always locked up in a drawer; for, as they truly say, it is nothing but paper and lines, which are not the least like the sea, and it is far better to trust to yourself, especially in parts where you have never been before. But, as they combine instinct with caution, progress is sometimes slow; and, instead of having a long afternoon at Cnidus, we did not anchor till five o'clock, and it was pouring with rain.

Desire for information tempted some of us ashore; the name of Asia others. By some mischance, we were landed on the broken edge of the town wall, and had to stumble upwards over vast blocks of dislodged stone, amid the rapture of competent observers, who had discovered that the iron clamps were those used in classical times, and that we were straining our ankles over masonry of the best period. Within the walls were darkness and much mud, such as there is within the Hades of Aristophanes, and heavy dropping drain, such as befouls the Limbo of Dante, and at first the great silence that befits a city dead a thousand years.

So I have never seen Cnidus, for the land was only an outline, and the sea ran into the sky. And who would expect visions from a dripping silhouette, when, time after time, the imagination has dwelt in vain desire amidst sun and blue sky and perfect colonnades, and found in them nothing but colonnades and sky and sun? But, that evening, under those weeping clouds, the imagination became creative, taking wings because there was nothing to bid it rise, flying impertinently against all archaeology and sense, uttering bird-like cries of 'Greek! Greek!' as it flew, declaring that it heard voices because all was so silent, and saw faces because it was too dark to see. I am ashamed of its outbreak, and will confine myself to facts, such as they are.

Cnidus, then, is only an outline. The high mountains of the peninsula are on the right, and on the left is the great Triopian promontory, joined to the mountains by a flat and narrow strip of sand. Thus the city is shaped like a dumb-bell – athletic similes are pardonable when the theme is Greek – having a throne on the mountains, a throne on Triopia, and a smooth causeway whereby she may pass between them. I do not know whether Greek art has ever embodied Cnidus as a maiden dominating the Aegean from a double seat of empire. It might very well be; for has not Eutychides personified Antioch bending over the side of a hill, to dip her feet in the waters of Orontes? Such conceptions, I ought to add, do not date from the best period of art, and therefore give no pleasure to those whose taste is really pure.

There are two harbours. Our steamer was in one, and the other was the Trireme harbour beyond the causeway, and our destination. We went to one or two temples, I think, and an agora; and I know we went to the theatre, for I fell off the stage into the orchestra, to the confusion of the competent observers, who, in the uncertain light, had mistaken the stage for the base of the harbour pier. The orchestra is planted with Jerusalem artichokes, and the mud in it is more glutinous than the mud outside.

Somewhere or other there must have been the temple of Apollo, and the temple of Poseidon, and the shrine of the nymphs, in whose honour all the men of the Dorian Hexapolis came yearly to race; and somewhere else there must have been the ruined house of the Cnidian Aphrodite. But I did see the home of the Goddess who has made Cnidus famous to us, for, up on the right, the mountain had been scarped and a platform levelled, and someone pointed it out and said: 'That is the precinct of the Infernal Deities, where they got the Demeter' – that Demeter of Cnidus, whom we hold in the British Museum now. She was there at that moment, warm and comfortable in that little recess of hers between the Ephesian Room and the Archaic Room, with the electric light fizzling above her, and casting blue shadows over her chin. She is dusted twice a week, and there is a railing in front, with 'No Admittance', so that she cannot be touched. And if human industry can find that lost arm of hers, and that broken nose, and human ingenuity can put them on, she shall be made as good as new.

I am not going to turn sentimental, and pity the exiled Demeter, and declare that her sorrowful eyes are straining for the scarped rock, and the twin harbours, and Triopia, and the sea. She is doing nothing of the sort. If her eyes see anything, it must be the Choiseul Apollo who is in the niche opposite; and she might easily do worse. And if, as I believe, she is alive, she must know that she has come among people who love her, for all they are so weak-chested and anaemic and feeble-kneed, and who pay her such prosaic homage as they can. Demeter alone among gods has true immortality. The others continue, perchance, their existence, but are forgotten, because the time came when they could not be loved. But to her, all over the world, rise prayers of idolatry from suffering men as well as suffering women, for she has transcended sex. And Poets too, generation after generation, have sung in passionate incompetence of the hundred-flowered Narcissus and the rape of Persephone, and the wanderings of the Goddess, and her gift to us of corn and tears; so that generations of critics, obeying also their need, have censured the poets for reviving the effete mythology of Greece, and urged them to themes of living interest which shall touch the heart of to-day.

There have been other finds in that mountain precinct – some fascinating terra-cotta pigs, for example, broad of back and steady poise, and a number of those interesting Katadesmoi, leaded tablets stamped with curses, which have thrown such a flood of light on the subject of classical vituperation. But we had no time to go up there, and plunged along, over a real ploughed field, to reach the Trireme harbour while there was yet a vestige of light.

The rain hammered down on our umbrellas, and filled our ears with fictitious uproar. It was only when we put the umbrellas down to speak or listen to each other, that we heard what was really happening. There were sounds then from the black and the illimitable grey – the bark of a dog, a sheep coughing in the wet, and the most certainly the sound of human voices. We put up our umbrellas again and hurried on; for human voices are alarming when they cease to be imaginary. It is not pleasant to meet new people in the dark.

The long ploughed field ended in a stone wall and a sharp slope of cliff. Looking down, I saw the Trireme harbour at last – a perfect curve of grey that bit into the black. It must face west; for it still shone, though not with colour, being to the eye without substance or perspective – a vast well that went through the middle of the earth into nothing. Some great building had fallen into the shallows; and pillars, capitals, and cornices were isolated mysteriously, as if in air. Only by the delicate smell and the delicate whisper of ripples on the sand, was it revealed to us that it was a harbour, and filled with the sea.

We had to turn at once and hurry back over the fields to our own harbour; for the rain was wetting us through, and it was quite dark now, and late, and voices were calling all about the hills. There was light of a kind by the boats, the light of phosphorescence, that was born when the ripples clashed and died when they subsided. And a small Japanese lantern, grotesquely incongruous, assisted us to embark.

Heads were counted, to see that no one was missing. There were ten already in the boats, and seven pressing to get in, stumbling about amid sea urchins and wet rocks ere they did so. And five more were coming up behind, all blurred out of the night. We were twenty-two in all; but that was hardly satisfactory, for we had started out twenty-one. Someone had joined us.

It is well known (is it not?) who that extra person always is. This time he came hurrying down to the beach at the last moment, and tried to peer into our faces. I could hardly see his; but it was young, and it did not look unkind. He made no answer to our tremulous greetings, but raised his hand to his head and then laid it across his breast, meaning I understand, that his brain and his heart were ours. Everyone made clumsy imitations of his gesture to keep him in a good temper. His manners were perfect. I am not sure that he did not offer to lift people into the boats. But there was a general tendency to avoid his attentions, and we put off in an incredibly short space of time. He melted away in the darkness after a couple of strokes, and we before long were back on the steamer, amid light, and the smell of hot meat, and the pity and self-gratulations of those who had been wise enough to stop on board.

It was indeed an absurd expedition. We returned soaked and shivering, without a photograph, without a sketch, without so much as an imprecatory tablet to link the place with reality and the world of facts. It lies a defenceless prey to the sentimental imagination and, as I am absolutely certain never to go there again, I do not see how it is to be rescued. I never cease to dry up its puddles, and brush away its clouds, and span it over with blue sky in which is hanging a mid-day sun that never moves. Even over that extra person the brain will not keep steady.

42

Roger Fry: Ciudad Rodrigo

Roger Fry's Sampler of Castile *(1923) is both a travel and a sketch book, with most of the chapters devoted to Castilian towns that Fry visited and illustrated. Indeed it is his sketchbook that involves Fry with the Chief of Police in Ciudad Rodrigo. The account follows Fry's chapter on Salamanca and alludes back to the opening chapter on the Spanish language where he complains of the indiscriminate Spanish use of the phrase 'muy bonito'. The chapter on Ciudad Rodrigo is accompanied with a sketch of the town from across the Agueda river.*

Whether it was the University tradition or what, I do not know, but somehow the people of Salamanca were unusually willing to enter into conversation. The shop people would keep me long after the transaction was over, elderly gentlemen would lean across café tables, and generally the conversation veered round to the wonders of Salamanca and its neighbourhood. Always too there lurked in the background the wonders of the Peña de la Francia, the low range of mountains just out of sight of the town, and the two mysterious and almost savage tribes that inhabit them – the Batuecas and the Jordes. These grew in my imagination by the piecing together of half- or mis-understood phrases to something monstrous and terrific. Later on, at Ciudad Rodrigo, my friend the Chief of Police told me all about the Jordes. Numbers of them come down twice a year to a sort of fair and there sell themselves almost as slaves, for they can barely exist in their mountain homes. He added that they were feeble, weakly creatures but 'muy bonitos' (a good sort). Perhaps all savages are 'muy bonitos' and it is only when civilized that man becomes a ferocious animal. But I never got to the Peña and never saw a Batueca or a Jorde, but I did go to the other much-praised sight of the country-side, Ciudad Rodrigo. It is some way off, almost down to the Portuguese frontier, on a line that I think leads nowhere in particular. But for once the time-table was propitious: by starting at 5 A.M. and getting back at 11 at night I could have a whole long day there. Had I trusted my Salamancan informants more implicitly and known what an enchanting place Ciudad Rodrigo was and how excellent its inn, I should have taken the means to stay a day or two.

The customary remoteness of the station meant half an hour's walk before 5.30, and no hope of any assistance whatever from the hotel people and, as I believed, no hope of food till I got to Ciudad at 9. But it was better than I thought, for I made the great discovery that morning, that if the hotels hardly stir before 8.30 or 9, there are people in Spain who get up really early or else stay up very late. There were workmen arriving somehow from the outlying desert, and to provide for these an old woman had already rigged up her booth in an open place near the station and was selling 'chorros'. The chorro is a splendid invention. A stiff paste of flour and water is squeezed out of a cylinder through a serrated circular opening into a huge pan of boiling oil, where it gets turned to lovely golden brown sticks, like brown Angelica stems. There is a delicious crisp crunch when one bites an end off, and the flavour is agreeably neutral. With a handful of these I was independent of contingent but improbable buffets for the three hours' journey.

There are few pleasures more satisfactory than that of being deposited by a little local train, still in the early morning of a fine day, outside some remote country town about which one has formed enticing anticipations. Sometimes, of course, it is almost the only entirely delightful moment of the day, and the subsequent disillusions spoil its record in the memory. But in this case every step towards the little town which lay a mile or so away confirmed my hopes. I was approaching from the upland side, and it lay along a low hill encircled by a wall which no doubt was originally of the high mediaeval type but had been lowered and remade according to the exigencies of later warfare. In fact it evidently resulted from our differences with Napoleon, so that one entered the town not through a handsome mediaeval archway but by a twisting lane between bastions and counterscarps and, for aught I know, all Uncle Toby's ' "curtains" and hornworks', and so through a narrow tunnel into the town itself.

And what a town! almost untouched, and filled with small provincial palaces built in a hard crystalline-brown stone with nearly as lovely a fracture as travertine. These palaces front the street with an almost

even face. The round-arched doorways have no moulding to spoil
the clean break from sunlit wall to blackness. The arches are built
with voussoirs as long or longer than the width of the doorway itself;
and these enormous blocks of stone are not marked out in any way,
the radiating joints of the well-cut masonry making the only pattern –
but how exquisite a one. Only farther up, and at rare intervals in
the façade, under the cornice perhaps, or round a window, there will
run a deeply-carved, intricate, foliated pattern of sixteenth-century
Gothic-Renaissance ornament.

In one of these palaces, though somewhat modernized, I had found a
most attractive inn, where, for once, one was almost welcomed, had
assured lunch and deposited some of my clothes, for the keen morning
chill was already gone, and then went out with ever-increased anticipa-
tion. I had begun to look round the Plaza Mayor, with its jolly little
Renaissance town hall, when a middle-aged man came up to me and
introduced himself as the Chief of the Police. My heart sank – what
had I done? was it against the law to have a sketch-book? were there
desperate military secrets hidden in the Napoleonic earthworks? or were
lonely strangers blackmailed before being allowed to leave the town?
But out of the voluble flow of my interlocutor's speech I gradually made
out that he was Chief of the Police indeed, but merely by way of an
expedient, at heart he was a desperate, though amateur, devotee of
painting – and – 'might he come with me round the town?' It was my
sketch-book that had betrayed me, and I was in for it; not indeed for the
blacker fates that had flashed across my apprehension, but for the other
fate of not being allowed to wander about just as the fancy might take
me. I should have to see the sights properly and under guidance. I
ventured one stammering appeal that I might be allowed first to go by
myself and then later on be shown in detail. But the civil authority was
inexorable; my words were brushed aside in a fresh flow of talk, and, but
for a short siesta after lunch, which my early start really justified, I was
to be tied to my new acquaintance through every minute of the day until
he saw me off by the train at 8 in the evening. My faint hopes that the
duties of a Chief of the Police might require some slight attention in the
course of the day were quickly dispelled by his account of the universal
peace, contentment, and friendliness to himself, of the whole population,
an account which everything I saw bore out.

I had to go to the town hall and be introduced to the Town Clerk, a
rather austerely polite gentleman, who had to show me the town charters
and market licences with the leaden seals of various fourteenth- and
fifteenth-century kings attached, and then to the police station, where, if
I was not locked up, I felt none the less the impossibility of escaping.

My guardian the while hurried off to his studio to arrange his own works in a satisfactory light. Thither I was piloted and made to give a professional opinion, with such technical advice as could trickle through the obstructions of my elementary Spanish. Indeed it was a great strain to keep on dodging doubtful irregular verbs and turning the corner of forgotten subjunctives all day long, and an even greater to pretend that I understood a respectable fraction of what was addressed to me.

However, we got to the Cathedral. Its dull modern classic façade is pitted all over with the marks of the comparatively innocuous shells which Napoleon's generals or Wellington (I forget which) hurled at it. On the south side, within a large closed porch, is one of the most superb early Gothic doorways I have ever seen. Its sculptures rival the best French work of the twelfth century. And inside, that fair and gay effect of logical simplicity of clear untroubled surfaces which belongs to the happy moment when the engineering business of vaulting had not gone too far and yet had enabled the builders to construct wide simple domical vaults in each bay. Once more I wondered why that craze for the even ridge-line of the vaulted roof, when so pleasant a space is spread for the imagination by this succession of flattened vaulted hollows. And as yet the ribs were not too prominent a feature, though oddly disposed here in eight radiating lines, four of which give on to the caps and four on to the summits of the supporting arches.

I was introduced to an elderly priest, who was positively affable. He sang me seventeenth-century chants from the immense hymn books on the lectern, regretted the decadence of modern taste which made it necessary for the Church to modernize the old music in the services, praised the magnificence of Vittoria's music, and showed me the choir-stalls. These in Spanish cathedrals generally add the last touch of boredom by their exaggerated attempt to astonish. How wearisome that profusion of late Gothic or Plateresque jugglery is. But at Ciudad Rodrigo, for once, they were interesting – early fifteenth century I guessed, and by some surprising original genius whose love of pure plastic forms had been, strangely enough, allowed full licence. Animals and nude figures in bold legible designs crouched under the miserere seats in attitudes of uncompromising freedom. Whenever we came to some peculiarly frank piece of mediaeval grossness, the priest would chuckle 'Muy ardito – muy ardito' (very daring) with evident pride in the unorthodox peculiarity of his church. Whether the civil authority of Ciudad had infected the religious with this genial spirit of tolerant humanity, or whether it was the other way about, I do not know – in any case it was an endearing peculiarity of its remote provincial civilization.

On the other side of the town the mediaeval walls still stand, and a pleasant walk takes one along their crest, with an enchanting view of the wide river valley beneath and the long undulating lines of distance beyond. The valley is richly and beautifully wooded, mostly with poplars, and the river itself is wide and clear. Having by now got not a single Spanish word left on my tongue, I persuaded my friendly guide to get his sketch-book and to come down to the further bank of the river and spend the afternoon sketching under the poplars. Even if no subject came to hand I should at least enjoy being silent in a foreign tongue for an hour or two, and in fact the afternoon passed delightfully enough in cool shade with the bell-like notes of orioles and the murmur of the river in our ears; and we went off at dusk to the distant station, my friend touchingly grateful for the happiness of a day spent in the company of a real professional artist, who could tell him more or less intelligibly how to prepare his own canvases. And there on the platform, for half an hour before the train's arrival, was gathered all the élite of Ciudad, from the Bishop downwards. It is the evening promenade, where one walks up and down and looks at the pretty girls who have come precisely to be looked at, and whom my friend assured me were, like the mountain savage, 'muy bonitas'.

43

Virginia Woolf: Street Haunting

It is fitting for the travel section of A Bloomsbury Group Reader *to end with an essay on London. Virginia Woolf's 'Street Haunting' is subtitled 'A London Adventure', the adventure being the purchase of a pencil. Starting from the illusion that one is not tied to a single mind, the narrator describes through an associative technique the perceptions of other lives in the streets and shops of a London winter evening. Woolf's essay was written for the* Yale Review *in 1930, then reprinted by a private press in America.*

No one perhaps has ever felt passionately towards a lead pencil. But there are cirumstances in which it can become supremely desirable to possess one; moments when we are set upon having an object, a purpose, an excuse for walking half across London between tea and dinner. As the foxhunter hunts in order to preserve the breed of horses, and the golfer plays in order that open spaces may be preserved from the builders, so when the desire comes upon us to go street rambling the pencil does for a pretext, and getting up we say, 'Really I must buy a pencil,' as if under cover of this excuse we could indulge safely in the greatest pleasure of town life in winter – rambling the streets of London.

The hour should be evening and the season winter, for in winter the champagne brightness of the air and the sociability of the streets are grateful. We are not then taunted as in summer by the longing for shade and solitude and sweet airs from the hayfields. The evening hour, too, gives us the irresponsibility which darkness and lamplight bestow. We are no longer quite ourselves. As we step out of the house on a fine evening between four and six we shed the self our friends know us by and become part of that vast republican army of anonymous trampers, whose society is so agreeable after the solitude of one's own room. For there we sit surrounded by objects which perpetually express the oddity of our own temperaments and enforce the memories of our own experience. That bowl on the mantelpiece, for instance, was bought at Mantua on a windy day. We were leaving the shop when the sinister old woman plucked at our skirts and said she would find herself starving one of these days, but 'Take it!' she cried, and thrust the blue and white china bowl into our hands as if she never wanted to be reminded of her quixotic generosity. So, guiltily, but suspecting nevertheless how badly we had been fleeced, we carried it back to the little hotel where, in the middle of the night, the innkeeper quarrelled so violently with his wife that we all leant out into the courtyard to look, and saw the vines laced about among the pillars and the stars white in the sky. The moment was stabilized, stamped like a coin indelibly, among a million that slipped by imperceptibly. There, too, was the melancholy Englishman, who rose among the coffee cups and the little iron tables and revealed the secrets of his soul – as travellers do. All this – Italy, the windy morning, the vines laced about the pillars, the Englishman and the secrets of his soul – rise up in a cloud from the China bowl on the mantelpiece. And there, as our eyes fall to the floor, is that brown stamp on the carpet. Mr Lloyd George made that. 'The man's a devil!' said Mr Cummings, putting the kettle down with which he was about to fill the teapot so that it burnt a brown ring on the carpet.

But when the door shuts on us, all that vanishes. The shell-like covering which our souls have excreted to house themselves, to make for themselves a shape distinct from others, is broken, and there is left of all these wrinkles and roughnesses a central oyster of perceptiveness, an enormous eye. How beautiful a street is in winter! It is at once revealed and obscured. Here vaguely one can trace symmetrical straight avenues of doors and windows; here under the lamps are floating islands of pale light through which pass quickly bright men and women, who for all their poverty and shabbiness wear a certain look of unreality, an air of triumph, as if they had given life the slip, so that life, deceived of her prey, blunders on without them. But, after all, we are only gliding smoothly on the surface. The eye is not a miner, not a diver, not a seeker after buried treasure. It floats us smoothly down a stream, resting, pausing, the brain sleeps perhaps as it looks.

How beautiful a London street is then, with its islands of light, and its long groves of darkness, and on one side of it perhaps some tree-sprinkled, grass-grown space where night is folding herself to sleep naturally and, as one passes the iron railing, one hears those little cracklings and stirrings of leaf and twig which seem to suppose the silence of fields all round them, an owl hooting, and far away the rattle of a train in the valley. But this is London, we are reminded; high among the bare trees are hung oblong frames of reddish yellow light – windows; there are points of brilliance burning steady like low stars – lamps; this empty ground which holds the country in it and its peace is only a London square, set about by offices and houses where at this hour fierce lights burn over maps, over documents, over desks where clerks sit turning with wetted forefingers the files of endless correspondences; or more suffusedly the firelight wavers and the lamplight falls upon the privacy of some drawing-room, its easy chairs, its papers, its china, its inlaid table, and the figure of a woman, accurately measuring out the precise number of spoons of tea which – She looks at the door as if she heard a ring downstairs and somebody asking, is she in?

But here we must stop peremptorily. We are in danger of digging deeper than the eye approves; we are impeding our passage down the smooth stream by catching at some branch or root. At any moment, the sleeping army may stir itself and wake in us a thousand violins and trumpets in response; the army of human beings may rouse itself and assert all its oddities and sufferings and sordidities. Let us dally a little longer, be content still with surfaces only – the glossy brilliance of the motor omnibuses; the carnal splendour of the butchers' shops with their yellow flanks and their purple steaks; the blue and red bunches of flowers burning so bravely through the plate glass of the florists' windows.

For the eye has this strange property: it rests only on beauty; like a butterfly it seeks out colour and basks in warmth. On a winter's night like this, when nature has been at pains to polish and preen herself, it brings back the prettiest trophies, breaks off little lumps of emerald and coral as if the whole earth were made of precious stone. The thing it cannot do (one is speaking of the average unprofessional eye) is to compose these trophies in such a way as to bring out their more obscure angles and relationships. Hence after a prolonged diet of this simple, sugary fare, of beauty pure and uncomposed, we become conscious of satiety. We halt at the door of the boot shop and make some little excuse, which has nothing to do with the real reason, for folding up the bright paraphernalia of the streets and withdrawing to some duskier chamber of the being where we may ask, as we raise our left foot obediently upon the stand, 'What, then, is it like to be a dwarf?'

She came in escorted by two women who, being of normal size, looked like benevolent giants beside her. Smiling at the shop girls, they seemed to be at once disclaiming any lot in her deformity and assuring her of their protection. She wore the peevish yet apologetic expression usual on the faces of the deformed. She needed their kindness, yet she resented it. But when the shop girl had been summoned and the giantesses, smiling indulgently, had asked for shoes for 'this lady' and the girl had pushed the little stand in front of her, the dwarf stuck her foot out with an impetuosity which seemed to claim all our attention. Look at that! Look at that! she seemed to demand of us all, as she thrust her foot out, for behold it was the shapely, perfectly proportioned foot of a well-grown woman. It was arched; it was aristocratic. Her whole manner changed as she looked at it resting on the stand. She looked soothed and satisfied. Her manner became full of self-confidence. She sent for shoe after shoe; she tried on pair after pair. She got up and pirouetted before a glass which reflected the foot only in yellow shoes, in fawn shoes, in shoes of lizard skin. She raised her little skirts and displayed her little legs. She was thinking that, after all, feet are the most important part of the whole person; women, she said to herself, have been loved for their feet alone. Seeing nothing but her feet, she imagined perhaps that the rest of her body was of a piece with those beautiful feet. She was shabbily dressed, but she was ready to lavish any money upon her shoes. And as this was the only occasion upon which she was not afraid of being looked at but positively craved attention, she was ready to use any device to prolong the choosing and fitting. Look at my feet, look at my feet, she seemed to be saying, as she took a step this way and then a step that way. The shop girl good-humouredly must have said something flattering, for suddenly her face lit up in an ecstasy. But, after all, the giantesses, benevolent though they were, had their own affairs to see to; she must make up her mind; she must decide which to choose. At length, the pair was chosen and, as she walked out between her guardians, with the parcel swinging from her finger, the ecstasy faded, knowledge returned, the old peevishness, the old apology came back, and by the time she had reached the street again she had become a dwarf.

But she had changed the mood; she had called into being an atmosphere which, as we followed her out into the street, seemed actually to create the humped, the twisted, the deformed. Two bearded men, brothers apparently, stone-blind, supporting themselves by resting a hand on the head of a small boy between them, marched down the street. On they came with the unyielding yet tremulous tread of the blind, which seems to lend to their approach something of the terror and inevitability of the fate that has overtaken them. As they passed, holding straight on, the little convoy seemed to cleave asunder the passers-by with the momentum of its silence, its directness, its disaster. Indeed, the dwarf had started a hobbling grotesque dance to which everybody in the street now conformed: the stout lady tightly swathed in shiny sealskin; the feeble-minded boy sucking the silver knob of his stick; the old man squatted on a doorstep as if, suddenly overcome by the absurdity of the human spectacle, he had sat down to look at it – all joined in the hobble and tap of the dwarf's dance.

In what crevices and crannies, one might ask, did they lodge, this maimed company of the halt and the blind? Here, perhaps, in the top rooms of these narrow old houses between Holborn and the Strand, where people have such queer names, and pursue so many curious trades, are gold beaters, accordion pleaters, cover buttons, or others who support life, with even greater fantasticality, upon a traffic in cups without saucers, china umbrella handles, and highly coloured pictures of martyred saints. There they lodge, and it seems as if the lady in the sealskin jacket must find life tolerable, passing the time of day with the accordion pleater, or the man who covers buttons; life which is so fantastic cannot be altogether tragic. They do not grudge us, we are musing, our prosperity; when, suddenly, turning the corner, we come upon a bearded Jew, wild, hunger-bitten, glaring out of his misery; or pass the humped body of an old woman flung abandoned on the step of a public building with a cloak over her like the hasty covering thrown over a dead horse or donkey. At such sights, the nerves of the spine seem to stand erect; a sudden flare is brandished in our eyes; a question is asked which is never answered. Often enough these derelicts choose to lie not a stone's throw from theatres, within hearing of barrel organs, almost, as night draws on, within touch of the sequined cloaks and bright legs of diners and dancers. They lie close to those shop windows where commerce offers to a world of old women laid on doorsteps, of blind men, of hobbling dwarfs, sofas which are supported by the gilt necks of proud swans; tables inlaid with baskets of many coloured fruit, sideboards paved with green marble the better to support the weight of boars' heads, gilt baskets, candelabra; and carpets so softened with age that their carnations have almost vanished in a pale green sea.

Passing, glimpsing, everything seems accidentally but miraculously sprinkled with beauty, as if the tide of trade which deposits its burden so punctually and prosaically upon the shores of Oxford Street had this night cast up nothing but treasure. With no thought of buying, the eye is sportive and generous; it creates; it adorns; it enhances. Standing out in the street, one may build up all the chambers of a vast imaginary house and furnish them at one's will with sofa, table, carpet. That rug will do for the hall. That alabaster bowl shall stand on a carved table in the window. Our merrymakings shall be reflected in that thick round mirror.

But, having built and furnished the house one is happily under no obligation to possess it; one can dismantle it in the twinkling of an eye, build and furnish another house with other chairs and other glasses. Or let us indulge ourselves at the antique jewellers, among the trays of rings and the hanging necklaces. Let us choose those pearls, for example, and then imagine how, if we put them on, life would be changed. It becomes instantly between two and three in the morning; the lamps are burning very white in the deserted streets of Mayfair. Only motor cars are abroad at this hour, and one has a sense of emptiness, of airiness, of secluded gaiety. Wearing pearls, wearing silk, one steps out on to a balcony which overlooks the gardens of sleeping Mayfair. There are a few lights in the bedrooms of great peers returned from Court, of silk-stockinged footmen, of dowagers who have pressed the hands of statesmen. A cat creeps along the garden wall. Love-making is going on sibilantly, seductively in the darker places of the room behind thick green curtains. Strolling sedately as if he were promenading a terrace beneath which the shires and counties of England lie sun-bathed, the aged Prime Minister recounts to Lady So-and-So with the curls and the emeralds the true history of some great crisis in the affairs of the land. We seem to be riding on the top of the highest mast of the tallest ship; and yet at the same time we know that nothing of this sort matters, love is not proved thus, nor great achievements completed thus; so that we sport with the moment and preen our feathers in it lightly, as we stand on the balcony watching the moonlit cat creep along Princess Mary's garden wall.

But what could be more absurd? It is, in fact, on the stroke of six; it is a winter's evening; we are walking to the Strand to buy a pencil. How then are we also on a balcony, wearing pearls in June? What could be more absurd? Yet it is nature's folly, not ours. When she set about her chief masterpiece, the making of man, she should have thought of one thing only. Instead, turning her head, looking over her shoulder, into each one of us she let creep instincts and desires which are utterly at variance with his main being, so that we are streaked, variegated, all of a mixture; the colours have run. Is the true self this which stands on the pavement in January, or that which bends over the balcony in June? Am I here, or am I there? Or is the true self neither this nor that, neither here nor there, but something so varied and wandering that it is only when we give the rein to its wishes and let it take its way unimpeded that we are indeed ourselves? Circumstances compel unity; for convenience's sake a man must be a whole. The good citizen when he opens his door in the evening must be banker, golfer, husband, father; not a nomad wandering the desert, a mystic staring at the sky, a debauchee in the slums of San Francisco, a soldier heading a revolution, a pariah howling with scepticism and solitude. When he opens his door, he must run his fingers through his hair and put his umbrella in the stand like the rest.

But here, none too soon, are the second-hand bookshops. Here we find anchorage in these thwarting currents of being; here we balance ourselves after the splendours and miseries of the streets. The very sight of the bookseller's wife with her foot on the fender, sitting beside a good coal fire, screened from the door, is sobering and cheerful. She is never reading, or has only the newspaper; her talk when it leaves bookselling, as it does so gladly, is about hats; she likes a hat to be practical, she says, as well as pretty. Oh no, they don't live at the shop; they live at Brixton; she must have a bit of green to look at. In summer a jar of flowers grown in her own garden is stood on the top of some dusty pile to enliven the shop. Books are everywhere; and always the same sense of adventure fills us. Second-hand books are wild books, homeless books; they have come together in vast flocks of variegated feather, and have a charm which the domesticated volumes of the library lack. Besides, in this random, miscellaneous company we may rub against some complete stranger who will, with luck, turn into the best friend we have in the world. There is always a hope, as we reach down some greyish-white book from an upper shelf, directed by its air of shabbiness and desertion, of meeting here with a man who set out on horseback over a hundred years ago to explore the woollen market in the midlands and Wales; an unknown traveller, who stayed at inns, drank his pint, noted pretty girls and serious customs, wrote it all down stiffly, laboriously for sheer love of it (the book was published at his own expense); was infinitely prosy, busy, and matter-of-fact, and so let flow in without his knowing it the very scent of the hollyhocks and the hay together with such a portrait of himself as gives him forever a seat in the warm corner of the mind's inglenook. One may buy him for eighteen pence now. He is marked three and sixpence, but the bookseller's wife, seeing how shabby the covers are and how long the book has stood there since it was bought at some sale of a gentleman's library in Suffolk, will let it go at that.

Thus, glancing round the bookshop, we make other such sudden capricious friendships with the unknown and the vanished whose only record is, for example, this little book of poems, so fairly printed, so finely engraved, too, with a portrait of the author. For he was a poet and drowned untimely, and his verse, mild as it is and formal and sententious, sends forth still a frail fluty sound like that of a piano organ played in some back street resignedly by an old Italian organ-grinder in a corduroy jacket. There are travellers, too, row upon row of them, still testifying, indomitable spinsters that they were, to the discomforts that they endured and the sunsets they admired in Greece when Queen Victoria

was a girl; a tour in Cornwall with a visit to the tin mines was thought
worthy of voluminous record; people went slowly up the Rhine and did
portraits of each other in Indian ink, sitting reading on deck beside a coil
of rope; they measured the pyramids; were lost to civilization for years;
converted negroes in pestilential swamps. This packing up and going off,
exploring deserts and catching fevers, settling in India for a lifetime,
penetrating even to China and then returning to lead a parochial life at
Edmonton, tumbles and tosses upon the dusty floor like an uneasy sea, so
restless the English are, with the waves at their very door. The waters of
travel and adventure seem to break upon little islands of serious effort
and lifelong industry stood in jagged column upon the bookshop floor. In
these piles of puce-bound volumes with gilt monograms on the back,
thoughtful clergymen expound the gospels; scholars are to be heard with
their hammers and their chisels chipping clear the ancient texts of
Euripides and Aeschylus. Thinking, annotating, expounding, goes on at
a prodigious rate all round us and over everything, like a punctual,
everlasting tide, washes the ancient sea of fiction. Innumerable volumes
tell how Arthur loved Laura and they were separated and they were
unhappy and then they met and they were happy ever after, as was the
way when Victoria ruled these islands.

The number of books in the world is infinite, and one is forced to
glimpse and nod and go on after a moment of talk, a flash of understanding, as, in the street outside, one catches a word in passing and from
a chance phrase fabricates a lifetime. It is about a woman called Kate that
they are talking, how 'I said to her, quite straight last night . . . if you
don't think I'm worth a penny stamp, I said . . .' But who Kate is, and to
what crisis in their friendship the penny stamp refers, we shall never
know; for Kate sinks under the warmth of their volubility; and here, at
the street corner, another page of the volume of life is laid open by the
sight of two men consulting under the lamp post. They are spelling out
the latest wire from Newmarket in the stop press news. Do they think,
then, that fortune will ever convert their rags into fur and broadcloth,
sling them with watch chains, and plant diamond pins where there is now
a ragged open shirt? But the main stream of walkers at this hour sweeps
too fast to let us ask such questions. They are wrapt, in this short passage
from work to home, in some narcotic dream, now that they are free from
the desk, and have the fresh air on their cheeks. They put on those bright
clothes which they must hang up and lock the key upon all the rest of the
day, and are great cricketers, famous actresses, soldiers who have saved
their country at the hour of need. Dreaming, gesticulating, often mutter-
ing a few words aloud, they sweep over the Strand and across Waterloo
Bridge whence they will be swung in long rattling trains, still dreaming,

to some prim little villa in Barnes or Surbiton where the sight of the clock in the hall and the smell of the supper in the basement puncture the dream.

But we are come to the Strand now, and as we hesitate on the curb, a little rod about the length of one's finger begins to lay its bar across the velocity and abundance of life. 'Really I must – really I must' – that is it. Without investigating the demand, the mind cringes to the accustomed tyrant. One must, one always must, do something or other; it is not allowed one simply to enjoy oneself. Was it not for this reason that, some time ago, we fabricated that excuse, and invented the necessity of buying something? But what was it? Ah, we remember, it was a pencil. Let us go then and buy this pencil. But just as we are turning to obey the command, another self disputes the right of the tyrant to insist. The usual conflict comes about. Spread out behind the rod of duty we see the whole breadth of the river Thames – wide, mournful, peaceful. And we see it through the eyes of somebody who is leaning over the Embankment on a summer evening, without a care in the world. Let us put off buying the pencil; let us go in search of this person (and soon it becomes apparent that this person is ourselves). For if we could stand there where we stood six months ago, should we not be again as we were then – calm, aloof, content? Let us try then. But the river is rougher and greyer than we remembered. The tide is running out to sea. It brings down with it a tug and two barges, whose load of straw is tightly bound down beneath tarpaulin covers. There is too, close by us, a couple leaning over the balustrade murmuring with that curious lack of self-consciousness which lovers have, as if the importance of the affair they are engaged on claims without question the indulgence of the human race. The sights we see and the sounds we hear now have none of the quality of the past; nor have we any share in the serenity of the person who, six months ago, stood precisely where we stand now. His is the happiness of death; ours the insecurity of life. He has no future; the future is even now invading our peace. It is only when we look at the past and take from it the element of uncertainty that we can enjoy perfect peace. As it is, we must turn, we must cross the Strand again, we must find a shop where, even at this hour, they will be ready to sell us a pencil.

It is always an adventure to enter a new room; for the lives and characters of its owners have distilled their atmosphere into it, and directly we enter it we breast some new wave of emotion. Here, without a doubt, in the stationer's shop people had been quarrelling. Their anger shot through the air. They both stopped; the old woman – they were husband and wife evidently – retired to a back room; the old man whose rounded forehead and globular eyes would have looked well on the frontispiece of some Elizabethan folio, stayed to serve us. 'A pencil, a pencil,' he repeated, 'certainly, certainly.' He spoke with the distraction yet effusiveness of one whose emotions have been roused and checked in full flood. He began opening box after box and shutting them again. He said that it was very difficult to find things when they kept so many different articles. He launched into a story about some legal gentleman who had got into deep waters owing to the conduct of his wife. He had known him for years; he had been connected with the Temple for half a century, he said, as if he wished his wife in the back room to overhear him. He upset a box of rubber bands. At last, exasperated by his incompetence, he pushed the swing door open and called out roughly, 'Where d'you keep the pencils?' as if his wife had hidden them. The old lady came in. Looking at nobody, she put her hand with a fine air of righteous severity upon the right box. There were the pencils. How then could he do without her? Was she not indispensable to him? In order to keep them there, standing side by side in forced neutrality, one had to be particular in one's choice of pencils; this was too soft, that too hard. They stood silently looking on. The longer they stood there, the calmer they grew; their heat was going down, their anger disappearing. Now, without a word said on either side, the quarrel was made up. The old man who would not have disgraced Ben Jonson's title-page, reached the box back to its proper place, bowed profoundly his good night to us, and they disappeared. She would get out her sewing; he would read his newspaper; the canary would scatter them impartially with seed. The quarrel was over.

During these minutes in which a ghost had been sought for, a quarrel composed, and a pencil bought, the streets had become completely empty. Life had withdrawn to the top floor, and lamps were lit. The pavement was dry and hard; the road was of hammered silver. Walking home through the desolation one could tell oneself the story of the dwarf, of the blind men, of the party in the Mayfair mansion, of the quarrel in the stationer's shop. Into each of these lives one could penetrate a little way, far enough to give oneself the illusion that one is not tethered to a single mind but can put on briefly for a few minutes the bodies and minds of others. One could become a washerwoman, a publican, a street singer. And what greater delight and wonder can there be than to leave the straight lines of personality and deviate into those footpaths that lead beneath brambles and thick tree trunks into the heart of the forest where live those wild beasts, our fellow men?

That is true: to escape is the greatest of pleasures; street haunting in winter the greatest of adventures. Still as we approach our own doorstep again, it is comforting to feel the old possessions, the old prejudices, fold us round, and shelter and enclose the self which has been blown about at so many street corners, which has battered like a moth at the flame of so many inaccessible lanterns. Here again is the usual door; here the chair turned as we left it and the china bowl and the brown ring on the carpet. And here – let us examine it tenderly, let us touch it with reverence – is the only spoil we have retrieved from the treasures of the city, a lead pencil.

Part IX

Memoirs

Bloomsbury's interest in autobiography is shown by the founding of the Memoir Club in 1920. Halfway through their careers, various members of the Group began to meet regularly for the humorously self-conscious purpose of reading their memoirs to one another. The ironic mode in which Bloomsbury regarded their Victorian past is manifest in a number of their memoirs, most of which were originally written for the club.

44

Vanessa Bell:
Notes on Virginia's Childhood

Vanessa Bell's notes on her sister's childhood were written for the Memoir Club after Virginia Woolf's death and then edited for a limited edition published in 1974. The Stephen children were all born within four years of one another. Vanessa, the eldest, born in 1879, was a year and a half older than Thoby, two-and-a-half years older than Virginia and three-and-a-half years older than Adrian. Vanessa's description of the beginnings of Virginia's writing as well as the development of free thought and speech in Bloomsbury is one of the most important records of the Group's early history. As with other Memoir Club papers, the memoir assumes an audience of old friends.

The more I see of children – and I am thankful to say I do manage to see more of them now – the more I realize that their world is quite unlike ours. It is so different from ours that, it seems to me, to describe it needs a peculiar kind of imagination and understanding. And I think any real account of a childhood would necessarily be long, for how much happens in an hour or a day of a child's life, and what changes come in a year! We were all so near in age that I cannot be very sure that many of my memories have any sort of truth. Why do I see her so clearly, a very rosy chubby baby, with bright green eyes, sitting in a high chair at the nursery table, drumming impatiently for her breakfast? She cannot have been more than two, and I therefore only about four and a half. But it is a vivid memory to me. How worried I was too, not much later, because she couldn't speak clearly; I feared she would never do so, which would certainly have been a misfortune. That cannot have lasted long, for we were not very old when speech became the deadliest weapon as used by her. When Thoby and I were angry with each other or with her, we used good straightforward abuse, or perhaps told tales if we felt particularly vindictive. How did she know that to label me 'The Saint' was far more effective, quickly reducing me to the misery of sarcasm from the grown-ups as well as the nursery world? One was vaguely aware that it was no good trying to retort in kind. No, our only revenge for such injuries, Thoby's and mine, was to make her, as we said, 'purple with rage'. I don't remember how we did this, I only remember watching her colour mount till it was the most lively flaming red – and then I suppose nurses interfered. Was it altogether painful to her? I am not sure.

I see us as children nearly always in the two nurseries almost at the top of the tall house in Hyde Park Gate. There we spent about ten months of the year, and in spite of the delights of our Cornish home I used sometimes to feel it almost unbearable so seldom to be in a wood in the spring – in the early summer, never. (Brighton was the nearest we usually got to such joys, and I have hated it ever since in consequence.) Not that we were often bored even in London; Kensington Gardens was comparatively wild in those days, and in the long grass between the Flower Walk and the Round Pond we had once had the thrill of finding the deserted corpse of a dog – a little black dog. Then four children can make a good deal of amusement and trouble for each other. Perhaps I should say three, for Adrian was still a baby or a delicate little boy, and Thoby the brother both Virginia and I adored. She has described him so fully that I need say nothing. But he and I had had an intimate friendship before she came on the scene, doing everything together, and later, though life was more interesting and exciting, it was also less easy. Even then she had the faculty of suddenly being able to create an atmosphere of tense thundery gloom. I think she always had this – perhaps it's a Stephen characteristic – but I had not been aware of it before she produced it. Suddenly the sky was overcast, and I in the gloom. It would last for endless ages – so it seemed to a child – and then go. But it was I who had been in the gloom – not the other two – and I suppose, though I cannot remember ever feeling it at the time, that it was simply the result of two little females and a male. Or was it something different and part of her temperament?

Children are jealous little creatures, and brothers and sisters in a large family have one great disadvantage over only children. No one ever says how nice Mary is or how lovely Jane, but always Mary is nicer than Jane and Jane prettier than Mary. It's inevitable, and comparisons are the easiest form of criticism, no doubt, but it may lead to trouble. I don't remember being jealous of the fact that her appearance and her talk had obviously the greatest success with the grown-ups. They laughed at her jokes but so did we all, and probably I was as much aware as anyone of her brilliance and loveliness to look at. She reminded me always of a sweet pea of a special flame colour. But then there was the unfortunate question of our godparents. We hadn't been baptised, but all the same we had godparents of a kind. Mine were very dull, a decrepit old cousin in Ceylon and Lady Vaughan Williams, the judge's wife, whom I couldn't bear. But Virginia had the American ambassador, James Russell Lowell, a great friend of our parents who was quite an important figure to us. He used to produce his chain purse and pull out of it 3d bits for each of us except Virginia, who got 6d. That wasn't very important though rather marked, but what really roused our jealousies was his giving her a bird, a real live bird in a cage. I suppose the poor man would have been much surprised had he known what evil passions he had caused.

One of the two nurseries in which we lived was the day, the other the night nursery, and in this we four children and a nurse slept and had our baths and did all else in what I think must by modern standards have been a very unhealthy atmosphere. Was the window ever open at night? I doubt it. There was a lovely bright fire to go to bed by, coal, food, hot water and babies being carried up many times a day. We were very snug, if stuffy, and of course told stories in bed. The only one I remember was a serial which went on night after night. The characters were real ones, those of our next door neighbours, the Dilke family, whom we mocked for not being able to pronounce the letter *R*. The story always began by my saying in an affected drawl, 'Clemente, dear child.' Virginia then took the part of Clemente and the séance would begin. The plot consisted in the discovery under their nursery floor of immense stores of gold. It then went on to describe the wonderful things they could buy in consequence, especially the food, which was unlimited, though mostly consisting of not then very ruinous eggs and bacon – our favourite dish. But as we got sleepier our ideas got vaguer, and vast oceans of wealth and sleep seemed to overwhelm one. The fire flickered, one by one we dropped off to sleep, and presently 'Clemente dear child' gave no answer. The story had to wait till next night. It was in these two nurseries that we all had whooping cough, for of course there was no question of one alone getting any infectious disease. I believe children on the whole love being ill, but that particular disease did seem to last a very long time. Probably the treatment was completely wrong; anyhow I think we stayed indoors most of the time and had special foods and lots of medicines and in the end emerged four little skeletons and were sent to Bath for a change. The rest of us quickly recovered, but it seemed to me that Virginia was different.

She was never again a plump and rosy child and, I believe, had actually entered into some new layer of consciousness rather abruptly, and was suddenly aware of all sorts of questions and possibilities hitherto closed to her. I remember one evening as we were jumping about naked, she and I, in the bathroom, she suddenly asked me which I liked best, my father or mother. Such a question seemed to me rather terrible; surely one ought not to ask it. I felt certain Thoby would have snubbed the questioner. However, being asked, one had to reply, and I found I had little doubt as to my answer. 'Mother,' I said, and she went on to explain why she, on the whole, preferred my father. I don't think, however, her preference was quite as sure and simple as mine. She had considered both critically and had more or less analysed her feelings for them which I, at any rate consciously, had never attempted. This seemed to begin an age of much freer speech between us. If one could criticize one's parents, what or whom could one not criticize? Dimly some freedom of thought and speech seemed born, created by her question.

Before Thoby went to school at the age of ten, he and I had done all our lessons together, but after that it was Virginia and I who shared ours. My mother taught us Latin, French and history – not very well, I think, and I am sure most mistakenly, both on her own account and on ours. What a relief it was when for a short time she went abroad with my father and we had a harmless, ordinary little governess. It is much too nerve-wracking to be taught by one's parents. But my father's lessons in arithmetic were the worse of the two, and how the poor man endured them I cannot think. Thoby was the only one of his children whom it can have been a pleasure to teach. Virginia all her life added up on her fingers and I am very little better. She always said that she had had no education, and I am inclined to agree with her, if by education is meant learning things out of books. If she had none, however, I had less, for she did at least teach herself or get herself taught Greek, and was given books to read by my father which may, for all I know, have had educational value.

However there were also classes. Music naturally, since we were girls, had to be drummed into us, and the piano mistress succeeded in reducing us to complete boredom. The singing class, on the other hand, had its amusing side in the shape of other children. Miss Mills, a well known teacher of the tonic sol-fa system in those days, was discovered by us to be intensely religious. So when one day she asked very seriously if any of us knew the meaning of Good Friday, Virginia began to giggle. Of course we hadn't the slightest idea, being little heathens. But when the prize girl of the class, a serious creature with a hooked nose and a fringe and the astonishing name of Pensa Filly, stepped forward and said something (I suppose accurately) about our Lord being crucified on that day, it was too much and Virginia had to be hurriedly banished, shrieking with laughter. It amused her very much too when Connor O'Brien, a fiery little Irish boy, burst into floods of tears because he wasn't top of the class; but when that happened it was he, kicking and screaming, who had to be removed by his shamefaced mother.

Then there was the dancing class with the celebrated Mrs Wordsworth in black satin. She had a stick and a glass eye at which she dabbed perpetually with a lace pocket handkerchief, and she croaked like a raven and made all the little girls jump up and down in a frenzy. But we were bored and sometimes retired to the W.C. and spent as long as we dared there. I don't know what the sixty or seventy other girls did meanwhile.

I cannot remember a time when Virginia did not mean to be a writer and I a painter. It was a lucky arrangement, for it meant that we went our own ways and one source of jealousy at any rate was absent.

Our happiest afternoons were spent in a small room handed over to us, opening from the large double drawing room. It was a cheerful little room, almost entirely made of glass, with a skylight, windows all along one side looking on to the back garden, a window cut in the wall between it and the drawing room, and a door (also half window) opening into the drawing room. Also another door by which one could retreat to the rest of the house. In this room we used to sit, I painting and she reading aloud. We read most of the Victorian novelists in this way, and I can still hear much of George Eliot and Thackeray in her voice. From this room too we could spy on the grown-ups. Naturally we produced a family newspaper, *The Hyde Park Gate News*. Virginia wrote most of it, and it lasted four or five years, I believe – I have copies of it from the years 1891 to 1895. She was very sensitive to criticism and the good opinion of the grown-ups. I remember putting the paper on the table by my mother's sofa while they were at dinner, and then creeping quietly into the little room to look through the window and hear the criticism. As we looked, she trembling with excitement, we could see my mother's lamplit figure quietly sitting near the fire, my father on the other side with his lamp, both reading. Then she noticed the paper, picked it up, began to read. We looked and listened hard for some comment. 'Rather clever, I think,' said my mother, putting the paper down without apparent excitement. But it was enough to thrill her daughter; she had had approval and been called clever, and our eavesdropping was rewarded. I think it must have been a good deal later that she sent a short story to *Tit Bits*, keeping it a deadly secret from all but me. *Tit Bits* was our favourite weekly, which we used to buy together with 3d worth of Fry's Chocolate, taking both to Kensington Gardens to read and eat together, lying in the grass under the trees on summer afternoons. The story was refused – as far as I remember, it was a wildly romantic account of a young woman on a ship – and the secret kept till this day.

45

E. M. Forster: Recollections

Edward Morgan Forster's great-grandfather was a successful banker and, like the great-grandfather of Vanessa and Virginia, a member of the upper middle-class evangelical Clapham Sect. His daughter Marianne Thornton (1797–1887) is the subject of Forster's last book, which he finished in 1956. Marianne Thornton, *subtitled 'A Domestic Biography', modulates into autobiography towards the end as Forster views his great-aunt through his own recollections. The chapter reprinted here was originally entitled 'My Recollections'. It describes the last years of 'Aunt Monie' on the East Side of Clapham Common. Among Marianne Thornton's nieces and nephews were Henrietta Synnot and Forster's father, who died the year after his only child's birth. At the time these recollections begin, Forster – known in the family as 'the Important One' – was living with his mother (née Alice Clara Whichelo) in the house that became Howards End. (His closing memories of Ansell there had been used earlier in his fiction.) Marianne Thornton left her great nephew £8,000, which enabled him to go to Cambridge and begin writing. 'She and no one else made my career as a writer possible,' Forster said in the last words of his biography, 'and her love, in a most tangible sense, followed me beyond the grave.'*

The time has come for me to put down a few recollections of the house on East Side. Family life was led on the first floor. Aunt Monie had a bedroom at the back, and she would sit on the edge of her low bed of a morning and entertain me to breakfast. Her déshabillé was dainty –

('My dear, an old woman's bad enough, but a dirty old woman – !'); clean dressing-gown, pretty cape, cap with a pale blue ribbon – and in the kindest way she would invite me to share her egg, dipping a bread-and-butter finger into its yolk and popping it into my expectant mouth. I enjoyed this for a time but alas for too short a time. I was growing at the rate of a month a day, she was static in her eighties, and she could not realize that eggy-peggy-leggy-jeggy would soon stale and might even nauseate. I behaved fairly well, thanks to my mother's admonitions. She would urge me to be nice before I went in, and she has recorded my attempts to get into intellectual touch with Aunt Monie, and my dejected expression when I realized I had failed. Anyhow I minded eggy-peggy less than my corkscrew curls. I had to wear these for the old lady's pleasure, and must have been almost the last of the moppets thus to be tormented. A pupil of Mr Richmond's made a repellent drawing of the curls and of me in their midst.

The bedroom communicated with the big front drawing-room which looked over a corner of Clapham Common. There were two wheeled chairs: one of them had great wheels on each side, and when she was strong enough she propelled herself in it, and she had 'lazy-tongs' which darted out and nibbled ineffectively at objects she had dropped on the floor. Once I came on her all alone in her chair shouting 'Nurse, nurse', and I slunk away frightened. I often wondered what was wrong with her. The room was covered with a brussels carpet, in whose corner a cat made messes, and it had a fireplace in front of which an enigmatic figure occasionally stood: 'Enty' (Henrietta Synnot) robed in a gown of plum-coloured silk with buttons all down it from the throat to the floor. I did not realize that Enty hated us, and was only there because she had had publicly proclaimed she should not be. I merely found her unresponsive. Once she gave me a Bible, whereupon my mother sobbed with rage. I learnt afterwards that when Enty disliked people she gave them a Hymn Book, and when she detested them a Prayer Book. So a Bible was the limit of limits. She also had a habit of sweeping out of the room uttering barbed words which were too incomprehensible to wound, 'A tortuous path is always futile. Good baa' was a classic farewell.

Upstairs was the Important One's peculiar realm – a darkling region, often overshadowed by Christmas. I would lie awake in excitement and be unable to enjoy the stocking when dawn broke. And I remember a healthier excitement – discovering up there at the age of four that I was able to read to myself. From that moment I never looked back. Printed words spread around me. No one taught me to read and no one managed to teach me to write. Pothooks and hangers remained unattainable. It was the nice picture-books in the Clapham upstairs that started me off towards freedom. 'Tiresome to be interrupted in my reading when the light is so good' I would priggishly say. 'Can't you tell the people I am busy reading, Havell?' I soon got on to the *Swiss Family Robinson* and loved it because the boys in it were happy, whereas Robinson Crusoe was always worrying over savages.

On the ground floor were the servants – a friendly enough company, and a numerous one, for Lady Inglis' legacy was still operating. Sarah Cook, Sarah Housemaid, White-Faced Emma, Mrs Ing etc. – I had tea with them and was usually popular, but when I cried 'Mrs Ing's a cat' she laid down the saucer from which she had been lapping and Sarah Cook looked very grave indeed. The most important figure of all – Nurse Havell – did not consort with us. She ate alone and worked alone. She was the power behind the wheeled chair and for all I know a beneficent one, but the letters of the period are full of anxious references to her; Havell has said this, that . . . Havell has told Monie when she had no right to that . . . has been playing fast and loose. She was certainly hand in glove with Henrietta Synnot, who has put up a tablet to her in the church at Milton.

Not much happened during these visits, which appear in retrospect as dun-coloured. I was not unhappy, I did not protest, but I caught the prevalent atmosphere, and realized without being told that I was in the power of a failing old woman, who wanted to be kind but she was old and each visit she was older. How old was she? Born in the reign of George the Fourth, my mother thought. 'More likely Edward the Fourth' cried I. Occasionally cousins were encountered – Brian Southey my senior whom I admired, and nasty Blowdie Wags who blew a whistle in my ear. I screamed, I screamed. News of this outrage spread through the Thornton clan, and Blowdie was widely condemned. My mother was furious with him for upsetting her darling but also annoyed with me for being a cry-baby. This horrid boy got me altogether on the hop, pointed his finger at me whenever we met, and was the first to demonstrate to me that I was a coward. Then there were some protective girl cousins, Ethel and Mabel Forster, whose pink dresses and kind offices won approval. But as I have already said once, not much happened at Clapham, and I could say this again. I seemed never to see the sun there: 'The room gets lighter or darker, but the sun never throws his rays in as he does at home.' Thus I sighed to my mother.

The truth is that she and I had fallen in love with our Hertfordshire home and did not want to leave it. It certainly was a lovable little house, and still is, though it now stands just outside a twentieth-century hub and almost within sound of a twentieth-century hum. The garden, the over-hanging wych-elm, the sloping meadow, the great view to the west, the cliff of fir trees to the north, the adjacent farm through the high tangled hedge of wild roses were all utilized by me in *Howards End*, and the interior is in the novel too. The actual inmates were my mother, myself, two maids, two or more cats, an occasional dog; outside were a pony and trap with a garden boy to look after them. From the time I entered the house at the age of four and nearly fell from its top to its bottom through a hole ascribed to the mice, I took it to my heart and hoped, as Marianne had of Battersea Rise, that I should live and die there. We were out of it in ten years. The impressions received there remained and still glow – not always distinguishably, always inextinguishably – and have given me a slant upon society and history. It is a middle-class slant, atavistic, derived from the Thorntons, and it has been corrected by contact with friends who have never had a home in the Thornton sense, and do not want one.

Aunt Monie had urged my mother to take the house (provided it was on gravel), so she had no grounds for complaint, and it had seemed to her quite proper that a beautiful young widow should bury herself in the wilds for the sake of a supposedly delicate son. All the same, there was this nagging desire to see us – me particularly. Her thirst for youth had become cannibalistic. My mother's letters fall into three classes – those in which she undertook to go to Clapham, those in which she excused herself from going, and those in which she fed the old lady with amusing bits of news about the Important One, in the hope of keeping her quiet. She was rather cynical – she held that it was as Morgan's mother that she mattered, and she could be proudly silent on the subject of Whichelo affairs. She was not very cynical – she was fond of naughty tiresome Monie, and grateful to her, and liked pleasing her.

Out of the endless trifles she now dished up I will select a few on the subject of Pink-Faced Emma. I might have chosen the Sailor-dollar sequence of letters, but it lacks variety. Pink-Faced Emma was our housemaid, and she was so called to distinguish her from Aunt Monie's White-Faced Emma.

Emma arrives:

> Morgan got much excited on Thursday at the thought of the new maids, he would watch for Emma at 4, she not being expected till 5.30. When time drew near he picked a huge yellow pansy to make himself smart. He asked her her name the moment she arrived and took her up to her room. At tea he said 'She calls me *Sir*, mamma, it is really very awkward. She doesn't know my name and now will she ever. She might ask me.' I think she must think he is mad, for he said to her 'Have you heard one of my long stories

about things that have never happened except inside my head – I'll tell you one, it is called "Excited maids under the Clothes line".' I can't imagine how he thinks of such sensational titles, he will write for the *Family Herald* I should think.[1]

Emma's folly:

We do lessons after breakfast and after dinner and then M. has his dancing lesson. I am teaching him the Polka and he is beginning to have quite a good idea of it. Unfortunately for me he instructs Emma in the afternoon and evidently she is but a sorry dancer – heavy footed for the drawing-room windows and doors rattle & the furniture screams. As the dancers grow wild they shout and play tambourines and musical boxes at the same time, so you may guess I pass a lively afternoon. Now they are very happy chatting, and he is determined the maids shall look for nineteen constellations this evening, poor things. He is quite annoyed with frivolous Emma for calling Jupiter a star.

Emma's further folly:

M. says to me several times today in a tone of mournful admiration 'how very sensible you are mamma, you can play games, Emma can't learn and does it wrong every time.' I can well believe it. I have always said (tho' not to M.) that she was deficient. The way she likes to amuse him is to make some foolish speech over and over again through the entire afternoon & then they both laugh as if they would have fits. The last speech is 'My name is Sir William Podgkins.' I ask what it means but they can't speak for laughter and then M. manages to say 'there is no meaning that is why we laugh.' Occasionally he wants variety, but E. could go on being amused by her own folly for ever.

Emma under instruction:

M. invited the maids to tea with him yesterday, and he said he must give them some amusement, so he armed himself with astronomical diagrams and said they had better do a little learning. He explained all and they

---

[1] Titles of other stories were: Dancing Bell, Chattering Hassocks, Screams, Scuffles in the Wardrobe, The Earring in the Keyhole, and The Adventures of Pussy Senior. What relation would these bear to the pictures painted at Battersea Rise by my little great-aunts? A brief analysis of Chattering Hassocks has survived: fifty lions and as many unicorns sit upon hassocks, and the lions put forward a plea for tolerance and for variety of opinion which I still support. 'Why didn't you finish baby's story about the talking hassocks?' Aunt Monie writes. 'It's much better than Alice in Wonderland.'

giggled like a pair of noodles. He then proposed Hide & Seek. He then took them both into the hall and instructed them in moves at chess. He flew all over the hall carpet saying 'Now I go like a knight, now like a castle &ct. He is chalking a map of South America, and implored me to help him before I went out yesterday 'for I know Emma won't think it matters a bit whether I put Patagonia in the place of Ecuador'.

Emma under examination:

Did I tell you of the conversation I overheard (I was supposed to be asleep) between Emma & Morgan.
E.   You know a good deal about stars, don't you Master Morgan?
M.   (humbly) No not very much. Do you?
E.   Oh no.
M.   *What* do you know about? (What indeed!!! Long pause.)
E.   Oh only what you have taught me.
M.   Botany?
E.   Yes, about the Great Bear & Little Bear.
M.   – scornfully – That's not Botany, that's Astronomy. Botany is about flowers and *Cology* about shells. I don't know very much of both those.
E.   Oh I think you know a great deal, Master Morgan.
M.   – very self-satisfied tone – Oh, do you.

Emma leaves. My cleverness and rudeness were more than she could stand. The break came gathering primroses. I sneered at her for picking them with short stalks, she jeered at me for picking so few. I hit at her basket and upset it, she hit at mine. I hit her, she hit me and tore my little coat. 'But I had to hit Master Morgan, ma'am, he hit me,' she explained mildly. I was sorry when she left and rather ashamed, for I knew it was my fault. She was such a suitable companion, and our chant of

> Oh the corns and bunians how they do grow,
> They hurt me so oh oh oh oh oh oh

still sometimes rings in my ears.

Aunt Monie loved all this nonsense and the way my mother put it, and before long there was little in our simple life that she did not know and upon which she did not advise. Occasionally she discussed the defects of my character. I was not a bad child, but I had been noticed too much by grown-ups, and I could be hysterical, pretentious and detestable. On this occasion I must have gone well over the edge:

I have not an idea what I should do if I had a child who indulged in that stile of talk, but I do think it ought to be stopped somehow, and I see no way of doing it except as Harti said 'Scold him when he's good and not when he's naughty', but when in one of his loving affectionate moods if you were to talk to him as if he were 20, and show him the evil consequences of saying what is not true for one thing and what will make mothers who have good children afraid of letting them play with a boy who says such shocking and such untrue things. You know I'm never for punishment which leads only to eye service as men-pleasers, but I do quite think that if you could convince that precocious little head of his that it really grieved you, he would reform – but if not with school looming in the distance I suppose he must look forward to the time when you will be his refuge from the torments his fellows will bestow upon what they call 'cheek'.

Or she meditates on my financial future:

Oh dear how I wish we knew beforehand what children are going to turn out, specially Mr Morgan Forster – as to getting his money when 21 or 25. If he *takes* it as they call it at 21 no provision is made for his children. If he waits till 25 he is to leave *his* money to you and his children, I'm afraid this will put it into his head to marry – like Charley Sykes who is to be executed on Tuesday next being just 21 & foolish enough to reverse the figures and be 12. The Important One I feel will have cleverness enough and to spare, & I could be almost as certain of his goodness & his general promise of all that one most wishes to see in a child. – His fits of crying for little things I look upon as more weak nerves than anything else.

Part of the trouble was that there were too few children in our lovely retreat. At the Park gate dwelt Baby Plum Bun or Sizzle, of inferior lineage and age, and through the rose hedge was Frankie Franklin of the farm. I admired Frankie when he attached himself to the wheel which turned the hay-cutter, and whirled round upon it Ixion-like, but did not get to know him well until later years: he only died in 1949 and I have actually spoken to five generations of that honoured family. Down in the rectory were nine daughters, to whom was presently added a future Lord Chancellor. And there were a few more children in the village, but we did not visit widely, for the pony backed when he thought we were going too far, and ran the trap into a hedge.

I depended a good deal for company upon the garden boys. With one of them, William (Mr Taylor), I am still in touch and he remembers, as I do, how he led me on the pony into the wilds of Botany Bay. But it is Ansell whom I remember best. This was a snub-nosed pallid even-tempered youth who came to us shortly before Aunt Monie died. He was reliable but not too reliable; ' 'e done it isself' was his explanation when the puppy was patterned in tar. My mother in her kindness let Ansell off every Wednesday afternoon so that he could play with me. We mostly played on a straw-rick which Mr Franklin abandoned to our fury. More kindness. We slid and we shouted. Ansell hid and left his billycock as a decoy. Not finding him I jumped on it and stove it in, and this did ruffle him. Once we built a hut between the rick and the hedge: ' 'ow 'ot it is in 'eer, I've got the 'eerdache already' said he. We stored apples there, and could not think what ate them.

Nor was his education neglected. I neglected no one's education. Each week, as we walked round the edges of the fields, I recounted to him what last I had read of the Swiss Family Robinson, and he retold it to me fairly well, except that he would call Fritz Frizz. Arithmetic defeated him. He never could state how many chickens his mother had, however much he waved his arms, and 'Ansell and the Chickens' survived as a family saying long after we left Hertfordshire. For me he has survived in other ways. He was the good sweet side of the odious Blowdy Wags, and probably did more than anyone towards armouring me against life. That is why I bring him in. He faded when a professional armourer was introduced in the person of a snobbish Irish tutor who prepared me for a preparatory school which was to prepare me for a public school which was to prepare me for the world, and who supposed he had obliterated the world of Emma and Ansell for ever.

46

Lytton Strachey: Lancaster Gate

Lytton Strachey's memoir of his early home was written for the Memoir Club in June 1922, after one by Virginia Woolf about her Hyde Park Gate home (on the other side of Kensington Gardens). Strachey's parents Sir Richard (1817–1908), a retired Indian administrator and scientist, and his second wife Jane Maria Grant (1840–1928) moved their family to Lancaster Gate in 1884, when Lytton was four, and he grew up there with his four brothers and five sisters. (For a view of the Strachey menage from the outside, see Leonard Woolf's memoir p. 378.) Among the people referred to in the memoir of a late Victorian drawing-room's atmosphere are the painter Frederic Leighton, the entertainer and author George Grossmith, four of Lytton's sisters – Dorothy, Philippa, Pernel, and Marjorie – and Lady Strachey's nephew Duncan Grant. Strachey's memoir was published posthumously by Michael Holroyd in Lytton Strachey by Himself *(1971).*

The influence of houses on their inhabitants might well be the subject of a scientific investigation. Those curious contraptions of stones or bricks, with all their peculiar adjuncts, trimmings, and furniture, their specific immutable shapes, their intense and inspissated atmosphere, in which our lives are entangled as completely as our souls in our bodies – what powers do they not wield over us, what subtle and pervasive effects upon the whole substance of our existence may not be theirs? Or is that all nonsense? Our fathers, no doubt, would have laughed at such a speculation; for to our fathers the visible conformations of things were unimportant; they were more interested in the mental and moral implications of their surroundings than in the actual nature of them; and their spirits, so noble and oblivious, escaped the direct pressure of the material universe. They could understand that it would make a difference whether one spent one's life in an ancient family seat in Gloucestershire or in a red-brick villa at Tooting – the social, personal, and traditional distinctions were obvious enough. But the notion that the proportions of a bedroom, for instance, might be significant would have appeared absurd to them; and so they were able to create, and to inhabit, South Kensington almost unconsciously, as if such conduct were the most natural thing in the world. Our view is different. We find satisfaction in curves and colours, and windows fascinate us, we are agitated by staircases, inspired by doors, disgusted by cornices, depressed by chairs, made wanton by ceilings, entranced by passages, and exacerbated by a rug.

In my case at any rate the impression caused by a house has been profound and extraordinary. I say impression, because as to more remote effects – such is the subtlety and complexity of the question – I hardly know what they may have been, or even whether there were any; but a memorable impression is beyond a doubt. Of all my dreams (and I am a confirmed dreamer) there is one alone which persistently recurs, only slightly varying in its details, with a curious iteration. For some reason or another – one of those preposterous and yet absolutely satisfying reasons which occur in dreams – we are back again, once more, just as we were, in Lancaster Gate. We are in the drawing-room, among the old furniture, arranged in the old way, and it is understood that we are to go there indefinitely, as if we had never left it. The strange thing is that, when I realize that this has come about, that our successive wanderings have been a mere interlude, that we are once more permanently established at number 69, a feeling of intimate satisfaction comes over me. I am positively delighted. And this is strange because, in my waking life, I have never for a moment, so far as I am aware, regretted our departure from that house, and if, in actuality, we *were* to return to it, I can imagine nothing which would disgust me more. So, when I wake up, and find myself after all at Gordon Square or Tidmarsh, I have the odd sensation of a tremendous relief at finding that my happiness of one second before was a delusion.

Apart from my pleasure at it, no doubt it is hardly surprising that Lancaster Gate should haunt me. For it was a portentous place, and I spent in it the first twenty-five years of my conscious life. My remembrances of Stowey House are dim and sporadic – Jim Rendel with a penny in a passage – a miraculous bean at the bottom of the garden – Beatrice Chamberlain playing at having tea with me, with leaves and acorns, under a tree. But my consecutive existence began in the nursery at Lancaster Gate – the nursery that I can see now, empty and odd and infinitely elevated, as it was when I stood in it for the first time at the age of four with my mother, and looked out of the window at the surprisingly tall houses opposite, and was told that this was where we were going to live. A calm announcement – received with some excitement, which was partly caused by the unusual sensation of extreme height, as I peered at the street below. The life that began then – my Lancaster Gate life – was to continue till I was twenty-eight – a man full grown – all the changes from childhood to adolescence, from youth to manhood, all the developments, the curiosities, the pains, the passions, the despairs, the delights, of a quarter of a century having taken place within those walls.

A portentous place! Yes, but exactly how portentous it is not easy to convey. Its physical size was no doubt the most obviously remarkable thing about it; but it was not mere size, it was size gone wrong, size pathological; it was a house afflicted with elephantiasis that one found one had entered, when, having mounted the steps under the porch, having passed through the front door and down the narrow dark passage with its ochre walls and its tessellated floor of magenta and indigo tiles, one looked upwards and saw the staircase twisting steeply up its elongated well – spiralling away into a thin infinitude, until, far above, one's surprised vision came upon a dome of pink and white glass, which yet one judged, with an unerring instinct, was not the top – no, not nearly, nearly the top. Below the ground-floor there was a basement, above it there was a drawing-room floor, and above that there were four floors of bedrooms; so that altogether the house contained seven layers of human habitation. But that was not all; all the rooms were high, but the height of the drawing-room was enormous; so that, if one had the courage to go up the stairs, one found, when one had surmounted the first floor, that one was on an airy eminence, surrounded by immeasurable spaces of yellow marbled wallpaper, and alarmingly near the dome; its pink lights seemed to glitter almost within one's reach, when, abruptly, one's course deviated; one turned to the left up six strangely broad steps, and came upon quite a new part of the building – the bedrooms, piled two and two on the top of one another, connected by quite an ordinary, small staircase, and forming a remote, towering outgrowth upon the monstrous structure below.

The house had been designed extraordinarily badly. The rooms that looked on to the street (one on each floor) were tolerable; all the rest were very small and very dark. There was not a scrap of garden, not even a courtyard; and so lugubrious was the outlook of the back rooms that the windows of most of them were of pink and white ground glass, so that one never saw out of them. In a London winter, very little light indeed came through those patterned panes. My mother, taking a hint from my father's office in the City, had 'reflectors' put up – huge plates of glassy material, slightly corrugated, which hung opposite the windows from chains. The windows themselves were so large that it was almost impossible to open them. Little circular ventilators were cut in them, working by means of cords. All this presented a peculiar spectacle, as one sat in the schoolroom – at the end of the passage on the ground-floor – or in 'the young ladies' room', behind the dining-room; a tiny apartment, far higher than it was either long or broad, with a gigantic mahogany door, and the vast window, pink and frosted, with its string and ventilator, and a dim vision of filthy yellow bricks, chains, and corrugations looming through the fog outside.

And besides the height and the darkness there were other strange inconveniences. There was the one and only bathroom, for instance, perched, with its lavatory, in an impossible position midway between the drawing-room and the lowest bedroom floors – a kind of crow's nest – to reach which, one had to run the gauntlet of stairs innumerable, and whose noises of rushing waters were all too audible from the drawing-room just below.

Then, in spite of its gigantic size, the house, somehow or other, seemed to have very few rooms in it. My father was the only person who had a sitting-room to himself. In the miserable little 'young ladies' room', Dorothy and Pippa, and Pernel, and later on Marjorie, led an oddly communal existence; privacy there, I suppose occasionally there must have been, but privacy arranged, studied and highly precarious. But, strangest of all, my mother had no room of her own. There was a large writing-table in the dining-room, and at that writing-table, amid the incessant *va-et-vient* of a large family, my mother did all her business – and she was a busy woman, with a multitude of outside interests, a large correspondence, and a curiously elaborate system of household accounts.

No doubt, in all large families, there is very little privacy; and one might say that Lancaster Gate was, in essence, the crowning symbol of the large family system. The one implied the other. The same vitality, the same optimism, the same absence of nerves, which went to the deliberate creation of ten children, built the crammed, high, hideous edifice that sheltered them. And so it was inevitable that the most characteristic feature of the house – its centre, its summary, the seat of its soul, so to speak – should have been the room which was the common meeting-place of all the members of the family – the drawing-room. When one entered that vast chamber, when, peering through its foggy distances, ill-lit by gas-jets, or casting one's eyes wildly towards the infinitely distant ceiling overhead, one struggled to traverse its dreadful length, to reach a tiny chair or a far-distant fireplace, conscious as one did so that some kind of queer life was clustered thick about one, that heaven knows how many eyes watched from just adumbrated sofas, that brains crouched behind the piano, that there were other presences, remote, aloof, self-occupied, and mysteriously dominating the scene – then, in truth, one had come – whether one realized it or no – into an extraordinary holy of holies. The gigantic door, with its flowing portière of pale green silk, swung and shut behind one. One stepped forwards in the direction of the three distant windows covered by their pale green limitless curtains, one looked about, one of the countless groups of persons disintegrated, flowed towards one, one sat and spoke and listened: one was reading the riddle of the Victorian Age.

I only mean to say that the Lancaster Gate drawing-room was, in its general nature, the concentrated product of an epoch; for certainly it was too full of individuality and peculiarity to be typical of anything. For one thing, it was too intelligent. I believe that it was not absolutely ugly; the decorations were undoubtedly, for the time, slightly advanced. But it is almost impossible for me to come to an impartial judgement on it. I know it far too well. To the entering stranger, puzzled and alarmed, the impression it produced may well have been one of mere confusion; to me, all was clear, all was articulate, every one of the innumerable details was accurately, intimately, and unforgettably known. At this moment I am perfectly certain that I could reconstruct the whole complexity, complete and exact in every inch. The details were indeed literally innumerable, but there was a climax – immediately obvious – in the arrangement of them. This climax occurred at the more distant of the two mantelpieces – on the right-hand wall, near the window end of the room – a very large high structure of a most peculiar kind. But I cannot hope to describe that bulk of painted wood with its pilasters and cornices, its jars and niches, its marble and its multi-coloured tiles. Designed by Halsey Ricardo, it combined, with an effect of emasculated richness, the inspiration of William Morris, reminiscences of the Renaissance, and a bizarre idiosyncrasy of its own. Guests, finding themselves for the first time face to face with this colossal complication, nearly always exclaimed 'What a magnificent mantelpiece!' It is difficult to see what else they could have done, for to have remained silent before an object so peculiarly conspicuous would have been decidedly marked. Standing by that mottled hearth, one had reached the citadel of the great room. Surveying it from that vantage-spot, one could see that it was a room that was utterly unromantic. It was a mere rectangular parallelepiped – a large ill-shaped box, crammed in between a whole series of exactly similar boxes, ranged on each side of it up and down the street. And yet, though there was no romance in it, there certainly *was* something that was not quite analysable. Was it the effect of its size or its ugliness or its absurdity? – I don't know; but familiar, incredibly familiar as it was to me, who had spent my whole life in it, there was never a time when I was not, in the recesses of my consciousness, a little surprised by it. It was like one of those faces at which one can look for ever without growing accustomed to. Up to my last hour in it, I always felt that the drawing-room was strange.

Strange indeed! Is it conceivable, after all, that I ever was really there? Is it conceivable that Dorothy, evening after evening, in that room, kissed me a hundred times, in a rapture of laughter and affection, counting her kisses, when I was six? that, in that same room, perhaps twenty years later, sitting on a sofa alone with Andrew, I suddenly kissed *him*, much to his surprise and indignation – 'My dear man! Really! One doesn't do those things!' – And that – but never mind.

It was a family room – (Andrew, I may mention, was my nephew) – and the family combinations and permutations in it were very various. Apart from the ordinary domestic moments, it was on Sunday afternoons, when my mother was invariably at home, that the family atmosphere, reinforced from without, reached its intensest and its oddest pitch. Then the drawing-room gradually grew thick with aunts and uncles, cousins and connections, with Stracheys, Grants, Rendels, Plowdens, Battens, Ridpaths, Rowes. One saw that it had indeed been built for them – it held them all so nicely, so naturally, with their interminable varieties of age and character and class – from Nina Grey in her faded airs of Roman Catholic aristocracy to Fanny Stanley and her lodging-house garrulity, from Uncle George, bent double with age and eccentricity, hideously sniffing, and pouring out his opinions upon architecture and Tasso to anyone who ventured within his reach, to Black Pat, youthful, horribly snouted, absurdly mendacious, who had come, it was clear, by arrangement, to meet Millie Plowden, and overdid his surprise when at last in yellow feathers she giggled into the room.

The crowd was at its largest at about six, and then it gradually thinned away. But somebody very often stayed on to dinner – Sir William Ward, perhaps, who, besides having been Governor of the Straits Settlements was an executor, of astonishing brilliancy, on the pianoforte. Pressed to play, he would seat himself at the piano and dash into a Chopin waltz with the verve of a high-stepping charger, when suddenly a very odd and discordant sound, rising and falling with the music, would make itself heard. It was something between a snore and a whistle, and nobody

could think what it could be. But the mystery was at last explained –
the ex-Governor suffered, in moments of excitement, from a curious
affection of the nose. While the family listened, a little hysterically, to this
peculiar combination of sounds, all at once yet *another* sound – utterly
different – burst upon their ears – the sound, this time, of rushing water.
There was a momentary shock; and then we all silently realized that
someone, in the half-way landing upstairs, was using the W.C.

There are various ways of 'seeing life'; but it seems to me that, in
one way or another, I saw a good deal of life in the drawing-room at
Lancaster Gate. And of course my experience then was not limited to an
enormous family: there was a constant succession of callers, there were
repeated dinner-parties and at homes. The preparations for an afternoon
party I have a queer vision of – a vision, as it happens, that can be
accurately dated. The room was bared, the chairs ranged round the walls,
and in the middle, walking up and down and showing themselves off
were Dorothy and Pippa dressed from head to foot in white muslin with
full flowing skirts, and black satin sashes round their waists, tied in
immense bows. They were in mourning – for the death of the German
Emperor; and that afternoon party must have been in the third week of
June 1888. Often, there were musical parties, and, in the days when
trousers were even more unfamiliar to me than they are now, I heard, to
my intense excitement, that Grossmith – the almost mythical Grossmith
of the *Sorcerer* and the *Pinafore* – was coming to sing and play. 'I know
what'll happen,' I whispered to Marjorie, in a great state of agitation, as
we waited for the guests. 'Just as Grossmith comes into the room, my
knickerbockers will fall down.' The grandest of the musical parties was
much later, given in combination by my aunt and my mother, with
Joachim and Piatti playing in their quartet. I can see at this moment, in
my mind's eye, the Olympian features of Sir Frederic Leighton, flushed
with anger, as he entered on that occasion. I can hear him explaining, in
heated accents, that he had made a mistake, had gone to the wrong
house, and had been driving over half London in consequence.

It must not be inferred from these entertainments that we were
fashionable or smart; on the contrary, if anything we were dowdy;
though on the other hand, we were not in the least Bohemian. Our conventionality, slightly mitigated by culture and intelligence, was impinged
upon much more seriously by my mother's constitutional vagueness and
immateriality, and by a vein in her of oddity and caprice. Her feeling for
what was right and proper was unsupported by the slightest touch of
snobbery; and, while it was very strong and quite unhesitating, it
was surprisingly peculiar to herself. That her daughters should go
into mourning for the German Emperor, for instance, appeared to her

essential; but her own dresses were most extraordinary, designed by herself, quite regardless of fashion. She had all her children christened, but she never went to Church – except in the country, when she went with the utmost regularity. She was religious in the payment of calls; but the arrangements of the household, from the point of view of social life, were far below the standard. We kept up the mere minimum of an appearance. Our butler, Frederick, the promoted gardener's boy of Stowey House, uncouth, simian, with a great mouth, ill-covered by a straggling moustache, was one of the most unpresentable of figures, and must have cast a chill upon the visitor to whom he opened the door for the first time. 'Why do the Stracheys allow their man to wear a moustache?' Marjorie, in hiding in the dining-room, once heard a military visitor inquire of another as they went down the passage together. Why did they indeed? But in truth my mother would no more have dreamt of ordering the unfortunate Frederick – one of the most excellent of creatures, in spite of his ugliness – to shave off his moustache than she would have dreamt of going without a butler altogether and having a parlour-maid. A butler, but an unpresentable butler, might have stood for the symbol of the Lancaster Gate establishment.

No doubt a contributing cause of our dowdiness was that we were only precariously well off. But, whatever the explanation, I think, as I look back, that the fact that we *were* dowdy was one of the redeeming elements in the situation. Few things could be imagined more terrible than a *smart* Lancaster Gate. As it was, there was something human in the untidyness and the dirt. It was a touch of nature that, in the hall, by the stairs, two bicycles should be grouped together, incompletely covered by a rug, that the dust was too thick on the red velvet in the alcove behind the cast of the Venus of Milo, and that, in the dining-room, my mother's writing-table, littered with papers, stood out obvious and unashamed during the largest dinner-parties. To the children, at any rate, nosing into corners, the full incorrectitude of the place stood revealed. Visitors, perhaps, might not particularly notice, but *we* knew by heart all the camouflaged abysses, taking a sardonic delight in the ruthlesssness of the introspective realism with which we plumbed and numbered 'filth-packet' after 'filth-packet' – for such was our too descriptive phrase.

What had happened was that a great tradition – the aristocratic tradition of the eighteenth century – had reached a very advanced stage of decomposition. My father and my mother belonged by birth to the old English world of country-house gentlefolk – a world of wealth and breeding, a world in which such things as footmen, silver, and wine were the necessary appurtenances of civilized life. But their own world was different: it was the middle-class professional world of the Victorians, in which the old forms still lingered, but debased and enfeebled, in which Morris wallpapers had taken the place of Adam panelling, in which the swarming retinue had been reduced to a boy in livery, in which the spoons and forks were bought at the Army and Navy Stores. And then, introducing yet another element into the mixture, there was the peculiar disintegrating force of the Strachey character. The solid bour-geois qualities were interpenetrated by intellectualism and eccentricity. Our family dinners expressed the complicated state of things. They were long and serious meals; but, unless there were visitors, we never dressed for them. At the end, the three mystic bottles of port, sherry, and claret were put at the head of the table and solemnly circulated – the port, sherry and claret having come from the grocer's round the corner. The butler and the liveried boot-boy waited on us, and the butler was Frederick, or, later, a figure even more characteristic of our subtle *dégringolade* – Bastiani – a fat, black-haired, Italianate creature, who eventually took to drink, could hardly puff up the stairs from the base-ment, and, as he handed the vegetables, exuded an odour of sweat and whisky into one's face. He disappeared – after a scene of melodramatic horror – to be replaced by Mr Brooks who, we could only suppose, must have been a groom in earlier life, since all his operations were accompanied by a curious sound of *sotto voce* hissing – or, of course, he might have been Sir William Ward, rather thinly disguised. Peering into the drawers of the sideboard, we discovered tangled masses of soda water-bottle wires, broken corkscrews, napkins, and the mysterious remains of disembowelled brushes. We took note of another filth-packet, observing at the same time, with gusto, that the glass stopper of the brandy decanter had been removed by Mr Brooks, and that a cork had been rammed into its place.

Disintegration and *dégringolade*, no doubt, and yet the total effect, materialized and enormously extended, was of a tremendous solidity. Lancaster Gate towered up above us, and around us, an imperturbable mass – the framework, almost the very essence – so it seemed – of our being. Was it itself, perhaps, one vast filth-packet, and we the mere *disjecta membra* of vanished generations, which Providence was too busy or too idle to clear away? So, in hours of depression, we might have unconsciously theorized; but nevertheless, in reality, it was not so. Lancaster Gate vanished into nothingness, and we survive. To me, that that régime would inevitably, someday, come to an end was a dreadful thought – one not to be dwelt upon – like death; what would, what *could* happen, when we went away from Lancaster Gate? Circumstances – a diminished income – brought about at length the unspeakable catastrophe: but I see now that, whatever had happened, however rich we might have continued, Lancaster Gate was in fact doomed. The disintegration would have grown too strong for it at last. Indeed the end, I think, had really come before we actually left it: Dorothy, with extraordinary courage, married a penurious French artist [Simon Bussy], and Lancaster Gate was shaken to its foundations. The new spirit was signalized by the omission – under the feeble plea of the difference in nationality – of a wedding service in a church – an omission which would have been impossible ten years earlier; but a family party to celebrate the occasion it was out of the question to omit. Once more the drawing-room was flooded by those familiar figures: even Uncle William in his coat and waistcoat of quaint cut and innumerable buttons – the very same that he might have worn in the forties in Holland House – even Mabel Batten, with that gorgeous bust on which the head of Edward the Seventh was wont to repose – were there. When the strange company had departed, something – though at the time we hardly realized it – had happened: it was the end of an age.

The actual events of life are perhaps unimportant. One is born, grows up, falls in love, falls out of love, works, is happy, is unhappy, grows old, and dies – a tedious, a vulgar, succession; but not there lies the significance of a personal history: it is the atmosphere that counts. What happened to me during my first twenty-five years of consciousness may well be kept to the imagination; what cannot be left to the imagination is the particular, the amazing, web on which the pattern of my existence was woven – in other words, Lancaster Gate. To imagine *that*! – To reconstruct, however dimly, that grim machine, would be to realize with some real distinctness the essential substance of my biography. An incubus sat upon my spirit, like a cat on a sleeping child. I was unaware, I was unconscious, I hardly understood that anything else could be. Submerged by the drawing-room, I inevitably believed that the drawing-room was the world. Or rather, I neither believed nor disbelieved; it *was* the world, so far as I was concerned. Only, all the time, I did dimly notice that there was something wrong with the world – that it was an unpleasant shape.

Of course, it would be absurd to pretend that I was permanently and definitely unhappy. It was not a question of unhappiness so much as of restriction and oppression – the subtle unperceived weight of the circumambient air. And there were moments, luckily, when some magic spring within me was suddenly released, and I threw off that weight, my spirit leaping up into freedom and beatitude. Coming home in the night in the summer once from the Temple with Clive, parting from him, excited, faintly amorous, opposite the sentry at St James's Palace, walking on in the early morning opalescence through sleeping Mayfair and down the Bayswater Road, where the County Council carts were sprinkling the pavements with pale blue disinfectant water – I arrived at last at number 69, a little weary, but not too weary to face with equanimity the long climb that lay in front of me before I reached my bed. Up and up I went, curling round the great dim ochre well, round and up, until the dome loomed over me, and, looking over the banisters, I hung high in mid space, then turned, went up the six broad steps, then passed bedroom after bedroom, up and up still, leaving the nursery floor behind me, until I reached the bedroom, which, for the moment, was mine – almost at the very top of the house – at the back – overlooking, from an incredible height, a mews and roof and chimneys. I opened the door and went in, and immediately saw that the second bed – there was invariably a second bed in every bedroom – was occupied. I looked closer: it was Duncan; and I was not surprised: he had lingered on, no doubt, till it was too late to go home, and had been provided with the obvious accommodation. I undressed, oddly exultant, in the delicious warm morning. As I was getting into bed I saw that all the clothes had rolled off Duncan – that he was lying, almost naked, in vague pyjamas – his body – the slim body of a youth of nineteen – exposed to the view. I was very happy; and, smiling to myself, I wondered why it was that I did not want – not want in the very least – what the opportunity so perfectly offered, and I got into bed, and slept soundly, and dreamt no prophetic dreams.

47

Virginia Woolf: Old Bloomsbury

Virginia Woolf's memoir of Old Bloomsbury was written, she says, at the instigation of Desmond MacCarthy's wife Molly (née Cornish), who was secretary of the Memoir Club. The opening scene continues less hyperbolically the last scene in her preceding memoir, where she called George Duckworth the lover of his half-sisters Vanessa and Virginia. 'Old Bloomsbury' was written around 1922 and recalls the three 'chapters' of Bloomsbury before the First World War: the first chapter ended with Thoby's death in 1906, and the second with the first Post-Impressionist Exhibition of 1910. Woolf's memoir swarms with people from the past and present. There are the three families referred to at the beginning: Leslie Stephen's daughter by his first marriage to Thackeray's daughter; the three children George, Stella, and Gerald Duckworth of Julia Stephen's first marriage; and the four Stephen children. Among the less known members of Bloomsbury mentioned are Saxon Sydney-Turner, a Treasury official; Ralph Hawtrey, an economist; and Lytton's younger brother James, who became Freud's English translator. Euphrosyne was an anonymous collection of undergraduate verse by Sydney-Turner, Clive Bell, Lytton Strachey, Leonard Woolf, and others. Before her marriage Virginia shared a house in Brunswick Square with Adrian, Keynes, Grant, and Leonard Woolf. Like Strachey's memoir, Virginia Woolf's is concerned with the atmospheres of rooms – at Hyde Park Gate, Gordon Square, James Strachey's college rooms, and Lady Ottoline Morrell's house in Bedford Square. 'Old Bloomsbury' and the preceding memoir on Hyde Park Gate were posthumously published in a collection of Virginia Woolf's memoirs entitled Moments of Being, edited by Jeanne Schulkind. (The editing of the memoir has been modified in some places.)

At Molly's command I have had to write a memoir of Old Bloomsbury – of Bloomsbury from 1904 to 1914. Naturally I see Bloomsbury only from my own angle – not from yours. For this I must ask you to make allowances. From my angle then, one approaches Bloomsbury through Hyde Park Gate – that little irregular cul-de-sac which lies next to Queen's Gate and opposite to Kensington Gardens. And we must look for a moment at that very tall house on the left hand side near the bottom which begins by being stucco and ends by being red brick; which is so high and yet – as I can say now that we have sold it – so rickety that it seems as if a very high wind would topple it over.

I was undressing at the top of that house when my last memoir ended, in my bedroom at the back. My white satin dress was on the floor. The faint smell of kid gloves was in the air. My necklace of seed-pearls was tangled with hairpins on the dressing table. I had just come back from a party – from a series of parties indeed, for it was a memorable night in the height of the season of 1903. I had dined with Lady Carnarvon in Bruton Street; I had seen George undoubtedly kiss her among the pillars in the hall; I had talked much too much – about my emotions on hearing music – at dinner; Lady Carnarvon, Mrs Popham, George and myself had then gone to the most indecent French play I have ever seen. We had risen like a flock of partridges at the end of the first act. Mrs Popham's withered cheeks had burnt crimson. Elsie's grey locks had streamed in the wind. We had parted, with great embarrassment on their side, on the pavement, and Elsie had said she did hope I wasn't tired – which meant, I felt, she hoped I wouldn't lose my virginity or something like that. And then we had gone on – George and I in a hansom together to another party, for George said, to my intense shame, I had talked much too much and I must really learn how to behave – we had gone on to the Holman Hunts, where 'The Light of the World' had just come back from its mission to the chief cities of the British Empire, and Mr Edward Clifford, Mrs Russell Barrington, Mrs Freshfield and I know not what distinguished old gentlemen with black ribbons attached to their eyeglasses and elderly ladies with curious vertebrae showing through their real but rather ragged old lace had talked in hushed voices of the master's art while the master himself sat in a skull cap drinking, in spite of the June night, hot cocoa from a mug.

It was long past midnight that I got into bed and sat reading a page or two of *Marius the Epicurean* for which I had then a passion. There would be a tap at the door; the light would be turned out and George would fling himself on my bed, cuddling and kissing and otherwise embracing me in order, as he told Dr Savage later, to comfort me for the fatal illness of my father – who was dying three or four storeys lower down of cancer.

But it is the house that I would ask you to imagine for a moment for, though Hyde Park Gate seems now so distant from Bloomsbury, its shadow falls across it. 46 Gordon Square could never have meant what it did had not 22 Hyde Park Gate preceded it. It was a house of innumerable small oddly shaped rooms built to accommodate not one family but three. For besides the three Duckworths and the four Stephens there was also Thackeray's grand-daughter, a vacant-eyed girl whose idiocy was becoming daily more obvious, who could hardly read, who would throw the scissors into the fire, who was tongue-tied and stammered and yet had to appear at table with the rest of us. To house the lot of us, now a storey would be thrown out on top, now a dining room flung out at bottom. My mother, I believe, sketched what she wanted on a sheet of notepaper to save the architect's fees. These three families had poured all their possessions into this one house. One never knew when one rummaged in the many dark cupboards and wardrobes whether one would disinter Herbert Duckworth's barrister's wig, my father's clergyman's collar, or a sheet scribbled over with drawings by Thackeray which we afterwards sold to Pierpont Morgan for a considerable sum. Old letters filled dozens of black tin boxes. One opened them and got a terrific whiff of the past. There were chests of heavy family plate. There were hoards of china and glass. Eleven people aged between eight and sixty lived there, and were waited upon by seven servants, while various old women and lame men did odd jobs with rakes and pails by day.

The house was dark because the street was so narrow that one could see Mrs Redgrave washing her neck in her bedroom across the way; also because my mother who had been brought up in the Watts-Venetian-Little Holland House tradition had covered the furniture in red velvet and painted the woodwork black with thin gold lines upon it. The house was also completely quiet. Save for an occasional hansom or butcher's cart nothing ever passed the door. One heard footsteps tapping down the street before we saw a top hat or a bonnet; one almost always knew who it was that passed; it might be Sir Arthur Clay; the Muir-MacKenzies or the white-nosed Miss or the red-nosed Mrs Redgrave. Here then seventeen or eighteen people lived in small bedrooms with one bathroom and three water-closets between them. Here the four of us were born; here my grandmother died; here my mother died; here my father died; here Stella became engaged to Jack Hills and two doors further down the street after three months of marriage she died too. When I look back upon that house it seems to me so crowded with scenes of family life, grotesque, comic and tragic; with the violent emotions of youth, revolt, despair, intoxicating happiness, immense boredom, with parties of the famous and the dull; with rages again, George and Gerald; with love scenes with Jack Hills; with passionate affection for my father alternating with passionate hatred of him, all tingling and vibrating in an atmosphere of youthful bewilderment and curiosity – that I feel suffocated by the recollection. The place seemed tangled and matted with emotion. I could write the history of every mark and scratch in my room, I wrote later. The walls and the rooms had in sober truth been built to our shape. We had permeated the whole vast fabric – it has since been made into an hotel – with our family history. It seemed as if the house and the family which had lived in it, thrown together as they were by so many deaths, so many emotions, so many traditions, must endure for ever. And then suddenly in one night both vanished.

When I recovered from the illness which was not unnaturally the result of all these emotions and complications, 22 Hyde Park Gate no longer existed. While I had lain in bed at the Dickinsons' house at Welwyn thinking that the birds were singing Greek choruses and that King Edward was using the foulest possible language among Ozzie Dickinson's azaleas, Vanessa had wound up Hyde Park Gate once and for all. She had sold; she had burnt; she had sorted; she had torn up. Sometimes I believe she had actually to get men with hammers to batter down – so wedged into each other had the walls and the cabinets become. But now all the rooms stood empty. Furniture vans had carted off all the different belongings. For not only had the furniture been dispersed. The family which had seemed equally wedged together had broken apart too. George had married Lady Margaret. Gerald had taken a bachelor flat in Berkeley Street. Laura had been finally incarcerated with a doctor in an asylum; Jack Hills had entered on a political career. The four of us were therefore left alone. And Vanessa – looking at a map of London and seeing how far apart they were – had decided that we should leave Kensington and start life afresh in Bloomsbury.

It was thus that 46 Gordon Square came into existence. When one sees it today, Gordon Square is not one of the most romantic of the Bloomsbury squares. It has neither the distinction of Fitzroy Square nor the majesty of Mecklenburgh Square. It is prosperous middle class and thoroughly mid-Victorian. But I can assure you that in October 1904 it was the most beautiful, the most exciting, the most romantic place in the world. To begin with it was astonishing to stand at the drawing room window and look into all those trees; the tree which shoots its branches up into the air and lets them fall in a shower; the tree which glistens after rain like the body of a seal – instead of looking at old Mrs Redgrave washing her neck across the way. The light and the air after the rich red gloom of Hyde Park Gate were a revelation. Things one had never seen in the darkness there – Watts pictures, Dutch cabinets, blue china – shone out for the first time in the drawing room at Gordon Square. After the muffled silence of Hyde Park Gate the roar of traffic was positively alarming. Odd characters, sinister, strange, prowled and slunk past our windows. But what was even more exhilarating was the extraordinary increase of space. At Hyde Park Gate one had only a bedroom in which to read or see one's friends. Here Vanessa and I each had a sitting room; there was the large double drawing room; and a study on the ground floor. To make it all newer and fresher, the house had been completely done up. Needless to say the Watts-Venetian tradition of red plush and black paint had been reversed; we had entered the Sargent-Furse era; white and green chintzes were everywhere; and instead of Morris wallpapers with their intricate patterns we decorated our walls with washes of plain distemper. We were full of experiments and reforms. We were going to do without table napkins, we were to have Bromo instead; we were going to paint; to write; to have coffee after dinner instead of tea at nine o'clock. Everything was going to be new; everything was going to be different. Everything was on trial.

We were, it appears, extremely social. For some months in the winter of 1904–5 I kept a diary from which I find that we were for ever lunching and dining out and loitering about the book shops – 'Bloomsbury is ever so much more interesting than Kensington,' I wrote – or going to a concert or visiting a picture gallery and coming home to find the drawing room full of the oddest collections of people. 'Cousin Henry Prinsep, Miss Millais, Ozzie Dickinson and Victor Marshall all came this afternoon and stayed late, so that we had only just time to rush off to a Mr Rutter's lecture on Impressionism at the Grafton Gallery ... Lady Hylton, V. Dickinson and E. Coltman came to tea. We lunched with the Shaw Stewarts and met an art critic called Nicholls. Sir Hugh seemed nice but there isn't much in him ... I lunched with the Protheroes and met the Bertrand Russells. It was very amusing. Thoby and I dined with the Cecils and went on to the St Loe Stracheys where we knew a great many people ... I called for Nessa and Thoby at Mrs Flower's and we went on to a dance at the Hobhouses'. Nessa was in a state of great misery today waiting for Mr Tonks who came at one to criticise her pictures. He is a man with a cold bony face, prominent eyes and a look of serenity and boredom. Meg Booth and Sir Fred Pollock came to tea ...' So it goes on; but among all these short records of parties, of how the chintzes came home and how we went to the Zoo and how we went to *Peter Pan*, there are a few entries which bear on Bloomsbury. On Thursday March 2nd 1905 Violet Dickinson brought a clergyman's wife to tea and Sydney-Turner and Strachey came after dinner and we talked till twelve. On Wednesday the 8th of March: 'Margaret [Duckworth] sent round her new motor car this afternoon and we took Violet to pay a series of calls, but we, of course, forgot our cards. Then I went on to the Waterloo Road and lectured (a class of working men and women) on the Greek Myths. Home and found Bell, and we talked about the nature of good till almost one!'

On the 16th March Miss Power and Miss Malone dined with us. Sydney-Turner and Gerald came in after dinner – the first of our Thursday evenings. On the 23rd March nine people came to our evening and stayed till one.

A few days later I went to Spain, and the duty which I laid on myself of recording every sight and sound, every wave and hill, sickened me with diary writing so that I stopped – with this last entry: May the 11th – 'Our evening: Gaye, Bell, D. MacCarthy and Gerald – who shocked the cultured.'

So my diary ends just as it might have become interesting. Yet I think it is clear even in this brief record in which every sort of doing is piled up higgledy-piggledy that these few meetings of Bloomsbury in its infancy differed from the rest. These are the only occasions when I do not merely say I had met so and so and thought him long-faced like Reginald Smith or pompous like Moorsom, or quite easy to get on with, but nothing much in him, like Sir Hugh Shaw Stewart. I say we talked to Strachey and Sydney-Turner. I add with a note of exclamation that we talked with Bell about the nature of good till one! And I did not use notes of exclamation often – and once more indeed – when I say that I smoked a cigarette with Beatrice Thynne!

These Thursday evening parties were, as far as I am concerned, the germ from which sprang all that has since come to be called – in newspapers, in novels, in Germany, in France – even, I daresay, in Turkey and Timbuktu – by the name of Bloomsbury. They deserve to be recorded and described. Yet how difficult – how impossible. Talk – even the talk which had such tremendous results upon the lives and characters of the two Miss Stephens – even talk of this interest and importance is as elusive as smoke. It flies up the chimney and is gone.

In the first place it is not true to say that when the door opened and with a curious hesitation and self-effacement Turner or Strachey glided in – that they were complete strangers to us. We had met them – and Bell, Woolf, Hilton Young and others – in Cambridge at May Week before my father died. But what was of much greater importance, we had heard of them from Thoby. Thoby possessed a great power of romanticizing his friends. Even when he was a little boy at a private school there was always some astonishing fellow, whose amazing character and exploits he would describe hour after hour when he came home for the holidays. These stories had the greatest fascination for me. I thought about Pilkington or Sidney Irwin or the Woolly Bear whom I never saw in the flesh as if they were characters in Shakespeare. I made up stories about them myself. It was a kind of saga that went on year after year. And now just as I had heard of Radcliffe, Stuart, or whoever it might be, I began to hear of Bell, Strachey, Turner, Woolf. We talked of them by the hour, rambling about the country or sitting over the fire in my bedroom.

'There's an astonishing fellow called Bell,' Thoby would begin directly he came back. 'He's a sort of mixture between Shelley and a sporting country squire.'

At this of course I pricked up my ears and began to ask endless questions. We were walking over a moor somewhere, I remember. I got a fantastic impression that this man Bell was a kind of Sun God – with straw in his hair. He was an [illegible] of innocence and enthusiasm. Bell had never opened a book till he came to Cambridge, Thoby said. Then he suddenly discovered Shelley and Keats and went nearly mad with excitement. He did nothing but spout poetry and write poetry. Yet he was a perfect horseman – a gift which Thoby enormously admired – and kept two or three hunters up at Cambridge.

'And is Bell a great poet?' I asked.

No, Thoby wouldn't go so far as to say that; but it was quite on the cards that Strachey was. And so we discussed Strachey – or 'the Strache', as Thoby called him. Strachey at once became as singular, as fascinating as Bell. But it was in quite a different way. 'The Strache' was the essence of culture. In fact I think his culture a little alarmed Thoby. He had French pictures in his rooms. He had a passion for Pope. He was exotic, extreme in every way – Thoby described him – so long, so thin that his thigh was no thicker than Thoby's arm. Once he burst into Thoby's rooms, cried out, 'Do you hear the music of the spheres?' and fell in a faint. Once in the midst of a dead silence, he piped up – and Thoby could imitate his voice perfectly – 'Let's all write Sonnets to Robertson.' He was a prodigy of wit. Even the tutors and the dons would come and listen to him. 'Whatever they give you, Strachey,' Dr Jackson had said when Strachey was in for some examination, 'it won't be good enough.' And then Thoby, leaving me enormously impressed and rather dazed, would switch off to tell me about another astonishing fellow – a man who trembled perpetually all over. He was as eccentric, as remarkable in his way as Bell and Strachey in theirs. He was a Jew. When I asked why he trembled, Thoby somehow made me feel that it was part of his nature – he was so violent, so savage; he so despised the whole human race. 'And after all,' Thoby said, 'it is a pretty feeble affair, isn't it?'

Nobody was much good after twenty-five, he said. But most people, I gathered, rather rubbed along, and came to terms with things. Woolf did not and Thoby thought it sublime. One night he dreamt he was throttling a man and he dreamt with such violence that when he woke up he had pulled his own thumb out of joint. I was of course inspired with the deepest interest in that violent trembling misanthropic Jew who had already shaken his fist at civilization and was about to disappear into the tropics so that we should none of us ever see him again. And then perhaps the talk got upon Sydney-Turner. According to Thoby, Sydney-Turner was an absolute prodigy of learning. He had the whole of Greek literature by heart. There was practically nothing in any language that was any good that he had not read. He was very silent and thin and odd. He never came out by day. But late at night if he saw one's lamp burning he would come and tap at the window like a moth. At about three in the morning he would begin to talk. His talk was then of astonishing brilliance. When later I complained to Thoby that I had met Turner and had not found him brilliant Thoby severely supposed that by brilliance I meant wit; he on the contrary meant truth. Sydney-Turner was the most brilliant talker he knew because he always spoke the truth.

Naturally then, when the bell rang and these astonishing fellows came in, Vanessa and I were in a twitter of excitement. It was late at night; the room was full of smoke; buns, coffee and whisky were strewn about; we were not wearing white satin or seed-pearls; we were not dressed at all. Thoby went to open the door; in came Sydney-Turner; in came Bell; in came Strachey.

They came in hesitatingly, self-effacingly, and folded themselves up quietly [in] the corners of sofas. For a long time they said nothing. None of our old conversational openings seemed to do. Vanessa and Thoby and Clive, if Clive were there – for Clive differed in many ways from the others [and] was always ready to sacrifice himself in the cause of talk – would start different subjects. But they were almost always answered in the negative. 'No,' was the most frequent reply. 'No, I haven't seen it'; 'No, I haven't been there.' Or simply, 'I don't know.' The conversation languished in a way that would have been impossible in the drawing room at Hyde Park Gate. Yet the silence was difficult, not dull. It seemed as if the standard of what was worth saying had risen so high that it was better not to break it unworthily. We sat and looked at the ground. Then at last Vanessa, having said perhaps that she had been to some picture show, incautiously used the word 'beauty'. At that, one of the young men would lift his head slowly and say, 'It depends what you mean by beauty.' At once all our ears were pricked. It was as if the bull had at last been turned into the ring.

The bull might be 'beauty', might be 'good', might be 'reality'. Whatever it was, it was some abstract question that now drew out all our forces. Never have I listened so intently to each step and half-step in an argument. Never have I been at such pains to sharpen and launch my own little dart. And then what joy it was when one's contribution was accepted. No praise has pleased me more than Saxon's saying – and was not Saxon infallible after all? – that he thought I had argued my case very cleverly. And what strange cases those were! I remember trying to persuade [Ralph] Hawtrey that there is such a thing as atmosphere in literature. Hawtrey challenged me to prove it by pointing out in any book any one word which had this quality apart from its meaning. I went and fetched *Diana of the Crossways*. The argument, whether it was about atmosphere or the nature of truth, was always tossed into the middle of the party. Now Hawtrey would say something; now Vanessa; now Saxon; now Clive; now Thoby. It filled me with wonder to watch those who were finally left in the argument piling stone upon stone, cautiously, accurately, long after it had completely soared above my sight. But if one could not say anything, one could listen. One had glimpses of something miraculous happening high up in the air. Often we would still be sitting in a circle at two or three in the morning. Still Saxon would be taking his pipe from his mouth as if to speak, and putting it back again without having spoken. At last, rumpling his hair back, he would pronounce very shortly some absolutely final summing up. The marvellous edifice was complete, one could stumble off to bed feeling that something very important had happened. It had been proved that beauty was – or beauty was not – for I have never been quite sure which – part of a picture.

From such discussions Vanessa and I got probably much the same pleasure that undergraduates get when they meet friends of their own for the first time. In the world of the Booths and the Maxses we were not asked to use our brains much. Here we used nothing else. And part of the charm of those Thursday evenings was that they were astonishingly abstract. It was not only that Moore's book [*Principia Ethica*] had set us all discussing philosophy, art, religion; it was that the atmosphere – if in spite of Hawtrey I may use that word – was abstract in the extreme. The young men I have named had no 'manners' in the Hyde Park Gate sense. They criticized our arguments as severely as their own. They never seemed to notice how we were dressed or if we were nice looking or not. All that tremendous encumbrance of appearance and behaviour which George had piled upon our first years vanished completely. One had no longer to endure that terrible inquisition after a party – and be told, 'You looked lovely.' Or, 'You did look plain.' Or, 'You must really learn to do your hair.' Or, 'Do try not to look so bored when you dance.' Or, 'You did make a conquest,' or, 'You *were* a failure.' All this seemed to have no meaning or existence in the world of Bell, Strachey, Hawtrey and Sydney-

Turner. In that world the only comment as we stretched ourselves after our guests had gone, was, 'I must say you made your point rather well'; 'I think you were talking rather through your hat.' It was an immense simplification. And for my part it went deeper than this. The atmosphere of Hyde Park Gate had been full of love and marriage. George's [first] engagement to Flora Russell, Stella's to Jack Hills, Gerald's innumerable flirtations were all discussed either in private or openly with the greatest interest. Vanessa was already supposed to have attracted Austen Chamberlain. My Aunt Mary Fisher, poking about as usual in nooks and corners, had discovered that there were six drawings of him in Vanessa's sketchbook and [had] come to her own conclusions. George rather suspected that Charles Trevelyan was in love with her. But at Gordon Square love was never mentioned. Love had no existence. So lightly was it treated that for years I believed that Desmond [MacCarthy] had married an old Miss Cornish, aged about sixty, with snow-white hair. One never took the trouble to find out. It seemed incredible that any of these young men should want to marry us or that we should want to marry them. Secretly I felt that marriage was a very low-down affair, but that if one practised it, one practised it – it is a serious confession I know – with young men who had been in the Eton Eleven and dressed for dinner. When I looked round the room at 46 I thought – if you will excuse me for saying so – that I had never seen young men so dingy, so lacking in physical splendour as Thoby's friends. Kitty Maxse who came in once or twice sighed afterwards, 'I've no doubt they're very nice but, oh darling, how awful they do look!' Henry James, on seeing Lytton and Saxon at Rye, exclaimed to Mrs Prothero, 'Deplorable! Deplorable! How could Vanessa and Virginia have picked up such friends? How could Leslie's daughters have taken up with young men like that?' But it was precisely this lack of physical splendour, this shabbiness! that was in my eyes a proof of their superiority. More than that, it was, in some obscure way, reassuring; for it meant that things could go on like this, in abstract argument, without dressing for dinner, and never revert to the ways, which I had come to think so distasteful, at Hyde Park Gate.

I was wrong. One afternoon that first summer Vanessa said to Adrian and me and I watched her, stretching her arms above her head with a gesture that was at once reluctant and yielding, in the great looking-glass as she said it – 'Of course, I can see that we shall all marry. It's bound to happen' – and as she said it I could feel a horrible necessity impending over us; a fate would descend and snatch us apart just as we had achieved freedom and happiness. She, I felt, was already aware of some claim, some need which I resented and tried to ignore. A few weeks later indeed Clive proposed to her. 'Yes,' said Thoby grimly when I murmured something to him very shyly about Clive's proposal, 'That's the worst of Thursday evenings!' And her marriage in the beginning of 1907 was in fact the end of them. With that, the first chapter of Old Bloomsbury came to an end. It had been very austere, very exciting, of immense importance. A small concentrated world dwelling inside the much larger and looser world of dances and dinners had come into existence. It had already begun to colour that world and still I think colours the much more gregarious Bloomsbury which succeeded it.

But it could not have gone on. Even if Vanessa had not married, even if Thoby had lived, change was inevitable. We could not have gone on discussing the nature of beauty in the abstract for ever. The young men, as we used to call them, were changing from the general to the particular. They had ceased to be Mr Turner, Mr Strachey, Mr Bell. They had become Saxon, Lytton, Clive. Then too one was beginning to criticize, to distinguish, to compare. Those old flamboyant portraits were being revised. One could see that Walter Lamb whom Thoby had compared to a Greek boy playing a flute in a vineyard was in fact rather bald, and rather dull; one could wish that Saxon could be induced either to go or to say something perhaps that was not strictly true; one could even doubt, when *Euphrosyne* was published, whether as many of the poems in that famous book were sure of immortality as Thoby made out. But there was something else that made for a change though I at least did not know what it was. Perhaps if I read you a passage from another diary which I kept intermittently for a month or two in the year 1909 you will guess what it was. I am describing a tea-party in James Strachey's rooms at Cambridge.

'His rooms,' I wrote, 'though they are lodgings, are discreet and dim. French pastels hang upon the walls and there are cases of old books. The three young men – [Harry] Norton, [Rupert] Brooke and James Strachey – sat in deep chairs; and gazed with soft intent eyes into the fire. Mr Norton knew that he must talk; he and I talked laboriously. The others were silent. I should like to account for this silence, but time presses and I am puzzled. For the truth is that these young men are evidently respectable; they are not only able but their views seem to me honest and simple. They lack all padding; so that one has convictions to disagree with if one disagrees. Yet we had nothing to say to each other and I was conscious that not only my remarks but my presence was criticized. They wished for the truth and doubted if I could speak it or be it. I thought this courageous of them but unsympathetic. I admired the atmosphere – was it more? – and felt in some respects at ease in it. Yet why should intellect and character be so barren? It seems as if the highest efforts of the most intelligent people produce a negative result; one cannot honestly be anything.'

There is a great change there from what I should have written two or three years earlier. In part, of course, the change was due to circumstances; I lived alone with Adrian now in Fitzroy Square; and we were the most incompatible of people. We drove each other perpetually into frenzies of irritation or into the depths of gloom. We still went to a great many parties: but the combination of the two worlds which I think was so [illegible] was far more difficult. I could not reconcile the two. True, we still had Thursday evenings as before. But they were always strained and often ended in dismal failure. Adrian stalked off to his room, I to mine, in complete silence. But there was more in it than that. What it was I was not altogether certain. I knew theoretically, from books, much more than I knew practically from life. I knew that there were buggers in Plato's Greece; I suspected – it was not a question one could just ask Thoby – that there were buggers in Dr Butler's Trinity [College], Cambridge; but it never occurred to me that there were buggers even now in the Stephens' sitting room at Gordon Square. It never struck me that the abstractness, the simplicity which had been so great a relief after Hyde Park Gate were largely due to the fact that the majority of the young men who came there were not attracted by young women. I did not realize that love, far from being a thing they never mentioned, was in fact a thing which they seldom ceased to discuss. Now I had begun to be puzzled. Those long sittings, those long silences, those long arguments – they still went on in Fitzroy Square as they had done in Gordon Square. But now I found them of the most perplexing nature. They still excited me much more than any men I met with in the outer world of dinners and dances – and yet I was, dared I say it or think it even? – intolerably bored. Why, I asked, had we nothing to say to each other? Why were the most gifted of people also the most barren? Why were the most stimulating of friendships also the most deadening? Why was it all so negative? Why did these young men make one feel that one could not honestly be anything? The answer to all my questions was, obviously – as you will have guessed – that there was no physical attraction between us.

The society of buggers has many advantages – if you are a woman. It is simple, it is honest, it makes one feel, as I noted, in some respects at one's ease. But it has this drawback – with buggers one cannot, as nurses say, show off. Something is always suppressed, held down. Yet this showing off, which is not copulating, necessarily, nor altogether being in love, is one of the great delights, one of the chief necessities of life. Only then does all effort cease; one ceases to be honest, one ceases to be clever. One fizzes up into some absurd delightful effervescence of soda water or champagne through which one sees the world tinged with all the colours of the rainbow. It is significant of what I had come to desire that I went straight – on almost the next page of my diary indeed – from the dim and discreet rooms of James Strachey at Cambridge to dine with Lady Ottoline Morrell at Bedford Square. Her rooms, I noted without drawing any inferences, seemed to me instantly full of 'lustre and illusion'.

So one changed. But these changes of mine were part of a much bigger change. The headquarters of Bloomsbury have always been in Gordon Square. Now that Vanessa and Clive were married, now that Clive had shocked the Maxses, the Booths, the Cecils, the Protheroes, irretrievably, now that the house was done up once more, now that they were giving little parties with their beautiful brown table linen and their lovely eighteenth-century silver, Bloomsbury rapidly lost the monastic character it had had in Chapter One; the character of Chapter Two was superficially at least to be very different.

Another scene has always lived in my memory – I do not know if I invented it or not – as the best illustration of Bloomsbury Chapter Two. It was a spring evening. Vanessa and I were sitting in the drawing room. The drawing room had greatly changed its character since 1904. The Sargent-Furse age was over. The age of Augustus John was dawning. His *Pyramus* filled one entire wall. The Watts' portraits of my father and my mother were hung downstairs if they were hung at all. Clive had hidden all the match boxes because their blue and yellow swore with the prevailing colour scheme. At any moment Clive might come in and he and I should begin to argue – amicably, impersonally at first; soon we should be hurling abuse at each other and pacing up and down the room. Vanessa sat silent and did something mysterious with her needle or her scissors. I talked, egotistically, excitedly, about my own affairs no doubt. Suddenly the door opened and the long and sinister figure of Mr Lytton Strachey stood on the threshold. He pointed his finger at a stain on Vanessa's white dress.

'Semen?' he said.

Can one really say it? I thought and we burst out laughing. With that one word all barriers of reticence and reserve went down. A flood of the sacred fluid seemed to overwhelm us. Sex permeated our conversation. The word bugger was never far from our lips. We discussed copulation with the same excitement and openness that we had discussed the nature of good. It is strange to think how reticent, how reserved we had been and for how long. It seems a marvel now that so late as the year 1908 or 9 Clive had blushed and I had blushed too when I asked him to let me pass to go to the lavatory on the French Express. I never dreamt of asking Vanessa to tell me what happened on her wedding night. Thoby and Adrian would have died rather than discuss the love affairs of undergraduates. When all intellectual questions had been debated so freely, sex was ignored. Now a flood of light poured in upon that department too. We had known everything but we had never talked. Now we talked of nothing else. We listened with rapt interest to the love affairs of the buggers. We followed the ups and downs of their chequered histories; Vanessa sympathetically; I – had I not written in 1905, women are so much more amusing than men – frivolously, laughingly. 'Norton tells me', Vanessa would say, 'that James is in utter despair. Rupert has been twice to bed with Hobhouse' and I would cap her stories with some equally thrilling piece of gossip; about a divine undergraduate with a head like a Greek God – but alas his teeth were bad – called George Mallory.

All this had the result that the old sentimental views of marriage in which we were brought up were revolutionized. I should be sorry to tell you how old I was before I saw that there is nothing shocking in a man's having a mistress, or in a woman's being one. Perhaps the fidelity of our parents was not the only or inevitably the highest form of married life. Perhaps indeed that fidelity was not so strict as one had supposed. 'Of course Kitty Maxse has two or three lovers,' said Clive – Kitty Maxse, the chaste, the exquisite, the devoted! Again, the whole aspect of life was changed.

So there was now nothing that one could not say, nothing that one could not do, at 46 Gordon Square. It was, I think, a great advance in civilization. It may be true that the loves of buggers are not – at least if one is of the other persuasion – of enthralling interest or paramount importance. But the fact that they can be mentioned openly leads to the fact that no one minds if they are practised privately. Thus many customs and beliefs were revised. Indeed the future of Bloomsbury was to prove that many variations can be played on the theme of sex, and with such happy results that my father himself might have hesitated before he thundered out the one word which he thought fit to apply to a bugger or an adulterer; which was Blackguard!

Here I come to a question which I must leave to some other memoir writer to discuss – that is to say, if we take it for granted that Bloomsbury exists, what are the qualities that admit one to it, what are the qualities that expel one from it? Now at any rate between 1910 and 1914 many new members were admitted. It must have been in 1910 I suppose that Clive one evening rushed upstairs in a state of the highest excitement. He had just had one of the most interesting conversations of his life. It was with Roger Fry. They had been discussing the theory of art for hours. He thought Roger Fry the most interesting person he had met since Cambridge days. So Roger appeared. He appeared, I seem to think, in a large ulster coat, every pocket of which was stuffed with a book, a paint box or something intriguing; special tips which he had bought from a little man in a back street; he had canvases under his arms; his hair flew; his eyes glowed. He had more knowledge and experience than the rest of us put together. His mind seemed hooked on to life by an extraordinary number of attachments. We started talking about [Marguerite Audoux's] *Marie-Claire*. And at once we were all launched into a terrific argument about literature; adjectives? associations? overtones? We had down Milton; we re-read Wordsworth. We had to think the whole thing over again. The old skeleton arguments of primitive Bloomsbury about art and beauty put on flesh and blood. There was always some new idea afoot; always some new picture standing on a chair to be looked at, some new poet fished out from obscurity and stood in the light of day. Odd people wandered through 46; Rothenstein, Sickert, Yeats, Tonks – Tonks who could, I suppose, make Vanessa miserable no more. And sometimes one began to meet a queer faun-like figure, hitching his clothes up, blinking his eyes, stumbling oddly over the long words in his sentences. A year or two before, Adrian and I had been standing in front of a certain gold and black picture in the Louvre when a voice said: 'Are you Adrian Stephen? I'm Duncan Grant.' Duncan now began to haunt the purlieus of Bloomsbury. How he lived I do not know. He was penniless. Uncle Trevor [Grant] indeed said he was mad. He lived in a studio in Fitzroy Square with an old drunken charwoman called Filmer and a clergyman who frightened girls in the street by making faces at them. Duncan was on the best of terms with both. He was rigged out by his friends in clothes which seemed always to be falling to the floor. He borrowed old china from us to paint; and my father's old trousers to go to parties in. He broke the china and he ruined the trousers by jumping into the Cam to rescue a child who was swept into the river by the rope of Walter Lamb's barge, the 'Aholibah'. Our cook Sophie called him 'that Mr Grant' and complained that he had been taking things again as if he were a rat in her larder. But she succumbed to his charm. He seemed to be vaguely tossing about in the breeze; but he always alighted exactly where he meant to.

And once at least Morgan [Forster] flitted through Bloomsbury lodging for a moment in Fitzroy Square on his way even then to catch a train. He carried, I think, the same black bag with the same brass label on it that is now in the hall outside at this moment. I felt as if a butterfly – by preference a pale blue butterfly – had settled on the sofa; if one raised a finger or made a movement the butterfly would be off. He talked of Italy and the Working Men's College. And I listened – with the deepest curiosity, for he was the only novelist I knew – except Henry James and George Meredith; the only one anyhow who wrote about people like ourselves. But I was too much afraid of raising my hand and making the butterfly fly away to say much. I used to watch him from behind a hedge as he flitted through Gordon Square, erratic, irregular, with his bag, on his way to catch a train.

These, with Maynard [Keynes] – very truculent, I felt, very formidable, like a portrait of Tolstoy as a young man to look at, able to rend any argument that came his way with a blow of his paw, yet concealing, as the novelists say, a kind and even simple heart under that immensely impressive armour of intellect – and Norton; Norton who was the essence of all I meant by Cambridge; so able; so honest; so ugly; so dry; Norton with whom I spent a whole night once talking and with whom I went at dawn to Covent Garden, whom I still see in memory scowling in his pince-nez – yellow and severe against a bank of roses and carnations – these I think were the chief figures in Bloomsbury before the war.

But here again it becomes necessary to ask – where does Bloomsbury end? What is Bloomsbury? Does it for instance include Bedford Square? Before the war, I think we should most of us have said 'Yes'. When the history of Bloomsbury is written – and what better subject could there be for Lytton's next book? – there will have to be a chapter, even if it is only in the appendix, devoted to Ottoline. Her first appearance among us was, I think, in 1908 or 9. I find from my diary that I dined with her on March the 30th 1909 – I think for the first time. But a few weeks before this, she had swooped down upon one of my own Thursday evenings with Philip [Morrell], Augustus John and Dorelia in tow: she had written the next morning to ask me to give her the names and addresses of all 'my wonderful friends'. This was followed by an invitation to come to Bedford Square any Thursday about ten o'clock and bring anyone I liked. I took Rupert Brooke. Soon we were all swept into the extraordinary whirlpool where such odd sticks and straws were brought momentarily together. There was Augustus John, very sinister in a black stock and a velvet coat; Winston Churchill, very rubicund, all gold lace and medals, on his way to Buckingham Palace; Raymond Asquith crackling with epigrams; Francis Dodd telling me most graphically how he and Aunt Susie had killed bugs: she held the lamp; he a basin of paraffin; bugs crossed the ceiling in an incessant stream. There was Lord Henry Bentinck at one end of the sofa and perhaps Nina Lamb at the other. There was Philip fresh from the House of Commons humming and hawing on the hearth-rug. There was Gilbert Cannan who was said to be in love with Ottoline. There was Bertie Russell, whom she was said to be in love with. Above all, there was Ottoline herself.

'Lady Ottoline', I wrote in my diary, 'is a great lady who has become discontented with her own class and is trying to find what she wants among artists and writers. For this reason, as if they were inspired with something divine, she approaches them in a deferential way and they see her as a disembodied spirit escaping from her world into one where she can never take root. She is remarkable to look at if not beautiful. Like most passive people she is very careful and elaborate in her surroundings. She takes the utmost pains to set off her beauty as though it were some rare object picked up in a dusky Florentine back street. It always seems possible that the rich American women who finger her Persian cloak and call it "very good" may go on to finger her face and call it a fine work in the late renaissance style; the brow and eyes magnificent, the chin perhaps restored. The pallor of her cheeks, the way she has of drawing back her head and looking at you blankly gives her the appearance of a marble Medusa. She is curiously passive.' And then I go on to exclaim rather rhapsodically that the whole place was full of 'lustre and illusion'.

When indeed one remembers that drawing room full of people, the pale yellows and pinks of the brocades, the Italian chairs, the Persian rugs, the embroideries, the tassels, the scent, the pomegranates, the pugs, the pot-pourri and Ottoline bearing down upon one from afar in her white shawl with the great scarlet flowers on it and sweeping one away out of the large room and the crowd into a little room with her alone, where she plied one with questions that were so intimate and so intense, about life and one's friends, and made one sign one's name in a little scented book – it was only last week that I signed my name in another little scented book in Gower Street – I think my excitement may be excused.

Indeed lustre and illusion tinged Bloomsbury during those last years before the war. We were not so austere; we were not so exalted. There were quarrels and intrigues. Ottoline may have been a Medusa; but she was not a passive Medusa. She had a great gift for drawing people under. Even Middleton Murry, it is said, was pulled down by her among the vegetables at Garsington. And by this time we were far from drab. Thursday evenings with their silences and their arguments were a thing of the past. Their place was taken by parties of a very different sort. The Post-Impressionist movement had cast – not its shadow – but its bunch of variegated lights upon us. We bought poinsettias made of scarlet plush; we made dresses of the printed cotton that is specially loved by negroes; we dressed ourselves up as Gauguin pictures and careered round Crosby Hall. Mrs Whitehead was scandalized. She said that Vanessa and I were practically naked. My mother's ghost was invoked once more – by Violet Dickinson – to deplore the fact that I had taken a house in Brunswick Square and had asked young men to share it. George

Duckworth came all the way from Charles Street to beg Vanessa to make me give up the idea and was not comforted perhaps when she replied that after all the Foundling Hospital was handy. Stories began to circulate about parties at which we all undressed in public. Logan Pearsall Smith told Ethel Sands that he knew for a fact that Maynard had copulated with Vanessa on a sofa in the middle of the drawing room. It was a heartless, immoral, cynical society it was said; we were abandoned women and our friends were the most worthless of young men.

Yet in spite of Logan, in spite of Mrs Whitehead, in spite of Vanessa and Maynard and what they did on the sofa at Brunswick Square, Old Bloomsbury still survives. If you seek a proof – look around.

48

Leonard Woolf: Coming to London

Leonard Woolf's memoir was written not for the Memoir Club but for a series published first by John Lehmann in the London Magazine *and then in a book called* Coming to London *in 1957. The contributors were asked to discuss their first encounters with London literary life. Among the authors in the series were V. S. Pritchett, Elizabeth Bowen, Christopher Isherwood, and Edith Sitwell. Another contributor was the novelist Rose Macaulay whose dinner party Woolf describes in his memoir. In 1960 Leonard Woolf began to publish the autobiographies that are the most extended and reliable account of Bloomsbury by one of its members. The title of the posthumously published fifth volume,* The Journey Not the Arrival Matters *(1969), is anticipated at the end of Woolf's memoir here.*

I 'came to London' embryonically, I presume, in February 1880, for I was born in the West Cromwell Road on November 25, 1880, and I have lived in London – except for seven years in Ceylon – ever since. Thus I am a Cockney born and bred, and to ask me to recall my first impressions of coming to London or any segment of it is like asking a humble herring to recall his first impressions of coming to the sea. I have lived in Kensington, Putney, Bloomsbury, Fleet Street and Westminster, and they have left the smell of London (including Gower Street station on the Underground 60 years ago) in my nostrils and its strange, austere, homelike spirit in my bones. I love it profoundly and, as with all real love that goes deep into the entrails, I hate it profoundly.

One of the things which I have been asked to deal with in this article is my 'first impressions of the London literary world'. My feelings towards that world are probably also ambivalent. It is sometimes represented as composed of literary personages, major and minor, endless talking, eating, and drinking in pubs and Soho restaurants, in rooms and flats and parties. Into that world, if it exists, I have not penetrated, and I can only remember two occasions upon which I felt that I was in the real London literary world, even though not of it. The first was when, latish in life, I was sometimes invited to the Sitwells, a dinner, say, with Osbert Sitwell or a party given by Edith Sitwell to meet Gertrude Stein. This was, of course, not in the least like the imaginary world of literary personages in Soho, but it was a literary world into which I went as an intruder feeling the inferiority complex of the amateur minnow among the great, confident, professional pike. To be led up to Gertrude Stein sitting on a kind of throne and to be given five minutes' conversation with her was what an old Edinburgh Writer to the *Signet* used to call 'an experience'. When he took me as a boy to see Abbotsford and halted me outside to survey that fantastic monument of literary fame and success, he said: 'This is an experience which ye'll do well to remember – O Ay, an experience ye'll do well to remember.' Gertrude Stein, I felt, was the same kind of experience.

My only other memory of entering the real London literary world recalls a more trivial and to me discreditable experience than a Sitwell party. Virginia and I accepted an invitation to dine with a well-known novelist whom we liked very much. We expected to dine with her alone or at most another guest, and late, dirty, and dishevelled we dashed from printing in the basement in a taxi to her flat – and found ourselves in a formal dinner of twelve or fourteen distinguished writers all in full evening dress. I suppose it was nervousness which made us fail the entrance examination to literary London. At any rate first, when one of those curious collective silences suddenly fell upon the company, Virginia's extremely clear voice was heard to say: 'The Holy Ghost?' to which the distinguished Catholic writer sitting on her left replied with indignation: 'I did not say Holy Ghost; I said the whole coast.' Almost immediately after, thinking that the distinguished lady writer sitting on my left had dropped her white handkerchief on the floor, I leant down, picked it up, and handed it to her, to find, to my horror, that it was the hem of her white petticoat which had protruded below her skirt. As soon as we decently could, we slunk off home, feeling that we had both disgraced ourselves in literary London.

Very different was my first meeting with a real literary personage. It was in a barber's shop and I must have been about 15. When I was 12 my father died and my mother no longer affluent, moved with her nine children to a house in Putney. One day I was having my hair cut in a shop near Putney station and Putney Hill when the door opened and everyone in the shop, including the man cutting my hair, turned and looked at the person who had come in. A tiny little man in a black cape and a black sombrero-like hat, below which hung lank curls, stood in the doorway. I had a sharp feeling of the fear and pain in his pale-blue eyes and pallid face. He stood silent in the doorway and looked at us and all of us looked at him. He turned and went out, and, as he shut the door, the hairdresser, beginning again to snip at my hair, said: 'That is Mr Swinburne, the writer; he lives at The Pines round the corner.' Swinburne, of course, lived with Theodore Watts-Dunton, the author of *Aylwin*, at The Pines, at the foot of Putney Hill, and could be seen occasionally walking up to Wimbledon Common and stopping now and then to kiss a baby in a pram. Our doctor, who was a famous rugger international half-back, was also Swinburne's doctor; he told me that when he was summoned by Watts-Dunton to come and see the poet, Swinburne could rarely be induced to say a word to him; he would sit very upright in a rather high chair and continually play an inaudible tune with his two hands on the polished dining-room table. The only other literary personage whom I met in those days was Compton Mackenzie, but he had not yet written anything and I had no idea that he would; we were both at St Paul's and I first met him in a football scrum on a cold wet November afternoon. We have often met since in much more pleasant and more literary surroundings. He once told me that I am included as one of the characters in one of his *Four Winds of Love* novels.

In 1894 I managed to win a scholarship and entered St Paul's School, where, under the highmastership of the savage and eccentric Mr Walker, the engines of education were applied violently and strangely to our tender minds. As classical scholars and potential winners of classical scholarships at Oxford or Cambridge, we were treated like Strasbourg geese, except that instead of being stuffed with food in order to fatten our livers, our minds were stuffed for eight or ten hours every day with the grammar, syntax, language and literature of ancient Greece and ancient Rome. No educational training and regimentation of the human mind could be more drastic, more ruthless than that to which we were subjected at St Paul's between the ages of 14 and 19, and when I went up to Trinity College, Cambridge, in 1899, I had an astonishingly thorough knowledge of the classical languages and literatures. And yet, though we spent so many hours every day in the study of some of the greatest literary masterpieces which have ever been produced, interest in or even recognition of literature as literature or of 'the arts' was certainly not in general encouraged. The mental atmosphere was eminently English, a kind of chastened and good-tempered barbarism, a contemptuous Philistinism, based upon a profound, devout veneration of the art of playing cricket or football and distrust of everything connected with the mind and intellect. Up to the age of 16, though my mind was, I think, eager and active, I lived intellectually in a trance, dimly aware that the pleasure I got from books, literature, even work was vaguely discreditable and should be concealed from my companions and teachers.

At the age of 16 I escaped from this land of the Philistines and its dim intellectual twilight with the help of one of the masters, A. M. Cooke, who was the brother of a distinguished journalist, E. T. Cook, editor of the *Daily News*. Cooke was a civilized, cultured, kindly, disillusioned schoolmaster, and an admirable teacher of the more intelligent boys. When I got into his form, he liked my English essays and got into the habit of walking round the playground with me during the 'breaks'. He talked to me as to an equal, sometimes about life and people, but more often about books and writing. He encouraged me to believe that a passion for great literature, even an aspiration to write oneself, was not discreditable. Under his gentle stimulation I read voraciously English and French masterpieces, and one of the things which I am peculiarly grateful that he taught me was to combine with the highest standards of judgement the widest possible catholicity of appreciation and enjoyment. It was characteristic of him that he gave me as a personal parting gift when I went up to a higher form Bacon's *Essays* bound in pale-blue leather by Zaehnsdorf while approving my love of Borrow, and that he was eager that I should enjoy both Montaigne and *Tristram Shandy*.

It was largely due to Cooke that I had a wide acquaintance with and intense enthusiasm for literature when I went up to Trinity College, Cambridge, at the age of 18. Cooke himself had been practically the only outlet for my enthusiasm and for my eagerness to talk about books. It is true that in my last year I had the great honour of being invited to join a small debating society which met on Saturday afternoons in the houses of the members in rotation. It had been founded by G. K. Chesterton and his friends when they were at school, and Chesterton and E. C. Bentley, the author of *Trent's Last Case* and inventor of the clerihew, often came to our meetings. Bentley was then at Oxford and President of the Union, and Chesterton on the *Daily News* rapidly making a name for himself by his brilliantly paradoxical articles. But he and our society were passionately interested, not in books, but politics. I cannot remember ever discussing literature, but we had a 'mock parliament' and my recollection is of Gilbert Chesterton, a tall and at that time comparatively slim young man, making inordinately long, rather boring, Liberal speeches on local government, public houses, foreign policy, etc., and, as he spoke, tearing up sheets of paper into tiny pieces which he scattered on the table in front of him.

When I got to Trinity, I was astonished and delighted to find that among many of my contemporaries and seniors a love of literature and a desire to write books, intensive criticism and aesthetic speculations were accepted as natural and creditable for intelligent persons. Here for the first time I entered what might be called a literary world, a provincial literary world – even though it was Cambridge University – but which yet had connexions with the great metropolitan literary world of London. In 1899, a literary constellation of some brilliance or promise of brilliance centred in Trinity and King's. Among my seniors who were in residence as Fellows or frequently came up and stayed in Cambridge and whom I got to know well were George and Bob Trevelyan, G. E. Moore, Bertrand Russell and Desmond MacCarthy of Trinity and Goldie Lowes Dickinson and E. M. Forster of King's. Lytton Strachey and Thoby Stephen came up to Trinity in the same year as I did and through them I got a glimpse of an old Victorian London literary world which was just on the point of extinction. Thoby was the son of Leslie Stephen, the author of *An Agnostic's Apology, English Thought in the Eighteenth Century*, and *Hours in a Library*, editor of the *Dictionary of National Biography* and of the *Cornhill*. I met Leslie Stephen when he came and stayed with Thoby in Cambridge and again once or twice in London at his house in Hyde Park Gate. To a nervous young man he was, when one first met him, a terrifying old man, for he was stone deaf and you had to talk to him down an ear trumpet and his bearded face looked as if it had been engraved for three score years and ten with all the sorrows of the world; and when not talking he occasionally groaned. In fact he was gentle and kind and went out of his way to put us at our ease and interest us. His talk enabled one to catch a last glimpse of that incredibly ancient London literary world of ladies and gentlemen which went right back to Thackeray and Dickens, to Mr and Mrs Carlyle, to Mill and Huxley. It was the world of the *Quarterly* and *Fortnightly* and *Cornhill*. It died with Leslie Stephen and John Morley, but later I met two relics or ghosts which survived from it into our dishevelled age, Thomas Hardy and Edmund Gosse.

Lytton was the son of Sir Richard Strachey, an extraordinarily eminent, intelligent, cultured, amusing Anglo-Indian soldier and administrator. When I knew him, he sat all day long, winter and summer, in a large chair in front of a large fire reading novels. Lytton's mother, Lady Strachey, was a remarkable woman and I came to have a great affection for her. She liked playing billiards with me or for hours reading aloud to

Lytton and me masterpieces of English prose or poetry. In their house in Lancaster Gate or some country house which they took for the summer she would sit at the head of the table around which her five sons and five daughters together with a certain number of their wives or husbands argued at the top of their Stracheyan voices with Stracheyan vehemence. Lady Strachey seemed entirely oblivious to or unaware of the terrific din. She delighted to tell one about the vanishing literary world in which she had been the intimate friend of Lord Lytton, Browning and Tennyson.

In 1904 I went for seven years to Ceylon as a Civil Servant. The literary world of London faded far away into the background of my youth and my memories. Then in 1911 I came back on a year's leave and decided not to go back to Ceylon, but to settle in London and try to earn a living by writing. I found a London which motor cars and taxis and new building seemed to have changed fundamentally from the London of my youth. I went to live in Brunswick Square and there I found what I suppose has to be described as a new literary world. It came in time to be called popularly Bloomsbury. It consisted of Vanessa and Clive Bell, Roger Fry, Duncan Grant, E. M. Forster, Maynard Keynes, Virginia and Adrian Stephen, Lytton Strachey. We all wrote books or painted pictures and I sat myself down in Brunswick Square and wrote *The Village in the Jungle*. On Morgan Forster's advice I sent it to his publishers, Edward Arnold. It was accepted and published in 1913.

So I reached the goal set me by the editor for this article, my first publication and the London literary world of Bloomsbury. I do not propose to say anything about either, because, as Montaigne said so many years ago, it is not the goal, not the destination, not the arrival which is interesting, but the journey.

49

John Maynard Keynes: Julian Bell

Keynes's formal memoir of Julian Bell was written for the King's College Annual Report *in November 1937. Keynes had known Vanessa and Clive's son since his birth, had lived next to Charleston since 1925, and been a fellow of King's while Julian was there.*

Julian Heward Bell was born in 1908, son of Clive and Vanessa Bell, grandson of Leslie Stephen, nephew of Virginia Woolf, first cousin once removed of 'J. K. S. [J. K. Stephen]' and H. A. L. Fisher. As he wrote himself in a poem 'Autobiography':

> I stay myself – the product made
> By several hundred English years,
> Of harried labourers underpaid,
> Of Venns who plied the parson's trade,
> Of regicides, of Clapham sects,
> Of high Victorian intellects,
> Leslie, Fitzjames.

He was at school at Leighton Park, was placed in the first division of the second class in the History Tripos of 1929 and the English Tripos of 1930, and held the Reginald John Smith Studentship in 1930 and the Augustus Austen Leigh Studentship in 1931. The four years after taking his degree were occupied in working for a fellowship, first of all with a dissertation on Pope's poetry and afterwards with one on some applications of Ethics to Aesthetics and Politics. In 1935 he was appointed Professor of English in the Chinese University of Hankow. The scrappy and belated news, which reached him, of events in Spain made him impatient to get home. He returned in 1937 eager to be of any use to the Government cause in Spain, revisited Cambridge and, in spite of efforts to dissuade him, joined the British Medical Unit in Spain as a lorry-driver. He was killed by a bomb from an insurgent aeroplane whilst driving his ambulance on the Brunete front on 18 July 1937. He is buried in the cemetery of Fuencarral, about two miles north of Madrid.

Julian Bell's interests and feelings were almost equally divided between politics and poetry. Like others of the post-war generation he moved uncertainly between the activism of political agitation and angry discontent and the quietism of reflective and sometimes abstract verse on the seasons, the countryside and, in particular, the observation of birds:

> Bare ploughland ridges sweeping from the down;
> Black hedges berryless; dead grass turned brown,
> And brown-tipped rushes on each field,
> And bare woods. Mists across the Weald,
> While the night soon
> Blurs afternoon.

He would live by himself for weeks on the Sussex downs observing and minutely describing the dress of nature, and would then return again to boisterous Bohemian parties and hot political disputations with a band of friends, the future holding no peace for him whenever his imagination had to pass from the specious present to consider it. He had the utmost openness of character and purity of motive, simple and gentle, with truth and sincerity stamped upon him, and was gradually learning to form his character and to express it. He developed slowly and had only lately begun to acquire a maturity whose final accomplishment, now cut off, might have greatly exceeded his apparent early promise. He published two small volumes of verse, *Winter Movement* in 1930 and *Work for the Winter* in 1936, from which future anthologists will probably wish to glean a few stanzas. He also edited in 1935 *We did not Fight: 1914–18 Experiences of War Resisters*, with a foreword by Canon H. R. L. Sheppard. In his introduction to this the transition of mind, characteristic of his generation, from non-resistant pacifism to believing that there might, nevertheless, be things which deserved and required a sacrifice, is already apparent. There was no inconsistency, but rather a deep inner consistency, between the inbred nonconformity with the right and duty of fearless individual judgement which led him to his first sympathies and that which impelled him past all dissuasions to an ultimate sacrifice which did not take him by surprise. The faith expressed in some sentences from his own introduction of 1935 is his best epitaph. Comparing the attitude of himself and his contemporaries with that of the idealist and absolutist conscientious objector he wrote: 'Those of my own generation who care about the human race and what happens to it have come to believe that only effective action counts . . . The attitude of the younger generation of war resisters has learned too much from its enemy, it has grown – even in peace-time – into a war mind: sometimes even into a war hysteria. Yet, with all its defects, I believe that the war-resistance movements of my generation will in the end succeed in putting down war – by force if necessary.'

50

Clive Bell: Maynard Keynes

Clive Bell's memoir of Keynes was published in Old Friends: Personal Recollections *(1956), ten years after Keynes's death and five years after Roy Harrod's authorized biography of Keynes. The affectionately critical tone of Bell's recollections also characterizes his Bloomsbury memoirs of Strachey, Fry, and Virginia Woolf, demonstrating once more that the Group was no mutual admiration society. Bell's memoir also reveals the interaction of ideas – moral, aesthetic, political, literary, economic – that accompanied the often involved personal relations of Bloomsbury. About those relations Bell was necessarily more reticent in print than memoirists such as Virginia Woolf and Lytton Strachey were able to be in the Memoir Club.*

In a memoir called 'My Early Beliefs' Lord Keynes, describing the company he kept at Cambridge, finds a word or phrase to fit each of his friends: 'Moore himself was a puritan and a precisian,' he writes, 'Strachey (for that was his name at that time) a Voltairean, Woolf a rabbi, myself a nonconformist, Sheppard a conformist and (as it now turns out) an ecclesiastic, Clive a gay and amiable dog, Sydney-Turner a quietist, Hawtrey a dogmatist and so on.' Now Clive may have been gay and amiable and a dog, but Maynard can have known it only by hearsay; for, oddly enough, at Cambridge we never met. Or did we meet for a moment, before dinner, before a debate? I think not; though I distinctly remember Edwin Montagu telling me that he had invited a brilliant freshman, just up from Eton, who would be of great value – when we had gone down – to the Liberal Party in the Union. That was in the late autumn of 1902, and that was the first I heard of Maynard. That we did not know each other may be accounted for perhaps by the fact that I spent a good part of my last, my fourth, year (October 1902–3) in London working at the Record Office, and when I was in Cambridge lived mostly with my old friends in Trinity, not accompanying Lytton Strachey on his excursions into King's. Be that as it may, certain I am that the first time I met Maynard to talk to was in the summer of 1906, when Lytton brought him to my chambers in the Temple. He was then, I surmise, sitting for the civil service examination, and wearing, I am sure, a light green Burberry and a bowler hat.[1]

Our acquaintance must have improved steadily. In February 1908 my elder son was born; and, as in those days it was customary for a young mother to remain in bed for perhaps a month after giving birth to a child, I took to inviting some agreeable friend who after dinner would entertain the convalescent with an hour's conversation. Maynard was one of the three or four who came. Nevertheless we cannot yet have been what I should call intimate since I remember feeling, not exactly shy, but conscious of the fact that this was the first time I had dined with him en tête-à-tête. He was still a clerk in the India Office, living in one of those dreary blocks of flats near St James's Park Station; but a few months later he returned to Cambridge, and though during the next year or two I saw him much in company I rarely saw him alone. He stayed with us in the country; he was with us at Guildford in July 1911 and he it was who, having as usual secured first look at *The Times*, told us that the Lords had passed the Parliament Act: when he took Asheham for the Easter holidays my wife and I stayed with him. Evidently in August 1913 we were on easy and amiable terms for we shared a tent on a camping-party, organized by the Oliviers of course – the Brandon Camp: I recall most vividly the discomfort. Maynard minded less, he was a better camper-out than I. On the other hand he was an even worse lawn-tennis player. We played occasionally on the hilly courts of Gordon Square – he and I, Gerald Shove, Phillip Morrell and sometimes Adrian Stephen. But Maynard was so feeble that though we always gave him for partner

---

[1] May I, while correcting one mistake, irrelevantly call attention to another? On page 79 of 'Two Memoirs' Maynard writes – 'Many years later he (D. H. Lawrence) recorded in a letter which is printed in his published correspondence, that I was the only member of Bloomsbury who had supported him by subscribing for Lady Chatterley.' This, if I am to be reckoned a member of Bloomsbury, is, like so many things that Lawrence said, untrue. My subscription copy, duly numbered 578 and signed, stands now in my book-case.

Phillip, by far the best of the bunch, we could not make a game of it. Maynard was dropped.

This must have been just before the first war, in the summer of 1914, when Maynard was lodging in Brunswick Square. During the winter he had served on a Royal Commission on Indian currency and consequently had begun to make friends in high places. A new Maynard, who accompanied but never displaced the old, was emerging – a man of great affairs and a friend of the great. Also, I fancy, it was about this time or a little earlier that he took to speculating. According to an account he once gave me – in whimsical mood I must confess – Maynard, who at Cambridge and in early London days had barely glanced at 'Stock Exchange Dealings', grew so weary – this is what he told me – of reading the cricket-scores in *The Times* that, while drinking his morning tea, he took to studying prices instead. You may believe it or not as you choose: anyhow it was a digression from what I was saying, that already before the war Maynard had come into contact with a part of the political and high official world. Some of us shook our heads, not over the new interests but over the new friendships. Would they not encourage the growth of what we were pleased to consider false values? Would he not soon be attaching more importance to means (power, honours, conventions, money) than to ends – i.e. good states of mind (*vide Principia Ethica passim*)? Would he not lose his sense of proportion? But when Maynard, having invited to dinner two of his big-wigs (Austen Chamberlain and McKenna I seem to remember), discovered at the last moment that all his Champagne had been drunk by Duncan Grant and his boon companions – Duncan's mid-day Champagne-parties in Brunswick Square were a feature of that memorable summer – he took it well enough. His sense of values appeared to be intact. And I will not doubt he realized that a subsequent party to which he and Duncan Grant invited the St John Hutchinsons – Mrs Hutchinson was Duncan's cousin – Molly MacCarthy and myself was much greater fun.

In September 1914 Maynard was with us at Asheham; and it pleases me to remember that the great man – and he was a great man – who enjoyed for years an international reputation for cool and detached judgement, rebuked me sharply for refusing to believe in the Russian-troops-in-England fairy tale and for surmising that the war would not soon be over. The fact is, of course, that Maynard's judgement would have been as sound as his intellect was powerful had it really been detached; but Maynard was an incorrigible optimist. I am not likely to forget the infectious confidence with which he asserted in 1929 that the Liberals were bound to have more than a hundred seats in the new House of Commons and would probably have a hundred and fifty (in fact they had 59); for he backed his opinion by a gamble on the Stock Exchange in which he involved some of his impecunious friends – I was not one of them. With considerateness as characteristic as his confidence, when he realized the awkwardness of the scrape into which his optimism had led them, he shouldered their liabilities. In 1939, towards the middle of July, when he was about to leave for a cure at Royat, he asked me whether I thought war would break out that autumn or whether there would be 'another hullabaloo'. ('Hullabaloo' seems to me quite a good name for Munich.) I said that, having committed ourselves, foolishly in my opinion, to defend Poland, and Hitler being obviously determined to invade Poland forthwith, I supposed war before winter was inevitable. This time Maynard did not exactly rebuke me, but he did call me a 'pessimist'.

During the 1914–18 war I saw a good deal of him, especially during the later part, when he and I, Sheppard and Norton, shared 46 Gordon Square. It seems not generally to be known – though Mr Roy Harrod has not attempted to conceal the fact – that Lord Keynes was a conscientious objector. To be sure he was an objector of a peculiar and, as I think, most reasonable kind. He was not a pacificist; he did not object to fighting in any circumstances; he objected to being made to fight. Good liberal that he was, he objected to conscription. He would not fight because Lloyd-George, Horatio Bottomley and Lord Northcliffe told him to. He held that it was for the individual to decide whether the question at issue was worth killing and dying for; and surely he was entitled to consider himself a better judge than the newspaper-men who at that time ruled the country. He was surprised and shocked when Mr Asquith gave way to their clamour. His work at the Treasury, which by 1917 had become of vital importance, kept him in contact with the more important ministers, and he saw right through Lloyd-George. He detested his demagogy. I remember his cutting from a French paper – *Excelsior* presumably – a photograph of 'the goat' as he always called him, in full evening dress and smothered in ribbons, speaking at a banquet in Paris; and I remember his writing under it 'Lying in state'. He pinned it up in the dining-room at forty-six. Later, in the supposed interests of the Liberal Party, he collaborated with 'the goat' who had become for certain left-wing papers and politicians a sort of 'grand old man'. No good came of that. As for his conscientious objection, he was duly summoned to a tribunal and sent word that he was much too busy to attend.

There are those who maintain that Maynard's importance during the war and familiarity with the great bred that cocksureness which was his most irritating characteristic. I do not agree. The influence of the great on Maynard was slight compared with Maynard's influence on them.

The cocksureness was always there; circumstances evoked and possibly stimulated it. Certainly the habit was provoking. It was also amusing. Late one night towards the end of the first war I remember his coming up to my room in Gordon Square where Norton and I were talking quietly about, as likely as not, the meaning of meaning. He was elated; he had been dining; what is more, he had been dining with cabinet ministers. The question had arisen – 'Who finally defeated Hannibal?' No one knew except Maynard and he told them it was Fabius Maximus: 'unus homo nobis cunctando restituit rem' he declaimed, and I hope he translated it for the politicians though for us he was good enough to leave it in the original. Of course it was not the cunctator but Scipio Africanus who finally defeated Hannibal at the battle of Zama, as I obligingly pointed out. Maynard disregarded my correction in a way that did perhaps ever so slightly suggest that someone who had been dining with cabinet ministers knew better, and continued to expatiate on the pleasures of the evening, his little historical triumph, the excellent cooking and above all the wine.

Maynard laid down the law on all subjects. I dare say I minded too much: many of his friends took it as a joke. But I do think it was silly of him; for by dogmatizing on subjects about which he knew nothing he sometimes made himself ridiculous to those who did not know him well and to those who did annoying. Cocksureness was his besetting sin, if sin it can be called. Gradually it became his habit to speak with authority: a bad habit which leads its addicts to assume that the rest of us are ready to assume that their knowledge must be greater than ours. Maynard knew a good deal about a great many things, and on several subjects spoke with warranted authority. Unfortunately he got into the habit of speaking with authority whether it was warranted or not. He acquired – I do not say he cultivated – a masterful manner; and when he spoke of matters about which he knew little or nothing with the confidence and disregard for other people's opinions which were perhaps excusable when he was talking about economics or probability or rare editions, instead of appearing masterly he appeared pretentious. That, too, was a pity, for he was not pretentious; he made no boast of his superior knowledge and expected no praise for it, he merely assumed it. For my part, I was exasperated most often by his laying down the law on painting and painters; but I will not draw an example of his misplaced self-confidence from his pronouncements on art, because, aesthetic judgements being always questionable, though I am sure that his were often wrong, I am far from sure that mine are always right. Instead, I will recall a conversation – or should I say an exposition? – which remains extremely clear in my memory, and provides an instance of misplaced self-confidence the misplacedness of which is not open to dispute.

He had been staying with one of his rich city-friends – for in those days (the early 'twenties') there were still rich men in England: he had been staying in Hampshire I think but I am not sure, certainly in the south, and he returned to Charleston, the house in Sussex which for a while he shared with my wife, myself and Duncan Grant, and told us all about it. It had been a shooting party; Maynard himself never handled a gun, but he told us all about it. He told us what is done and what is not done; he told us when you might shoot and when you might not shoot, he told us how to shoot and what to shoot. And as he was under the impression – all this happened long before he had a farm and a wood of his own – that his party had been shooting grouse in Hampshire or thereabouts with rifles, you can imagine the sort of nonsense he made of it. Now it so happens I was brought up in a sporting family: I have possessed a game-licence since I was sixteen and walked with the guns since I was a child; and I do believe I have killed every game-bird in the British Isles except a capercailzie and some of the rarer duck. But if you suppose that these facts would have daunted Lord Keynes, all I can say is – you have got the great economist wrong.

My insistence on Maynard's cocksureness may have given the impression that he was spoilt by success. If so, I have given a false impression. Maynard floated happily on a sea of power and glory and considerable wealth, but never went out with the tide. Two stout anchors held him fast to shore: his old friends and Cambridge. This Mr Roy Harrod has made clear in his excellent biography. Cabinet Ministers and *The Times* might praise, but if he had an uneasy suspicion that Lytton Strachey, Duncan Grant, Virginia Woolf and Vanessa Bell did not share their enthusiasm, public flattery might appear something to be ashamed of. When he came to Charleston with Lady Keynes for the first time after his peerage had been announced he was downright sheepish. 'We have come to be laughed at' he said. And what was Cambridge thinking? Maynard cared passionately for his country, but I believe he was at greater pains to improve the finances of King's than to rescue those of the British Empire. If this be a slight exaggeration, that artistic temperament, from which I should like to be supposed to suffer, must bear the blame; but that stern, unbending economist, Mr Roy Harrod, has made it clear to all who read that Keynes valued the good opinion of his old friends far above that of the majority or the great. Mr Harrod, it seems to me, gives an excellent account of his subject – I had almost said his 'hero' – which should be read for its own sake and perhaps as a corrective to mine. Nevertheless

I understand the feelings of those old and intimate friends who say – 'Maynard was not really like that, he was not like that at all.' That is what old friends will always say of official biographies; and they will be right. Mrs Thrale, who knew Johnson far longer and far more intimately than Boswell knew him, doubtless said as much. And of course Mrs Thrale was right. Only she forgot that it was Boswell's business to write a biography, to depict a man in all his activities and in his relations to all sorts of people, while it was her privilege to record a personal impression.

I, too, am recording a personal impression. I am trying to remember little things that have escaped the notice of my betters. Such things are trivial by definition, and sometimes derogatory; but, though they may be beneath the dignity of history, they matter a good deal in daily life. My recollections, I foresee, run the risk of appearing spiteful. To counteract this appearance I could of course pile up well merited compliments. But of what use would it be for me to expatiate on the power of Maynard's intellect and his services to humanity when writers far better qualified have done it already and done it with authority? Nevertheless, to escape the charge of malignity, let me say here and now what maybe I shall have occasion to repeat. Maynard was the cleverest man I ever met: also his cleverness was of a kind, gay and whimsical and civilized, which made his conversation a joy to every intelligent person who knew him. In addition he had been blest with a deeply affectionate nature. I once heard him say, humorously but I believe truly, at dinner, before a meeting of the memoir club, 'If everyone at this table, except myself, were to die tonight, I do not think I should care to go on living.' He loved and he was beloved. He did not love, though he may have rather liked, me; and I did not love him. That should be borne in mind by anyone who does this sketch the honour of a reading.

In great things he was magnificently generous; generous to his country, generous to his college, generous to servants and dependents, particularly generous to his less fortunate friends (I know two charming young men who may or may not know that they were educated – and highly educated – partly at his expense). In small things, however, like many who have enjoyed the advantages and disadvantages of a serious, non-conformist upbringing, he was careful. Also, financier that he was, he loved a bargain. One summer's evening in 1919 he returned to Charleston from a day in London bearing a heavy parcel which contained innumerable minute tins of potted meat. He had bought them at a sale of surplus army-stores and he had bought them at a penny a piece. The private soldiers had not liked the stuff, and therein had shown good taste. I teased Maynard by pretending that the meat had been condemned as unfit for human consumption: and indeed, the bargain-hunter himself could barely keep it down. But at a penny a tin. . . . Again, I remember being with him at Lewes races, and asking a farmer of my acquaintance for 'a good thing'. Maynard did not want 'a good thing'; what he wanted was the best bet. He wanted a bargain in odds. This rather complicated notion puzzled my friend, and we left him puzzling. For I did not attempt to explain that what Maynard had in mind was that there might be some horse in some race against which the odds were longer than need be, or rather, book-makers being what they are, less short than might have been expected. If there were a starter at a hundred to one which might just as well have been offered at sixty-six to one, that horse, though standing no apparent chance of winning, was the horse for Maynard's money. What he wanted was not a winner but a bargain.

Lytton Strachey used to say – 'Pozzo has no aesthetic sense.'[2] That was an exaggeration perhaps. What may be said confidently is that he had no innate feeling for the visual arts. Had he never met Duncan Grant he would never have taken much interest in painting. He made a valuable collection because generally he bought on good advice; when he relied on his own judgement the result was sometimes lamentable. Lamentable it would have been had he relied on his own judgement to the end when he wrote that piece in *The New Statesman* about Low's drawings; for in the original version, not only had he compared Low with Daumier, he had likened him to Daumier, had almost equalled him with Daumier. What he insisted on retaining is sufficiently tell-tale.

> We all know that we have amongst us today a cartoonist in the grand tradition. But, as the recognition, which contributions to evening papers receive by word of mouth round the dinner-table, cannot reach the modest cartoonist, one welcomes a book like this as an opportunity to tell Low how much we think of him and how much we love him. He has the rare combination of gifts which is necessary for his craft – a shrewd and penetrating intelligence, wit, taste, unruffled urbanity, an indignant but open and understanding heart, a swift power of minute observation with an equally swift power of essential simplification, and, above all, a sense and talent for beauty, which extracts something delightful even out of ugliness. One may seem to be piling it on, but Low really has these things,

[2] Mr Roy Harrod writes in a note: 'For many years in Bloomsbury Keynes was familiarly known by the name of Pozzo, having been so christened by Strachey after the Corsican diplomat, Pozzo di Borgo – not a diplomat of evil motive or base conduct, but certainly a schemer and man of many facets.' But it was not only, nor chiefly, of the Corsican diplomat that Lytton and those who used the nickname were thinking. The Italian word 'pozzo' has more than one meaning, and to English ears carries various suggestions.

and it is a great addition to our lives to meet the tongue and eye of a civilized man and true artist when we open the *Evening Standard*.

Last summer Low and Kingsley Martin made a trip to Bolshieland, and this agreeable book is the outcome. Low's pencil and charcoal sketches are reproduced by some process which, whatever it may be, looks like lithograph and thereby reinforces the comparison between Low and the lithographers of the old *Charivari* of Paris – Gavarni and Daumier and their colleagues. They are *illustrations* in the literal sense of the word – pictures of the inside and of the outside of things at the same time. (Review of 'Low's Russian Sketchbook' – *New Statesman and Nation*, Dec. 10, 1932)

What one tried to point out, and Maynard could not understand, was that no two artists – to be for a moment polite and dishonest – could be much more unalike than Daumier and Low. To begin with, Low is not an artist. He possesses a prodigious knack of inventing visual equivalents for political situations and ideas; and ekes out their meaning with tags which have often the neatness of epigrams. It is a remarkable gift. But those equivalents have no aesthetic value – no value in themselves. The line is as smart and insensitive as the prose of a penny-a-liner. Daumier, who was one of the great draughtsmen of the nineteenth century, lacked entirely that gift which in old days made us buy the *Evening Standard* to see what Low was up to. Having made a beautiful drawing, which might or might not suggest some crude bit of social or political criticism, Daumier as often as not, could think of no legend to put under it. The drawing, you see, was not an illustration of something else but a work of art complete in itself. So he left the business of putting in the patter to Philipon or some other clever fellow in the office. This distinction to Maynard seemed fanciful, as it must seem to anyone who has no real feeling for visual art. Even in literature his untutored judgement was not to be trusted. During the last war he returned from America with a find – a great new novel. He had discovered a modern master, and he had brought the masterpiece home with him. It was Bemelmans' *Now I Lay Me Down to Sleep*, a piece of comicality that might, or might not, while away an hour in the train.

That Maynard Keynes has benefited all the arts by the creation of the Arts Council is a title to glory and a notorious fact which proves nothing contrary to what was said in the last paragraph. It would prove, if further proof were needed, that he was one of those uncommon human beings who have devoted great powers of organization to good purposes. Maynard's gifts were always at the service of civilization, and by long and affectionate association with artists – do not forget that Lady Keynes was a brilliant ballerina and an interesting actress – he came to realize acutely that of civilization the arts are an essential ingredient. Also this achievement, the creation of the Arts Council in time of war, of a war in which he was playing an important and exhausting part, proves – but again what need of proof? – his boundless energy and versatility, as well as his capacity for making something solid and durable out of a hint. God forbid that anyone should imagine that I am suggesting that it was I who gave the hint. At that time anxious questionings as to the future of the arts in a more or less socialist state were to be heard on all sides. I drag myself into the picture only because I recall a conversation with Maynard which led to my writing, at his suggestion, an article in *The New Statesman* of which, at that time, he was part-proprietor and, unless I mistake, a director. My argument was that, much as I disliked the idea of a Ministry of Fine Arts, the creation of such a Ministry would be, when private patronage had been destroyed by economic egalitarianism, the only means of saving the arts from extinction. The argument was neither striking nor novel; what was remarkable was that Maynard, in the midst of his preoccupations, should not only have devised but realized an institution which might nourish the arts without handing them over to civil servants and politicians. So far his contrivance has worked and worked well. Whether it will continue to evade the embrace of death – of politicians I mean – remains to be seen.

Those who have said that Maynard Keynes had no aesthetic sense may seem to have forgotten his prose. He had a fine, lucid style in which he could state persuasively and wittily the interesting things he had in mind. When he attempted to express the more delicate shades of feeling or to make a picture out of observations rather than ideas, he was, in my opinion, less convincing. Those famous portraits of Clemenceau, Wilson and Lloyd-George have never seemed to me quite the masterpieces they have seemed to other, and perhaps better, judges. They are lively and telling but scarcely subtle I think. To my taste his best book is *Essays in Persuasion*, and the best portrait he ever drew that of Alfred Marshall. In that long biographical notice, reprinted in *Essays in Biography*, his knowledge and his culture, which, though limited, had been garnered and sifted by an extraordinarily powerful understanding, are most skilfully employed to enlighten what in other hands might have appeared a dull subject. The result, if not precisely beautiful, is more than pleasing: in the exact sense of the word it is admirable.

I said that his culture was limited: such judgements are always relative, and perhaps I should try to be more explicit. As has been intimated, in the visual arts his taste was anything but sure and his knowledge amounted to nothing. Some believe he appreciated music, but I have never discovered the foundations of their belief. Literature is another matter. At Eton Maynard had been reared on the classics, and of the Greek and Latin authors remembered as much as clever people who have enjoyed what are called the advantages of a public school education can be expected to remember. I have heard that he was a fair German scholar, but of that I cannot speak. He had very little French and no Italian. Of English he had read much, both verse and prose. He liked poetry; but he enjoyed it as a well educated man of affairs rather than as an artist or an aesthete. One had only to hear him read aloud – and he was fond of reading poetry aloud – to feel that the content was what he really cared for. His commerce with the English historians would have been more profitable if his memory had been more retentive. He had a capacity for forgetting, and for muddling, dates and figures, that was astonishing and sometimes rather tiresome – tiresome because, with his invincible cocksureness, he could not dream of admitting that he mistook. To the end of his life he continued to study – or perhaps, towards the end, merely to take an interest in – mathematics and philosophy. Presumably he understood Wittgenstein as well as anyone understood him – except Professor Ayer. He never called himself a Logical Positivist. Of his economic theories and constructions, that is to say of the great work of his life, I am too ignorant to speak. I should be able to say more about his theory of Probability than that it served him ill at Monte Carlo, since in the years before the first war I often heard him talk about it. And after that war, when he took up the manuscript of his old dissertation with a view to making a book, he would – I suppose because we were living in the same house – occasionally hand me a much corrected sheet saying – such was his lack of memory – 'can you remember what I meant by that?' Alas, figures and symbols had crept into the argument and my miserable inaptitude for sums made me unhelpful. Anyhow I am not equipped to criticize so abstruse a theory, but I understand that [Frank] Ramsay made a rent which caused all the stitches to run.

I dare say most readers will think I have said enough to disprove my statement that Maynard's culture was limited. Maybe I used the wrong word and should have said 'provincial'. To explain what I mean by that, perhaps I may be allowed to draw on my homely but vivid memories. At Charleston it was our habit to sit after dinner in an oblate semi-circle before a curious fire-place, devised and constructed by Roger Fry to heat with logs a particularly chilly room: strange to say, it did. Each of us would be reading his or her book, and someone was sure to be reading French. Also it so happened that, just after the old war, stimulated I think by Aldous Huxley, I had become interested in the life and through the life the plays of Alfieri; wherefore, Alfieri leading on, I might be reading some early nineteenth-century Italian. Thus, towards bed-time, could spring up talk about French or Italian ways of thinking, feeling and living. In such discussions one could not but be struck by Maynard's inability to see a foreign country from inside. France, Italy, America even, he saw them all from the white cliffs of Dover, or, to be more exact, from Whitehall or King's combination room. Compared with (say) Roger Fry, who was often of the company, he seemed ludicrously provincial. And that may be what I had in mind when I called his culture limited.

In spite of all the little annoying things that have stuck in my memory, my recollection of Maynard, vivid and persistent, is that of a delightful companion. I miss him; and I understand the feelings of those who more than miss, of those for whom the wound caused by his death never quite heals and may at any moment become painful. What I miss is his conversation. It was brilliant: that is an obvious thing to say but it is the right thing. In the highest degree he possessed that ingenuity which turns commonplaces into paradoxes and paradoxes into truisms, which discovers – or invents – similarities and differences, and associates disparate ideas – that gift of amusing and surprising with which very clever people, and only very clever, can by conversation give a peculiar relish to life. He had a witty intellect and a verbal knack. In argument he was bewilderingly quick, and unconventional. His comment on any subject under discussion, even on a subject about which he knew very little, was apt to be so lively and original that one hardly stopped to enquire whether it was just. But in graver mood, if asked to explain some technical business, which to the amateur seemed incomprehensible almost, he would with good-humoured ease make the matter appear so simple that one knew not whether to be more amazed at his intelligence or one's own stupidity. In moments such as these I felt sure that Maynard was the cleverest man I had ever met; also, at such moments, I sometimes felt, unreasonably no doubt, that he was an artist.

That Maynard Keynes was a great man is generally admitted; but in private life no one could have been less 'great-manish'. He was never pompous. His greatness no doubt revealed itself most impressively in economics – the work of his life – in organization and negotiation; but of greatness in such matters I am not competent to speak. Nor yet, alas! am I entitled to speak of what to some was his most memorable quality: for me his cleverness was what counted most, but to a few privileged men and women who knew him through and through his supreme virtue was his deeply affectionate nature. He liked a great many people of all sorts and to them he gave pleasure, excitement and good counsel; but his dearest friends he loved passionately and faithfully and, odd as it may sound, with a touch of humility.

Part X

Afterwords

Four very different kinds of afterwords end *A Bloomsbury Group Reader*. Roger Fry's critical retrospective concludes a selection of his widely ranging writings on art. Desmond MacCarthy's retrospective consolation takes the form of a dedicatory letter to himself. E. M. Forster's afterword continues a novel he wrote many years before. And Virginia Woolf's celebration of reading returns us again to the common reader.

51

Roger Fry: Retrospect

Fry combined aesthetics and autobiography at the end of the collected writings he published under the title Vision and Design *in 1920. Tracing his critical progress from the old masters to post-impressionism, Fry restates his convictions about the unity in great art of aesthetic emotion and what Clive Bell called significant form – of vision, that is, and design. 'Retrospect' is thus one of the best summaries of Bloomsbury aesthetics. It was originally illustrated with plates of a Derain still life, Seurat's La* Baignade, *and Raphael's* The Transfiguration.

The work of re-reading and selecting from the mass of my writings as an art critic has inevitable brought me up against the question of its consistency and coherence. Although I do not think that I have republished here anything with which I entirely disagree, I cannot but recognize that in many of these essays the emphasis lies in a different place from where I should now put it. Fortunately I have never prided myself upon my unchanging constancy of attitude, but unless I flatter myself I think I can trace a certain trend of thought underlying very different expressions of opinion. Now since that trend seems to me to be symptomatic of modern aesthetic, and since it may perhaps explain much that seems paradoxical in the actual situation of art, it may be interesting to discuss its nature even at the cost of being autobiographical.

In my work as a critic of art I have never been a pure Impressionist, a mere recording instrument of certain sensations. I have always had some kind of aesthetic. A certain scientific curiosity and a desire for comprehension have impelled me at every stage to make generalizations, to attempt some kind of logical co-ordination of my impressions. But, on the other hand, I have never worked out for myself a complete system such as the metaphysicians deduce from *a priori* principles. I have never believed that I knew what was the ultimate nature of art. My aesthetic has been a purely practical one, a tentative expedient, an attempt to reduce to some kind of order my aesthetic impressions up to date. It has been held merely until such time as fresh experiences might confirm or modify it. Moreover, I have always looked on my system with a certain sus-picion. I have recognized that if it ever formed too solid a crust it might stop the inlets of fresh experience, and I can count various occasions when my principles would have led me to condemn, and when my sensibility has played the part of Balaam with the effect of making temporary chaos of my system. That has, of course, always rearranged itself to take in the new experience, but with each such cataclysm it has suffered a loss of prestige. So that even in its latest form I do not put forward my system as more than a provisional induction from my own aesthetic experiences.

I have certainly tried to make my judgement as objective as possible, but the critic must work with the only instrument he possesses – namely, his own sensibility with all its personal equations. All that he can con-sciously endeavour is to perfect that tool to its utmost by studying the traditional verdicts of men of aesthetic sensibility in the past, and by constant comparison of his own reactions with those of his con-temporaries who are specially gifted in this way. When he has done all that he can in this direction – and I would allow him a slight bias in favour of agreement with tradition – he is bound to accept the verdict of his own feelings as honestly as he can. Even plain honesty in this matter is more difficult to attain than would be admitted by those who have never tried it. In so delicate a matter as the artistic judgement one is liable to many accidental disturbing influences, one can scarcely avoid tem-porary hypnotisms and hallucinations. One can only watch for and try to discount these, taking every opportunity to catch one's sensibility unawares before it can take cover behind prejudices and theories.

When the critic holds the result of his reaction to a work of art clearly in view he has next to translate it into words. Here, too, distortion is inevitable, and it is here that I have probably failed most of accuracy, for language in the hands of one who lacks the mastery of a poet has its own tricks, its perversities and habits. There are things which it shies at and goes round, there are places where it runs away and, leaving the reality which it professes to carry tumbled out at the tail of the cart, arrives in a great pother, but without the goods.

But in spite of all these limitations and the errors they entail it seems to me that the attempt to attain objective judgements has not altogether failed, and that I seem to myself to have been always groping my way towards some kind of a reasoned and practical aesthetic. Many minds have been engaged alongside of mine in the same pursuit. I think we may claim that partly as a result of our common efforts a rather more intelligent attitude exists in the educated public of to-day than obtained in the last century.

Art in England is sometimes insular, sometimes provincial. The pre-Raphaelite movement was mainly an indigenous product. The dying echoes of this remarkable explosion reverberated through the years of my nonage, but when I first began to study art seriously the vital movement was a provincial one. After the usual twenty years of delay, provincial England had become aware of the Impressionist movement in France, and the younger painters of promise were working under the influence of Monet. Some of them even formulated theories of naturalism in its most literal and extreme form. But at the same time Whistler, whose Impressionism was of a very different stamp, had put forward the purely decorative idea of art, and had tried in his 'Ten o'clock', perhaps too cavalierly, to sweep away the web of ethical questions, distorted by aesthetic prejudices, which Ruskin's exuberant and ill-regulated mind had spun for the British public.

The Naturalists made no attempt to explain why the exact and literal imitation of nature should satisfy the human spirit, and the 'Decorators' failed to distinguish between agreeable sensations and imaginative significance.

After a brief period during which I was interested in the new possibilities opened up by the more scientific evaluation of colour which the Impressionists practised, I came to feel more and more the absence in their work of structural design. It was an innate desire for this aspect of art which drove me to the study of the Old Masters and, in particular, those of the Italian Renaissance, in the hope of discovering from them the secret of that architectonic idea which I missed so badly in the work of my contemporaries. I think now that a certain amount of 'cussedness' led me to exaggerate what was none the less a genuine personal reaction. Finding myself out of touch with my generation I took a certain pleasure in emphasizing my isolation. I always recognized fully that the only vital art of the day was that of the Impressionists whose theories I disbelieved, and I was always able to admit the greatness of Degas and Renoir. But many of my judgements of modern art were too much affected by my attitude. I do not think I ever praised Mr Wilson Steer or Mr Walter Sickert as much as they deserved, and I looked with too great indulgence on some would-be imitators of the Old Masters. But my most serious lapse was the failure to discover the genius of Seurat, whose supreme merits as a designer I had every reason to acclaim. I cannot even tell now whether I ever saw his work in the exhibitions of the early nineties, but if I did his qualities were hidden from me by the now transparent veil of pointillism – a pseudo-scientific system of atmospheric colour notation in which I took no interest.

I think I can claim that my study of the Old Masters was never much tainted by archaeological curiosity. I tried to study them in the same spirit as I might study contemporary artists, and I always regretted that there was no modern art capable of satisfying my predilections. I say there was no modern art because none such was known to me, but all the time there was one who had already worked out the problem which seemed to me insoluble of how to use the modern vision with the constructive design of the older masters. By some extraordinary ill luck I managed to miss seeing Cézanne's work till some considerable time after his death. I had heard of him vaguely from time to time as a kind of hidden oracle of ultra-impressionism, and, in consequence, I expected to find myself entirely unreceptive to his art. To my intense surprise I found myself deeply moved. I have discovered the article in which I recorded this encounter, and though the praise I gave would sound grudging and feeble to-day – for I was still obsessed by ideas about the content of a work of art – I am glad to see that I was so ready to scrap a long-cherished hypothesis in face of a new experience.

In the next few years I became increasingly interested in the art of Cézanne and of those like Gauguin and van Gogh who at that time represented the first effects of his profound influence on modern art, and I gradually recognized that what I had hoped for as a possible event of some future century had already occurred, that art had begun to recover once more the language of design and to explore its so long neglected possibilities. Thus it happened that when at the end of 1911 [1910], by a curious series of chances, I was in a position to organize an exhibition at the Grafton Galleries, I seized the opportunity to bring before the English public a selection of works conforming to the new direction. For purposes of convenience it was necessary to give these artists a name, and I chose, as being the vaguest and most non-committal, the name of Post-Impressionist. This merely stated their position in time relatively to the Impressionist movement. In conformity with my own previous prejudices against Impressionism, I think I underlined too much their divorce from the parent stock. I see now more clearly their affiliation with it, but I was none the less right in recognizing their essential difference, a difference which the subsequent development of Cubism has rendered more evident. Of late the thesis of their fundamental opposition has been again enforced in the writings of M. Lhote.

If I may judge by the discussions in the press to which this exhibition gave rise, the general public failed to see that my position with regard to this movement was capable of a logical explanation, as the result of a consistent sensibility. I tried in vain to explain what appeared to me so clear, that the modern movement was essentially a return to the ideas of formal design which had been almost lost sight of in the fervid pursuit of naturalistic representation. I found that the cultured public which had welcomed my expositions of the works of the Italian Renaissance now regarded me as either incredibly flippant or, for the more charitable explanation was usually adopted, slightly insane. In fact, I found among the cultured who had hitherto been my most eager listeners the most inveterate and exasperated enemies of the new movement. The accusation of anarchism was constantly made. From an aesthetic point of view this was, of course, the exact opposite of the truth, and I was for long puzzled to find the explanation of so paradoxical an opinion and so violent an enmity. I now see that my crime had been to strike at the vested emotional interests. These people felt instinctively that their special culture was one of their social assets. That to be able to speak glibly of Tang and Ming, of Amico di Sandro and Baldovinetti, gave them a social standing and a distinctive cachet. This showed me that we had all along been labouring under a mutual misunderstanding, i.e. that we had admired the Italian primitives for quite different reasons. It was felt that one could only appreciate Amico di Sandro when one had acquired a certain considerable mass of erudition and given a great deal of time and attention, but to admire a Matisse required only a certain sensibility. One could feel fairly sure that one's maid could not rival one in the former case, but might by a mere haphazard gift of Providence surpass one in the second. So that the accusation of revolutionary anarchism was due to a social rather than an aesthetic prejudice. In any case the cultured public was determined to look upon Cézanne as an incompetent bungler, and upon the whole movement as madly revolutionary. Nothing I could say would induce people to look calmly enough at these pictures to see how closely they followed tradition, or how great a familiarity with the Italian primitives was displayed in their work. Now that Matisse has become a safe investment for persons of taste, and that Picasso and Derain have delighted the miscellaneous audience of the London Music Halls with their designs for the Russian Ballet, it will be difficult for people to believe in the vehemence of the indignation which greeted the first sight of their works in England.

In contrast to its effect on the cultured public the Post-Impressionist exhibition aroused a keen interest among a few of the younger English artists and their friends. With them I began to discuss the problems of aesthetic that the contemplation of these works forced upon us.

But before explaining the effects of these discussions upon my aesthetic theory I must return to consider the generalizations which I had made from my aesthetic experiences up to this point.

In my youth all speculations on aesthetic had revolved with wearisome persistence around the question of the nature of beauty. Like our predecessors we sought for the criteria of the beautiful, whether in art or nature. And always this search led to a tangle of contradictions or else to metaphysical ideas so vague as to be inapplicable to concrete cases.

It was Tolstoy's genius that delivered us from this *impasse*, and I think that one may date from the appearance of 'What is Art?' the beginning of fruitful speculation in aesthetic. It was not indeed Tolstoy's preposterous valuation of works of art that counted for us, but his luminous criticism of past aesthetic systems, above all, his suggestions that art had no special or necessary concern with what is beautiful in nature, that the fact that Greek sculpture had run prematurely to decay through an extreme and non-aesthetic admiration of beauty in the human figure afforded no reason why we should for ever remain victims of their error.

It became clear that we had confused two distinct uses of the word beautiful, that when we used beauty to describe a favourable aesthetic judgement on a work of art we meant something quite different from our praise of a woman, a sunset or a horse as beautiful. Tolstoy saw that the essence of art was that it was a means of communication between human beings. He conceived it to be *par excellence* the language of emotion. It was at this point that his moral bias led him to the strange conclusion that the value of a work of art corresponded to the moral value of the emotion expressed. Fortunately he showed by an application of his theory to actual works of art to what absurdities it led. What remained of immense importance was the idea that a work of art was not the record of beauty already existent elsewhere, but the expression of an emotion felt by the artist and conveyed to the spectator.

The next question was, Of what kind of emotions is art the expression? Is love poetry the expression of the emotion of love, tragedy the expression of pity and fear, and so forth? Clearly the expression in art has some similarity to the expression of these emotions in actual life, but it is never identical. It is evident that the artist feels these emotions in a special manner, that he is not entirely under their influence, but sufficiently withdrawn to contemplate and comprehend them. My 'Essay in Aesthetics' here reprinted, elaborates this point of view, and in a course of unpublished lectures I endeavoured to divide works of visual art according to the emotional point of view, adopting the classification already existing in poetry into Epic, Dramatic, Lyric, and Comedic.

I conceived the form of the work of art to be its most essential quality, but I believed this form to be the direct outcome of an apprehension of some emotion of actual life by the artist, although, no doubt, that apprehension was of a special and peculiar kind and implied a certain detachment. I also conceived that the spectator in contemplating the form must inevitably travel in an opposite direction along the same road which the artist had taken, and himself feel the original emotion. I conceived the form and the emotion which it conveyed as being inextricably bound together in the aesthetic whole.

About the time I had arrived at these conclusions the discussion of aesthetic stimulated by the appearance of Post-Impressionism began. It became evident through these discussions that some artists who were peculiarly sensitive to the formal relations of works of art, and who were deeply moved by them, had almost no sense of the emotions which I had supposed them to convey. Since it was impossible in these cases to doubt the genuineness of the aesthetic reaction it became evident that I had not pushed the analysis of works of art far enough, had not disentangled the purely aesthetic elements from certain accompanying accessories.

It was, I think, the observation of these cases of reaction to pure form that led Mr Clive Bell in his book, *Art*, to put forward the hypothesis that however much the emotions of life might appear to play a part in the work of art, the artist was really not concerned with them, but only with the expression of a special and unique kind of emotion, the aesthetic emotion. A work of art had the peculiar property of conveying the aesthetic emotion, and it did this in virtue of having 'significant form'. He also declared that representation of nature was entirely irrelevant to this and that a picture might be completely non-representative.

This last view seemed to me always to go too far since any, even the slightest, suggestion of the third dimension in a picture must be due to some element of representation. What I think has resulted from Mr Clive Bell's book, and the discussions which it has aroused on this point is that the artist is free to choose any degree of representational accuracy which suits the expression of his feeling. That no single fact, or set of facts, about nature can be held to be obligatory for artistic form. Also one might add as an empirical observation that the greatest art seems to concern itself most with the universal aspects of natural form, to be the least preoccupied with particulars. The greatest artists appear to be most sensitive to those qualities of natural objects which are the least obvious in ordinary life precisely because, being common to all visible objects, they do not serve as marks of distinction and recognition.

With regard to the expression of emotion in works of art I think that Mr Bell's sharp challenge to the usually accepted view of art as expressing the emotions of life has been of great value. It has led to an attempt to isolate the purely aesthetic feeling from the whole complex of feelings which may and generally do accompany the aesthetic feeling when we regard a work of art.

Let us take as an example of what I mean Raphael's *Transfiguration*, which a hundred years ago was perhaps the most admired picture in the world, and twenty years ago was one of the most neglected. It is at once apparent that this picture makes a very complex appeal to the mind and feelings. To those who are familiar with the Gospel story of Christ it brings together in a single composition two different events which occurred simultaneously at different places, the Transfiguration of Christ and the unsuccessful attempt of the Disciples during His absence to heal the lunatic boy. This at once arouses a number of complex ideas about which the intellect and feelings may occupy themselves. Goethe's remark on the picture is instructive from this point of view. 'It is remarkable', he says, 'that anyone has ever ventured to query the essential unity of such a composition. How can the upper part be separated from the lower? The two form one whole. Below the suffering and the needy, above the powerful and helpful – mutually dependent, mutually illustrative.'

It will be seen at once what an immense complex of feelings interpenetrating and mutually affecting one another such a work sets up in the mind of a Christian spectator, and all this merely by the content of the picture, its subject, the dramatic story it tells.

Now if our Christian spectator has also a knowledge of human nature he will be struck by the fact that these figures, especially in the lower group, are all extremely incongruous with any idea he is likely to have formed of the people who surrounded Christ in the Gospel narrative. And according to his prepossessions he is likely to be shocked or pleased to find instead of the poor and unsophisticated peasants and fisherfolk who followed Christ, a number of noble, dignified, and academic gentlemen in impossible garments and purely theatrical poses. Again the representation merely as representation, will set up a number of feelings and perhaps of critical thoughts dependent upon innumerable associated ideas in the spectator's mind.

Now all these reactions to the picture are open to anyone who has enough understanding of natural form to recognize it when represented adequately. There is no need for him to have any particular sensibility to form as such.

Let us now take for our spectator a person highly endowed with the special sensibility to form, who feels the intervals and relations of forms as a musical person feels the intervals and relations of tones, and let us suppose him either completely ignorant of, or indifferent to, the Gospel story. Such a spectator will be likely to be immensely excited by the extraordinary power of co-ordination of many complex masses in a single inevitable whole, by the delicate equilibrium of many directions of line. He will at once feel that the apparent division into two parts is only apparent, that they are co-ordinated by a quite peculiar power of grasping the possible correlations. He will almost certainly be immensely excited and moved, but his emotion will have nothing to do with the emotions which we have discussed since in the former case, ex-hypothesi, our spectator has no clue to them.

It is evident then that we have the possibility of infinitely diverse reactions to a work of art. We many imagine, for instance, that our pagan spectator, though entirely unaffected by the story, is yet conscious that the figures represent men, and that their gestures are indicative of certain states of mind and, in consequence, we may suppose that according to an internal bias his emotion is either heightened or hindered by the recognition of their rhetorical insincerity. Or we may suppose him to be so absorbed in purely formal relations as to be indifferent even to this aspect of the design as representation. We may suppose him to be moved by the pure contemplation of the spatial relations of plastic volumes. It is when we have got to this point that we seem to have isolated this extremely elusive aesthetic quality which is the one constant quality of all works of art, and which seems to be independent of all the prepossessions and associations which the spectator brings with him from his past life.

A person so entirely preoccupied with the purely formal meaning of a work of art, so entirely blind to all the overtones and associations of a picture like the *Transfiguration* is extremely rare. Nearly everyone, even if highly sensitive to purely plastic and spatial appearances, will inevitably entertain some of those thoughts and feelings which are conveyed by implication and by reference back to life. The difficulty is that we frequently give wrong explanations of our feelings. I suspect, for instance, that Goethe was deeply moved by the marvellous discovery of design, whereby the upper and lower parts cohere in a single whole, but the explanation he gave of this feeling took the form of a moral and philosophical reflection.

It is evident also that owing to our difficulty in recognizing the nature of our own feelings we are liable to have our aesthetic reaction interfered with by our reaction to the dramatic overtones and implications. I have chosen this picture of the Transfiguration precisely because its history is a striking example of this fact. In Goethe's time rhetorical gesture was no bar to the appreciation of aesthetic unity. Later on in the nineteenth century, when the study of the Primitives had revealed to us the charm of dramatic sincerity and naturalness, these gesticulating figures appeared so false and unsympathetic that even people of aesthetic sensibility were unable to disregard them, and their dislike of the picture as illustration actually obliterated or prevented the purely aesthetic approval which they would probably otherwise have experienced. It seems to me that this attempt to isolate the elusive element of the pure aesthetic reaction from the compounds in which it occurs has been the most important advance of modern times in practical aesthetic.

The question which this simile suggests is full of problems; are these chemical compounds in the normal aesthetically gifted spectator, or are they merely mixtures due to our confused recognition of what goes on in the complex of our emotions? The picture I have chosen is also valuable, just at the present time, from this point of view. Since it presents in vivid opposition for most of us a very strong positive (pleasurable) reaction on the purely aesthetic side, and a violently negative (painful) reaction in the realm of dramatic association.

But one could easily point to pictures where the two sets of emotions seem to run so parallel that the idea that they reinforce one another is inevitably aroused. We might take, for instance, Giotto's *Pietà*. In my description of that, it will be seen that the two currents of feeling ran so together in my own mind that I regarded them as being completely fused. My emotion about the dramatic idea seemed to heighten my emotion about the plastic design. But at present I should be inclined to say that this fusion of two sets of emotion was only apparent and was due to my imperfect analysis of my own mental state.

Probably at this point we must hand over the question to the experimental psychologist. It is for him to discover whether this fusion is possible, whether, for example, such a thing as a song really exists, that is to say, a song in which neither the meaning of the words nor the meaning of the music predominates; in which music and words do not merely set up separate currents of feeling, which may agree in a general parallelism, but really fuse and become indivisible. I expect that the answer will be in the negative.

If on the other hand such a complete fusion of different kinds of emotion does take place, this would tend to substantiate the ordinary opinion that the aesthetic emotion has greater value in highly complicated compounds than in the pure state.

Supposing, then, that we are able to isolate in a work of art this purely aesthetic quality to which Mr Clive Bell gives the name of 'significant form'. Of what nature is it? And what is the value of this elusive and –

taking the whole mass of mankind – rather uncommon aesthetic emotion which it causes? I put these questions without much hope of answering them, since it is of the greatest importance to recognize clearly what are the questions which remain to be solved.

I think we are all agreed that we mean by significant form something other than agreeable arrangements of form, harmonious patterns, and the like. We feel that a work which possesses it is the outcome of an endeavour to express an idea rather than to create a pleasing object. Personally, at least, I always feel that it implies the effort on the part of the artist to bend to our emotional understanding by means of his passionate conviction some intractable material which is alien to our spirit.

I seem unable at present to get beyond this vague adumbration of the nature of significant form. Flaubert's 'expression of the idea' seems to me to correspond exactly to what I mean, but, alas! he never explained, and probably could not, what he meant by the 'idea'.

As to the value of the aesthetic emotion – it is clearly infinitely removed from those ethical values to which Tolstoy would have confined it. It seems to be as remote from actual life and its practical utilities as the most useless mathematical theorem. One can only say that those who experience it feel it to have a peculiar quality of 'reality' which makes it a matter of infinite importance in their lives. Any attempt I might make to explain this would probably land me in the depths of mysticism. On the edge of that gulf I stop.

52

Desmond MacCarthy:
To Desmond MacCarthy *Aet.* 22

Desmond MacCarthy's honest, rueful dedication to a younger self of the journalism collected by a friend in 1931 was written when MacCarthy was in his fifties. MacCarthy hopefully called the collection of Portraits *'Volume One' (1931), but there was never a second. Four additional volumes of criticism were published by MacCarthy before he died, however, and three more appeared posthumously.*

I dedicate this book to you, young man, and you will not be pleased. You will suspect me of laughing at you: I admit to a certain malice. It was you who prevented me from collecting my contributions to the press during the past thirty years, with the result that when I finally made up my mind to do so, I found I had written more than I could read. If Logan Pearsall Smith, whose friendship, in the beginning, I owe to you, had not undertaken to choose for me, this volume and those which are to follow, would never have been got together. When I tried to do the work myself you were at my elbow, blighting that mild degree of self-complacency which is necessary to an author preparing a book for publication. I was afraid of you, for I knew I had nothing to print which would gratify your enormous self-esteem. Why, I ask, did everything I wrote seem to you, not necessarily worthless, but quite unworthy of you? I respect your high standards, but you have behaved to me like an over-anxious mother who prevents her daughter from making the most of herself at a party because she is not indisputably a queen among the rest.

How angry you were in 1900 when I hinted that you would be doing splendidly if you ever wrote nearly as well, say, as Andrew Lang? Your dismay convinced me that you would, in that case, never have touched a pen – and yet you were not conceited. You were only hopeful.

Now, I am not writing this letter for your eyes alone, but for young men of your age who long to write books and have to live by literary journalism. That was our case. It is an agreeable profession – provided you get enough work, or your circumstances do not require you to undertake more than you can do; but it had dangers for such as you: the journalist must ever be cutting his thoughts in the green and serving them up unripe, while his work as a critic teaches him to translate at once every feeling into intellectual discourse. But artists know what a meddlesome servant the Intellect can be, and in the Kingdom of Criticism the Intellect learns to make itself Mayor of the Palace. Moreover, to frequent newspaper offices, to live always close to the deafening cataract of books is chilling to literary endeavour. So many good books, let alone the others, are seen to be unnecessary.

Of course you are disappointed with what I have done, though I admit that of each essay as it was written you were by no means an austere judge. Still, I always felt that your praise was conditional upon there being something much better to come – and I have disappointed you. Why? Partly, I maintain, because your hopes (I do you the justice of not calling them expectations) were excessively high. Parents would not be surprised at the difficulty of dissuading their children from the life of letters, if they remembered that there is hardly a masterpiece which a would-be author of your age would not blush to have written. He admires parts of the masterpiece – qualities in it – adoringly, but he hopes that he will be able to make its merits his own and avoid all its defects. Impossible! as critics know.

By the bye you never intended me to become a critic, did you? I slipped into it. The readiest way of living by my pen was to comment upon books and plays. At first the remuneration was never more than thirty shillings a week; but the work was easy to me, for I found, whenever I interrogated you (though you continued to insist that there was within you something which ached to find expression), your head was humming with the valuable ideas of others. They were more audible than your own; they were useful to me. Some day, when you came upon a hushed space in life, away from journalism, away from the hubbub of personal emotions, I know you fully intended to listen to yourself; and discovering what you thought about the world to project it into a work of art – a play, a novel, a biography. But confess, you were too careless to prepare that preliminary silence, and too indolent to concentrate. Meanwhile how delightful you found it to imbibe literature at your leisure! And so you read and read. I must say I was grateful to you afterwards, for as a critic I should have run dry long ago if you had not been so lazy.

53

E. M. Forster: A View without a Room

Forster's brief continuation of A Room with a View *was written for the* New York Times *on the fiftieth anniversary of his novel. This is not the only time Forster revisited a novel – he wrote an introduction to* The Longest Journey *and some notes for* A Passage to India *when they were reprinted years later – but it is his only speculation on the futurity of his characters. The characters mentioned are the heroine and hero Lucy Honeychurch and George Emerson, their parents Mrs Honeychurch and Mr Emerson, Lucy's cousin and chaperone Charlotte Bartlett, Lucy's brother Freddy, and her ex-fiancé Cecil Vyse.*

A Room with a View was published in 1908. Here we are in 1958 and it occurs to me to wonder what the characters have been doing during the interval. They were created even earlier than 1908. The Italian half of the novel was almost the first piece of fiction I attempted. I laid it aside to write and publish two other novels, and then returned to it and added the English half. It is not my preferred novel – *The Longest Journey* is that – but it may fairly be called the nicest. It contains a hero and heroine who are supposed to be good, good-looking and in love – and who are promised happiness. Have they achieved it?

Let me think.

Lucy (Mrs George Emerson) must now be in her late sixties, George in his early seventies – a ripe age, though not as ripe as my own. They are still a personable couple, and fond of each other and of their children and grandchildren. But where do they live? Ah, that is the difficulty, and that is why I have entitled this article 'A View without a Room'. I cannot think where George and Lucy live.

After their Florentine honeymoon they probably settled down in Hampstead. No – in Highgate. That is pretty clear, and the next six years were from the point of view of amenity the best they ever experienced. George cleared out of the railway and got a better-paid clerkship in a government office, Lucy brought a nice little dowry along with her, which they were too sensible not to enjoy, and Miss Bartlett left them what she termed her little all. (Who would have thought it of Cousin Charlotte? I should never have thought anything else.) They had a servant who slept in, and were becoming comfortable capitalists when World War I exploded – the war that was to end war – and spoiled everything.

George instantly became a conscientious objector. He accepted alternative service, so did not go to prison, but he lost his government job and was out of the running for Homes for Heroes when peace came. Mrs Honeychurch was terribly upset by her son-in-law's conduct.

Lucy now got on her high horse and declared herself a conscientious objector too, and ran a more immediate risk by continuing to play Beethoven. Hun music! She was overheard and reported, and the police called. Old Mr Emerson, who lived with the young couple, addressed the police at length. They told him he had better look out. Shortly afterwards he died, still looking out and confident that Love and Truth would see humanity through in the end.

They saw the family through, which is something. No government authorized or ever will authorize either Love or Truth, but they worked privately in this case and helped the squalid move from Highgate to Carshalton. The George Emersons now had two girls and a boy and were beginning to want a real home – somewhere in the country where they could take root and unobtrusively found a dynasty. But civilization was not moving that way. The characters in my other novels were experiencing similar troubles. *Howards End* is a hunt for a home. India is a Passage for Indians as well as English. No resting-place.

For a time Windy Corner dangled illusively. After Mrs Honeychurch's death there was a chance of moving into that much loved house. But Freddy, who had inherited it, was obliged to sell and realize the capital for the upbringing of his family. An unsuccessful yet prolific doctor, Freddy could not do other than sell. Windy Corner disappeared, its garden was built over, and the name of Honeychurch resounded in Surrey no more.

In due course World War II broke out – the one that was to end with a durable peace. George instantly enlisted. Being both intelligent and passionate, he could distinguish between a Germany that was not much worse than England and a Germany that was devilish. At the age of fifty he could recognize in Hitlerism an enemy of the heart as well as of the head and the arts. He discovered that he loved fighting and had been starved by its absence, and also discovered that away from his wife he did not remain chaste.

For Lucy the war was less varied. She gave some music lessons and broadcast some Beethoven, who was quite all right this time, but the little flat at Watford, where she was trying to keep things together against George's return, was bombed, the loss of her possessions and mementos was complete, and the same thing happened to their married daughter, away at Nuneaton.

At the front George rose to the rank of corporal, was wounded and taken prisoner in Africa, and imprisoned in Mussolini's Italy, where he found the Italians sometimes as sympathetic as they had been in his tourist days, and sometimes less sympathetic.

When Italy collapsed he moved northward through the chaos towards Florence. The beloved city had changed, but not unrecognizably. The Trinità Bridge had been destroyed, both ends of the Ponte Vecchio were in a mess, but the Piazza Signoria, where once a trifling murder had occurred, still survived. So did the district where the Pension Bertolini had once flourished – nothing damaged at all.

And George set out – as I did myself a few years later – to locate the particular building. He failed. For though nothing is damaged all is changed. The houses on that stretch of the Lungarno have been re-numbered and remodelled and, as it were, remelted, some of the façades have been extended, others have shrunk, so that it is impossible to decide which room was romantic half a century ago. George had therefore to report to Lucy that the View was still there and that the Room must be there, too, but could not be found. She was glad of the news, although at that moment she was homeless. It was something to have retained a View, and, secure in it and in their love as long as they have one another to love, George and Lucy await World War III – the one that would end war and everything else, too.

Cecil Vyse must not be omitted from this prophetic retrospect. He moved out of the Emersons' circle but not altogether out of mine. With his integrity and intelligence he was destined for confidential work, and in 1914 he was seconded to Information or whatever the withholding of information was then entitled. I had an example of his propaganda, and a very welcome one, at Alexandria. A quiet little party was held on the outskirts of that city, and someone wanted a little Beethoven. The hostess demurred. Hum music might compromise us. But a young officer spoke up. 'No, it's all right,' he said, 'a chap who knows about those things from the inside told me Beethoven's definitely Belgian.'

The chap in question must have been Cecil. That mixture of mischief and culture is unmistakable. Our hostess was reassured, the ban was lifted, and the Moonlight Sonata shimmered into the desert.

54

Virginia Woolf: The Love of Reading

The Common Reader was devoted, Virginia Woolf said in her fore-word, to the pursuit of reading by private people. The last essay of The Common Reader, Second Series *(1932) completes that purpose with an essay entitled 'How Should One Read a Book?' The essay was first published in the* Yale Review. *Before rewriting it for book publica-tion, however, Woolf abridged the essay to accompany a booklist pub-lished by the Hampshire Bookshop of Northampton, Massachusetts in 1932. The abridgement is entitled 'The Love of Reading', and like the revised essay it emphasizes both the double nature of reading and its complex pleasure.*

At this late hour of the world's history books are to be found in every room of the house – in the nursery, in the drawing room, in the dining room, in the kitchen. And in some houses they have collected so that they have to be accommodated with a room of their own. Novels, poems, histories, memoirs, valuable books in leather, cheap books in paper – one stops sometimes before them and asks in a transient amazement what is the pleasure I get, or the good I create, from passing my eyes up and down these innumerable lines of print?

Reading is a very complex art – the hastiest examination of our sensations as a reader will show us that much. And our duties as readers are many and various. But perhaps it may be said that our first duty to a book is that one should read it for the first time as if one were writing it. One should begin by sitting in the dock with the criminal not by mounting the bench to sit among the Judges. One should be an accomplice with the writer in his act, whether good or bad, of creation. For each of these books, however it may differ in kind and quality, is an attempt to make something. And our first duty as readers is to try and understand what the writer is making from the first word with which he builds his first sentence to the last with which he ends his book. We must not impose our design upon him; we must not try to make him conform his will to ours. We must allow Defoe to be Defoe and Jane Austen to be Jane Austen as freely as we allow the tiger to have his fur and the tortoise to have his shell. And this is very difficult. For it is one of the qualities of greatness that it brings Heaven and earth and human nature into conformity with its own vision.

The great writers thus often require us to make heroic efforts in order to read them rightly. They bend us and break us. To go from Defoe to Jane Austen, from Hardy to Peacock, from Trollope to Meredith, from Richardson to Rudyard Kipling is to be wrenched and distorted, to be thrown violently this way and that. And so, too, with the lesser writers. Each is singular; each has a view, a temperament, an experience of his own which may conflict with ours but must be allowed to express itself fully if we are to do him justice. And the writers who have most to give us often do most violence to our prejudices, particularly if they are our own contemporaries, so that we have need of all our imagination and understanding if we are to get the utmost that they can give us.

But reading, as we have suggested, is a complex art. It does not merely consist in sympathizing and understanding. It consists, too, in criticizing and in judging. The reader must leave the dock and mount the bench. He must cease to be the friend; he must become the judge. And this second process, which we may call the process of after-reading, for it is often done without the book before us, yields an even more solid pleasure than that which we receive when we are actually turning the pages. During the actual reading new impressions are always cancelling or completing the old. Delight, anger, boredom, laughter succeed each other incessantly as we read. Judgement is suspended, for we cannot know what may come next. But now the book is completed. It has taken a definite shape. And the book as a whole is different from the book received currently in several different parts. It has a shape, it has a being. And this shape, this being, can be held in the mind and compared with the shapes of other books and given its own size and smallness by comparison with theirs.

But if this process of judging and deciding is full of pleasure it is also full of difficulty. Not much help can be looked for from outside. Critics and criticism abound, but it does not help us greatly to read the views of another mind when our own is still hot from a book that we have just read. It is after one has made up one's own opinion that the opinions of others are most illuminating. It is when we can defend our own judgement that we get most from the judgement of the great critics – the Johnsons, the Drydens and the Arnolds. To make up our own minds we can best help ourselves first by realizing the impression that the book has left as fully and sharply as possible, and then by comparing this impression with the impressions that we have formulated in the past. There they hang in the wardrobe of the mind – the shapes of the books we have read, like clothes that we have taken off and hung up to wait their season. Thus, if we have just read say Clarissa Harlowe for the first time we take it and let it show itself against the shape that remains in our minds after reading Anna Karenina. We place them side by side and at once the outlines of the two books are cut out against each other as the angle of a house (to change the figure) is cut out against the fullness of the harvest moon. We contrast Richardson's prominent qualities with Tolstoy's. We contrast his indirectness and verbosity with Tolstoy's brevity and directness. We ask ourselves why it is that each writer has chosen so different an angle of approach. We compare the emotion that we felt at different crises of their books. We speculate as to the difference between the eighteenth century in England and the nineteenth century in Russia – but there is no end to the questions that at once suggest themselves as we place the books together. Thus by degrees, by asking questions and answering them, we find that we have decided that the book we have just read is of this kind or that, has this degree of merit or that, takes its station at this point or at that in the literature as a whole. And if we are good readers we thus judge not only the classics and the masterpieces of the dead, but we pay the living writers the compliment of comparing them as they should be compared with the pattern of the great books of the past.

Thus, then, when the moralists ask us what good we do by running our eyes over these many printed pages, we can reply that we are doing our part as readers to help masterpieces into the world. We are fulfilling our share of the creative task – we are stimulating, encouraging, rejecting, making our approval and disapproval felt; and are thus acting as a check and a spur upon the writer. That is one reason for reading books – we are helping to bring good books into the world and to make bad books impossible. But it is not the true reason. The true reason remains the inscrutable one – we get pleasure from reading. It is a complex pleasure and a difficult pleasure; it varies from age to age and from book to book. But that pleasure is enough. Indeed that pleasure is so great that one cannot doubt that without it the world would be a far different and a far inferior place from what it is. Reading has changed the world and continues to change it. When the day of judgement comes therefore and all secrets are laid bare, we shall not be surprised to learn that the reason why we have grown from apes to men, and left our caves and dropped our bows and arrows and sat round the fire and talked and given to the poor and helped the sick – the reason why we have made shelter and society out of the wastes of the desert and the tangle of the jungle is simply this – we have loved reading.

Further Reading

The following list of shorter writings by the Bloomsbury Group is not exhaustive. Selections from works marked with an asterisk have been included in *A Bloomsbury Group Reader*. The dates are of first publication.

Clive Bell

Landmarks in Nineteenth-Century Painting, London: Chatto & Windus; New York: Harcourt, Brace, 1927.

Enjoying Pictures: Meditations in the National Gallery and Elsewhere, London: Chatto & Windus; New York: Harcourt, Brace, 1934.

*Old Friends: Personal Recollections, London: Chatto & Windus, 1956; New York: Harcourt, Brace, 1957.

*Pot-Boilers, London: Chatto & Windus, 1918.

*Since Cézanne, London: Chatto & Windus; New York: Harcourt, Brace, 1927.

E. M. Forster

*Abinger Harvest, London: Edward Arnold; New York: Harcourt, Brace, 1936.

*Collected Short Stories of E. M. Forster, London: Sidgwick & Jackson, 1948; *The Collected Tales*, New York: Alfred Knopf, 1947.

The Life to Come and Other Stories, edited by Oliver Stallybrass, London: Edward Arnold, 1972.

*Two Cheers for Democracy, London: Edward Arnold; New York: Harcourt, Brace, 1951.

Roger Fry

*Characteristics of French Art, London: Chatto & Windus, 1932; New York: Brentano's, 1933.

Last Lectures, Cambridge: Cambridge University Press; New York: Macmillan, 1939.

A Sampler of Castile, London: Hogarth Press, 1923.
Transformations, London: Chatto & Windus, 1926; New York: Brentano's, 1927.
Vision and Design, London: Chatto & Windus, 1920; New York: Brentano's, 1921.

John Maynard Keynes

Collected Writings of John Maynard Keynes, 30 volumes, edited by Donald Moggridge and others, London and Cambridge, UK: Macmillan and Cambridge University Press; New York: Cambridge University Press, 1971–89.
Essays in Biography, London: Macmillan; New York: Harcourt, Brace, 1933.
Essays in Persuasion, London: Macmillan; New York: Harcourt, Brace, 1931.

Desmond MacCarthy

Criticism, London and New York: Putnam, 1932.
Drama, London and New York: Putnam, 1940.
Experience, London: Putnam, 1935.
Humanities, London: Macgibbon and Key, 1953.
Memories, London: Macgibbon and Key, 1953.
Portraits, London and New York: Putnam, 1931.
Remnants, London: Constable, 1918.
Shaw, London: Macgibbon and Key, 1951.
Theatre, London: Macgibbon and Key, 1954.

Lytton Strachey

Books and Characters: French and English, London: Chatto & Windus; New York: Harcourt, Brace, 1922.
Characters and Commentaries, London: Chatto & Windus; New York: Harcourt, Brace, 1933.
Lytton Strachey by Himself: A Self-Portrait, edited by Michael Holroyd, London: Heinemann; New York: Holt, Rinehart & Winston, 1971.
Portraits in Miniature and Other Essays, London: Chatto & Windus; New York: Harcourt, Brace, 1931.
The Really Interesting Question and Other Papers, edited by Paul Levy, London: Weidenfeld and Nicolson; New York: Coward, McGann & Geoghegan, 1972.
Spectatorial Essays, edited by James Strachey, London: Chatto & Windus; New York: Harcourt, Brace, World, 1964.

Leonard Woolf

Essays on Literature, History, Politics, Etc., London: Hogarth Press, 1927.
Stories of the East, London: Hogarth Press, 1921.

Virginia Woolf

The Captain's Death Bed and Other Essays, London: Hogarth Press; New York: Harcourt, Brace, 1950.

*The Common Reader, First and Second Series, London: Hogarth Press; New York: Harcourt, Brace, 1925, 1932.

*The Complete Shorter Fiction of Virginia Woolf, edited by Susan Dick, 2nd edition, London: Hogarth Press; New York: Harcourt, Brace, Jovanovich, 1989.

*The Death of the Moth and Other Essays, London: Hogarth Press; New York: Harcourt Brace, 1942.

*The Essays of Virginia Woolf, 6 volumes, edited by Andrew McNeillie, London: Hogarth Press; New York: Harcourt, Brace, Jovanovich, 1986–.

*Granite and Rainbow, London: Hogarth Press; New York: Harcourt, Brace, 1958.

*The Love of Reading, How Should One Read a Book? Smith College Library, Northampton, Massachusetts, 1985.

The Moment and Other Essays, London: Hogarth Press, 1947; New York: Harcourt, Brace, 1948.

*Moments of Being, edited by Jeanne Schulkind, 2nd edition, London: Hogarth Press; New York: Harcourt, Brace, Jovanovich, 1985.

Index of Names

Ackerley, J. R. 288
Adelphi Theatre 281
Aeschylus 184, 235, 324
Alfieri, Vittorio 184, 392
Alma-Tadema, Lawrence 121
Archer, William 188
Aristophanes 257, 308
Aristotle 185
Arnold, Matthew 213–18, 417
Arnold, Thomas 5
Arts Council 390–1
Athenaeum 102, 182, 225, 226
Audoux, Marguerite 369
Austen, Jane 227, 239, 240, 246,
    274, 287, 293, 295, 416
Ayer, A. J. 392

Babur, Emperor 53–7
Bach, Johann Sebastian 104
Bacon, Francis 376
Baldwin, Stanley 139–40, 143, 148,
    149
Barclay, Florence 162
Barrow, Isaac 293
Bazille, Frédérick 261
Beethoven, Ludwig van 414
Behn, Alphra 274
Bell, Clive 102, 182, 226, 353, 355,
    360–2, 364–5, 367, 368–9, 378,
    379, 382, 397; Art, 102, 211,
    403–4, 406–7; 'Artistic Problem',
    102–6; 'Ibsen', 182–8; 'Maynard

Keynes', 382–93; *Old Friends*,
    382; *Pot-Boilers*, 182; *Since
    Cézanne*, 102, 225; 'Wilcoxism',
    225–8
Bell, Julian 378–81, 383
Bell, Vanessa 331, 336, 358,
    359–60, 362, 364–5, 367–8,
    371–2, 378, 379, 383, 387;
    Notes on Virginia's Childhood,
    331–5
Bemelmans, Ludwig 390
Bennett, Arnold 106, 233, 234,
    239–46
Bentley, E. C. 376
Bewick, Thomas 293
Bible 254, 306, 404–5
Biographie Universelle 293
Bloomsbury Group 10, 12, 51, 95,
    126, 165, 173, 203, 211, 213,
    233, 251, 280, 297, 329, 331,
    355–72, 378, 382, 397
Bomberg, David 228
Bonnard, Pierre 227
Borrow, George 375
Boswell, James 388
Boudin, Eugene 227
Bowdler, Thomas 255
Braque, Georges 227
Bridges, Robert 192, 194
Brill, A. A. 189
British Broadcasting Corporation
    280